ANALYZING TEXT AND DISCOURSE

ANALYZING TEXT AND DISCOURSE

Nine Approaches for the Social Sciences

Edited by
Anders Björkvall
Kristina Boréus
Per-Anders Svärd

2nd Edition

1 Oliver's Yard
55 City Road
London EC1Y 1SP

2455 Teller Road
Thousand Oaks, California 91320

Unit No 323-333, Third Floor, F-Block
International Trade Tower Nehru Place
New Delhi 110 019

8 Marina View Suite 43-053
Asia Square Tower 1
Singapore 018960

Editor: Kate Keers
Editorial Assistant: Becky Oliver
Production Editor: Tanya Kapoor
Copyeditor: Diana Chambers
Indexer: KnowledgeWorks Global Ltd
Marketing Manager: Ben Sherwood
Cover Design: Shaun Mercier
Typeset by KnowledgeWorks Global Ltd

Editorial Arrangement © Anders Björkvall, Kristina Boréus, and Per-Anders Svärd (2024)

Chapter 1 © Kristina Boréus, Anders Björkvall, Per-Anders Svärd and Göran Bergström (2024)
Chapter 2 © Kristina Boréus and Sebastian Kohl (2024)
Chapter 3 © Mats Lindberg (2024)
Chapter 4 © Jussi Kurunmäki and Jani Marjanen (2024)
Chapter 5 © Alexa Robertson (2024)
Chapter 6 © Linda Ekström, Göran Bergström and Hugo Faber (2024)
Chapter 7 © Kristina Boréus and Charlotta Seiler Brylla (2024)
Chapter 8 © Anders Björkvall (2024).

Apart from any fair dealing for the purposes of research, private study, or criticism or review, as permitted under the Copyright, Designs and Patents Act, 1988, this publication may not be reproduced, stored or transmitted in any form, or by any means, without the prior permission in writing of the publisher, or in the case of reprographic reproduction, in accordance with the terms of licences issued by the Copyright Licensing Agency. Enquiries concerning reproduction outside those terms should be sent to the publisher.

Library of Congress Control Number: 2023942866

British Library Cataloguing in Publication data

A catalogue record for this book is available from the British Library

ISBN 978-1-5296-0196-1

ISBN 978-1-5296-0195-4 (pbk)

Contents

About the Editors and Contributors   vi

1. Analysing Text and Discourse in the Social Sciences   1
   Kristina Boréus, Anders Björkvall, Per-Anders Svärd and Göran Bergström

2. Content Analysis   24
   Kristina Boréus and Sebastian Kohl

3. Analysis of Ideas and Ideological Thought   52
   Mats Lindberg

4. Conceptual History   85
   Jussi Kurunmäki and Jani Marjanen

5. Narrative Analysis   111
   Alexa Robertson

6. Three Poststructural Approaches to Discourse Analysis   135
   Linda Ekström, Göran Bergström and Hugo Faber

7. Critical Discourse Studies   168
   Kristina Boréus and Charlotta Seiler Brylla

8. Multimodal Discourse Analysis   199
   Anders Björkvall

References   238
Index   264

About the Editors and Contributors

About the Editors

Anders Björkvall is Professor of Swedish at Örebro University, Sweden. He has published widely within the fields of multimodality, social semiotics, discourse analysis, genre and literacy studies, and the ethnography of artefacts and texts. He is also one of the founding editors of the journal *Multimodality & Society* (SAGE). Recent publications include the chapter 'The emotional civil servant: On the multimodal construction of affect in "platform of values" texts of Swedish public authorities' in *Organizational Semiotics: Multimodal Perspectives on Organization Studies* (2023); 'Feeling Safe While Being Surveilled: The Spatial Semiotics of Affect at International Airports' in *Social Semiotics* (2023, with S. Van Meerbergen and G. Westberg); and 'Semiotics of Destruction: Traces on the Environment' in *Visual Communication* (2022, with A. Archer).

Kristina Boréus is Professor of Political Science at Uppsala University, Sweden. She has studied ideology and ideological change, discrimination against migrants and other groups, racism and right-wing populism. This work has resulted in several books and articles, including *Migrants and Natives – 'Them' and 'Us.' Mainstream and Radical Right Political Rhetoric in Europe* (SAGE, 2020) and 'Why Are Care Workers from the Global South Disadvantaged? Inequality and Discrimination in Swedish Elderly Care Work', with A. Behtoui, A. Neergaard and S. Yazdanpanah in *Ethnic and Racial Studies* (2020). Her current research focuses on climate-related city transformation. In that area, she has published 'Breaking through banal consumerism? Representations of post-consumerist perspectives in mainstream press media,' with K. Bradley and S. Tornhill in *Journal of Consumer Culture* (2023).

Per-Anders Svärd holds a PhD in political science and is a Senior Lecturer at the School of Humanities, Education and Social Science, Örebro University, Sweden. He is also an Associate Fellow of the Oxford Centre for Animal Ethics. His research has mainly focused on critical animal studies, animal ethics and the political history of the human–animal relationship, covering topics like animal welfare regulation, slaughter and animal experimentation from a post-Marxist and psychoanalytically informed discourse theoretical perspective. He is a co-founder and co-editor of the open access journal *Politics and Animals* and a board member of the *Centre for Marxist Social Studies* in Sweden.

About the Contributors

Göran Bergström is an Associate Professor in Political Science, Department of Political Science, at Stockholm University, Sweden. For a long time, he was Director of Education. He has studied ideological change in Education Policy with a particular focus on the Swedish Labour Party. Recent publications include articles in pedagogical content knowledge, more specifically how the content knowledge is developed in social science/civics research projects (with Linda Ekström, *Nordidactica – Journal of Humanities and Social Science Education*, 2015). He has also studied how central core values in the Swedish educational system has been interpreted among school leaders (with Linda Ekström, in *Utbildning och Demokrati*, 2016, and with Madestam and Sundström, in *Scandinavian Journal of Public Administration*, 2018). Göran Bergström edited the first edition of *Analyzing Text and Discourse* (with Kristina Boréus, SAGE, 2017) as well as the book's Swedish counterpart, *Textens mening och makt* (with Kristina Boréus, Studentlitteratur, 2018).

Linda Ekström is a senior political science lecturer at Södertörn University, Sweden. Her main research interests are educational policies and social science didactics. She has previously worked, together with Göran Bergström, with discursive psychology while studying principals' interpretations of the concept of 'equity.' In two ongoing studies, she uses discursive psychology to study social studies teachers' perceptions of how social studies education can promote democratic competencies among vocational students.

Hugo Faber is a PhD candidate in Political Science at Södertörn University, Sweden. He studies climate and energy issues with a specific focus on the power, discourses and politics involved in phasing out fossil and nuclear energy. Recent publications include 'How Does Falling Incumbent Profitability Affect Energy Policy Discourse? The Discursive Construction of Nuclear Phaseouts and Insufficient Capacity as a Threat in Sweden' (2023, in *Energy Policy*) and 'Legitimacy Under Institutional Complexity' (with Naghmeh Nasiritousi, 2021, in *Review of International Studies*).

Sebastian Kohl is Professor of Sociology at Freie Universität Berlin, Germany. He specialises in economic, historical and urban sociology as well as in comparative political economy of housing and insurance markets. His work uses both classical quantitative methods and quantitative text analysis of large text corpora. His research has been published in *Urban Studies, Socio-Economic Review, Housing*

Studies, *Review of International Political Economy* and the *British Journal of Sociology*. His book *Homeownership, Renting and Society* appeared with Routledge in 2017.

Jussi Kurunmäki has a PhD in political science, and he holds the title of Docent both in political science (Stockholm University) and political history (University of Helsinki). He is currently senior research fellow at the Department of History and Ethnology at University of Jyväskylä. His main fields of research are the theory and methods of conceptual history, nineteenth- and twentieth-century conceptual histories of political representation, democracy, and ideology. His coedited books in English include *Time, History and Politics* (2003), *Rhetorics of Nordic Democracy* (2010), *Democracy in Modern Europe: A Conceptual History* (2018). Together with Jani Marjanen, he has edited a special issue on the political rhetoric of isms in *Journal of Political Ideologies* (2018).

Mats Lindberg is Professor in Political Science at Örebro University. For three decades he has been lecturing (at several Swedish universities) on political and social theory, as well as the philosophy of science. His dissertation (Uppsala University, 1979, second edition, 2013) was a theory-critical analysis of Karl Marx's *Capital*, which has been followed up by the new Introduction to the Swedish translation of Marx's *Capital* (2013) and the chapter on 'Sweden' in the *Routledge Handbook on Marx's Capital* (forthcoming, 2026). He has written a widely read ideology-critique of Swedish social democracy (1975) and has made critical analyses of the concepts of the state (1982, 1985), Civil Society (1995) and Local Self-Government (1999) (all in Swedish). He is one of the introducers of Jürgen Habermas to the Swedish public (1984) and the initiator of The Swedish Network in Political Theory (since 1993). At Lund University he was the initiator in 2014 of a digitalisation project of the production of the renowned Swedish political scientist Herbert Tingsten, influential liberal chief editor in the late 1940s and 1950s. Lindberg's latest publications regard the structure of ideological thought and the method of rationalistic idea-criticism (2018). He is currently doing research on political Islam, especially the organisation, ideology and rhetoric of the Muslim Brotherhood in Europe and Sweden (2023).

Jani Marjanen is a university lecturer in Political History at the University of Helsinki. His research focuses on discourses of patriotism and civil society in the eighteenth and nineteenth centuries, the conceptual history of ideology and isms (together with Jussi Kurunmäki), digital humanities approaches to analysing digital newspapers and parliamentary records, and the theory and method of conceptual history. He has served as one of the editors of *Contributions to the History of Concepts* and on the board of the History of Concepts Group. He has co-edited *The Rise of Economic Societies in the Eighteenth Century* (Palgrave, 2012) and *Contesting*

Nordicness (De Gruyter, 2021). His most recent article is 'Quantitative Conceptual History: On Agency, Reception, and Interpretation' (2023).

Alexa Robertson is Professor of Media and Communication at Stockholm University and holds a PhD in Political Science. The red thread running throughout her work is the question of how media representation is conceived and effected in a world of diversity and transborder communication flows, with a focus on storytelling. Her books include *Screening Politics* (Routledge, 2018), *Media and Politics in a Globalized World* (Polity, 2015), *Global News: Reporting Conflicts and Cosmopolitanism* (Peter Lang, 2015), and *Mediated Cosmopolitanism: the world of television news* (Polity, 2010). She is principal investigator of the SRC-funded project *Infojämlikhet: Information Inequality in a Global Perspective*, and teaches courses at the Master's level on global media studies, media and politics, politics and popular culture, and research design.

Charlotta Seiler Brylla is Professor of German at Stockholm University in Sweden where she teaches German language and linguistics. Her research interests lie in the fields of political discourse analysis, discourse semantics, lexicology, as well as comparative language and culture studies. Currently, her research projects focus on the communication of right-wing populist supporters, the semiotics of anti-semitism in contemporary Sweden, and East–West discourses in Germany. Her recent work includes the multi-authored book *Voices of Supporters: Populist parties, social media and the 2019 European elections* (Koller et al., 2023).

1

Analysing Text and Discourse in the Social Sciences

Kristina Boréus, Anders Björkvall, Per-Anders Svärd and Göran Bergström

The Bible ... The Quran ... the battle song The Internationale ... the films documenting the horrors of German concentration camps after the Allied Forces liberated them in 1945 ... Nelson Mandela's speech in court in 1964, where he stated that he was prepared to die for a free and equal society ... the photo of a drowned three-year-old child washed up on a Turkish shore in 2015 ... the widespread images of Greta Thunberg cross-legged, striking from school outside the Swedish parliament building ...

These are all examples of texts – in the wide meaning of the word used in this book – that have undoubtedly had influence on society, public debate and people's lives at different times in history. Myriad texts are produced and consumed. Some have historical impacts on processes and events, like those exemplified above. Others are part of people's mundane lives, like the text on a box of cereals, the road signs we pass when walking or driving, or the advertising that large parts of the world's population are exposed to every day.

Thus, texts are crucially important in modern societies. For that reason, they are also important objects of analysis for the social sciences. Through their different disciplines, people in societies are researched. The objects of study include power, politics, families, oppression, governments, equality, inequality, crime, economic markets, traditions, migration, conflict, consensus and many other social phenomena. Obviously, when such phenomena are studied, texts are crucial artefacts.

Just to illustrate the importance of texts with an example from the list of social phenomena, take governments. They make decisions formulated in texts and express their proposals textually to parliaments as well as to the public in social media. There are texts that regulate what governments may and may not do. In government institutions, large amounts of texts circulate every day. Governments are criticised in texts such as articles by political opponents and satirical television programmes.

Before we turn to what a text is, we will exemplify how textual analysis might be applied when the object of study is the first one in the list above: power. Power is often examined in social research and several power-related issues will be used throughout the book to exemplify how texts can be analysed in the social sciences. The examples here illustrate how the complex objects of study of the social sciences are constructed in different ways and how these differences imply different tasks for textual analysis.

Steven Lukes (2005) describes power as having three dimensions (or faces). According to the *first dimension of power*, power is about making somebody do what they would not otherwise have done. A typical example is when a decision is taken by a political body and those in opposition must yield to the majority. When using such a concept of power, texts like voting protocols and texts that express opinions could be analysed. The *second dimension of power* is broader: the usage of *non-decision making*, when some issues are never put to a vote, perhaps due to shifty agenda-setting techniques, is also power. In this case, crucial texts can exist outside the arenas of decision making – e.g., petitions from groups whose issues are excluded from the decision-making process. Other relevant texts to analyse might be the interview transcripts that we as researchers produce when asking members of the excluded groups about their issues. The *third dimension of power*, according to Lukes, is about manipulating people to want things that are not really in their interest. When such power over the minds and souls of people is studied, other texts become relevant. It might be assumed, for instance, that mass media plays an important role in making people hold certain beliefs. In this case, mass media texts would be important to study. Pictures might be interesting to analyse from all the mentioned perspectives, but presumably most important for the third dimension of power. Images can influence us in partly unconscious ways, avoiding our shield of critical thinking – which is why they are so important in advertising.

The social sciences also use other concepts of power, such as that formulated by Michel Foucault. According to Foucault, studying power is not about finding out which agents have power over others, the way that Lukes conceptualised it. In Foucault's conceptualisation, individuals do not have power – they are instead *locations of power* (Foucault, 1980). Power is diffused, always shifting and present, almost everywhere, not least in the details – what Foucault refers to as the *micro-physics of power*. Power exists between people and within people as self-discipline. When studying power, one should analyse how it is exercised, its technologies – is it, for example, exercised by arms, by linguistic means or through different forms of surveillance and control? The way that power is institutionalised should also be investigated: institutions like families, prisons and mental hospitals create different conditions for power (Foucault, 1994: xv–vi). An example of how texts can be used to study technologies of power and their institutionalisation is provided when Foucault, in one of his major studies, *Madness and Civilization* (2001 [1967]), examines the shifting meaning of 'madness' in European culture, law, medicine and other contexts from the Middle Ages until the end of the nineteenth century. He uses not only texts that describe madness, but also texts that describe how those considered mad were treated. Thus, Foucault uses reports by inspectors of the institutions where 'the mad' were confined that describe how they were treated – which can be understood as descriptions of the technologies of power used within institutions – to interpret how madness was understood. Such descriptions could give us important clues about how people with mental diseases were conceptualised at different points in time – e.g., as criminals who needed 'correction' or as animals that could not be corrected but needed to be locked up.

According to a conceptualisation of power based in *critical realism*, a theory of science referred to by Norman Fairclough as related to critical discourse studies (CDS, see Chapter 7), power is a potential: defined as possibilities created within the social structures in which agents (individuals or groups) act. Analysing texts becomes a first necessary step in assessing how power is reproduced and how it changes (Fairclough, 1992: 113). If the aim is to study how power changes in academia, for example, we need to analyse policy documents and texts in which universities describe what they do and ask how the content of such documents and texts has changed over time. We also need to study which groups are allowed to influence important decisions in academia, such as the distribution of research grants and the content of education (see Fairclough, 2015 [1989]: 73–6). To analyse the texts is to study the 'empirical' domain (Bhaskar, 2008 [1978]: 56), which is necessary for getting at the mechanisms that affect power relations, which are to be found in the 'real' domain. Fairclough has often referred to the shifts in power relations between university staff, politicians, students and commercial interests as a result of changes in capitalism (Fairclough, 2015 [1989]: 63–7).

As the examples show, texts can hardly be avoided in the study of power or other social phenomena, although social practices need to be studied through other methods too: it might be necessary to observe what people do and to study society in other ways than through the analysis of texts. It might also be indispensable to study the distribution of goods such as money, arms or the ownership of the means of production. But text studies of one kind or the other are crucial to the sciences of people and societies. As with any method, a student who wants to learn to use text analysis needs to get a grasp of basic ideas and techniques. The aim of this book is to function as a guide in that learning process. The rest of this chapter is meant as a manual for reading and using the book. To begin with, we explicate the central concepts of text, genre and discourse.

Multimodal texts, genres and discourses

When most people talk about *text*, they refer to chunks of writing inscribed on something, like a piece of paper or a screen. However, when texts are used as research data, as in this book, the lay definition needs to be further elaborated and the concept of text needs to be related to other key concepts in discourse studies: *genre, discourse* and *multimodality*. All texts, genres and discourses are multimodal in that they involve more *communicative modes* than language alone, such as image, layout and colour. This multimodal perspective stems from *semiotics*, which is the science of *signs*, also beyond those of language. Since semiotics forms the foundation for many of the perspectives presented in this book, its basic assumptions are briefly presented before text, genre, discourse and multimodality are introduced in more detail.

Charles Sanders Peirce and Ferdinand de Saussure are considered the founding fathers of semiotics (even though Saussure used the word *semiology* rather than semiotics). Three concepts are of key importance in order to understand Saussure's assumptions: the sign along with its two parts, the *signifier* and the *signified*. The signified is any type of meaning – an idea in people's heads. An example of a signified can be 'a vehicle with wheels'. The signifier, on the other hand, is what expresses the meaning – for instance, the sounds or the letters that form the spoken word *car* in English. However, 'a vehicle with wheels' can also be expressed by a photo of such a thing, which is a key point in semiotics.

One more semiotic principle is of importance. Saussure claimed that the *arbitrariness* between the signified and the signifier is the 'first principle' of signs (Saussure, 2013: 78): the meaning of 'a vehicle with wheels' could have been expressed by any other combination of sounds or letters than the English 'car' – for instance, *macchina*, as in Italian, as long as members of the social group in which the sign is used agree upon the choice of signifier. This absolute arbitrariness has been challenged. In Charles Sanders Peirce's semiotic theory, three types of signs – *symbolic, indexical* and *iconic* (Peirce, 1998: 13–18) – are arbitrary only to some degree, and in recent years Gunther Kress (2010) has argued that signs are above all *motivated* rather than arbitrary. Put briefly, in Kress's *social semiotics*, signs are constantly remade as sign-makers make use of the signifying materials for meaning-making (called *semiotic resources* and *modes*) that they find most appropriate for making the meanings they want to make at a specific time and place, and in a specific social context. This way, sign making, as described by Kress, is always a social activity and a direct result of how people interpret their social, societal context. In this perspective, meanings of signs are also viewed as *meaning potentials* (or *semiotic* potentials; see van Leeuwen, 2005: 4) rather than more or less fixed by conventions, which will be further elaborated upon in Chapter 8 on multimodal discourse analysis.

With these understandings of semiotics as a backdrop, text as used in this book can be defined through a number of properties that all texts possess. First, texts have *materiality*. They are written, printed, recorded, etc. on something and with something: on paper with a pencil, on a screen with a keyboard or a digital stylus, or on a wall with spray paint. Even speech has materiality in the sense that its meanings are carried on sound waves. Second, texts have *finality*: they have an identifiable beginning and end. This finality is marked by material means such as capital letters and interpunctuation, but also by layout such as frames or by the finality of, say, the wall or paper sheet that texts are exposed on. However, their finality is also related to a third fact: texts are (more or less) *cohesive* and *coherent*. Cohesion refers to how texts are delimited and kept together through their internal composition or by means such as the repetition of words or expressions within the text (see Halliday and Hasan, 1976). Being coherent means that they have themes that are rationally organised and can be followed in given cultural contexts, thus allowing members of a cultural sphere to recognise the text as a meaningful entity.

Fourth, and this is where *multimodality* comes in, texts are not strictly linguistic entities. Instead, they are multimodal, which Roland Barthes (1977) was among the first to point out in the 1960s, even though the term 'multimodality' was not coined until later by other researchers (cf. Hodge and Kress, 1988; Kress and van Leeuwen, 2021). In many texts today, such as social media texts or graffiti, the words are often inferior to other means of communication such as image, colour, drawing and painting. Even more traditional monomodal texts, such as government reports, parliament protocols or formal business letters, often employ various typefaces, tables and diagrams that are not strictly linguistic. More precisely, language alone rarely contributes to all the semiotic work required for communication; other communicative modes such as image, colour, music or gesture are often just as important. Bateman et al. (2017: 132) explain:

> The reason for maintaining, or rather re-instating, the term 'text' for this diversity is to draw attention to a specific property shared by all of these communicative or signifying artefacts or actions: i.e. the property that *they are structured in order to be interpreted*. (Italics in the orginal)

In the present book, all texts are treated as multimodal, even though in most chapters the main focus is on their linguistic properties.

Lastly, but perhaps most importantly, texts are *functional*. In fact, this property of texts is superior to all the others: texts are (multimodally) designed the way they are, or, in the words of Bateman et al. (2017), have the structure that they do because they serve certain functions rather than others. This functionality of texts is also what makes them a key object of analysis in the social sciences: texts have societal functions which they both perform and reflect.

The theorisation of texts as functional in the field of discourse studies comes mainly from semiotics and linguistics (e.g., Jakobson, 1960; Halliday and Matthiessen, 2014). In these fields, the 'function in structure' approach to language and texts (cf. van Leuwen, 2005: 75) has been very influential. It is also a cornerstone of discourse studies, in which the interrelations between texts and social practice are at the core of the analysis (see below).

Roman Jakobson (1960) recognises six functions of language, including the *referential* function (what a message is about with regard to its context); the *emotive* function (oriented towards the speaker's attitudes towards what is being said); and the *conative* function (when the speaker is trying to do something with and towards an addressee). He also discusses a *phatic* function (keeping a conversation going and avoiding silence) along with a *metalingual* (checking so that all involved can handle the code: 'do you know what I mean?') and a *poetic* function. All these functions have implications for a functional view of texts (also in the wider sense of the term, as discussed above), but not all of them are equally relevant when texts are approached from a social science perspective. However, the referential function directly relates texts to *goings-on* in the world, and a focus on the emotive and conative functions shows how social actors and groups express attitudes towards such goings-on and also how they use texts to 'act on' the world and on other persons, and try to influence them or exercise power through texts.

With Jakobson's text functions as a background, Michael Halliday's (1978; Halliday and Matthiessen, 2014) functional view of texts and language has been used extensively in the field of critical discourse studies, CDS (cf. Fowler, (2013 [1991]): 68–70; Fairclough, 1992, 1995, 2003). Halliday identifies only three so-called *metafunctions*, but they all relate, in part, to the ones described above as relevant to text analyses in the social sciences. The *ideational* or *representational* metafunction is about the potential of multimodal texts to represent versions of *states* (static) and goings-on (dynamic) in the world (cf. Jakobson's referential function). For instance, texts can represent a chain of historical events, the actors that made things change and the (new) states of affairs after these events. Importantly, these events and goings-on can not only be represented in one way, but in many different versions depending on the interests of the persons and groups behind the texts, and the discourses that the texts draw on (see below). This is also why analyses of the ideational metafunction in texts have been so prominent in critical studies: which version of the world prevails in different texts?

The *interpersonal* metafunction has to do with how we create and maintain our social relations with others – e.g., through expressing an opinion or an attitude towards something, asking a question, giving an order or making a joke. Language is thus used not only for representation, but also for expressing and evoking attitudes and emotions, and trying to affect the feelings, actions and behaviours of others (again, cf. Jakobson's emotive and conative functions). This function of texts is also relevant for many analyses in the social sciences, not least those that focus on rhetorical aspects of, for instance, political communication.

Halliday also identifies a third, *textual*, metafunction that, in a way, is instrumental to the other two. The textual metafunction connects the other two into interpretable, communicative texts. Put differently, the textual metafunction has to do with how words and clauses combine into cohesive texts, something that was touched upon above with regard to the properties of texts (Halliday and Hasan, 1976).

Texts also relate to different types of conventions – that is, the composition of texts and their design are not arbitrary but motivated (Kress, 2010) in relation to the *social action* or practices that they are part of (Miller, 1984; cf. Björkvall, 2020). This way, texts that are part of similar social actions tend to share certain properties. This is the *genre* dimension of texts. For instance, advertisements in lifestyle magazines tend to present the product or service (in its lifestyle context) advertised saliently at the top of the page, often visually represented. Possible logos or written messages that anchor the product advertised tend to be presented at the lower part of the page. As mentioned, this composition is not there by chance; it is motivated in relation to the social action of trying to sell a particular product or service to audiences of a certain type in a specific medium (lifestyle magazines).

The social actions that texts are part of in given cultures, along with motivated, conventionalised textual properties, make it possible to recognise ads as ads and not as something else. As a result, in this book, genres are perceived as social constructs used to achieve something in society. In other words, texts do not 'belong' to genres; they are the materialisation (see above) of genres as part of social actions. Of course, genres are also multimodal. Printed advertising, as in the example above, is a highly multimodal genre, and so are, for example, the workplace interview with all its gestures and gazes and the parliamentary debate, not to mention social media genres such as the 'selfie' (Zhao and Zappavigna, 2017).

The final basic concept to be introduced in this section is that of *discourse*. In Chapter 6 on discourse analysis, there is a detailed explanation of different concepts of discourse. Common to those concepts is that the term 'discourse' refers to semiotic practices related to wider societal practices that include more than the use of language and other sign systems. Another kind of definition of discourse is based on the assumption that human interaction and multimodal texts always include specific perspectives. These can be perspectives on, for instance, gender, ethnicity, social justice, economic efficiency, and these perspectives can be referred to as 'racist discourses', 'neoliberal discourses', and so on.

Texts are concrete manifestations of discourses. More technically expressed, multimodal texts 'realise' discourses, which is the reason why researchers and students in the social sciences need access to robust text analytical methods.

To sum up, texts are material artefacts with identifiable functions that are reflected in their representations of goings-on in the world, in how they create and maintain social relations, and in their compositional design. Texts are also multimodal by definition, always combining different materialities and semiotic modes for meaning-making. In other words, a transcript of a parliamentary debate is a text, but so is a local TV commercial or an Instagram post combining a photo of, for example, a smiling cyclist, with any type of caption.

Further, as part of their functionality, texts are part of purpose-driven social actions. This is the genre aspect of texts: texts are conventionalised materialisations of social actions, which gives them recognisable properties in terms of above all composition and design. Members of cultures and subcultures recognise that, for example, the research paper is different from the undergraduate textbook.

Finally, texts are never neutral but contain many, sometimes conflicting, perspectives as part of social practices and wider societal contexts. Such perspectives can, according to one definition, be called discourses. Multimodal texts realise such discourses; thus, they offer a way for researchers and students in the social sciences to investigate societal issues, conflicts and (power) struggles through the analysis of texts.

Approaches to textual analysis

To analyse something is to identify and scrutinise its components. Different approaches to textual analysis are about identifying and studying different parts of texts, different phenomena that relate to the functions of texts mentioned above. The book presents nine broad, partly overlapping, approaches.

Content analysis is used both within the humanities and the social sciences. By conducting content analysis, a student might make comparisons based on quantifications of different elements in texts, which may be useful, for example, if the purpose is to study changes over time. If it is found that the frequencies of certain words in certain genres, such as editorials, change over time, this could be a sign of ideological change. And so could the finding that the villains in thrillers and crime films are represented by new groups of people over time. The approach is sometimes divided into qualitative and quantitative content analysis. In this book, we treat these varieties as different in degree rather than in kind.

Analysis of ideas and ideological thought is an approach with methodological roots and a long and venerable ancestry in theology, history, philosophy, law, literature and political science. The key concepts are ideology and ideas; the focus is on intentional action. Ideologies are analysed as consisting of ideas that guide the actions and interactions that make up society with its institutions, social relations and power relations. The aim is to identify, interpret, describe and classify the ideological content in thought and language not only in existing institutions and social fields, but also in debates, movements and organisations striving for preservation or change of the social order.

Conceptual history has its roots in a critique of social history as well as of the history of ideas. Its point of departure is that concepts are continuously disputed and that conceptual change affects social processes. Conceptual change mirrors historical change, but shifting concepts also has an impact on societal developments. Reinhart Koselleck (2004) claims that there are concepts filled with experience to the extent that they affect our very expectations. The changing meaning of terms can be studied over shorter as well as longer periods of time, and it is possible to analyse how conceptual change affects whole systems of thought. Historical but also contemporary texts might be analysed.

From its origins as a method used almost exclusively by historians, *narrative analysis* has spread to all branches of the social sciences and beyond. It involves the explication of stories as a way of gaining insights into ideological power and 'common-sense' understandings of the way the world works. A student might be interested in which components constitute a narrative, in what order different kinds of events take place and what roles there are in the story. Or they might want to study how something is narrated – e.g., whether the story-teller keeps their distance from the characters in a story or if they seem engaged with their destinies.

Discourse analysis – henceforth often DA – is also used both within humanities and the social sciences. Aspects of discourses that might be studied are the frames for what ought (not) to be said in a particular context, which categories are in use and what is taken for granted but not explicitly expressed. The overarching purpose of DA is often to study issues related to power, an example being how different categories of people (like 'the mad' in Foucault's analysis referred to above) are discursively constructed and how this might affect their possibilities to act. DA comes in many kinds and the first of three chapters devoted to this broad strand of analysis presents three poststructural discourse analytical approaches (more on poststructuralism below) referred to as political discourse theory (PDT), discursive psychology and the 'What is the problem represented to be?' approach (WPR).

Another discourse analytic approach, *critical discourse studies*, CDS (also referred to as critical discourse analysis, CDA) has its own chapter in the book. CDS is presented here as an umbrella of linguistically inspired methods for analysing text and discourse – mostly developed by linguists, such as Ruth Wodak and Norman Fairclough – and used with a critical purpose. The techniques presented in the chapter can also be used without such a critical aim. The methods are suitable for revealing implicit rather than explicit meanings of texts. The chapter demonstrates methods for analysing metaphors, choice of words and the perspective chosen to describe goings-on in the world through grammatical choices.

In the chapter on *multimodal discourse analysis*, we present tools for analysing many visual resources and their ideational, interpersonal and compositional aspects. Interest in studying both pictures as such and multimodal texts – for example, how writing and pictures interact on a website – has been growing lately. Although both verbal language and pictures can represent reality, and are used to create and maintain social relations, they do so in different ways. In verbal language, aspects such as the grammar of a clause are used to express offers or demands; in pictures, an important way in which this is done is by humans' different ways of looking at the viewer.

The different approaches presented in this book have grown out of different academic traditions, and studies inspired by them are more or less clearly anchored in particular theories of science. In some of the chapters, we discuss issues to do with the theory of science. We deal with two general aspects, epistemology and ontology, and how texts relate to them. In the next section we introduce a few basic ideas that will be revisited in coming chapters.

Textual analysis, language and learning about the world

As we have stated, texts are *material artefacts* produced by humans. As such, texts are empirically visible residues of people's social interaction. Textual analysts argue that by attending to the texts of a particular society, we may reconstruct important features of the ideational, cultural and political worlds from which these texts emerged.

The relationship between texts and society, however, is not entirely straightforward. As textual analysts, we need to reflect on our assumptions about the world and the nature of knowledge. This means addressing issues of *ontology* – i.e., *what the world is like* – and *epistemology* – i.e., *what we can know* about the world. Importantly, we need to ask what role texts play in society and what we can learn from examining them.

A key epistemological question is what constitutes reliable knowledge about the world. For textual analysts, this translates into a question of what conclusions we can draw from the materials we study. Can we ever retrieve a text's pure 'truth', or are we restricted to making subjective interpretations of it? Should we limit our efforts to reporting about a text's easily verifiable surface properties, or are we allowed to use our interpretative skills and imagination to speculate about its deeper meanings? The answers to these questions differ depending on what metatheoretical perspective we take on science. Here, we will look at a few prominent perspectives – namely, empiricism, constructionism, poststructuralism and critical realism – and what they imply for textual analysis.

The *empiricists*, close to the school of *logical positivism* that emerged in the late 1920s (Carnap, 2003), claim that our senses hold the key to knowledge. Influenced by the natural sciences, empiricists argue that reliable knowledge can only come from observation. Of course, people believe in many things that cannot be observed directly – like gods, justice, love, and the like – but empiricists insist that we bracket such beliefs from the realm of proper *scientific* knowledge (Benton and Craib, 2011). Moreover, empiricists argue that accurate knowledge requires a *neutral observation language*, a descriptive language based on sensory experience that would be 'objective' and 'value-free' (Kitcher, 2002). Such a language, it is claimed, is indispensable to reach the goal of science – namely, to objectively *explain* and even *predict* natural and social events in terms of universal 'covering laws' (Hempel, 1970).

The empiricist commitments to observation, neutral language and law-like explanations have served the natural sciences well, but they pose a problem for many forms of textual analysis. Since textual analysts often deal with non-observable phenomena (like 'ideologies', 'discourses', 'narratives' or 'affects'), they face a challenge in meeting the strict empiricist criteria for science. Moreover, when textual analysts stress the role of language in shaping people's worldviews and apprehend the researcher as a co-constructive agent, they further blur the line between 'pure' science and the messy, opinionated worlds of culture and politics.

Concerns like these, however, may not invalidate the scientific ambitions of textual analysis as much as they highlight crucial *ontological* differences between the natural and the social world. Two differences stand out: first, while the study objects of natural science do not speak, it is impossible to understand *humans* and their *societies* without attending to the dimensions of meaning and language (Norton, 2004). As thinking, speaking and interpreting creatures, people cannot escape this dimension of meaning-making; it is present in everything they do (Chouliaraki and Fairclough, 1999; Fairclough et al., 2002). Second, while societies may well be *rule-governed* – meaning that we can often observe structured patterns in people's behaviour – they are far from *law-governed* in the empiricist sense (Glynos and Howarth, 2007).

Here, we meet with a curious paradox: we know that people often act according to unquestioned social norms, but we also know that when people become aware of these norms, perhaps by reading or conducting social scientific studies, this magical force dissipates. From this moment on, people face a *choice* between reproducing the old pattern and acting differently. Unlike natural science then, social science holds the potential to annul the 'laws' that it discovers *in the very act of discovering them* (Oren, 2006). Although textual or linguistic analyses cannot directly affect the physical world, they *can* change people's *relationships* with their worlds. Here, we begin to discern why studying language and texts is indispensable to understanding society. We also see that an overly restrictive empiricist outlook would prohibit us from addressing many questions of academic interest and great human concern. This is why other theories of science have opted to treat language as central – even claiming that the basis of knowledge lies *within* language and not *outside* of it.

According to the *constructivist* view, we never have access to a reality unfiltered by language. From this perspective, language is not a neutral medium for communicating existing facts. Instead, it is language that produces the categories through which we perceive the world as consisting of distinct 'facts' or 'things' (Barthes, 1993; Berger and Luckmann, 1966). Constructivists argue that things in the world never 'speak' to us to convey their pre-existing, inherent meaning.

Instead, *we impart meaning to things* by naming them and talking about them (Burr, 2003; McGowan, 2006).

Poststructuralism pursues these constructivist themes to their fullest extent (Sayyid and Zac, 1998; Howarth, 2000). Informed by Nietzschean scepticism, poststructuralists take an *anti-essentialist* and *anti-foundationalist* stance, dismissing the existence of any 'facts' or 'truths' independent of language (Nietzsche, 1976; Rorty, 1989). For example, when we speak of ourselves as individual, self-contained subjects ('I did that') or express a particular identity ('I am a woman'), poststructuralists claim that we confuse causes with effects. There is no unchanging, unified 'I' that is the sovereign author of its own actions. Nor is there an eternal 'womanhood' that expresses itself through particular individuals. Rather, it is the doing itself – the 'performance' – of individuality or femininity that *produces* the perception of a 'self' or a 'woman' as the originator of the act (Haar, 1971; Butler, 2006: 28–9).

Poststructuralists also emphasise the radical undecidability and antagonism inherent in all systems of meaning. For example, they stress that no term in language has meaning on its own. Terms only acquire their identities in relation to what they are *not* ('I' means 'not you'; 'woman' means 'not man', and so on). There is no term in language that is purely self-identical that could serve as an 'anchor' for the meaning of other terms. Differently put, no single term can structure a linguistic system without being structured in turn (Derrida, 2001). This is why poststructuralists stress the *contingency* of linguistic constructions – i.e., that meaning can always change – and underscore that *power* and *hegemony* (the elevation of a particular worldview to the status of 'common sense') always play a role in determining the outlooks of different groups, movements, societies or cultures (Laclau and Mouffe, 1990, 2001).

Just like the meaning of any particular word is determined by its position in a sentence or a paragraph, poststructuralists argue that objects and subjects obtain their identities by being positioned in ever-changing networks of social practices (Howarth and Stavrakakis, 2000). Knowledge about the social realm comes from analysing these discursive networks and *deconstructing* them – i.e., laying bare their internal make-up and interrogating their conditions of emergence (see Chapter 6).

Another attempt to justify an epistemology more permissive to textual interpretation is the *critical realism* of Roy Bhaskar (1998, 2008). Against empiricism and positivism, which Bhaskar rebuked as the ruling 'ideology' of the scientific community at the time, he proposed a three-tiered, 'layered' view of reality that would allow us to maintain a belief in the power of science while steering clear of both naive empiricism and postmodern scepticism. Starting with the vexing question of *what the world must be like for science to work*, critical realists hypothesise that there must be a set of basic mechanisms operating to bring order to the universe. However, the foundational forces at work in this *real domain* are not immediately observable. We can only posit their existence by mapping the patterns that arise from their complex and conflictual interplay. Unfortunately, we cannot observe everything occurring in this *actual domain* either. Only some of these events lend themselves to human observation in the *empirical domain*. From the clues we can glimpse at this level – for example, in the texts that people produce – we must work backwards to posit plausible hypotheses of what the world is like (Collier, 1994; Bhaskar, 2008).

Critical realists share many of the assumptions that constructivists and poststructuralists make about the sense-making powers of language. However, given their commitment to an ultimate ontological 'ground', critical realists stress the interrelations between language use and other, more readily determined, social structures like the legal system or the economic mode of production. The tradition of critical discourse studies (CDS) (see Chapter 7), in particular, has emphasised this need for studying 'texts in context' (Fairclough, 1992, 1995, 2003).

Differences in ontology and epistemology, then, determine the kinds of questions that researchers believe they can answer and the kinds of research methods that are appropriate. Most notably, while empiricists cling to the hope of a neutral observation language, constructivists, poststructuralists and critical realists maintain that researchers are always, to some extent, involved in *producing* what they study.

Fundamental differences in moral and political outlooks often accompany this line of separation. Where empiricists strive to avoid value judgements, constructivists, poststructuralists and critical realists often see their work as inexorably normative. Although the latter group of analysts are typically sceptical of absolute moral and political truths, they often align themselves with an emancipatory ethos. Poststructuralists, for example, have often expressed their vision of freedom as an ever-expanding horizon of human possibilities and framed their critical stance as 'the art of *not* being governed or better, the art of not being governed *like that and at that cost*' (Foucault, 1997: 28, emphasis added). Similarly, the abiding normative concern of critical realism is 'human emancipation understood as the replacement of unneeded and unwanted sources of determination with needed and wanted ones' (Hartwig, 2008: ix). In concrete textual analyses – as will become evident in the following chapters – these normative attitudes often come to the fore in efforts to unravel the texts that bind us in subjection to given assumptions and to point beyond these obstacles to hitherto undiscovered realms of human freedom. Table 1.1 summarises important aspects of three influential meta-theories of science.

Textual analysis and interpretation

The verb 'to interpret' has two meanings in this book. On one hand, it refers to the fact that *texts* must be interpreted: they must be understood and the potential meanings of what is stated must be identified. On the other hand, it refers to the

Table 1.1 Prominent meta-theories of science

	Ontology	Epistemology	Methodologies
Empiricism	Reality is law-governed, observable (through the senses) and observer-independent.	Knowledge comes from rigorous observation and should be expressed in a neutral language where facts are separated from values.	Quantitative approaches aiming for explanation of regularities in the world: deductive (experimental testing of hypotheses) and inductive (generalisation, modelling, postulation of covering laws).
Poststructuralism	Reality cannot be observed directly. We only have access to discursively constructed versions of the world.	Knowledges (in plural) are products of language use and social power relations. Researchers participate in the social construction of the world but may also use the rules of language and meaning-making to elucidate how particular constructions work.	Qualitative, interpretative approaches aiming for understanding of particular settings or epochs: inductive and retroductive (qualitative interviews, document/archival studies, observation, case studies etc.).
Critical realism	Reality is stratified; real and observer-independent mechanisms give rise to actual events, of which some are empirically observable.	Surface appearances can be misleading, which is why research must be a process of hypothesising about the underlying causes of our observations. The gap between the world and the language we use to represent it requires reflexive awareness of the theory-dependence of all research.	Quantitative and qualitative approaches aiming to explain observables by positing plausible hypotheses: inductive, deductive and retroductive (mixed methods).

step in the research process that follows the textual analysis where the meaning of the *results* is interpreted – i.e., their significance for the social scientific problem that the analysis was meant to shed light on. In this section, we will only discuss interpretation in the first sense.

All elements of a multimodal text, as well as the text as a whole, are in need of interpretation. Interpretation is a more or less complex process. The complexity is due to the research problem one is working on, the nature of the text itself and the kind of analytical approach chosen. In a content analysis where words are encoded, interpretation problems might not occur. In a discourse analysis in which both explicit and implicit meanings are important, the interpretation problems are likely to be more challenging.

When interpreting a text, different contextual aspects can be in focus: the text producer, the discourse that the text is a manifestation of, and the readers of the text – that is, readers in an extended sense including listeners and viewers, depending on the medium. The text producer might be a single person or an organised group of people, like an NGO, a board or a government. The *empirical reader* is the person who actually reads a text. For an advertisement, this could be, for instance, a 52-year old woman in a rural area on the Indian east coast, without a university degree. However, the *model reader* (cf. Eco, 1984, 1994) – the text-internally constructed reader – can be someone else: a younger woman with a university degree, living in an urban area in India. Such tensions between empirical readers and model readers of a text are very common, and a result of the dynamic nature of texts. However, they also add to the complexity of interpretation, as well as the methodological tools required by the analyst.

From these descriptions, three main strategies of interpretation can be formulated: one that relates the interpretation to the producer of the text; one that relates it to the model or empirical readers; and one that relates it to the discourse without focusing on particular agents. Neither of these strategies is pure: normally, one does a little bit of everything but with different emphasis.

However, we start by introducing a fundamental insight from *hermeneutics*, the art and theory of reading and interpreting – namely, the role of the *prejudices* with which every reader approaches a text. Hans-Georg Gadamer (1900–2002) stresses that every reader comes to a text with prejudices (Gadamer, 1989). The analyst is interpreting a text from their particular historical horizon. Without prejudices, interpretation is not possible, which is a key point. Our understanding of the world, the social context in which we exist, our education, our genre knowledge, all influence our interpretation. Gadamer describes the analyst's own historically and socially conditioned prejudices as the starting point from which it is at all possible to appreciate texts from other times and cultures. The meaning of the text changes, since different readers interpret it differently in different historical contexts. It is impossible to reconstruct exactly what the author wanted to say with the text. The text and we as socially and historically conditioned interpreters are what matters (Gadamer, 1989).

The *producer-oriented strategy* of interpretation is primarily focused on the meaning of the text from the perspectives of its producer(s). The *meaning potential* is regarded as closely connected to what the person or groups of people who formulated it wanted it to mean. In hermeneutics, Friedrich Schleiermacher (1768–1834) is often referred to as a researcher who considered interpretation to be a reconstruction of what the text producer meant – a form of interpretation that Gadamer opposed (Schleiermacher, 1998). Historians of ideas often use this way of reading when studying texts by dead authors. Art might also be interpreted that way.

In relation to this kind of interpretation, Quentin Skinner gives us some sophisticated advice, the essence of which is, first, that it is essential to understand what kind of *speech act* that was carried out by producing the text: what is being *performed* by this particular act of using language? Did the author write a piece of social satire, a scientific report, a political pamphlet or something else? In a similar vein, this can be formulated as 'which social action is being performed, and, accordingly, which genre conventions are drawn upon by the producer(s) of a text?' What kind of speech acts were, or are, usually carried out by producing texts of a particular kind, and which genres become relevant? What is an author of news articles, economic reports or medical records supposed to be writing (Skinner, 1988a)?

Second, the meaning of the text must be interpreted in relation to the given author's language use and way of arguing. Skinner (1988b) stresses the importance of not reading one's own (the interpreter's) meaning into the terms used in the text. This is crucial when studying old texts, but the vocabulary does not need to be that old for the interpreter to fall into linguistic traps. Third, knowledge of context is very important for good interpretations. The context should, however, not be seen as decisive for what is expressed in texts, but rather be of help for determining the *generic* frames inside which reasonable interpretations can be made.

Stuart Hall (1994) also has advice to offer to those interpreting texts from the perspective of the text producer. He is less interested in particular individuals (such as Mary Wollstonecraft, John Stuart Mill or whatever author's texts are being interpreted) and more interested in societal structures and the positions created by them for different agents. He concentrates on what resembles Skinner's first point. What might, say, a journalist on a TV channel in a particular part of South Africa in the early 2020s be doing when publishing a TV news report? What frames are created by technical issues, the format of the news programme, the owners of the TV channel and other social structures?

When interpreting images and other visual elements in multimodal texts, we also use knowledge about genre conventions to understand what the text producer wanted to convey. We know that text inside a balloon above somebody's head in a comic tells us what the person says, and that the cartoonist wants to convey that the person is in pain and dizzy when they draw a circle of little stars around the head of a character who has just been beaten over the head. This example illustrates the importance of a knowledge of conventions – more precisely, genres – for the interpretation of texts, while the genres in themselves partly decide what speech acts are possible.

The purpose of the *reader-oriented strategy* can be to understand which meaning a particular text has for its empirical readers. The meaning of the text is determined by its reception, just as stated by Gadamer, which, in terms of methods, requires reception studies. In media reception studies, it might be asked how certain groups of people – the poorly educated, the highly educated, people in blue- or white-collar jobs, female, male, young or old – tend to interpret a certain news item. Hall explains that different social groups interpret what they read, hear and watch according to different frames of interpretation and sets of values. This interpretation strategy is thus about learning about the prejudices of others and how they meet with texts.

Of relevance to some studies in this context is the concept of *preferred reading* (Hall, 1994), which refers to the reading that a text producer intended the addressees to make, or, more loosely, to a dominant reading that most people would have made at the time. But people also interpret messages in ways other than those intended by text producers and might produce oppositional readings, using alternative frames of reference. Related is Eco's (1994) aforementioned concept of the model reader, a type of reader identity set up by the design of a text, which any empirical reader of a text must relate to in one way or another. Just as with preferred reading, model reader identities can be accepted by empirical readers, or be questioned or rejected.

According to the *discourse-oriented strategy* the meaning potential of a text is above all found in discourses which it draws on or realises. In discourse analysis this is the most common strategy of interpretation. The meaning of a particular text is thus understood through other texts that it is *interdiscursively* related to and from discourses that the text realises (Fairclough, 1995). It works the other way round as well: the discourse as a whole is interpreted and understood from interpretations of many single texts. Discursive patterns – such as how categories are used or the kind of claims and evaluations that are made when particular subject matters are treated in particular contexts – are studied in a systematic fashion and these patterns are related to a wider social reality. An example of an interpretation of patterns in discourses not primarily interested in agents around the text is Fredric Jameson's the *political unconscious*. Jameson makes Marxian interpretations of fiction written in certain social conditions and finds in them expressions of social contradictions being symbolically processed in narratives (Jameson, 1989). This interpretation strategy is also used for images, symbols and multimodal texts. Recurrent images of the nation's flag as well as photos of triumphant members of the national team lifting the victory trophy towards the sky may be interpreted as *banal nationalism* (Billig, 1995) – i.e., an everyday recurrent message that 'we' belong to the same nation that we naturally feel is ours, which we esteem and want to defend. Individual images of flags could not be interpreted in this way: every single image gets its potential meaning by being part of a social practice in which flags and other national symbols are often depicted.

Table 1.2 summarises the three interpretation strategies. In practice, interpretations normally focus on several aspects. Yet, a researcher working with texts should be aware of whose meaning they are trying to reconstruct: the meaning potential mainly set up by the producers of the text; the way it is or was understood by its empirical readers, or the preferred readings and model reader; or, more abstractly, the meaning that could be drawn from the discourse that the text realises by anyone versed in this discourse.

Table 1.2 Interpretation strategies

Interpretation strategy	Whose meaning making is in focus?	What aspects should be studied?	Examples of use
Producer-oriented strategy	The text producers as individuals or groups of people.	The producer's particular social position and the speech acts and social actions likely to be performed in certain genres from that position; the producer's normal language use; genres.	The history of ideas; interpretations of art and literature; critical analysis of genres of governance and power in organisations.
Readers-oriented strategy	The empirical readers; model reader construed as a strategy in the text.	Reception of texts; preferred readings; constructions of text internal reader identities.	Media reception studies; interpersonally oriented studies of addressivity in texts.
Discourse-oriented strategy	Meaning created through discourse.	Discursive patterns regarding particular subject matters in particular contexts and the discourse in relation to its social context.	Discourse analysis.

Goals of textual analysis in the social sciences

According to this book, the overarching goal of a textual analysis within the social sciences should be that it *contributes to shedding light on a social scientific research problem*. For an analysis to be relevant to the social sciences, it needs to ask questions relating to the study objects of these disciplines or formulate research aims of relevance. For instance, it is perfectly possible to analyse a political text from certain linguistic perspectives, answering questions of interest within the field of linguistics that lack relevance for politics as studied within political science. Then it is not a social scientific study. To reach the goal of enlightening a social scientific problem, any study needs to fulfil some criteria regarding validity or trustworthiness and reliability. This section discusses such criteria with regard to textual analysis for social scientific purposes.

To answer research questions, methodological tools are needed. It is important both to know how to use different tools and to choose the right ones for the task. When wood needs to be chopped, it is probable that the clumsiest axe user will do a better job than an expert user of sewing machines. But, unlike the woodcutter who can fall back on centuries of experience of wood cutting during which axes of all sorts were developed, the social scientist who wants to analyse texts lacks precise tools to choose between for particular research questions. Instead, there are more general tools that in most cases need to be honed to precision and often are combined with other available tools. The tool metaphor illustrates the aspect of a good study that is referred to as *validity*. In the empiricist perspective, a method is valid if it measures what is intended to be measured in a particular study. Is the frequency of mosque visits a valid way of measuring the strength of religiosity in a community? Presumably, in many cases, but in others not at all, as in a predominantly Christian community. Or take the research aim to compare the views on 'madness' or mental illness at two points in time. This could be done by comparing corpora from different points in time. There are more or less valid methods for making this comparison. Should we compare the lengths of sentences in the texts in the two corpora in a simple content analysis? Or perhaps use narrative analysis to compare in what order events are told in narratives that might be found in the texts? There is reason to doubt that either of these strategies would be valid: why would they tell us anything about the views on mental illness expressed in the texts? Comparing how special terms for mental illness are used, how people categorised as mentally ill are described, what treatment is proposed for them and what evaluative expressions are used about them could produce more valid results. Turning to some kind of DA or perhaps conceptual history might prove fruitful.

Yet another aspect of validity is the choice of texts to analyse for answering a particular research question. If, for example, one wants to conduct textual analysis to pin down views on 'madness' in today's societies, what kind of texts should be studied? Perhaps texts related to modern psychiatry or to fiction and film. This indicates that we would need to narrow the research aim to specific areas.

Theoretical ideas also play a part when it comes to validity. Is it sufficient to investigate who got a majority for their propositions and who was voted down to know who exercised power in the university board? 'Yes, it is a valid method for analysing power,' an adherent of power's first dimension would answer. 'No,' someone who prefers the second or third dimension of power would argue, 'that is not a valid way of measuring power.'

The meaning of the concept of validity in relation to many qualitative studies, especially those with a constructivist take on research, is more complex. Some authors see validity in qualitative research as one aspect of the broader concept of *trustworthiness* and claim that validity should be differently interpreted depending on the research paradigm – e.g., constructivism or critical realism. Several ways of validating qualitative studies, of which some are more relevant to textual analysis than others, are proposed. One way is to address a phenomenon from multiple directions, *triangulation*, which could speak for the use of different kinds of textual analysis on the same texts. It is also important to be critically self-reflexive when interpreting texts. How does my own societal position affect my interpretations? In critical research, validity could be judged on a study's ability to transform sociopolitical situations of concern (Rose and Johnson, 2020).

Good validity is not enough to make a study credible or trustworthy. Even though it might be preferable to use an axe clumsily than to try out a sewing machine on wood, some ability to handle an axe is necessary to get the wood chopped. It is, for example, crucial to hit the wood rather than other nearby objects. In other words, there is a need for precision. This is true also for the research study. This aspect is referred to as *reliability*. When this concept is used in the context of an empiricist view of science, the way to obtain high reliability is to be sufficiently accurate in measuring and counting. The concept may also be used in a broader sense, suitable for most studies, and refer to operations other than measuring and counting. It then refers to being accurate and precise in all steps of the study. For most textual analyses, interpretation is a matter of reliability. Whatever interpretation strategy is used, the reading must be careful enough for the purpose.

A way of testing reliability is to compare the results of independent studies of the same phenomenon which were carried out in the same way (see Chapter 2). If different persons conduct them and reach the same results, they have a high degree of *intersubjectivity*. How strongly good intersubjectivity is emphasised varies with the theory of science: it is particularly highly valued from an empiricist point of view. In the social sciences and the humanities, that interpret human communication and activities, this ideal is controversial. Even if complete intersubjectivity is seen as an impossible ideal, however, good research should still be transparent and the results well argued for. The reader should be able to reconstruct the steps taken by the researcher to reach the conclusions. For this to be possible, interpretations of written texts should be argued for with the help of quotes and records of the texts. The interpretation of pictures can be argued for by using descriptions of the image, references to its context and the meaning that certain camera angles, for instance, have in a particular genre.

Another aspect of reliability is *intrasubjectivity*. Good intrasubjectivity implies that the same person gets the same results from the same kind of analysis of the same material at different points in time. The purpose is to guarantee that the researcher is judging consistently. This is particularly important when comparisons are made. If the differences found between corpora from different points in time are best explained by the researcher having judged the texts of the corpora in different ways, there is a reliability problem at hand. In that case, the result is due to differing researcher judgements and not to differences in the texts. Table 1.3 summarises the criteria for goal-fulfilling textual analysis discussed above.

About choosing between approaches

A methods reader presenting several different approaches begs the question: How does one choose an approach and method for one's study? In this section we offer some reflections on that question. Our message can be summarised as follows: (1) let the research problem or research questions guide the methodological choices; (2) always choose methods appropriate for the particular study; (3) choose

Table 1.3 Criteria for textual analysis for social scientific purposes

Criterion	Aspects and meaning
Formulation of adequate research questions/ research aims	• Questions and aims should relate to the study objects of the social sciences
Validity/trustworthiness	• Choice of adequate analytical tools and honing them to precision in order to answer a research question or to fulfil a research aim • Well-motivated choice of texts for answering a research question or fulfilling a research aim • Triangulation • Self-reflexiveness • Awareness of the implications of the choices of theoretical perspectives or concepts for the design of the study
Reliability	• Being accurate and precise in all steps, including counting, measuring and interpreting texts • Intersubjectivity (= the possibility for other researchers to repeat the study and reach the same results; particularly important from an empiricist view of science) • Transparency in all steps of the study, including interpretation • Well-argued results • Intrasubjectivity (= the result of the researcher themselves having judged all parts of a corpus consistently)

the simplest possible way to answer the research questions; and (4) adapt the tools for analysis when necessary. These points are valid not only for textual studies but for social science studies in general.

The research question should always guide the choice of methods. What is the best way to answer it? That said, research questions or research aims tend to come in at different phases of the research project in different disciplines. While studies in political science or sociology tend to be guided by research questions formulated at a relatively early stage, in historical studies, as well as in anthropological and ethnographic ones, the questions to be answered or the aims to be fulfilled by the study are often developed later in the process, when work in the archive or field is already well under way.

Furthermore, some researchers feel acquainted with particular approaches that rather guide the choice of research questions and aims than the other way around. Discourse analysis, conceptual history and other approaches might be understood as the researcher's point of departure, rather than as methods to choose between. It is nevertheless crucial that the chosen method/approach is appropriate with regard to the research questions or aims. By 'appropriate' we refer to methods and approaches that fit the available time to spend on the project, researcher knowledge and other resources. For a small project conducted by a student who has no previous knowledge of discourse analysis, a qualitative content analysis with a simple coding frame might be a better choice than DA.

Simplicity is a virtue in the social sciences. The use of a more complex method does not in itself enhance the quality of any project. A simpler method to reach an answer is time saving and might allow for analysing a larger corpus. The use of simpler methods also usually makes it easier to describe the study in a manner that is transparent to readers.

As already indicated in the discussion of validity above, the analytical tools and ways to conduct textual analysis described in this book – such as the construction of coding frames and coding schemes in content analysis, semasiological analyses in conceptual history and the questions developed to guide the discourse analytical 'What's the Problem Represented to be?' approach – can rarely be used for analysis without adaptation to the research aims and questions of particular studies. 'Foucault never worked that way' might be a relevant critique if a researcher claims to be copying Foucault's kind of studies, but it is irrelevant for a study that uses Foucauldian ideas as its point of departure, but develops the analytical tools in a way that suits the particular research project. While being 'true' to a particular author or approach is not important; being very transparent to the readers about how the study has been conducted is.

How to use this book

This book is primarily meant for students in higher education and researchers in the social sciences. For those who choose to analyse different kinds of texts in their Bachelor's or Master's theses, this book will presumably be the only methodological handbook necessary. If needed, some of the 'Suggested readings' can be added. For PhD students and other researchers unfamiliar with textual analysis, the book can be used as an overview of methods and as a gateway to further reading. Each chapter can be read on its own, but we suggest that readers engage with this introductory chapter first.

Each of the following chapters presents a particular approach to textual analysis. The chapters are all organised in the same way:

- *Background*. This section offers an overview of the approach, situates it in a broader social-scientific context and lays out key theoretical concepts.
- *Analysis*. In this section, the authors demonstrate how to apply the approach in social scientific studies. Examples are hands-on and help readers to use the analytical tools in their own work. Existing studies are often used as illustrations of what the approach can do.
- *Critical reflections*. This part considers the pros and cons of the approach so that readers may make informed methodological choices - e.g., in relation to reliability/validity, interpretative strategies and epistemological issues.
- *Approach and the study of society*. This section highlights the potential uses of the approach in social scientific enquiries, such as, for example, the study of power relations, or the mapping of social, political or ideological change.

- *Summary*. This section has two parts. The first part considers for what purpose the approach is and is not useful. The second part summarises the conceptual structure and practical 'workflow' of the approach in a step-by-step fashion. Readers can use the summaries as checklists for their own studies or read the bullet points for an overview before they engage with the whole chapter.
- *Suggested reading*. This part contains commented suggestions for readers who want to broaden their understanding of the method or dig deeper into certain aspects.
- *Exercises*. Students who want to move beyond theoretical understanding to practical mastery of the approaches can work with the exercises included in each chapter. The exercises are all about trying out the methods on real texts. Teachers using this book in their classes can similarly use the exercises as a basis for course assignments, group work or seminar discussions.

The book ends with a full reference list and an index of the many terms explained in the different chapters.

Suggested reading

A student interested in learning the basics about the concept of power as used within the social sciences could well start with Lukes's (2005) influential book. Avelino (2021) is a brief and comprehensive text that presents seven points of contestation over the concept of power in social theory.

To learn more about the concepts and theories of texts and multimodality, Per Ledin and David Machin's book *Introduction to Multimodal Analysis* (2020) is an accessible introduction.

A good introduction to the theories of science is *Philosophy of Social Science* by Ted Benton and Ian Craib (2011).

For scholars who want to engage with the issue of what is good social scientific research and how it could be planned – e.g., as indicated by Table 1.3 – *Designing Social Research* by Norman Blaikie and Jan Priest (2019) is a recommended read.

2

Content Analysis

Kristina Boréus and Sebastian Kohl

Background

In 1743, a collection of 90 hymns called *Songs of Zion* appeared in Sweden. Although the collection passed state censorship, it was later accused of undermining the Swedish state church clergy and being dangerously popularised and to benefit an oppositional religious group. A number of scholars got involved in a controversy over whether the songs really had a subversive content. After counting some religious symbols in the suspect songs and the same symbols in established songbooks, they found no difference. This was probably the first well-documented content analysis (Dovring, 2009). In the late 1800s, what was referred to as 'quantitative newspaper analysis', an early form of content analysis, was already conducted in the United States. The sociologist Max Weber (1864–1920) predicted in 1910 that researchers would now start to measure quantitative changes in newspaper content (Weber, 2009 [1924]). During the Second World War, the British intelligence service used content analysis of Nazi Germany's propaganda directed at the German people to draw conclusions about the country's new weapons of mass destruction – the method proved to work (George, 2009 [1959]). During the second half of the twentieth century, the new medium of TV sparked an interest in analysing more than written text: pictures and film sequences could also be studied! In the 1950s, what came to be referred to as 'qualitative', in contrast to 'quantitative', content analysis was developed (Schreier, 2014). In the twenty-first century, the development of computer software and the existence of large amounts of text in digitised form have created new opportunities.

Quantitative and qualitative content analysis

By 'content analysis', we refer to a method of text analysis that systematically breaks down and categorises parts of text content to answer specific research questions, a process usually called 'coding'. There are references to 'quantitative' as well as 'qualitative' content analysis in the methods literature. In the social sciences, quantitative studies generally focus on quantities: how much is there of what the researcher is looking for? Qualitative studies attend to the qualities or features of the object under study: what is it like?

Some authors define 'content analysis' as an intrinsically quantifying method – e.g., Shapiro and Markoff (1997) – while others, such as Schreier (2014), distinguish between quantitative and qualitative content analysis. *Quantitative content analysis* is then understood as a method of counting or measuring something in texts because it is assumed that the fact that something occurs to a greater or lesser extent in texts indicates something outside the texts. *Manifest textual aspects* – i.e., explicit expressions – are counted. Quantitative content analysis is essentially deductive in the sense that the analytical tools are generated from the research questions rather than from the texts that are analysed. As the approach is usually understood, it is rooted in an empiricist approach to science (see Chapter 1).

While quantitative content analysis is relatively well delimited as an approach, this is not true of *qualitative content analysis*. Some researchers, such as Mayring (2019), define the latter method as a hybrid between quantitative and qualitative research, while others see it as more thoroughly qualitative (Schreier et al., 2019). The term is also used for analyses where quantification is involved but more complex textual interpretations are required – see, e.g., the description of *summative content analysis* as a type of qualitative content analysis in Hsieh and Shannon (2005). Schreier (2014: 170) describes qualitative content analysis as a method for systematically describing the meaning of qualitative data by successively categorising parts of texts using a *coding frame*. She understands the method as at least partly inductive, meaning that even when the researcher starts from predetermined broad themes or research questions, they allow categories to emerge from the coding process. Kuckartz (2014) describes three kinds of qualitative content analysis (which he refers to as 'qualitative *text* analysis') – namely, thematic, evaluative and type-building text analysis. We present his take on type-building content analysis in this chapter.

We argue that the most fruitful way to deal with the distinction between quantitative and qualitative content analysis is to consider the difference as relative rather than absolute. If counting or measuring is more prominent and advanced, the analysis is more quantitative than if counting and measuring activities are subordinate and rudimentary. More qualitative content analyses rely on complex interpretations of the texts, while less qualitative analyses use less intricate interpretations. The important thing is, however, to be able to explain how the results of the analyses were arrived at, not to categorise studies as either quantitative or qualitative.

Uses of content analysis

Content analysis is used in both the social sciences and the humanities. It is popular in media and communication studies, in its quantitative as well as in its qualitative forms. Qualitative content analysis has gained popularity, not least in the health sciences. Any text can be analysed: reality TV, advertising, newspaper editorials, novels, stamps, tweets, cartoons, psychologist–patient interviews, textbooks, religious documents, tourist brochures, etc. Many different elements of the texts can be categorised, counted or measured, such as particular words, images, metaphors, arguments of a certain type, headline sizes or references to a particular phenomenon. Before we go into detail about how to work with content analysis, we will present some types of studies for which content analysis is suitable.

Classifying text content

Qualitative content analysis is always inductive to some extent, meaning that the researcher goes through the texts early on to determine what topics or other kinds of content it contains instead of using a coding scheme that determines what to look for from the start. The findings might be used to construct classifications or typologies. An example is Fernández Galeote et al. (2022) who classified avatar identities in certain computer games into different types (see Sample study 4 below). Another example is Hatakka et al. (2017) who used thematic qualitative text analysis to construct a typology for the discursive strategies that nationalist-populist anti-immigration parties use when accused of racism.

Studying frequencies and proportions

Quantitative content analyses measure the extent of some kind of text content. The reason for this measuring is often related to a critical research interest in comparing text content with frequencies of certain phenomena (crime, people of different gender) in society or with some standard for fair representation or unbiased reporting. An example is Kagan et al.'s (2020) analysis of the film industry's gender gap. An idea behind the study was that, in an equal society, films would have as many female as male characters in central roles. However, previous studies had confirmed that men were overrepresented as active, speaking characters in films, while women were stereotypically portrayed in peripheral roles. Subtitles from many films were analysed to study the social interaction between movie characters. The results showed that, although the gender gap had decreased over time, it was still considerable. There were more men than women in central roles (an extreme example being that all the *Lord of the Rings* movies have ten male characters in the top ten roles). One way to study interaction was to analyse all instances of three people interacting. In 77 per cent of all such interactions, men were in the majority. (The researchers claim that their way of testing the gender gap in central film roles is superior to the famous Bechdel test (Bechdel, 1986: 22), which any film passes if (1) there are at least two female characters in it, who (2) talk to each other, about (3) something besides a man.)

Another analysis of representativity is Jacobs et al. (2021). The researchers conducted a content analysis of the tone of the economic news by counting positive and negative words in the reporting. Their results indicate that the tone of economic news outside the business section in the 32 high-circulation US newspapers they analysed, strongly and disproportionately tracks the fortune of the richest households in the country. The growth of the welfare of the rich is accompanied by positive language, whereas the lower-income population is mentioned less and uncorrelated with positive language. This, the authors argue, is due to journalists' tendency to report on economic aggregates, such as the total growth of the economy, while not paying attention to distribution. This journalistic habit produces class-biased economic news because aggregate economic expansion and contraction have been closely tied to the ups and downs of the top incomes since the mid-1980s. Thus, when the economy expands, the richest gain. However, when the economy as a whole is doing well, inequality rises since other income groups do not gain.

Examining how something is represented and evaluated
Another use for content analysis is to study how something is evaluated or represented. The research question might consider to what extent something is valued positively or negatively, whether there is any difference in the evaluation between different sources, or whether the same source evaluates different phenomena differently. Sample study 3 below on media coverage of 'stay-at-home-mothers' poses questions about the portrayal and evaluation of women who made the transition from a paid job to staying at home with their children.

For evaluative purposes, negative or positive statements or descriptions may be counted. In their analysis of over 20,000 novels, Archer and Jockers (2016) found that best-selling novels follow a clear pattern of how positively or negatively the plot is described along the storyline. Many bestsellers exhibit a 'rhythmic beat' structured around two bumps of positive emotions, one when the central puzzle is solved in the middle and one when there is a happy end. An automated approach of content analysis of this kind is called 'sentiment analysis', which looks up sets of terms of different evaluative connotations in a given corpus. The Linguistic Inquiry and Word Count (LIWC) is one of the largest repositories for sentiment dictionaries in multiple languages and is standardly used to measure evaluative connotations in texts.[1]

Comparing corpora or time periods
Content analysis is suitable for comparing corpora. The comparison may concern, for example, how different actors express themselves or how phenomena

---
[1] www.liwc.app/dictionaries

are constructed in different national media cultures. Laver and Garry (2000), for example, show how political ideas in party manifestos or other party documents can be systematically compared.

Comparing texts from earlier periods with texts from later ones is a method used to examine change – or the lack thereof – in attitudes and ideas. In Boréus (1997), ideological change in Swedish public debate between 1969 and 1989 was studied through various content analyses of mass-media debate, political speeches and other materials. Expressions of neoliberal ideas and counter-ideas were counted, and the results showed that the debate had undergone a shift from more social democratic, social liberal and leftist ideas, to more neoliberal notions. Sample study 1 below counts the frequency of expressed ideas of certain types with a similar purpose: identifying whether social democratic parties in Europe have undergone a 'neoliberalisation' over time (Fagerholm, 2013).

Analysis

In this section, we first review some steps and concepts in content analysis, after which we present parts of four content-analytical studies: one typical quantitative content analysis, one network analysis, one analysis that uses both quantitative and qualitative techniques to study how a phenomenon is evaluated, and one type-building qualitative text analysis in the vein of Kuckartz (2014).

Analytical steps and key concepts

Choosing and collecting texts

After formulating research questions, the first task is choosing and collecting the texts to be analysed. Quantitative analyses have the advantage that a large amount of texts can be analysed – particularly in the case of computerised studies – since the analysing techniques are simpler than in the case of qualitative studies. In any kind of content analysis, it is advisable to start by examining a small number of texts in order to get an idea of what kinds of texts can provide relevant information. In a media study, a number of choices need to be made: What parts of a newspaper or what TV programme genre will be analysed? What particular papers or programmes will be included? From what time period will the texts be drawn? It might be necessary to reduce the material by taking samples. (Chapter 6 in Krippendorff, 2019, gives a detailed account of sampling methods.) Big datasets and texts from the Internet provide particular selection challenges and certain sampling problems, and ethical selection biases might need to be taken into account.

Sources

What data sources are available for content analysis? A first, classic type is newspaper texts. In many countries, newspapers themselves or research projects are making available increasingly large historical news corpora (i.e., digitised collections of articles), such as *The New York Times* or *The Times Archive*, the huge *British Newspaper Archive*, many even local historical newspapers chronicled by the Library of Congress, the Swedish Media Archive (Retriever Research), Gallica.fr for most major French historical newspapers, Spiegel/Zeit/FAZ archives in Germany, NZZ in Switzerland and the Gale platform for various long-run newspaper archives, available through several university libraries. Probably the most commonly used providers of many outlets across many countries are the Nexis, Factiva or Europress database that many universities have licensed access to. In these archives, one can either perform word-based frequency searches of the entire corpus or find a selection of relevant articles using search strings and Boolean conjunction words such as AND, OR and NOT. It is often possible to *truncate* – i.e., to include different inflections of words and composite words by ending or beginning part of a word with an asterisk (*).

Another important source type is television, radio and film. In some cases, public service television offers access to their archives, as does the American Public Media Archive (https://americanarchive.org/) or, on the European side, the Swedish Media Database (https://smdb.kb.se), or the British media collection (www.bl.uk/subjects/news-media).

A third source is written fiction. Much used by quantitative researchers in literature (Jockers, 2014), these data also contain a wealth of social historical and sociological insights. Older material is freely available from, for example, the Gutenberg Project, Wikipedia or Project Runeberg (http://runeberg.org/). When using Google Books through its online visualisation tool called Ngram Viewer, users can employ complex search strings in a corpus of both fictional and non-fictional works (https://books.google.com/ngrams).

A fourth, frequently used source are texts produced in political processes, such as party manifestos in Sample study 1 below. A large body of bills, motions, parliamentary debates, committee reports, press releases and organisational reports from the post-1945 period is available digitally in OECD countries. Many governing bodies and public agencies collect official documents in searchable databases like the British parliamentary corpus (Hansard) from 1803 to 2005, the Comparative Agenda Project (www.comparativeagendas.net), the digital corpus of the European Parliament, the US congressional records at Congress.gov and all French parliament debates since the French revolution. Legal databases are available in many countries, and Hathi-Trust and the Internet Archive (archive.org) are important providers of historical digitised books. Organisations like the Sunlight Foundation (e.g., Open States, Capitol Words) contribute to the growing number of digitised texts.

Fifth, there are a number of new web-based data sources such as microblogs and social media. Political scientists have used Twitter data to predict election outcomes. Twitter offered researchers (limited and currently not free-of-charge) downloads of text data, and most statistical software, such as R, Stata or Python, offers packages for importing them. Many Twitter data collections are already available through archival institutions, such as the Internet Archive or the Library of Congress (Bail, 2014). The geographical location of tweets and the networks of Twitter users created through retweets, followers and hashtags also allow researchers to link content data to other data. These social media have been prominently used, for instance, to study censorship behind China's Great Wall (King et al., 2013).

A sixth type of source are websites where users upload information and make it available to a wider audience, such as buyers' and sellers' platforms (zillow.com or eBay.com), contact pages and so on. For example, Rudder (2014) has demonstrated the lack of success of overly long or grammatically incorrect messages on the online dating website OkCupid. Google Trends offers an interface for downloading aggregates of its search results (https://trends.google.com). A few providers offer official cooperation with researchers, while others at least allow their content to be webscraped for non-commercial purposes (see Munzert et al., 2014 for how to do this in R).

Finally, researchers can use text material they themselves produced in qualitative research processes such as transcripts of interviews or focus group conversations, ethnographic diaries or even their own research or reading notes. The list of sources above is definitely not exhaustive, as so many materials can be bearers of representational content that can be potentially analysed, but it does mention frequently used sources for content analysis in the social sciences.

Coding: manual or computerised

Texts can be coded manually – i.e., by humans alone, or with the help of the computer, or a mixture of both. Qualitative content analysis, such as Kuckartz's (2014) qualitative text analysis, requires complex interpretation and needs to be done manually. QDA (Qualitative Data Analysis) software is very helpful when coding, but each decision about how to code still has to be taken by the researcher. The advantage of manual analysis is that it allows for more complex judgements and interpretations. Validity is potentially high, meaning that the coding is more likely to measure what it is supposed to measure. The obvious disadvantage is that it is time-consuming and that good intercoder reliability is sometimes hard to achieve.

By computerised coding, we refer to the use of software that searches for words or word combinations according to predetermined principles so that no human being has to read the texts to code them. The researcher uses a *dictionary* of terms – e.g., nouns for locating topics or adjectives for locating sentiments – and runs it automatically over a corpus. The advantage of computer analysis is that vast amounts of digital text can be processed consistently and reliably. The disadvantage is that the validity could be low.

Constructing the analytical tools

The next step is to construct an analytical instrument that shows what should be registered in the material. In manual quantitative content analysis, a fully developed *coding scheme* should tell us exactly what to note in the analysed texts. The basic idea of a coding scheme is to guide the coder so that all texts are analysed in the same way. The word 'code' refers to elements in texts – e.g. certain words being recorded as numbers (see Table 2.2). More complex coding schemes are often accompanied by separate *coding instructions* describing how to assess unclear cases. In manual coding, a *code form* (on paper or on the computer) where the codes can be filled in during the coding process, might be helpful.

Before constructing a coding scheme for manual coding or a dictionary for computerised coding, it is wise to first become familiar with the material by reading all of it (if it is manageable) or going through representative parts of it (if the corpus is too big to be read in its entirety). Just as with any textual analysis, some genre awareness is indispensable. Knowledge of the discourse of which the texts are manifestations and of the social context in which they were produced is also necessary in most cases.

After the coding scheme and the coding instructions for the quantitative analysis have been sketched out, they need to be tested on parts of the material. This process almost always reveals a need to modify the coding scheme and clarify the instructions. It is also appropriate to conduct some double coding (see below) at an early stage to check whether the analytical tools are developed enough to enable consistency in assessing the material.

In qualitative content analysis, the sorting tool is often referred to as a 'coding frame' (Schreier, 2014), but can also be referred to as a 'coding scheme', which is the word we will use henceforth for all kinds of manual content analysis, or *category guidelines* (Kuckartz, 2014). A coding scheme for a qualitative analysis might consist of a number of open-ended questions that should be systematically answered for each text. In qualitative text analysis, as described by Kuckartz (2014), the coding scheme is developed stepwise and its development is an integrated part of the analysis. The process is described below.

Determining recording and sampling units

Constructing a coding scheme for a quantitative content analysis means deciding what to count. The phenomena that are recorded and counted are called 'recording units' (Krippendorff, 2019). These units can be certain words, metaphors, themes, images, arguments of a certain type or anything else that can be discerned in texts of various kinds. The recording units can vary in their attributes, which is why they are also called *variables*. For example, a particular phenomenon may be referred to neutrally, appreciatively or in a disparaging way. These varying properties can be called 'variable values'.

The *sampling unit* (Krippendorff, 2019) or *context unit* (McMillan, 2009) is a text unit for which notes are made for the presence of any recording unit. For example, the coding instruction may specify that the occurrence of certain expressions should be noted once for each political speech in a material consisting of such speeches. In this case, every speech is a sampling unit. However, the speeches can also be broken down so that each section or each sentence constitutes a sampling unit. In a study of what people (gender, age, class, etc.) most often appear in advertisements, it would be appropriate to treat each advertisement as a sampling unit. A sampling unit on the Internet could be a web page, but this would require further specification, including how many of the levels that it is possible to click into that should be examined (McMillan, 2009: 65–6).

In more qualitative analyses using open-ended questions, the recording units are not necessarily fixed from the start, nor do they come with predetermined variable values. Even so, as the analysis proceeds, each category is linked to some part or *segment* of a text during coding: to a word, sentence, page or an entire text (Kuckartz, 2014). When developing the coding scheme and working inductively with a text, particular themes might be 'discovered' and linked to an appropriate text chunk, like a paragraph. When using a predetermined coding scheme, each segment is worked through much in the same way as in quantitative analysis.

Testing the analytical instruments

Once a preliminary coding scheme has been designed, conducting a *pilot study* on a limited part of the data is advisable. This means carrying out an analysis in accordance with the principles for the entire study, thus testing the coding scheme and instructions. In this way, problems with the analytical instruments may be corrected before the whole data set is analysed. In a qualitative text analysis, the stepwise construction of the coding scheme works as an ongoing test of its appropriateness and a separate pilot study is not called for.

Coding

In quantitative content analysis, enough work should have been put into the development of the coding scheme and the coding instructions, including preliminary reliability checks, for few problems to arise during the coding procedure.

The coding in qualitative analysis is different as the work in itself constitutes a constructive part of the analysis. Here, we will look at the coding procedure in a type-building text analysis, where the outcome is meant to be a typology of something (such as avatar-types in Sample study 4 below), as recommended by Kuckartz (2014).

A first step is to read all texts to be analysed, posing preliminary questions in relation to the research question. Say that we are conducting a type-building analysis of how animals are represented in relation to human characters in films. In this case, it could be asked what humans and animals do together or to each other in the films. Other things to look for would suggest themselves during this initial process. Using *memos* – attaching notes to particular parts of the studied texts to advance the analysis – is recommended. Many QDA software packages have memo functions of this kind. The next step is to summarise the text in relation to the research questions.

After this preliminary work, the construction of categories starts. The coding might be inductive, growing out of the interpretation of the texts in relation to the research question, or deductive as when the classification is based on existing typologies (say, of the roles of animals in relation to human characters in films as found in previous research). Often a combination is used. The inductive coding of animal roles could, for instance, be combined with the application of existing taxonomies, such as those for animals of different kinds and breeds. The same animal in a film might thus be coded deductively – e.g., as a horse – and by categories growing out of the interpretation of the text – e.g., as the main human character's friend.

In the next step, inductively constructed categories are grouped together to form more abstract ones. Perhaps a typology of many animals' roles has grown out of the coding: animals that appear as carriage horses, hunting dogs or draught buffalos could be grouped together as 'working animals', while other animals like cats, family dogs or children's guinea pigs are classified as 'pets' and the game bird or insects collected for food belong in the category 'prey'. The working animal, pet and prey categories might then be sorted into one single category at a higher level of abstraction, perhaps as 'animals under human dominion', in contrast to animals in roles such as wild animals that could be classified as 'animals free from human usage'. When part of the material has been analysed in this stepwise fashion, and the categories seem to be at the right level, one should end up with a functional coding scheme to use throughout the rest of the code work.

Testing coding consistency

Computer-based analysis is completely consistent – the computer loses neither energy nor concentration, something that easily happens to human coders. Since the goal of the analysis is to find patterns, the coding scheme must be used consistently. If the aim is to compare one set of texts with another, both sets must be coded in exactly the same way, otherwise, the results will reflect differences in assessment by the coders rather than differences between the texts themselves. To ensure consistency, a single coder may carry out *double coding* in order to check *intrasubjectivity* (or *intracoder reliability*) – i.e., the consistency between the same person's coding of the same material on different occasions. This involves recoding parts of the material and comparing the results of the two rounds. Sufficient time should elapse between the coding rounds, so the coder will not remember how the individual assessments were made. (If the coder remembers which assessment they made on the first occasion, the double coding is not a check on the clarity of the analytical instrument.)

If the results do not match well, it is a sign that the coding has not been consistent. The remedy is to clarify the instructions for the coding scheme to improve consistency. Since the analytical instrument may need to be reworked, double coding should be done early. If poor inconsistency is detected when it is too late to rework the coding scheme, the results for two codes that have proved difficult to distinguish can be merged into a new code with a new name and description. If some codes prove to have been too difficult to code consistently, the coding results for those particular codes should be left out, as they cannot be relied on.

If more than one person has coded different parts of the material, it is important to check that all coders have made similar judgements – i.e., that *intersubjectivity (intercoder reliability)* is satisfactory. To check for consistency, all coders can code the same selected small part of the material. This is particularly important when coding is not only done by experts, but is outsourced for 'crowdcoding' via commercial platforms (see, e.g., Horn, 2019). Crowdcoding has the advantage of scaling coding exercises to include more material, even across multiple languages, but comes at the risk of lower intercoder reliability.

What is an acceptable degree of intra- or intercoder variation depends on the extent to which inconsistencies affect the results of interest. For example, if the aim is to count relatively precisely how many articles dealt with a particular theme, a high degree of consistency should be strived for. If the research objective is to procure a rough measure of differences – e.g., which newspaper had the most coverage of a particular theme – and the difference found between the newspapers is large, a higher degree of deviation is acceptable. There are several ways of reporting the consistency between different codings, and different views on which measures are most appropriate (see Krippendorff, 2019, Chapter 12). The basic idea is to determine what proportion of the agreement in the assessments is unlikely to have been the result of chance.

Methods other than double coding can also be used to achieve consistency in the analysis. For example, different coders can compare their assessments, make joint decisions, discuss divergent codings to adapt the coding scheme and instructions, or code in multiple rounds to increase intercoder reliability.[2] Such methods are commonly used in qualitative content analysis.

Compiling, presenting and interpreting the results
Once the texts have been coded, the results are summarised. A common and simple way to summarise quantitative analyses is to calculate the frequencies of the recording units. The research question may be related to relative frequencies – e.g., how often women are interviewed compared to men. More sophisticated

---

[2] Olson et al. (2016) contains a very detailed process of how to make sure intercoder reliability is given in grounded theory studies.

statistical analyses – e.g., factor analysis – can also be conducted if the coding has been planned to make such an analysis possible. Computer calculations may also be carried out on manually coded material. In other cases, figures can be used. An example where this is necessary is in network analysis (see Figure 2.2). In a type-building analysis, the resulting typology could be presented in a table. Once the results have been presented, it remains to interpret them in relation to the research questions.

Content analysis and software

Software can be brought into the research process at different stages and in different ways. There is software to help with manual coding, specialised software for computerised content analysis – i.e., where the software does the coding – software for unsupervised methods – i.e., topic modelling, where an algorithm produces topics inductively – and software for statistical analysis of the generated variables. There is also special software for network analysis, as in one of the sample studies presented below.

We recommend using some kind of *Qualitative Data Analysis* (QDA) software (also called *Computer Assisted Qualitative Data Analysis Software*, CAQDAS) for any manual coding endeavour that is more complicated than counting words, at least if the study is a bit more extensive. This advice applies to all significant research undertakings (definitely for writing a doctoral thesis and maybe for working on a Master's thesis). It also applies to researchers who plan to work qualitatively with larger amounts of text in the future. QDA programs such as ATLAS.ti, MAXQDA and NVivo have convenient coding features that allow researchers to save, redo and reorganise the coding in time-saving ways. There is also free software on the Internet for such tasks. Even standard applications like Excel or self-programmed command prompts in R allow for qualitative coding. R also offers a Qualitative Data Analysis package, which is closer to the program interface known from other qualitative coding tools.

Coding is still manual with QDA software: the coder makes exactly the same interpretative work as if they were working with paper and coloured pencils or marking up a Word file. Compared to such methods, coding with QDA software may save much effort, help prevent mistakes and increase reliability.

Some software packages have built-in reliability checks to facilitate double coding. These applications can also be used to search for specific words in large text sets and to code automatically. However, if only words are coded, other programs that facilitate the production of dictionaries for computerised coding are probably the better choice. QDA software can also be used for coding and structuring the excerpts of literature reading. Table 2.1 summarises the different features of software for content analysis.

After this review of the basic steps in content analysis, we will present four sample studies. In these analyses, the researchers have chosen recording units that

Table 2.1 Types of programs for different tasks in content analysis studies

Task performed	Examples of software
Manual coding with more complex recording units than words (e.g. expressions of ideas); organisation of qualitative research data	ATLAS.ti, MAXQDA, NVivo, freeware[a]
Computerised coding (searching words and creating dictionaries, coding without reading the texts)	R (with the packages quanteda, tm, openNLP), Python
Statistical calculations using coding results	R, SPSS, Stata, SAS, Python

Note: (a) There is a wide range of free software that can replace many features of commercial software, e.g. Free QDA, Coding Analysis Toolkit, RQDA, TAMS, QDA Miner Lite, ConnectText. If you search for 'Computer assisted qualitative data analysis' you will find many more.

differ in scope. There are also differences in how the coding schemes were constructed and how the reliability issue was addressed.

Sample study 1: Counting expressions of ideas as a measure of ideological change

In our first sample analysis (Fagerholm, 2013), the researcher did not construct the coding scheme or carry out the coding himself, but used an existing database of already coded texts. An advantage of such an approach is that the researcher avoids extensive groundwork; the disadvantage is that the researcher cannot choose what to code and cannot influence the reliability of the coding.

The recording units of the study were expressions of political ideas or policy positions expressed in election manifestos retrieved from the Manifesto Project Database (https://manifesto-project.wzb.eu/), henceforth the *manifesto database*. Beginning in 1979, a series of international projects made a concerted effort to encode 56 variables in the election manifestos of most post-1945 parties in the OECD and later also many Latin American countries (Volkens et al., 2011). The data, consisting of original texts as well as PDF files and already coded[3] plain text files and coded categories, is freely available,[4] and although a number of problems, such as intercoder reliability, have been identified, they are considered the best available in the field.[5] The coded manifestos can also be linked to variables

---

[3] For both manual and computerised coding, it is important that the programs can read the text, which requires the files to be in PDF with identified text, Word or plain text format (.txt files). For quantitative analysis, comma-separated files (CSV) are common, where a comma separates columns in Excel. The advantage of the .txt and .csv formats is that almost any program can read them, but there are many formats they cannot handle, such as italic letters.

[4] All data and all the manifestos can be downloaded with a package in the R program called manifestoR.

[5] A variable in the manifesto database also shows which person coded what (and when) so that it is possible to compute coder reliability.

regarding party organisation, parties and the political system in the different countries (Giger and Schumacher, 2015). The codes represent the relative proportion of *quasi-sentences* expressing a particular policy position, where a quasi-sentence is the smallest meaningful part of a sentence and constitutes a sampling unit.

Of the 56 variables, many relate to the classic political divide between left and right on matters of distributive justice. Using some of these variables, Fagerholm (2013) constructed a composite index designed to measure how neoliberal a party is. Scholars describe a policy shift towards neoliberalism since the 1970s, but while this seems to hold for conservative parties (Harvey, 2005), Fagerholm tries to find out whether a similar shift has taken place in nineteen European social democratic parties between 1970 and 1999.

Fagerholm selected a number of variables that capture classical social democratic/socialist standpoints as well as neoliberal ones. For the first type of variable, he chose, among others, one that deals with whether parties defend the interests of the working class (a variable called per701 in the manifesto database). Other variables included the one to be coded when a manifesto presents social justice and equality as a central political goal (per503) to be achieved through a comprehensive and universal welfare state (per504).

As expressions of neoliberal policy positions, variables included per401 (to be coded when a free market economy is advocated) and per402 (to be coded when a policy considered to favour private enterprise is proposed). Table 2.2 shows an extract from the manifesto database coding scheme and coding instruction for these two variables, among others. Variable names are on the left, and descriptions of each code along with instructions on how to code the quasi-sentences are on the right.

Based on the selected variables, Fagerholm calculated a socio-economic left–right measure based on the following formula: 'SocioeconSN = (SocioeconN − SocioeconS)/(SocioeconN + SocioeconS)', where S and N stand for 'socialist' and 'neoliberal', respectively. Consider a socialist and a neoliberal policy position, both of which can range between 0 and 100 per cent of a party manifesto: the index measures the difference between the amount of neoliberal and socialist statements in relation to their sum. The index ranges from −1 at one extreme, if there are only socialist statements, to +1 if there are only neoliberal ones, while 0 represents a threshold between left and right. The descriptive statistics for the composite measure for all parties, both social democratic and conservative, are shown in Table 2.3.

As expected, the conservative parties generally have a positive mean (μ). In contrast, the social democrats have a negative one, although both party groups show a large internal variation, as shown by the high standard deviation (σ). A breakdown into two periods, pre-1970 and post-1970, shows a shift among the social democratic parties from a very high leftist value of −0.710 to a more moderate −0.395. However, the growing standard deviation reveals that this trend only applies to some parties – the Italian PSI/PDS, the Finnish SDP, the Walloon PS-B and the Flemish SP – while others undergo election-specific but not permanent shifts that

Table 2.2 Extract from the coding scheme with coding instructions in the Manifesto Project Dataset Codebook[a]

Domain 4: Economy

per401	**Free Market Economy** Favourable mentions of the free market and free market capitalism as an economic model. May include favourable references to: • Laissez-faire economy; • Superiority of individual enterprise over state and control systems; • Private property rights; • Personal enterprise and initiative; • Need for unhampered individual enterprises.
per402	**Incentives: Positive** Favourable mentions of supply side oriented economic policies (assistance to businesses rather than consumers). May include: • Financial and other incentives such as subsidies, tax breaks etc.; • Wage and tax policies to induce enterprise; • Encouragement to start enterprises.
per403	**Market Regulation** Support for policies designed to create a fair and open economic market. May include: • Calls for increased consumer protection; • Increasing economic competition by preventing monopolies and other actions disrupting the functioning of the market; • Defence of small businesses against disruptive powers of big businesses; • Social market economy.
per404	**Economic Planning** Favourable mentions of long-standing economic planning by the government. May be: • Policy plans, strategies, policy patterns etc.; • Of a consultative or indicative nature.
per405	**Corporatism/Mixed Economy** Favourable mentions of cooperation of government, employers, and trade unions simultaneously. The collaboration of employers and employee organisations in overall economic planning supervised by the state. Note: This category was not used for Austria up to 1979, for New Zealand up to 1981, and for Sweden up to 1988.

Source: Party Programme Project, https://manifesto-project.wzb.eu/coding_schemes/mp_v5
Note: (a) In addition, there are long general coding instructions on the Party Programme Project website: https://manifesto-project.wzb.eu/information/documents/handbooks

Table 2.3 Coding of the expressed ideology of Western European parties in different time periods

	All parties			Social dem. parties[a]			Cons. parties		
Period	μ	σ	N	μ	σ	N	μ	σ	N
1945-1999	-.261	.520	1586	-.499	.401	364	.162	.471	172
1945-1969	-.293	.536	537	-.710	.228	120	.126	.540	71
1970-1999	-.245	.511	1049	-.395	.426	244	.187	.417	101

Source: Fagerholm (2013: 547), 'Western European Parties along Socioecon$_{SN}$: an overview'.
Note: (a) Covers all parties coded as social democratic by CMP. Some of these parties are not included in this study, mainly due to reasons such as political insignificance or short-livedness.

sometimes form a zigzag course. The Swedish SAP, for example, moved strongly to the right in the 1994 elections but does not show any permanent trend.

Sample study 2: Counting expressions of ideas and relating them to actors: discursive network analysis

Discursive network analysis is a type of content analysis that connects what is said with the individuals or organisations that say it. It thus anchors topics, positions or feelings in the social reality that creates them.

The approach was used by Leifeld (2016) to study newspaper discourses on the privatisation of pensions in German politics in the 1990s, when there was a heated debate on the transition from a pension system in which people working today pay to those who have retired ('pay-as-you-go') to one based on capital coverage (funded pensions). The aim of the research was to understand why the liberal capital coverage system was eventually introduced, despite initial strong opposition from the left.

The approach is associated with a free and easily accessible computer program (www.philipleifeld.com/software/software.html), with which the author analysed all articles in three major politically non-radical newspapers that contained the term 'pension' between 1993 and 2001 (Leifeld, 2016). The truncation '*' allows a search for 'pension' regardless of the ending of the word. The idea of this approach is to be able to code not only opinions for or against particular policy positions, such as 'We must privatise the pension system', but also to register who made the suggestion, with which organisational affiliation and at what date. In the selected 1,876 articles, 246 organisations were found to make 7,249 positive or negative statements about pension reform. In this study, each newspaper article constituted a sampling unit, while policy positions (expressed in one or more sentences) counted as recording units.[6] The latter were coded using 68 different variables.

On the computer, this step looks like in Figure 2.1 below. The big window shows the original newspaper text and the grey highlighted text is the text excerpt coded as 'funded pension system' (*Kapitaldeckungsverfahren*), expressed by the Greens (*Die Grüne*) who supported ('Agreement: Yes') this kind of pension system.

The program saves the manual coding and offers a range of possible outputs in CSV (comma-separated values: see footnote 3) format, Excel format or in file formats that can be used directly by standard network analysis programs such as Netdraw or UCINET.

The study's main finding was that the traditional opposition groups on the left that had been against the funded pension schemes disintegrated in the early 2000s. Around 2000, a policy coalition for a funded pension scheme began to dominate discursively. The changing policy coalitions were able to 'neoliberalise' the old German pension system. The network visualisation of the pension debate

---

[6] There are no explicit coding instructions. The idea is that each policy position has specific and clear expressions in the text.

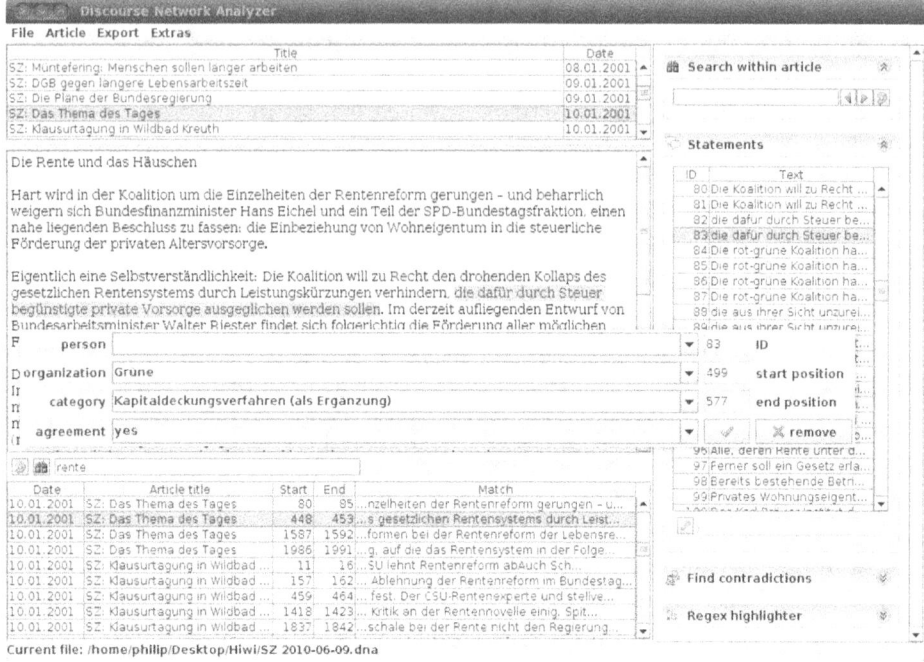

Figure 2.1 DNA window and analysis

Source: DNA (Discourse Network Analyzer) instruction manual, www.philipleifeld.com/software/software.html

between January and May in 2001 in Figure 2.2 below shows the outcome after this discursive shift.

As the study shows, adding the actor, organisation and time dimensions significantly expands the repertoire of quantitative content analysis. Time trends for topics could thus be produced for all actors or specific groups of actors who spoke about pension reform. Two types of networks can be considered, created by the actor and content dimension: the first type describes actors (organisations or individuals) as nodes and uses the number of shared positions as links. Networks are usually characterised by different arrangements of entities (nodes), represented as points, and relations (connections) between them, represented as lines. In typical visualisation algorithms – i.e., where the coding result is displayed as a figure, such as Figure 2.2 – this information is used to group nodes with thicker – i.e., stronger – connections so that, for example, polarised debates create two opposite clusters with strong intracluster connections and weak intercluster connections. In the pensions debate, financial institutions such as banks and employers' associations appear on one side as a policy coalition in favour of pension privatisation through capital-funded schemes (with pension savings channelled through banks and insurers). In contrast, trade unions and left-wing parties appear on the other side of the visualisation, the public pension side, in favour of state-funded pension programmes.

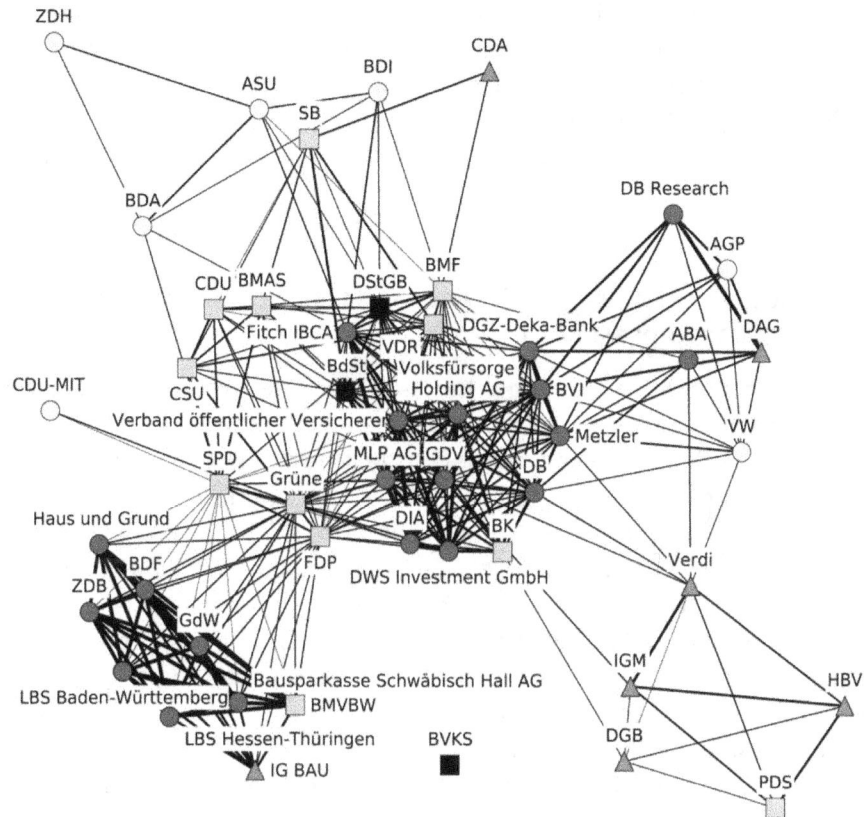

Figure 2.2 Discourse network in the German pension debate, January to May 2001

Source: Leifeld (2013: 189), 'Figure 7: Normalized Actor Congruence Network between January and May 2001'.

Connections express the number of shared statements between nodes, which are organisations (financial = dark circles; social = dark triangles; liberal = light circles; parties/state = grey squares). The visualisation algorithm brings together ideologically related actors in clusters. Compared to the networks of the 1990s, the then central social and state actors had been replaced by a financial–industrial cluster linked to state institutions, while social actors had been relegated to the periphery. Although this network is based only on positively shared policy opinions, the analysis also makes it possible to examine differing opinions.

The second type of network consists of content nodes – in this case, policy proposals that are linked by actors who share a common view. The visualisation describes the discursive landscape of a debate by clustering shared positions. For example, if one defends the retreat of the state from the pension system, one is usually also in favour of a more active role for banks. Both of these networks can be tracked over time in terms of cluster composition and cohesion, and specialised computer software makes it possible to create a 'network movie' of data to track – for example, how more and more actors started supporting the privatisation reforms. A final dimension that can be explored is the interaction between the organisational and individual levels: actors from the same organisation can make conflicting public statements, and intra-organisational cohesion can have an impact on how the organisation moves in the inter-organisational discursive network.

Sample study 3: Counting different aspects of content to analyse how something is presented

Two researchers studied how 'stay-at-home-mothers' were constructed in British press coverage in the period 2008–2013 (Orgad and De Benedictis, 2015). The stay-at-home mothers, who emerged as a distinct type in British public discourse during the 2008 recession, were mothers who had moved from professional work to home life, often because they had lost their jobs in the economic crisis. The authors studied the construction of stay-at-home mothers based on the assumption that the ideal of womanhood has increasingly been cast in neoliberal identity terms linked to the market and consumerism. The central research question was whether being a stay-at-home mother was portrayed as negative (given the importance of female labour for the economy) or whether the reporting supported the women's transition to domestic life. The study is a manual content analysis that tends towards the qualitative in that some variables require relatively complex interpretation.

The empirical material consisted of 299 news articles from the British press. The researchers developed a coding scheme based on reading some of the material, the theoretical literature and the research questions. A total of 30 articles were coded in a pilot study, which led to adjustments to the scheme and a final scheme that included nine variables. The first four were background variables, including publication – i.e., which journal and whether the article topic was personal, social or economic. The other five variables were designed to capture how the mothers were constructed and what values the reporting expressed. We reproduce here the three variables that were essential to the article findings:

- *Class*, where a division was made into *upper class/elite*, *upper middle-class* and *working-class* for the women appearing in the articles.
- *Framing* focused on whether becoming a stay-at-home mother was presented as a voluntary choice or as a result of coercion.
- Finally, *tone* examined whether the mothers were portrayed in a positive or negative light.

For these three variables, the coder could also choose the option of *mixed/neither/unclear* or *neither/unclear*. Each article constituted a sample unit and the coders decided for each article – for example, the social class of the portrayed stay-at-home mother. The recording unit is harder to define. Different aspects of content (the category of people involved, framing, tone, etc.) were noted to examine how the stay-at-home mothers were represented and evaluated. (The article presents more detailed coding criteria than reported above, which probably means that the coders had access to specific coding instructions.) A double coding was performed. The relationships between variables were analysed in SPSS.

The results are presented in quantitative terms, many in graphs showing changes over the period. Some results are illustrated with quotations from typical articles. As it turned out, being a mother caring for the home was not portrayed as a bad thing. The framing analysis showed that only 18 per cent of the articles portrayed becoming a stay-at-home mother as a forced decision, while 63 per cent portrayed it as a free choice. The article offers several examples of stories where the stay-at-home mother praises her new life. A *Times* article about several women who had held senior positions in media companies and law firms but had become unemployed due to the recession, described how these women struggled with their changed roles, but then discovered new values in life. According to the article's author, the more she watched her son 'picking up new bits of his world, the less tedious it feels to be there when he's doing so. It's as if my brain is switching away from the rapid pace of office life, and falling into step with the mind of my son' (Orgad and De Benedictis, 2015: 429).

Another finding, based on the tone variable, is that the descriptions of stay-at-home-mothers became increasingly positive over time. These results indicate that the news reporting supported rather than challenged women's transition from the workplace to the home. However, it was mainly upper- and upper-middle class women who were described in positive terms. The women were also said to be white, heterosexual and married (which was not coded for, but probably became apparent when reading the articles). The few articles on working-class women were overwhelmingly negative in tone (81 per cent compared to only 26 per cent of the articles on upper- and middle-class women). According to the authors' interpretation, the positive and negative tone of the articles 'functions as a significant divisive discursive feature, which separates and polarises middle-class mothers whose "choice" to opt out of the workforce is largely endorsed and commended, and their counterparts, working-class mothers whose similar "choice" is criticised and derided' (Orgad and De Benedictis, 2015: 430).

Sample study 4: Categorising content to create typologies: type-building qualitative coding

Playing digital games might motivate people to engage with the climate crisis, according to Fernández Galeote et al. (2022). The relationship between players and their avatars – the figures through which a player exists in the game and which is the mediator of the player's identity – is of particular interest. Previous research suggests that the relationship that players form with their avatars can have cognitive and behavioural effects on players in their life outside the game.

The study analysed 80 games in which players can act to mitigate or adapt to climate change. The researchers attempted to classify the avatar identity types, what climate issues the players got to tackle through these identities and how their actions related to the ultimate goals of the games. The content analysis was performed by one of the authors with special expertise in both designing and playing digital games. Using only one analyst's perspective is not ideal from the point of reliability, but the authors argue that the particular skills of the analyst made up for this limitation. To get a better understanding of the games, game manuals, game-play videos and forum posts by players were also consulted. Different aspects of the games were coded by slightly different coding strategies. Here, we concentrate on how the avatar identities were studied.

An avatar identity was captured by coding both what the avatar should achieve in the game and the rules and norms that influence or decide how the player acts to achieve the goal through the avatar. The goal of the avatar is also the ultimate goal of the game, or how a player wins, finishes or prolongs the game. The norms were studied with regard to several aspects – e.g., if the game focused on individual or collective action and whether the avatars' behaviour explicitly impacted the world. These norms were captured by studying messages in the games and cataloguing what a player can and ought to do to progress through the game.

A type-building coding in several steps was carried out in an inductive fashion (motivated by the scarcity of research in the area; if more research had existed, deductive coding based on previous results could have been applied). In the first step of the coding, the game-playing analyst attributed values to each game's primary avatar and made short summaries of them. In the next step, the avatar identities were clustered according to the games' goals and norms – i.e., how the players were prompted to act and for what purpose. This resulted in 23 clusters of avatars from the 80 games. In the final step, six types were constructed from these clusters and given names and descriptions.

The most common avatar type, referred to by the researchers as 'authority', was one where the avatar is provided with extensive power over a collective – e.g., being decision-maker in a town – a power that is limited by conflicting interests and/or environmental issues such as mitigation challenges, the goal being to pursue community or business development. The second most common identity was the 'climate hero', an avatar with access to special means or superpowers, having to address climate challenges in the game world. Another type was the 'climate self', avatars that 'lived' in what resembled real-world societies and could choose to reduce their greenhouse gas emissions by changing lifestyles or opt for better climate policies, the objective being to change players' behaviour in the real world. A rather rare, but potentially important, identity was the 'climate citizen' who could perform citizen-like behaviour in the game world, including using democratic means to address climate challenges within the game. The norms that regulated what this kind of avatar could do resembles the means available to many real-world citizens.

According to the authors, all six types contain potential benefits for climate change engagement. The 'climate authority' games explore how to handle conflicting interests in complex settings and point to the need to reach agreements. While the 'climate hero's' behaviour cannot be emulated in real life, heroes can inspire and motivate real-world action. The 'climate self' identity directly engages players to strive for changes in their own lives, while the 'climate citizens' show similarities with many players' options in real life.

The study has traits of critical research. For example, the authors start out from the fact that the production and playing of games have detrimental environmental effects in terms of high energy consumption. They claim that it is crucial to question whether and how digital games can do more good than harm, implying that offering avatar identities that can engage players in climate issues may be one way.

Critical reflections

Like other research methods, content analysis has its limitations and challenges to meet and working with content analysis means making certain choices.

The invisible does not count

A limitation of quantitative content analysis is that it tends to focus on the explicit rather than the implicit – i.e., only the manifest content of texts is coded. But the unspoken can also be very important. The fact that some things remain unsaid *may* be a sign that they are insignificant, but they can also belong to the domain of the 'obvious' that does not need to be stated. These two cases cannot be distinguished by ordinary content analysis. This is, however, a truth with modification. Software and computer development have made capturing some kinds of implicit content possible. In quantitative text analysis, topic modelling can be used to identify implicit topics and infer latent variables based on the co-occurrences of words in different texts (Ramage et al., 2009).

A problem with deductive coding is that textual features other than those captured by the coding scheme do not emerge. A coding scheme that has not grown out of the texts inductively does not allow the texts to 'speak' to the analyst – or, rather, they only speak about things that the researcher has decided to look for. The problem, then, is not only that latent or implicit messages escape quantification, but also that a precise and targeted analytical tool renders invisible even the manifest textual content that might have been registered in an inductive analysis. This problem can be reduced by reading at least parts of the textual material in an open fashion early on, as well as by gaining knowledge of the general discourse and social context where the texts appear.

Validity issues

Validity problems are often the result of taking recording units out of context. If large amounts of material are to be coded and if high reliability is desired, the coding process cannot be too cumbersome and time-consuming. Hence, less contextual information can be dealt with.

Validity problems may also accrue from the character of the text sample (Gemenis, 2013). Manifesto coding, for example, has been criticised by the argument that what parties say in election manifestos does not measure their real policy preferences but only their rhetorical stances. Moreover, a problem in national comparative studies is that different manifesto cultures exist in different countries and the manifestos play different roles. A final problem is that party manifestos often remain silent on certain positions because of strategic considerations, even if the party holds a strong position on the issue. That silence may falsely register as a lack of policy even when there is a firm stance. These contextual factors have to be taken into consideration when formulating the research question that the content analysis is meant to answer.

There are particular validity problems associated with computerised content analysis where the coding units are single words, one being that many words are ambiguous. Examples in English are 'bank', 'rock' and 'plain'. Each of these words has two or more distinct meanings. There are also ambiguous words with different but related meanings – e.g., 'wing' as part of a bird or aeroplane, or a section of a building. This problem is not very difficult to handle, however. One can either avoid ambiguous words in coding or back up a computerised analysis with a manual coding of such words. If software of the kind used in corpus linguistics is at hand, creating a *concordance* (see Chapter 7) will be helpful for that task. Laver and Garry (2000) also point out that one meaning of an ambiguous word usually dominates in specific genres. When the word 'banks' occurs in political manifestos, it rarely refers to river banks but typically to financial institutions.

Vague words are more problematic – i.e., those that have diverse but not clearly defined meanings. This applies in particular to evaluative words whose meaning is contested (cf. Connolly, 1983 on essentially contested concepts and the section 'Semantic struggles' in Chapter 7). What does 'democracy' mean? Most likely a form of governing that the text producer evaluates positively. But what 'democracy' refers to varies. For one text producer, it may be a political system where the majority make far-reaching decisions about finances and other aspects of social life. For another, the term connotes any form of government that meets minimal criteria regarding periodical elections, the freedom to form political parties and absence of media censorship. To determine the meaning of such a term for a particular text producer (if it is at all possible to determine) often requires relatively complex interpretations and comprehensive discourse knowledge.

Interpretation issues

What is really 'there' in a text? In the case of simple assessments, such as whether a particular word is there or not, this is rarely a problem. When it comes to counting the expressions of certain ideas, which is what was done in different ways in both the first, second and third sample studies, however, one immediately runs into questions about interpretation. What might it mean to find an 'idea' expressed in a text? It could mean that I, as the researcher and person I am, tend to see certain expressions as manifestations of certain ideas. But if I am concerned primarily with something outside of myself, this may not be particularly interesting. Here, the different interpretive strategies presented in Table 1.2 are relevant. If the researcher is familiar with the discourse, the interpretation problems may not be acute, but in other cases improving one's knowledge of both the text producers and the relevant discourses is necessary.

Content analysis and the study of society

How can content analysis be used in the study of power, politics, oppression or other objects of study in the social sciences? Several of the studies referred to in this chapter have obvious links to larger social science issues. The network study in Sample study 2 shows how state actors were replaced by a financial–industrial cluster as an important political bloc in the debate on German pensions (Leifeld, 2016). Since it is likely that power in debate is linked to power over policy outcomes, the study indicates a political power shift. The avatar analysis in Sample study 4 aimed at enhancing knowledge about how gamers could be engaged in the climate crisis that threatens and already affects societies all over the globe (Fernández Galeote et al., 2022). Many other studies using content analysis as a method are also motivated by social scientific research problems, some of which have been referred to in this chapter – e.g., the study of the film industry's gender gap (Kagan et al., 2020) and that of the content of economic news and its potential consequences for class issues and economic policies (Jacobs et al., 2021).

Generally speaking, the strength of quantitative content analysis lies in its ability to provide an overview of significant amounts of text and a basis for comparison. Given that the ability to generalise and to examine patterns and changes over time in society are central to social science, quantitative content analysis can provide a kind of general information that not all the other analytical approaches presented in this book can. Qualitative content analysis, for its part, enables a deeper understanding of texts in context. The construction of categories, like in the type-building sample study of the avatars, might also be followed up by more extensive studies – e.g., of how mitigation of global warming is mediated by games for those living parts of their lives in fictional game worlds.

Summary

On the usefulness of content analysis

- The chapter has presented the principles of quantitative and qualitative content analysis – i.e., analyses in which elements of texts are counted, measured or categorised for specific research purposes.
- Quantitative content analysis is particularly suitable for finding patterns in more extensive materials and for comparisons, and can be combined with other types of analysis.
- If the texts to be studied are available in a database or can be scanned, very large amounts of material can be analysed with the help of the computer.
- Manually conducted content analyses allow for more advanced assessments and interpretations, but for processing less material than computerised analyses.
- Quantitative content analysis is carried out deductively, while inductive work is more prominent in qualitative content analysis.
- A consequence of choosing content analysis of a more deductive kind when the analysis is carried out manually is that one becomes locked into a particular way to carry out the analysis relatively early on.
- Many research questions cannot be answered with statements about 'more' or 'less' and consequently cannot be answered by quantitative content analysis. In many situations, it is not important *how many times*, but rather *in which way*, something is expressed.
- Content analysis, particularly the quantitative approach, is ill-suited for analysing implicit aspects, like the unspoken conditions of a debate or the kind of tacit knowledge that everyone takes for granted.
- Like other highly structured analytical approaches, content analysis diverts interest away from things in the material that are not deemed noteworthy in advance.
- Quantitative content analysis tends to be insensitive to the context in which the counted units are located, which may impair validity.

How to do it

- The selection of texts must be made with regard to the research question and to the ambitions for generalisation.
- Researchers should familiarise themselves with the corpus early on by reading through some of the texts (or, if possible, all of them) and by acquiring sufficient knowledge of their genre and context.
- An analytical tool called a coding scheme for manual analysis together with more or less detailed instructions on how to use it, or a dictionary for computer-aided analysis should be developed. In type-building text analysis, the coding scheme is constructed stepwise by finding categories in the texts that are then grouped under more overarching categories.
- Before the final version of the coding scheme is adopted, the scheme should be tested in several rounds on parts of the data and a pilot study should be carried out.
- The recording units – i.e., what is counted – can be of many different kinds and must be determined in relation to the research questions.
- The sample unit is the unit of text (an entire text, a sentence, etc.) in which the recording units are registered.
- Special software is available for computer-based content analysis. For manual content analysis where the coding units are more complex than single words, QDA software is very helpful.
- Consistency is paramount in coding: intrasubjectivity is about one coder's consistency; intersubjectivity is about different coders assessing the texts in the same way. To improve consistency, double coding or similar methods may be used. Reliability is not a problem in computer-based analyses, but validity may be.

- The results can be presented in charts, tables or other ways.
- The overall result should be interpreted in relation to the research problem at hand.

Suggested reading

A good introduction to qualitative content analysis is Schreier (2014). Kuckartz (2014) provides accessible and detailed explanations of how to conduct what he refers to as thematic, evaluative and type-building qualitative text analysis. Krippendorff (2019) defines and delineates quantitative content analysis and expounds on all the steps of what he considers good content analysis. The book includes an evaluation of different types of reliability tests and presents computerised methods. A very rich anthology is Krippendorff and Bock (2009). More than 50 contributions address, among other things, the history of content analysis, the problems of text selection, issues of reliability and validity, questions of inference from analysis of texts to contexts, and computerised versus manual coding. The book contains many interesting examples of quantitative content analytical studies of texts in many different genres. A good introduction to the statistical program R and quantitative text analysis for students in the humanities is Jockers (2014).

Exercises

Exercise 1: Climate change debates in US congressional hearings: a network analysis

Climate change policies are subject to political polarisation in the United States. Already in the 2000s, in particular during the 109th (3 January 2005 to 3 January 2007) and 110th Congresses (3 January 2007 to 3 January 2009), there were 341 pieces of climate legislation, for many of which there were Congressional hearings. These transcripts have been used to study partisan polarisation over climate change issues (Fisher et al., 2013), as the testimonies in hearings allow connecting actors of different interest and partisan groups with their propositions regarding climate change.

The task

Visit Philip Leifeld's github-page and follow the instructions there to install Java11 and the Discourse Network Analyzer (https://github.com/leifeld/dna/releases). On the same page, you also find a 'sample.dna' file with a selection of the climate-change hearings, including the original codings the authors tagged on the texts. Take a look at the typology of propositions and actors the authors employ in the coding scheme: how many different types of organisations and positions can you discern (check the 'attribute manager' in the menu)? Use the 'filter' function at the bottom right to locate an organisation or person you recognise and find the respective text. Do you agree with the coding decisions of the authors when you read the coded texts? Finally, check out the various export functions in the menu and export a CSV-file of an organisation-to-organisation network matrix,

(Continued)

(Continued)
including all agreement statements. Take a look at the resulting matrix using Excel. Choose one of the Congressional hearings of the recent 117th Congress[7] and apply the coding scheme the authors have developed. Do you find new levels of polarisation?

The texts

Congressional hearings of the two houses of Congress as well as joint hearings are available at www.govinfo.gov/app/collection/chrg. Navigate to the relevant committee and date to identify hearings related to climate change issues. Then import the hearings into the DNA program in order to start the coding process.

Exercise 2: A qualitative content analysis of political (lack of) climate crisis awareness

According to a Google Ngram analysis of English language literature, the term 'climate crisis' has been on the rise since the beginning of the new century but was still marginal compared to 'climate change' in 2019. This can be interpreted as a sign of rising climate crisis awareness in parts of the English-speaking public sphere (Kunelius and Roosvall, 2021). Is there a corresponding rising awareness in political rhetoric? In this exercise, you study how a political party shows/does not show awareness of the climate crisis and how it proposes/does not propose to deal with it.

The task

Formulate a research question – e.g., 'How has [Party X]'s rhetoric and policy proposals with regard to global warming changed between [date 1] and [date 2]?' Compare a number of relevant texts from the two points in time. Start inductively by working with some of the texts and formulating questions to pose to all texts while you read. These questions will result in a coding scheme with coding questions – e.g., 'How does the party refer to the ongoing climate change?', 'What policies for mitigating global warming does the party propose?' Compare the results of the coding for the two points in time in order to answer your research question. Discuss reliability and validity aspects of your study.

The texts

Use comparable party documents from the two points in time, such as election manifestos that might be available from the manifesto database (https://manifesto-project.wzb.eu/), election material such as election films or party-leader speeches from different general elections, or parliamentary bills.

---

[7] See here for a list of relevant hearings: www.eesi.org/articles/view/on-the-hill-in-2022-a-breakdown-of-climate-energy-and-environmental-congressional-hearings

Exercise 3: A type-building text analysis of relationships between humans and other animals in fiction

Non-human animals are present in all sorts of fiction and their relations with humans vary widely. These relations are expressed in narratives, in metaphors, by images and in many other ways that vary with the text genre (Tidwell, 2016). The relationships described or depicted are also specific to the species, so are, for example, human-horse relations imagined to be of particular kinds (Nyman, 2016). The purpose of this exercise is to choose some aspect(s) of human-animal relationships and construct a relationship typology in a chosen text genre.

The task

Formulate a research question about human-animal relationships in some genre – e.g., 'How are emotional relationships between humans and animals represented in Ugandan movies from period X?', and pick out a number of texts (in this example, particular films) to analyse. Go through the texts and summarise them with regard to your research question. Formulating some preliminary questions will help, in the example perhaps about what emotions the human characters show towards animals they meet (fear, joy, love, etc.) and what emotions the animals express when confronted with humans (anger, stress, affection, etc.). In the next step, create categories by inductively coding parts of the material. The emotional relationships could perhaps be sorted as mutually positive, mutually negative or unbalanced – e.g., the human shows joy and the animal shows fear. Then try to sort the categories into more overarching ones, creating a system with categories and subcategories. This can be done in two, three or more steps, depending on your research objective. If you have chosen to work with only a few texts, you may want to code all of them in this step. If you have many texts you could stop when it seems unlikely that you will find more relation types. When you have constructed a fruitful typology, label and describe the categories of interest for your research question. Also write coding instructions. Use the typology and instructions to code the entire corpus. Finally, present the typology and the results with regard to how common the categories are in the corpus. Discuss how the typology could be used in research.

The texts

Use more or less fictional texts in any suitable genre: Western films, children's books, nursery rhymes, novels, YouTube channels, paintings in your nearest art museum or whatever you find interesting.

3

Analysis of Ideas and Ideological Thought

Mats Lindberg

Background

Ideas, politics and society

Terms like 'ideas' and 'ideologies' are commonplace in ordinary language. In a news programme the question may be raised about what kind of ideology is guiding the Labour Party in the UK. At a political demonstration, we can get to hear a speaker argue that media and advertising are full of pro-capitalist ideology, making shallow consumerism the meaning of life. We can also hear our neighbour describe her working place as full of sexist *ideas* fitted into the walls. The methodological approach presented in this chapter offers analytical tools for the systematic description of such ideas or ideologies (*descriptive ideational analysis*), making a rational criticism of them possible (*critical ideational analysis* or *idea-criticism*).

In the common-sense examples above, the words 'ideas' and 'ideologies' allude to a specific social and political phenomenon: *ideological thought*. Ideological thought influences the preferences and behaviour of individuals. It is *action orienting* and *action guiding* – that is, motivating and directing, but also legitimating, the social and political actions and interactions of people. Thus, ideological thought is part of the interactions, structures, institutions and norms that a society consists of. Everyday ideological thought, as well as elaborated idea systems – ideologies – consists of three basic kinds of ideas: *values* (visions, preferences, ends or goals), *descriptions* (value-loaded beliefs and judgements about the surrounding world) and *prescriptions* (recommendations for action).

As the initial examples show, the notion of ideological thought here is broader than what is common in political science or regular political language, where the notion of ideology is mainly tied to political parties or outright political action (see, for example, Lasswell and Kaplan, 1950; Seliger, 1976; Goffman,1986; Freeden, 2003; Fairclough and Fairclough, 2012; Heywood, 2021; Ball et al., 2021). Here, I will combine the political perspective with a sociological and cultural one. The result is a *broad notion of ideological thought* as a central, component part of society (see, e.g., Parsons, 1951; Habermas, 1991; van Dijk, 1998; Bourdieu, 2013 [1977]). Consequently, ideological thought as it is understood here may be found in both public and private communication and discourse, in political or commercial messages, as well as in literature, film or the social media. (For details, see Lindberg, 2018a: 285–9, 297–302, easy to reach via open access.)

Usually, the ideological thought-content in communication and discourse – the specific values, beliefs and norms – is barely noticed as such by the participants themselves; it exists as habitual common sense or the natural way to see things. Sometimes, however, the ideological thought-content becomes visible as such and is overtly argued for. It becomes openly politicised and debated. In that case, an ideological contestation may occur between various agents of the social and political spectrum.

Conflictual ideas are found in any society. Republican conservatism and Democratic liberalism in the US build up regimes with different values, policies and propensities for action. Furthermore, feminists contest patriarchal ideas; anti-racists contest racist ideas; Hindus contest Islamic ideas; Islamists contest modern, liberal ideas; leftists contest right-wing ideas; socialists contest capitalist ideas; democrats contest populist ideas (whether left-wing or right-wing populist ones), and vice versa. Sometimes such debates even grow to *idea struggles*. Depending on the political culture in various countries or times, such idea struggles may be civilised or rude. Today, we witness a return of stark ideological contestations throughout the world, leading to cleavages and polarisation. Large-scale idea struggles or 'cultural wars' are ravaging many societies, making a genuinely *democratic process* difficult (Dahl and Shapiro, 2021: 37).

In this situation, it is more important than ever to have tools to lay bare and analyse the ideological positions and arguments in such debates and struggles, and make the thought-content on both sides transparently visible. Equally important is to make possible a critical assessment of their empirical or moral validity. The methodological approach presented here delivers tools for such descriptive and critical analysis. Thus, the ultimate aim of this approach is to enhance *rationality* and *enlightened understanding* among citizens (see Dahl and Shapiro, 2021: 37–8, 85; Richardson, 2002: 75–84).

In sum: ideas and ideological thought – as the inner, action-guiding thought-content of verbal communication and discourse – consist of values, descriptions and prescriptions (recommendations or norms). They are parts of the conflictual or cooperative communicative actions and interactions of which society is constituted. The approach here suggests that the analyst should focus on ideological regularities in thought and language used by agents from different sides of the social and political spectrum – that is to say, how values, descriptions and action-guiding recommendations are expressed and how they structure the debate or discourse on current issues. In the following, this general view will be specified before the practicalities of actual analysis are described.

A general theory of ideological thought-content: the VDP-triad

Ideological thought, as sketched above, is built up in a specific way; it has a specific inner *morphology* (to borrow Michael Freeden's term). Elsewhere, I have outlined this inner morphology in a 'general theory' of ideological thought-content (Lindberg, 2018a: 277–8). According to this general theory, ideological thought-content consists of three generic dimensions:

- moral, political or cultural *values*, goals, ends or preferences (V);
- value-loaded *descriptions*, attitude-loaded cognitive beliefs or judgements (D);
- *prescriptions*, recommendations for action or norms (P).

The methodological approach here is based on this triadic, inner morphology. The general theory proposes that all ideological thought consists of these three kinds of ideas, combined in overt or covert argumentative sequences. Often, they occur in elaborated *idea systems* or *ideologies* and are explicitly expressed as such in text or talk. But equally often, such systems of ideas must be sifted out by the analyst from a mass of verbal flow, wherein the ideas are implicitly present or reside as latent suggestions. We will return to all of this later.

According to the general theory, the combination of values (V), descriptions (D) and prescriptions (P) produces *action-guiding thought*. To take an example. If a future sustainable eco-system on the earth is held as the (action-motivating) *value* (V), and is combined with the (action-orienting) *description* that emission of carbon dioxide threatens the sustainability of the global ecosystem (D), the accompanying (action-directing) *prescription* urges us to slow down or stop the emission of carbon dioxide (P). When the three kinds of ideas are combined like this, I call them a *VDP-triad*. All action-guiding or ideological thought, according to the general theory, consists of VDP-triads with this basic morphological pattern. From this view, an analytical model is derived: *the VDP-model*. The VDP-model is used to discern, describe and classify the ideological thought-content that is inherent in any piece of communication and discourse, whether in a single text or in a larger system of texts (see Lindberg, 2018a: 297–302, 324–7; 2018b: 515).

The basic three kinds of ideas are found in systematic form in the main *political philosophies* or *political ideologies* of our time. In our culture, these elaborated and systematised idea systems serve as sources of social thought and political argument. As we have seen, they permeate communication in public and private discourse, and even figure as the foundation of political constitutions or legislation. Political ideologies and philosophies are also *objects to believe in* or to be critical of. Thus, the debates and arguments between their believers and critics are legion, historically as well as today. The most important political philosophies and influential ideologies in modern society are systematically presented in authoritative and well-known textbooks (see, for example, Sabine and Thorson, 1973; van Dyke, 1995; Freeden, 2003; Bloor, 2010; von Beyme, 2013a, b, c; Heywood, 2021; Ball et al., 2021). Sources like these are often indispensable to students who wish to track ideological influences in the material they study.

Ideas, actions and institutions

In social and political theory, as well as in empirical sociology and political science, ideas and ideologies are conceived as embedded in the communicative interactions in society. Patterns of communicative action make up social relations, including power relations, and make them persist or change over time. To take a commonplace example: Christmas celebration is void without a Christmas tree and the action-guiding notions of 'Christmas' and 'Christmas celebration' that give meaning to this cultural institution. In public life, the British Parliament resides in particular buildings and its work is guided by legislation, precedents and norms, together with the ideological significance of Parliament as the representative of the British people against the monarch. The social actions and interactions that make up institutions are normally habitualised and hard to notice. But in periods of change or conflict, overt argumentation about the purpose and meaning of an institution occurs, often with arguments fetched from the basic political philosophies mentioned above (see Habermas, 1991; Archer, 2000; Bourdieu, 2013).

Carl J. Friedrich, in his magisterial *Man and his Government*, makes the following summary:

> Ideologies are action-related systems of ideas (...) related to the existing political and social order and intended either to change or defend it. The ideas an ideology contains are as such action-related, and may or may not be very true and appropriate (...). (Friedrich, 1963: 89)

In Friedrich's political science world of political realism, there is always a *plural set of social and political ideologies* in a society. These are brought forward by a plural set of social or political agents or networks, normally involved in political struggle and ideational strife as well as collaboration. Most existing institutions and norms are contested from various sides of the political spectrum.

As Friedrich points out, *the truth or falsity of an ideology is not important for the possibility of being believed in* and thus of being effective or operative in a society. Thus, unfortunately, *truth* is not necessary nor ultimately cherished in the real world of politics, especially not in wartime. Instead, we must realise the perhaps disappointing fact that ideologies are successful, not because they are true, but because they are held to be true.

Comprehensive and field-specific ideologies

The main comprehensive ideologies

If an elaborate system of ideas suggests an institutional and cultural configuration for the whole society, I will term it a *'comprehensive ideology'*. Comprehensive ideologies exist as self-proclaimed idea traditions that have emerged at different times in history. In the Western world, they make up a dozen or so main types. The liberal, conservative and cooperative socialist idea traditions developed in the aftermath of the French Revolution of 1789; later, in the nineteenth century they were joined by Marxist 'scientific socialism' and the Catholic 'Social doctrine of the Church'. In the twentieth century, new sociopolitical idea traditions emerged, such as democratic socialism (social democracy), left liberalism (welfare liberalism), Leninist communism (Marxism–Leninism), Italian Fascism, national socialism (Nazism) and Christian democracy. Prominent newcomers were ecologism and feminism. Comprehensive political Islam (or Islamism) was similarly constructed in the twentieth century by iconic ideologues in Egypt, Pakistan and Iran. All these political ideologies have several variants and subdivisions. They are generalised and stylised in the textbooks mentioned above.

Comprehensive ideal types

The generalised and stylised ideologies listed above do not exist in the world in their pure form. When we encounter these ideologies in textbooks and speak of them as elaborated ideologies or *isms*, we speak, in fact, of stylised reconstructions – *ideal types*. What exists in the real world are manifestos, pamphlets or books written by prominent ideologues and brought forward by movements, networks or organisations with leaders and activist cadres. Each of them offers their view of the world or their own ideological tale, as well as a system of core ideas together with an ideologically value-loaded vocabulary. In short, the various main ideologies describe, explain and interpret 'the world' differently, and they each contain specific values (V), descriptions (D) and prescriptions (P).

This leads to a basic methodological prerequisite in ideational analysis. The specific *political language* and *political vocabulary* of an ideology or an actor, whether a person or an organisation, is a basic thing to master. The specific vocabulary is the key to understanding the inner thought-content. The stylised ideal types we find in textbooks summarise the specific vocabularies and the specific thought-content we need to be attentive to. The ideal types serve as hypotheses or points of departure for all idea analyses and deliver the analytical categories for ideological classification and political understanding. For example, with a thorough knowledge of the ideal types of feminism, liberalism or Islamism, it is easy to discern specific feminist, liberal and Islamist words and sentences in a text and start the search for their inner thought-content. A certain problem must be noted: the same word – for example, 'freedom' or 'justice' – may have quite different meanings in different ideologies. The meanings of words in political language are always actor-dependent and context-dependent. This fact makes it even more important to acquire a basic, general knowledge of the main political languages and vocabularies and their corresponding thought-content. (For further discussion, see the section 'The importance of understanding a text in its historical context' in Chapter 4.)

Field-specific and organisation-specific ideologies

Comprehensive ideologies have also influenced ideas in more partial domains of society. Hence, we meet *field-specific ideologies*, but also *organisation-specific* ideologies. Like their comprehensive counterparts, these ideologies are also built up by VDP-triads and involved in idea struggles. In the workplace, for example, the ideas of capitalist ownership and management have been challenged by ideas of 'economic democracy' or variants of 'syndicalism'. Ideas about 'corporatist balance' and 'shared influence' have also figured in this debate. Concerning the internal democracy in political parties or organisations, there may be struggles between radicalising and moderating strands, or between centralists and decentralists, inside every party or social movement. In family life, the ideas of patriarchy and matrimonial equality, or different schools of child-rearing, make up field-specific ideologies of their own, often resulting in accompanying idea struggles (even on the societal level with consequences for legislation). This also goes for fields like healthcare, education, social work, housing, immigration, environment and city planning. Field-specific or organisation-specific ideologies and idea struggles make up intriguing objects of research in their own right. They enjoy relative autonomy in relation to the comprehensive ones, and, depending on the context, such analyses may demand a keen sensitivity to the particular situation and its actors and conflicts.

Like the comprehensive ideologies, field-specific ideological thought is part of the communication and interaction that make up the configuration of the society and its subfields. We encounter it in habitual thought or ongoing public debates over values and norms. The task for the methodological approach here, as we saw above, is to interpret and describe the ideas and the ideological thought found in different realms and subfields of society.

Political language and the source material

The choice of sources depends on the focus of the research and the chosen research problem. We find ideological thought-content in cultural products like film and literature; in personal sources like Facebook posts or email; in school books, educational policies or curricula; in political party manifestos or social movement platforms; in official government documents or legislation; in manuals for social work or ecological sustainability; in public policy reports or parliamentary debates; in legislation; in speeches and texts by political leaders, ideologues, theorists or media pundits; or in the messages and opinions of the usual media flow. Moreover, researchers may also produce their own source material. When needed, it is possible to use *personal interviews* or *participant observation*. Such efforts are often planned with the purpose to lay bare the values, beliefs and norms (the V, D and P) of some actor, whether a person or an organisation. *Quantitative questionnaires* may concern the attitudes and beliefs of the whole electorate or a certain segment of it. So, the general theory and the VDP-triad may be used in both qualitative and quantitative studies.

Analysis

The three basic kinds of ideas and their combination

The theoretical foundation for the notion of three basic kinds of ideas
The notion of the three basic kinds of ideas in ideological thought is elaborated out of many intertwined fields of knowledge. They occur in linguistic philosophy (expressive, constative and regulative speech acts); general social theory, frame analysis and empirical social science (values, beliefs and norms); but also in linguistic discourse studies, rhetoric theory (Aristotle's common topics) and even in some Marxist elaborations. They all more or less express the same three basic kinds of action-guiding ideas, although with slightly different names. From this widespread, common view I have fetched the building blocks of the general theory here. From political theory I have chosen the following shorthand terms: 'values', 'descriptions' and 'prescriptions' (for the details, see Lindberg, 2018a: 292–302; 2018b: 498–503, 509–12).

The argumentative combination of values, descriptions and prescriptions
None of the three basic kinds of ideas, taken one by one, is sufficient to guide actions. They need to be combined to acquire an action-guiding capacity or force. A value (V) without a description of the situation (D) is void of practical meaning. For example, the value 'goodness' is empty without a description (D) of someone to be good to. A famous example is the robbed and wounded traveller on the road to Jericho, as in the biblical parable of the Good Samaritan. But the Samaritan's cognition of the wounded traveller (D) will remain meaningless without an action-motivating value (V) – in this case, goodness. On the other hand, the same sight of the wounded traveller (D) may lead to quite different actions if the observer is another person, holding another value (V). If her action-motivating value is selfish greed – all values are not noble – she may rob the wounded traveller once more and steal the last parcels of his belongings.

Thus, values, descriptions and prescriptions need to be combined to attain an action-guiding force. In real life, they are combined in argumentative sequences. For example, the members of the Society for Homeless Cats in Huddersfield (which I happen to be acquainted with) are motivated by certain moral *values* or compelling emotions regarding suffering animals (V). Besides, they are oriented by certain evaluative *descriptions* regarding the difficult situation for lost cats in the city (D). The V and the D in combination are logical grounds for the *prescription* 'Take care of the lost cats in the city!' (P). Another example is the young couple next door (who I happened to overhear). I heard the woman say, expressing a value (V): 'I thought we would share the housework equally!' And she continued, expressing a description (D): 'You haven't done your share.' A logical creature, she concluded, expressing a prescription (P): 'From now on, I expect you to do your share!'

The notion of practical reasoning

In the examples above, the action-guiding force emerged out of the combination of the V and the D, leading up to a specific prescription P. This argumentative combination formed a VDP-triad and gave it a substantial action-guiding force. In the triad, the argumentative premises (V and D) lead up to, or argumentatively support, the practical conclusion (P).

In this way, the combination receives a quasi-logical character, as a sequence of *practical reasoning* or a *practical argument* (also called informal logic; see Vedung, 1982; Audi, 2001; Walton, 2008; Fairclough and Fairclough, 2012; Bowell and Kemp, 2015). When combined in this way, ideas make up VDP-triads (see Figure 3.1 and Table 3.1 below).

But the argumentative pattern of practical reasoning is found not only in ideological thought in everyday communication or in field-specific ideologies, as in the examples above. It is also found in public debates or in the comprehensive political ideologies exemplified above. These comprehensive systems of ideas consist of *large-scale VDP-triads of practical reasoning*, normally combining several values, bundles of descriptions and characteristic recommendations for action. In classical liberalism of the eighteenth and nineteenth centuries, for example, the values of basic human rights together with the values of economic and political freedom (V) were combined with descriptive views and narratives of the disastrous organisation of the economy and the polity (mercantilism and autocratic monarchy) (D), which together led to a whole set of prescriptions (P) to institute free markets, freedom of speech and widened suffrage. (The reader may, as an exercise, put forward her own favourite example(s) of the main ideologies of today, viewed as large-scale VDP-triads, and deconstruct them down to their basic elements.)

The formal VDP-model of simple practical reasoning

When starting an actual analysis of the ideological content of a text, the notions of V, D and P are important as our first guideline or hypothesis; at least some of them ought to be there in the text. The second main guideline or hypothesis is the notion of practical reasoning; there ought to be at least some sequence of practical reasoning in the material.

I will complement the Huddersfield and the young couple examples of practical reasoning above with an example from an elementary textbook in political science (from my time as a young student) by the Swedish political theorist Stefan Björklund, *Politisk teori* (Political theory) (1970: 28–31). The example accounts for the argument from one side in the public debate about a local government reform in Sweden in the 1960s. It is stylised by Björklund to an argumentative, deductive sequence of practical reasoning (informal logic) and is somewhat reformulated here:

> V: 'The citizenry ought to have the greatest possible democratic influence on local government.'
> D: 'The old and small municipalities offer better conditions for local democratic influence than the proposed, new, large ones.'
> ---
> P: 'Keep the old and small municipalities!'

Here, the prescription derives from the value of strong local democracy. But how do we get from the value (V) to the prescription (P)? If we think of it, the action motivating force inherent in the initial value (V) is very fuzzy. If we do not know the context, the value is in itself void of action-guiding direction. What is needed is a specific descriptive assertion (D) of the context to situate and orient the political action. In this case, the descriptive assertion says that we are in a situation of institutional change, and that the old and small municipalities are potentially more democratic than the proposed new, large ones. We can also see that the description (D) is an assertion that can be empirically true or false. If the description (D) is held to be true by the actor, and if the value (V) is still cherished, the argument leads up to the prescription (P): 'Keep the old and small municipalities!' (see Lindberg, 2018b: 515–19).

In the example on local democracy above, we met a sequence of practical reasoning in its most simple form. It illustrates the typical formal pattern of practical arguments. In the VDP-model, this pattern can be represented as a quasi-logical, reasoned deduction or 'informal logic' (see Walton, 2008). According to the general theory used here, the formal pattern of practical reasoning makes up the inner, morphological structure of all ideological thought (see Figure 3.1).

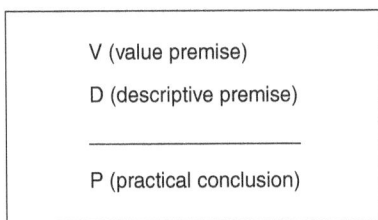

Figure 3.1 The formal VDP-model of simple, practical reasoning, presented as an argumentative-logical deduction of informal logic

Types of descriptions (D)

Situational descriptions (Dsit) and means–ends descriptions (Dme)

There are two main kinds of descriptive statements to be aware of. The first and most common one concerns the *situation* – i.e., its objects or characteristics, or the problems, possibilities or causal relations inherent to it (D*sit*). Descriptions of situations pervade all political language and ideological thought. The second kind, equally significant, consists of accounts of *means–ends relationships* and descriptions of means or methods for achieving certain goals (D*me*).

Situational descriptions (D*sit*) are easy to understand. Means–ends relations (D*me*) may be more difficult. How do they qualify as descriptions? The fact is that they are. They are assertions of actual, causal linkages. In communication and discourse they often hold central positions among the D-factors of the argument. They state relations like 'the booze → will destroy your life', 'equal parenting → makes it possible for women to work', 'more immigrants → will destroy public finances', or 'education for all → strengthens the country's economic competitiveness'. Statements of means–ends relations (D*me*), combined with a value (V), directly inform practical conclusions or direct prescriptions (P). In our cases above: 'Stop drinking!', 'Strive for equal parenting!', 'Curb immigration!' or 'Promote education for all!'

The double-sidedness of descriptions: cognitions and evaluations

There is a more complicated, general aspect of all descriptions (D), however. This difficulty arises because most descriptions are grammatically formulated in the present indicative and carry both a cognitive component and an attitudinal component. They simultaneously exhibit a double nature as *cognitive assertions* (D*cog*) and *evaluative judgements* (D*eval*), making them at the same time both descriptive and evaluative. They are *value loaded*, as has been said. The evaluative side always contains an attitude to some object, be it a person, an institution or a policy suggestion. Therefore, descriptive statements in actual and situated political language are never neutral; rather, they function as arguments in themselves. Their value loading is often, but not always, carried forward by specific words that signal an underlying attitude.

An obvious example of the double-sidedness is the descriptive sentence in an editorial in *The Times*: 'The GDP has increased with 7% compared to 2022.' The cognitive assertion (D*cog*) is easy to grasp. But the descriptive sentence may also contain an evaluative attitude (D*eval*). The value loading in this case is most likely positive, since no one normally is negative to economic growth, at least not in *The Times*. The value-loaded subtext, though, can be sensed by the readers and imagined by the analyst. It reads: 'And this is good!'

Another example may be a little trickier to sort out. We can hear an MP in a debate in Parliament say: 'The EU has a target of reducing greenhouse gas emissions by at least 50% by 2030.' This seems to be a perfect descriptive assertion (D*cog*). The sentence points to an observable fact (D*cog*), a target suggested in an EU report. Nonetheless, there may be an evaluative attitude attached to it by the speaking MP. But which one? The MP may approve this target from the EU if she is a climate activist (positive [D*eval*]). But if we do not know this, we must be open to the possibility that she is a climate-change denier who thinks of the EU target as a suggestion that will hamper economic growth and restrict personal freedom (negative [D*eval*]). In other words, we cannot infer the attitude *from the grammatical construction as such*. The attitude must be inferred by *interpretation* using (a) the rest of the MP's presentation in the search for a positive or negative attitude, or (b) other texts or talks by her, or (c) the common vocabulary in the discursive debate situation, or (d) the already known positions of the MP or her party. Note that in both the examples above, *the text itself* is not the key to the hidden value loading. Instead, it is *the context*, which we will return to below.

The case of only descriptive statements

In fact, much ideological thought consists only of descriptive statements. Whole narratives may be built up in this way, giving them a seemingly objective or neutral appearance. The value loading may nevertheless be sensed by participants in the discursive situation and hopefully also by the analyst. Whether intuitively sensed or rationally sifted out, the value loading may reside in word choices, perspectives, metaphors or illustrations. It may also reside in the moral of the narrative as such. This is equally common in a film or a book, as in a report from a think tank or in a policy document. This means that many texts *have an ideological content without explicitly stating any values (V) or prescriptions (P)*. The values and prescriptions may instead be carried forward by implicit value loadings (D*eval*) or by the implied moral sense of the narrative as a whole. It is very important to be attentive to all such latent associations.

Narratives that only contain descriptive statements may be tricky for the analyst. How can you go ahead to find the missing values and prescriptions? The challenge is to grasp both sides of the descriptions. For a start, you can look for the moral or the argumentative point of the whole text, which reveals the aim or the intent. But the main thing is to go on and find the double-sided character of the descriptive statements and expose it in clear words. This means breaking apart the descriptions into their cognitive (D*cog*) and their evaluative components (D*eval*). Breaking apart the two aspects of any description (D) and reformulating it in *two separate statements* is the method to clear the ambiguity and bring forward the double-sided thought-content. If the value loading resides in the subtext, you also get hold of the actual *value* (V) that, even if not manifestly outspoken, loads the descriptions with approving or disapproving attitudes. Having exposed the value (V), it should be logically possible to establish the presence of some implicit prescription (P), even if the narrative only contains descriptive statements. This demonstrates the power of the VDP-model as a tool to bring forward the latent or unspoken prescriptions (P) in a text.

If the value loading of the descriptions is not found directly, and if the implicit values (V) and prescriptions (P) don't show up easily, they can be searched for in (a) *other locations* in the text at hand, (b) *other texts* in the agent's textual system and (c) in *surrounding texts* by other authors/agents in the intertextual discursive situation or debate.

The distinction between values (V) and evaluations (Deval)

Finally, we must highlight the tricky distinction between an evaluative descriptive statement (D*eval*) and a value statement (V). Compare these two statements regarding health: 'Apples are healthy' (D*eval*) and 'Health is important!' (V). The former is an evaluative assessment regarding the properties of apples, parallel to 'This car is fast' (D*eval*). The latter statement, 'Health is important!', is a value-statement (V) parallel to 'Speed is important!' (V). The distinction between an evaluative assessment (D*eval*) and an expressed value (V) may be hard to notice. Typically, the analyst must reformulate the inherent value (V) into a perfect value statement to make it visible as such.

From the US, we can discuss Donald Trump and his slogan 'Make America great again!' At first glance, this seems like a simple prescription (P), with an exclamation mark and all. But a closer look reveals that Trump's subtextual associations contain a strong value under the grammatical surface. The value is: 'America is (in its essence) great!' – perhaps with the addition 'and must always be (in its essence) great' (V). Furthermore, the sentence contains a tragic narrative under the linguistic surface, probably the following descriptive assertion or evaluative assessment: 'America once was great, but is it no more' (D). Thus, what initially appears as a simple prescriptive sentence (P) actually contains a value statement (V) and a descriptive statement (D) – that is to say, a full sequence of practical argumentation or a VDP-triad. This illustrates again the usefulness of the VDP-model.

The two levels of ideological thought

Now we come to something extremely important for the analyst to observe. In all established ideologies and all everyday ideological thought, we find two main levels. On one hand, we have the *fundamental level*, where we find the basic, comprehensive philosophical worldviews that define the meaning of (wo)man, society and history, along with a set of fundamental moral values or ideals. On the other hand, we have the more concrete *operative level*, encompassing concrete situations and practical problems. I will illustrate these two levels with the ideology of European Christian democracy. On the fundamental level, we find religious values and moral principles. On the operative level, we find everyday positions on the balance between the public sector and the family. The values and views on the fundamental level function like 'compass directions' and inform the policy choices on the operative level (see Lindberg, 2018b: 519–21).

This distinction between the fundamental and the operative level is always floating, though. The border between them is permeable and fluctuating. Moreover, the levels themselves may have sublevels. Nevertheless, the notion of two main levels is basic for all idea analysis and has several consequences.

The value dimension divided into 'values' and 'goals'

A first consequence of the distinction between the fundamental and the operative level regards the notion of values (V). Up to now, we have been speaking of the 'value dimension' as such. The distinction between fundamental and operative levels of thought, however, demands a subsequent division between, on one hand, general values or ideals, and on the other hand, concrete goals or ends on the operative level. I will thus suggest a terminological change and speak of 'values' (V) on the fundamental level and 'goals' (G) on the operative level.

Values are like general compass directions; they are like visions with no definite end-state. The values of 'Health', 'Goodness' or 'Equality', for example, indicate directions, but hardly a practical limit. You cannot have too much of 'Health', 'Equality' or 'Goodness' (if you hold any of these values). The same goes for all other moral or political fundamental values like 'Justice', 'Freedom', 'God's will' or 'Nature'. (See Brecht, 1959, Chapter VIII, for the thirteen main fundamental values of modern political thought.)

When values are defined on the operative level as practical goals, they are specified into end states that can or should be reached. An example is: 'Only two degrees Celsius global warming until 2050' (G). This goal is situated on the concrete and operative level of discourse and turns the agent's attention to detailed descriptions of the most effective means or methods to reach it. Thus, on the operative level of thought, we meet concrete and practical goals instead of values – hence, GDP-triads instead of VDP-triads.

Hierarchical chains of values, descriptions and prescriptions

Values and goals appear in argumentative–logical chains, from logically higher (more abstract) levels to the logically lower (more concrete) levels. The operative goal of 'not more than two degrees Celsius global warming' (G) is derived from the logically higher (more abstract) value of an undisturbed ecosystem (V). Similarly, the operative goal of 'low body mass index (BMI)' is derived from the fundamental value of 'Health'. The chain consists of argumentative–logical connections between the levels since the values on the fundamental level are supportive warrants for the concrete goals on the operative level. At the same time, the operative goal can be regarded as an argumentative–logical derivation from the fundamental value. These chains between levels are systematic links in idea systems. They are also present in the main political ideologies.

Accordingly, there is also a systematic connection between high-level normative conclusions (P), which we may call principles, and the operative level. This connection is not obvious at first sight. For example, the high-level prescription 'Take care of the ecosystem!' (P) may be transposed to the operative level to function as an action-motivating goal (G). Thus, a new sequence of practical reasoning may commence on the operative level. New concrete, operative descriptions (D*op*) give birth to several new concrete, operative prescriptions like 'Diminish fossil fuel emissions!', 'Fly less!' or 'Eat less meat!' (P*op*). Depending on the level of refinement an almost infinite row of even more specialised descriptions and prescriptions may emerge (see Tables 3.1 and 3.2). (A confusing thing is perhaps that I speak of the fundamental or basic level as (logically) 'higher'. My problem has been to combine two strands of thinking: ideology theory and argumentative–logical theory. I have not found a better solution and the reader may have to excuse me.)

A two-level analytical scheme of ideological thought

When we combine the two levels of thought (fundamental and operative) with the three basic kinds of ideas (V, D and P), we end up with an extended, *two-level analytical scheme of ideological thought*. We receive a six-field table of analytical concepts. The scheme contains six basic kinds of ideas to search for: three on the fundamental level and three on the operative level. It also suggests the possibility of VDP-triads on the fundamental level and GDP-triads on the operative level (see Table 3.1).

Table 3.1 The extended, two-level analytical scheme of ideological content and the six main kinds of ideas

	Values	Descriptions	Prescriptions
Fundamental level	Moral, social, cultural or political *values* (V).	a) *Philosophical assumptions* about human nature, history or society (D). b) Broad *descriptive generalisations* or assumptions of the state or the market, or other broad institutional complexes (D). (Held to be true or valid.)	General *principles* of social and political action (P) (as suggested in the traditions of social and political philosophy, theory and ideology). (Held to be valid or appropriate.)
Operative level	Concrete situation-specific or problem-specific *goals* (G).	Concrete descriptive or evaluative accounts of: a) the situation, including its objects, causal relationships, problems or possibilities (D*sit*); b) the means-ends relations or suggested means or methods to solve problems (D*me*). (Held to be true or valid).	Concrete, situation-specific or problem-specific or means-ends specific *prescriptions* for action (P). (Held to be valid or appropriate.)

Initially, we learned to use the VDP-model in the search for the *three basic kinds* of ideological thought – V, D and P. Now we have six kinds of ideological thought to look out for: three on the fundamental level and three on the operative level. While all six may not be present at the same time in a text, the scheme indicates what six basic kinds of ideas *may* be found. The point of the six-field scheme is that it prompts us to search for all six potential ideas to find out which are present and which are not. Metaphorically, the scheme provides the analyst with an efficient fishing net or a forceful metal detector to sweep over the verbal surface. Some texts under investigation may consist of ideas and VDP-triads only on the fundamental level, while other texts only proffer ideas and GDP-triads on the operative level. Most often the analyst encounters single statements and argumentative sequences on both levels. Which will be the case, and in which combination, is an empirical question, as we will see in the next section.

The combination of VDP-triads

The two-level analytical scheme can be used to discern and identify single ideas on the two levels of thought in a text. But equally important, of course, is the search for triads of practical reasoning. These may also occur on the two levels of thought. The interesting thing is that they are linked by logical connections. Just as the value 'Health' on the fundamental level is connected to the goal 'low BMI' on the operative level, the scheme suggests that there are logical connections between whole VDP-triads on the fundamental level and GDP triads on the operative one. A *complete idea system* consists of both fundamental and operative ideas of the six kinds, as well as argumentative triads on both levels.

As an example of a complete idea system, we will turn to a lifestyle magazine which I happened to catch sight of. The lavish layout seemed to suggest the fundamental value of 'Health' (V) already on the cover. When browsing through the text, I soon found the implicit, general, descriptive assertion that 'overweight is detrimental to health' (D*fund*) signalled all over the texts and the illustrations. By using the logic of the VDP-model it was not difficult to derive the permeating, albeit latent, general prescription: 'Mind your weight!' (P*fund*).

Further into the text, the argument became more explicit and moved to the operative level where three operative sublevels were found, concerning exercise and diet. In this way, the magazine in fact presented – perhaps unconsciously, but surely informatively – a whole *idea system* of how to keep fit and healthy. As with all idea systems, this one was anchored in the fundamental level of thought, but the most interesting ideas were found at the operative level. The results of the closer analysis of the operative level are presented in Table 3.2.

In Table 3.2, we can see that the idea system consists of three sublevels on the operative level with connected triads, one on each sublevel. We can also see that the prescription (P*fund*) on the fundamental level appear as a goal (G) on the operative level. Furthermore, the triads on the three operative sublevels are connected

Table 3.2 The stylised inner structure of the operative level of the idea system found in the lifestyle magazine (presupposing the fundamental level presented in the text)

	Goals	Descriptions	Prescriptions
Operative level (sublevel 1)	'Mind your weight!' (G). (Fetched from the fundamental level's [P*fund*].)	'To mind your weight the BMI is a handy measure' (D*me*)	'Keep your BMI between 20 to 25!' (P*op*)
Operative level (sublevel 2)	'Keep your BMI between 20 to 25!' (G)	'Exercising every day enhances metabolism and burns calories' (D*me*) 'Dieting helps control calorie intake' (D*me*)	'Exercise and diet!' (P*op*)
Operative level (sublevel 3)	'Exercise and diet' (G)	'Two gym sessions per week is enough' (D*me*) 'The LFHC diet is phenomenal' (D*me*)	'Two sessions at the gym a week! And always diet by LFHC!' (P*op*)

to one another since the prescription (P) in a higher operative triad reappears as the goal (G) in a more concrete operative triad. *The triads, thus, are bound together or linked.* The idea system receives its action guiding force through these links, that is, the argumentative–logical connections of the triads. (This fact may take some time to digest, so look through Table 3.2 again. To grasp the inner links of the idea system, it may be useful to read it both horizontally and vertically. Do not forget the fundamental level, presented above.)

The argumentative-logical structure of the idea system in the magazine is an example of how all idea systems are built up in real life (seen from the analytical point of view) and we meet such systems everywhere. As with all ideas, some of them may be explicitly stated, while others are merely implied. And just like the VDP-triads themselves, idea systems may be incomplete, with missing factors and non-reasoned conclusions. Many of them are thus in need of analytical reconstruction to be understandable or at least an analysis that points out the missing factors and links.

Three necessary, basic analytical distinctions

Before starting an actual textual analysis using the schemes above, three basic analytical distinctions must be observed. They are central to the methodological approach presented here, but also for the other approaches of this book.

The first distinction emerges from general semantics and is the distinction between *sentences* as grammatical constructions and *statements* as the inner meaning of the sentences. It is the equivalent to the distinctions between term and concept, word and meaning, or symbol and idea. As is well known, the term *signifies* the concept that in turn *refers to* an object (material or immaterial) outside the text. The connection between explicit sentences and their intended meanings – the statements – may be clear and unequivocal, as in lucid and well-kept prose. But sometimes the connection is diffuse, fragmented or sloppy, rendering the inner meaning unclear (see Naess, 1966; Vedung, 1982; Ogden and Richards, 2013 [1923]).

The second distinction is the analytical distinction between language levels, mainly between the *political language* of the actor on one hand, and the *analytical language* of the researcher on the other (Lindberg, 2018a: 333–8). What one actor calls 'freedom fighters', another calls 'terrorists'; what one calls 'the conspiracy of the liberal elite' another calls 'democratic decision-making'; what one calls 'indigenous people' another calls 'natives', and so on. This means that the researcher's analytical language must rise above the contested word use in the debate. If the analyst describes a certain group as terrorists (instead of freedom fighters), the analyst is accepting the perspective of one of the contenders and in fact becomes implicated as a part of the investigated object. To get a distanced perspective, you must *always stay away from specific words of political language, especially when they are involved in a debate or idea struggle*. The value loadings of contested words appear clearly when they are compared to their contenders. So, as an analyst you must get a clear grasp of the always contested meanings of words and concepts, otherwise you risk being duped by the seemingly neutral vocabulary here and there, and become side-taking or one-eyed yourself.

The third distinction is about the difference between the *descriptive* and the *critical* modes of analysis. All idea analyses must start with interpretation and description, clarifying and laying bare the thought-content of the ideas in a text. Only after the specific thought-content is clarified, you will have something specific to criticise. Then, your criticism can be either empirical, moral or logical. Are the descriptive assertions (D) empirically correct, or at least empirically probable? Are the values in themselves morally acceptable (either from the point of view of the analyst or from the points of view of other moral positions)? Are the prescriptions logically sound and valid as argumentative conclusions? In this way, the VDP-model is a powerful tool for transparent clarifying as well as rational criticism, contributing to enhanced rationality and enlightenment in society (Richardson, 2002: 75–84; see also Vedung, 1982; Walton, 2008; Bowell and Kemp, 2015; Lindberg, 2018a: 323–30). With these three analytical distinctions on board, we can now move further into the uncertain waters of interpretation.

The difficulties of interpretation

Political language is not easy to interpret and make sense of. Political language is by nature full of latent meanings, associations and subtexts (see, for example, Edelman, 1977, 1988; Simpson, 1993; Crowley and Hawhee, 1999; Martin, 2014). To this we must add a set of difficulties that emerge from the conscious/unconscious use of field-specific rhetoric, fully understood only by the insiders of a specific context. In real life, the VDP-triads are always embedded in or expressed by context-specific political language, whether on the national level, the community level, the organisational level or the group level. Abbreviations for complex processes – for example, 'Watergate', '9/11' or 'the red wall' – are commonplace (and these are the simple ones), as well as subtextual associations or references. Normally, it is no simple task to detect the meaning of such idioms. Moreover, the analyst must decide *what* meaning to focus on. For example, is the aim to interpret the ideas held by an individual author or an organisation, or is the objective to map the contours of a broader social field from which the ideas in a text have been drawn? (See Table 1.2 and the section on 'Textual analysis and interpretation' in Chapter 1 for further discussion about different interpretative strategies.) In all cases, successful interpretation requires that the analyst possesses both textual and contextual, detailed knowledge about the word-use and the debates under study.

Difficulty 1: Unorganised or fragmented practical reasoning

Sometimes, the interpretation and analysis of the ideological content is easy. The pattern of practical reasoning presents itself in a neat and well-ordered fashion. This is often the case in government reports or in the public debate in daily newspapers. However, in much everyday discourse this is not the case. Here, single ideas may be dispersed throughout the text flow, rendering the VDP-triads hard to see. Some Ps may hang loose by themselves and the seemingly logical value premise (V) or descriptive premise (D) may be missing. In such cases, it may take several close readings to sift out and assemble the missing factors of the VDP-triads. In extreme cases, a total *reconstructive interpretation* is needed to establish the intended meaning of the text, based on scarce evidence or textual fragments (see Vedung, 1982: 99–122).

Nonetheless, the task of the analyst is to single out and lay bare the values, descriptions and prescriptions in the textual flow, however vague or hidden. They normally reside somewhere in the text (otherwise the text would lose its action guiding or ideological meaning), or they may be found in adjacent texts or in the surrounding discursive debate, already known to the audience. In any case, one should not underestimate unorganised or fragmented messages. They may be astonishingly effective in front of the right audience.

No matter how fragmented the text is, the basic analytical questions apply: (1) Which single ideas are there in the text, manifestly expressed or latently suggested? (2) What sequences of normative argument figure in the text? (3) Which kind of ideological content is contained in the message (according to the ideal types of the main ideologies of our culture and their variants and subvariants)? These steps will be illustrated below in the analysis of the Women's Equality Party in the UK.

Difficulty 2: Multilayered and ambiguous sentences

In many texts, the three kinds of ideas are textually present, although involved in multilayered meanings or ambiguous associations. Indeed, words in social and political language often are ambiguous to begin with. What do they point to? What do they really mean? Rhetorically skilled politicians are experts in exploiting ambiguities or choosing synonyms with varying value loadings or varying suggestive empirical associations. As argued above, the analytical distinction between the grammatical sentence and the inner meaning – the intended statement – is important to observe. The general method of ideational interpretation is to start with words and sentences and then search for their intended meanings.

Difficulty 3: The importance of the context
The starting point is always the words and sentences as they empirically appear in their grammatical and rhetoric form. The vocabulary used in front of a specific audience may be very natural for the speaker and the listener, and quite effective when the audience shares the speaker's language use and is privy to its implied associative meanings. If the analyst is lucky, she is herself acquainted with the discursive conventions at hand, but if she is not familiar with the discourse, the associative references can be hard to discern. It normally takes a thorough background knowledge of the language use of a social or political context (sometimes even a good slang dictionary) to grasp even quite common meanings, associations and references. Take, for example, the political language employed at a rally held by charismatic leaders like Nigel Farage or Jeremy Corbyn. Often a laborious reading of other texts (the textual system) by the authors/actors themselves, or of surrounding texts in the debate situation, is needed. As I pointed to above, the contestations with other ideas and vocabularies are often the key to the intended meanings, and the actual communicative idioms are always context bound. The significance of the context becomes especially obvious when you are about to analyse texts from unfamiliar social milieus, from distant geographic areas or from distant historical periods, and have to start your journey of understanding from scratch.

As an example, we can return to Donald Trump's slogan 'Make America great again!' As noted, the slogan's meaning and appeal depends on a complex set of references. Taken by itself, as a grammatical sentence, it is in fact extremely vague or ambiguous. The same simple sentence could in principle have been a socialist slogan, or a song by Bruce Springsteen and Barack Obama. Words in themselves are in principle devoid of meaning. They are just carriers of messages (Evans, 2009; Ogden and Richards, 2013) and it is the message that counts. Knowledge of the context, therefore, is indispensable in all interpretation. It simply takes some time and training to be acquainted with the language use and vocabulary of (a) a specific author/agent; (b) a specific genre or system of texts in an ideological camp; or (c) a specific discursive situation, with its varying degrees of conflict or consensus, and its varying shades and nuances of words.

As an analyst, you should always treat your suggested interpretation like a hypothesis. You can never be totally sure of its veracity. The only thing you can do is to check it again and again, and try to establish a case for or against it. There is seldom a final verdict to wait for, only a continued discussion among peers and colleagues. This insight is in itself a part of the truth-seeking, scientific attitude (see Lindberg, 2018b: 524–9).

Difficulty 4: Grammatical multifariousness
The three basic kinds of ideas – V, D or P – may reside in sentences of multifarious grammatical forms. Take, for example, the UN Declaration of Human Rights, where the first article starts with the famous statement that 'All human beings are born free and equal in dignity and rights'. This grammatically descriptive sentence (present tense in the indicative) is, of course, meaningless or outright wrong if it is interpreted as an empirical statement of facts (D). Most people on this planet are not born free and equal at all. Upon closer inspection, however, we find that the claim is not formulated on the empirical (operative) level of thought at all, but on the philosophical (fundamental) level, and furthermore, that it is actually *a value statement or an ideal* (V). To make the value statement manifest, we could reconstruct the intended meaning to something like this: 'We, here assembled for this purpose, hold as our fundamental value: All human beings are born free … ', and so on. This is an interpretation which is also, in fact, supported by the Preamble of the Declaration.

A value claim (V) in a text can thus be stated in seemingly descriptive sentences like 'Health is important' and still serve as a value statement in a sequence of practical reasoning. You might even meet value claims in questions like 'How can you put up with yourself without taking care of your health?', a long sentence that mainly expresses the value 'Health', but perhaps also the value of moral responsibility for your body. The lesson is that *it is not the sentence type or the linguistic syntax that decides which of the three basic kinds of ideas we are confronted with.* The ideological thought-content must be grasped via the arguments of practical reasoning at hand. For this, the VDP-model is the analytical tool. There are no shortcuts on the arduous road to establish a *reasonable interpretative hypothesis* of the thought-content in a text, be it poetry or political language.

Difficulty 5: Long sentences and verbose reasoning
A recurrent problem for the analyst are longish sentences or narrations. To be able to analyse them in the light of the VDP-model, the ideas need to be reconstructed, shortened and stylised. Such shortening and stylising are parts of the analytical process, laying bare the backbone of the ideological thought-content. It takes some experience and acquaintance to be good at it. A reading protocol might be helpful. There you can write down the stylised forms for the intended values, descriptions or prescriptions. (We have already met such stylised forms in the examples of practical reasoning above.) In the process of reconstructive stylising, the VDP-model should serve as a guideline. Only clear and short statements will express the ingoing single ideas and their combinations into triads.

Difficulty 6: Incomplete VDP-triads

The task of interpretation is also complicated by the fact that a text may contain only one or two of the three factors of the VDP-triad. In such cases, the sequence of practical reasoning might be incomplete on the surface of the text, but perhaps not in its subtext or in its implicit, suggested meaning. If this is the case, the analyst must try to find the missing links. As already noted, two ways to do this suggest themselves: the first is to search for the *implicit assumptions* or the self-evident, silent commonplaces that inhere between the lines or hide behind the words. The second is to search for them in *other texts* of the author–agent, or in the *intertextual discursive situation* consisting of texts from other participants in the direct or indirect debate.

The lack of explicit value claims is particularly common. We can meet a text where an evident descriptive account (D) is present ('The Ebolavirus is spreading') and an equally evident prescription (P) is pronounced ('Start vaccination at once!'). But why this is important might not be manifestly stated, most likely because it is self-evident to the audience. In cases like this we can derive the value by working backwards from the practical conclusion (P), moving over the descriptive account (D) to reach the value position. Then the *implicit value premise* (V) ('Health for the whole population') may emerge logically. This may seem like nit-picking, but in the research context it may be the starting point for a critical analysis. Is vaccination really accessible for 'the whole population', or does it only reach the elite segment? And if so, why?

After working through all these analytical concepts and interpretative pitfalls, it is time to meet some real-life ideas. We will undertake an analysis of a specific, illustrative example – namely, the Policy Document of the British Women's Equality Party (WE).

Illustration: The Policy Document of the Women's Equality Party (WE) of the UK

The Women's Equality Party (WE) was founded in the UK in 2015 with the purpose to 'bring about equality for women'. They slightly updated their platform in 2017 (available at: www.womensequality.org.uk). What is their ideology? Is this a revolutionary feminist project or one of gradual, democratic reform? Or might even the label 'feminism' be questioned?

WE labels itself as a 'mainstream party' (WE, Policy Document, p. 4) and presents itself as a network of women working in the tradition of gradual democratic reformism. They strive for parliamentary seats and for cooperation with the established parties. They do not label their ideology and policy 'feminist' even though their Policy Document suggests profound gender equality goals and profound institutional changes, launching a heavy critique of the lack of gender equality in Britain. The institutions under attack range from informal habits to existing legislation and public policies. Hence, the chosen strategy of the WE is a mix of awareness-raising campaigns and legislative proposals. (I recommend the reader

The seven core objectives of the party

The opening chapter of the party platform is called 'The WE model' (presented after the tightly loaded preamble). There we meet the overarching goal, the 'remit' of the party, together with its 'seven core objectives'. Since we are speaking of goals and objectives, we are situated on the operative, fairly concrete and practical level of ideology. I quote (with my own italics):

> The Women's Equality Party is a focused mainstream party. WE will never take a party line on issues outside our remit: *to bring about equality for women*. Our policies are designed to further these seven core objectives:
>
> - WE are pushing for *equal representation* in politics, business, industry and throughout working life.
> - WE expect *equal pay* and equal opportunity to thrive.
> - WE are campaigning for *equal parenting and caregiving*, and shared responsibilities at home to give everyone equal opportunities both in family life and in the workplace.
> - WE urge an *education* system that creates opportunities for all children and an understanding of why this matters.
> - WE strive for *equal treatment* of women by and in *the media*.
> - WE seek an *end to violence* against women.
> - WE are working for *equality in healthcare* and medical research to ensure better health outcomes and access and provision of treatment and support.
>
> (WE Policy Document, p. 4)

The seven core objectives then make up the headings of the seven main chapters of the Policy Document. Each chapter heading consists of the words italicised by me above, but is phrased as a catchy political demand, or, in my terminology, a prescription (P). We thus find: *'Equal representation!'* (P1), *'Equal pay!'* (P2), *'Equal parenting and caregiving!'* (P3), and so on (although without the exclamation marks). I will term them P1–P7. The party promises to 'work for', 'tackle', 'press for', 'enable', 'urge', 'seek', 'strive for', 'address' or 'push for' specific policy measures and specific institutional changes in the direction of the general goal (G) 'equality for women'.

An immediate reflection may be that 'equality for women' sounds more like a fundamental value (V) and not a general, operative goal (G). This is, of course, a point of discussion; the reader will meet my hypothesis of interpretation on this point later. The organisation of the Policy Document in seven chapters, under headings closely related to each of the 'seven core objectives', makes the structure of the policy document extremely clear and the ideological message easy to grasp – an impressive example of political pedagogy.

From where do the seven core objectives come?

So far, so good. But at a closer look we confront a puzzling fact. These seven objectives are seemingly derived from the general goal 'to bring about equality for women' (G). But why are there seven objectives, and why exactly *these* seven? Let us use the analytical reading glass of the VDP-model and take a closer look at the two opening sentences of the quotation above about the remit to bring about equality for women.

The connection between the general goal (G) and the seven core objectives (P1–P7) is not visibly spelled out. There is a gap in the text between the general goal 'to bring about equality for women' and the subsequent sentence starting with 'Our policies are designed to further these seven objectives'. This is an important gap, obviously filled with an underlying meaning. The general message is grasped by most people and consequently they do not bother to dig deeper into it – but we will, since we are aiming for certainty. To reconstruct the underlying meaning residing in this logical gap we need the formal VDP-model as the analytical tool.

Seven descriptions of seven social fields
We know that a prescription (P), as a practical conclusion, needs to be anchored in a value premise (V) and a descriptive premise (D). Therefore, seven prescriptions – 'objectives' – ought to have seven descriptive accounts (D) as their premises. We have not seen them yet, although most readers will intuitively imagine them. For the platform to be argumentatively convincing, though, we need to find the seven missing descriptions in the following text.

The solution is nearby. The seven missing D-factors of the opening sentences are present in the following way. In the party platform, each chapter is filled with factual information from *seven social domains*. The seven chapters contain thorough descriptive assertions and evaluative assessments of *the situation of deficient gender equality* ($Dsit$) in seven domains of the British society, together with descriptions and evaluations of available *policy means* (Dme) to reach the goal of gender equality in the respective domains. The descriptions of the situations and the available policy means are supported by statistics and known facts, making up seven basic descriptive complexes or narratives, one in each chapter. I term them D1–D7 and they correspond to the seven objectives described above. Together, the seven argumentative complexes make up a fairly comprehensive descriptive ($Dcog$) and evaluative ($Deval$) account of contemporary British society from the point of view of gender equality (a rather impressive effort in itself). This descriptive account is the kernel of the party's ideological message.

If I shorten and stylise the seven descriptive complexes, they assert the following: there is no equal representation in the UK in politics, business and beyond (D1); there is no equal pay between the sexes (D2); there is no equal parenting and care-giving of children and elderly parents (D3); the education system is unequal or has unequal effects (D4); the treatment of women in the media is not only unequal but also degrading (D5); there is an appalling level of violence against women and girls in British society, including rape, prostitution and trafficking (D6); and there is a striking inequality in health, healthcare and medical research to the detriment of women (D7). Here, I have simplified and stylised the seven descriptive complexes to the bare bones, to clarify the descriptive factors that go into the practical reasoning sequences in the party's Policy Document.

The VDP-triad of the policy document

The puzzle of the non-reasoned hole (or logical gap) in the opening is thus resolved by the fact that the seven objectives are founded on seven descriptive accounts. The comprehensive account of the gender situation in Britain is built up by seven descriptive complexes, D1–D7. These seven descriptive complexes function as seven distinct descriptive premises (D), one of them in each of the seven chapters. We know from the above that the value premise was the general goal 'to bring about equality for women' (G) ranging over all seven chapters. Together, these descriptive premises, chapter by chapter, lead up to the seven practical conclusions P1–P7, which are the same as the seven core objectives of the opening. We have thus found the overarching argumentative sequence of practical reasoning in the party manifesto. We get the following GDP-triad:

> G: 'To bring about equality for all women.'
> D: 'There is unequal representation, unequal pay, unequal parenting, unequal education system ... etc.' (D1- D7).
> --
> P: 'Push for equal representation, equal pay, equal parenting, equal education ... etc.' (P1-P7).

We can see that the seven core objectives of the opening now appear as seven practical conclusions (P1–P7) derived from the general goal (G) on one hand and the seven descriptive complexes (D1–D7) as the descriptive premises (D) on the other. This is the major backbone of practical reasoning on the level of the whole platform. It is the kernel of the ideological content in the political message from the Women's Equality Party. The formal VDP-model has shown its fruitfulness in an actual analysis. (In the Exercises below, the reader will be urged to investigate further into the ideological secrets of the programme.) But there is more to come, some of which, I think, is really eye-opening.

Digging still deeper: finding the fundamental philosophical assumptions

The analysis above, like the rhetorical build-up of the platform, regards the operative level of ideological thought. We have not yet touched upon the fundamental level, which is hardly visible in the manifesto. Initially, I mentioned a preamble which we have not yet examined. It starts as follows:

> Nowhere in the world do women enjoy full equality. This represents a shameful waste of potential, for women and for the countries that fail to harness their talents and the societies living at odds instead of mutual respect. This also represents a huge opportunity. WE believe that England, Scotland, Wales and Northern Ireland should not lag behind other countries but instead should take the lead and be the first countries in the world where all genders are equal. The policies set out in this document are a blueprint for enabling women and girls to achieve their full potential. (WE Policy Document, p. 3)

In the first sentence, we seem to find a fundamental value, 'full equality'. But is it really the *utmost* fundamental value? Does it not sound too similar to the general operative goal (G) that we noted above ('equality for all women')? To be really fundamental, we ought to find a value that explains why 'full equality' is important and why it should be valued. A closer reading reveals one such higher value in the preamble. The lack of equality for women in the world is said to be a 'shameful waste of potential' for women (and for countries) and an obstacle to women's achievement of 'their full potential'. In my view, this is the fundamental, political–philosophical value we are looking for. The value is simple: *every woman's achievement of her full potential* (V). If we jump over some interpretative and simplifying steps, we arrive at the following sequence of practical reasoning on the *fundamental level* of the ideology of the Policy Document:

V: 'Every woman's achievement of her full potential.'
D: (a) 'Nowhere in the world do women enjoy full equality.' (D*sit*)
   (b) 'This lack of equality is also found in Britain.' (implied) (D*sit*)
   (c) 'The lack of equality for women in all countries (including Britain) prevents all women (in Britain) from achieving their full potential.' (D*me*)

P: 'Bring about equality for all women (in Britain)!'

Bringing in the two-level analytical scheme

We have thus reached a result concerning both the operative level and the fundamental level of the Policy Document. Let us combine them in our two-dimensional scheme to get hold of the full, inner structure of the party's *system of ideas*, or the structure of the *ideological thought-content* that resides in the Policy Document (see Table 3.3)

Table 3.3 The two-level structure of the ideological thought of the WE Policy Document

	Values	Descriptions	Prescriptions
Fundamental level	Every woman's achievement of her full potential (V).	a) Nowhere in the world do women enjoy full equality (D*sit*). b) The lack of equality for women all over the world disables them to achieve their full potential (D*me*).	Bring about equality for all women! (P).
Operative level	Bring about equality for all women (in Britain) (G).	In Britain there is unequal representation, unequal pay, unequal parenting, unequal education system ... etc. (D1-D7).	Push for equal representation, equal pay, equal parenting, equal education ... etc. (in Britain) (P1-P7).

As the reader will notice while working through the WE Policy Document (or doing the exercises on the document below), the party programme is more complex than the rough analysis in Table 3.3 reveals. The fundamental level is more complicated, in fact, and the operative level is distinctly divided into three sub-levels: the platform level, the chapter level and the section level. This will be indicated in the exercises.

Another question arises when analysing the fundamental level of the party's ideology. Does the party, in its fundamental ideological thought, start out from a comprehensive feminist ideology? Or is it rather a comprehensive liberal ideology – that is, liberalism writ large and expanded into the realm of gender equality? This question will also be taken up in the exercises.

Critical reflections

The error of idealism

Although synthesised and rejuvenated by me (see Lindberg, 2018a: 277–85; 2018b: 435–8), the methodological approach here has a long history. The study of *ideas*, whether philosophical, cultural or political, is an old tradition of scholarship and research. Nevertheless, or for this reason, the tradition shows some typical mistakes or limitations. A first mistake, which is easily committed, is idealism. Idealism is the mistaken notion (nurtured by Platonism, Hegelianism and postmodernism) that the realm of ideas, culture or language is the self-sufficient, ultimate reality in human society or the ultimate causal factor. From the point of view of empirical social science, though (as, for example, Lasswell and Kaplan, 1950; Seliger, 1976; Archer, 2000; Norris and Inglehart, 2011; Bourdieu, 2013 [1977]), there are no self-sufficient or ultimate causal factors, especially not ideas, as may be indicated by idealistic notions of 'culture', 'language', 'spirit of the time' or 'spirit of the nation'. Instead, the Aristotelian, materialist maxim holds: 'Nothing comes out of nothing.' This means that the historically given ideas of the cultural heritage of any given time or place – even the language – are carried forward by actors; wilful individuals and interacting networks who are reusing and recombining already existing ideational elements of thought. All this takes place in *specific historical situations*. Already existing ideational elements make it possible for intentional actors to combine them into new wholes that are socially and politically effective and functioning at least for the time being. Just think of Martin Luther's rereading of the Bible and his formation of a new Christian theology and language; the emergence of Protestant republicanism in the English Civil War of the 1640s and the formation of a new political philosophy and language; the nationalist republicanism of the 'Young Turks' of 1908; the Islamism of the Muslim Brotherhood in the 1930s in Egypt; the welfare liberalism of the 1940s in the UK; the 'New Left' of the 1960s or the 'New Right' of the 1980s. Moral: the focus on the inner structure and meaning of an idea system – as in the methodological approach of this chapter – is no excuse for forgetting the historically contingent, constructed character of all ideas, situated in historical, structural, cultural or biographical contexts (see, for example, Archer, 2000; Bourdieu, 2013 [1977]).

Mistaking the agent

A second typical error is vagueness about who is the actor, and hence who is the author, sender or speaker. This error often comes out of an unclear problem formulation and the corresponding flaws in the choice of source material. It makes a lot of difference whether a political message comes from an official party conference or from a diverging opposition within the party; or if the public document you are reading is a parliamentary report to be discussed or an enacted new legislation; or if the leaked documents from inside an organisation is a total or a haphazard sample.

It is all too common to meet studies with imprecise research questions about 'the view of the world in the 1960s', 'the political attitudes of immigrants' or 'attitudes to gender in the healthcare system'. The researcher, though, is bound to be precise, both regarding the chosen question and the chosen source material. If you are about to investigate attitudes to gender in the healthcare system, for example, you must specify both the agents (doctors, nurses or patients; male or female, or both) and the source material (internal documents, interviews or official information), as well as the research problem (what is the relevance of the attitudes to gender) and your basic analytical concepts (how do you define 'gender' and how do you operationalise or scale the attitudes).

The mistake of holism

A third error is the mistake of holism. This mistake is close to the other two and concerns mistaking the part for the whole. Holism comes in two versions. The *consensus version* suggests that there is only one dominant way of thinking, or only one worth mentioning, forgetting that there is always an ideational struggle going on in any organisation or social field. Investigations into 'The view of sex in the 1960s' or 'The view of child upbringing in the 1950s' suggest the existence of a holistic, general spirit of the time. To be empirically balanced and informative, such studies ought instead to be designed as 'The alternative views of sex in the 1960s' or 'The idea struggle over child-upbringing in the 1950s'.

The *elitist version* of the mistake of holism consists of forgetting the general public, letting the ideas of the elite represent the ideas of the society or of the times. Studies like 'The view of insanity in the early twentieth century' in the elitist version normally concentrate on academic and upper-class mentalities, forgetting other segments of the population or regarding them as less interesting. The ideas of the (often male) elite (in literature, magazines or official documents) are presented as the ideas of the time, while the actual ideas of the lower middle class, the workers, ethnic minorities, outsiders, the opposition or simple commoners (including women and people of colour) are not included in the investigation. The sad thing, I would argue, is that this is a habituated or invisible *point of view*; a class-based (or perhaps even gender- or colour-based) prejudice in the academic community about who is important and who is not. (On non-conscious points of view and hidden values in the academic community, see the classic account in Myrdal, 1996 [1944], Vol II: 1035–70.)

Analysis of ideas and ideological thought and the study of society

The approach is designed to lay bare the social and political thought of political parties, social movements, interest organisations, lobby groups, media agencies, pundits or public intellectuals, as well as the general debate in social media. What kind of *ideas* do they propose or disseminate? Consequently, which societal change – or preservation – do they strive for? Knowledge of such things is essential to understand the aspirations of the actors in society – for example, a newly elected president or a new owner of Twitter, and thus what can be expected in the future.

The primary task in the study of ideas is thus *descriptive ideational analysis*: what ideas and argumentative sequences (VDP-triads) guide social and political actors or are involved in the policy suggestions or alternatives for the future? The aim is to clarify which standpoints and alternatives are at hand. However, some actors deliberately hide their goals and try to win success with devious or misleading information strategies and rhetoric – you do not need to have read Mark Twain's *Huckleberry Finn* to know that. In these all-too-common cases, a descriptive ideational analysis will have to expose the actual thought-content of the ideas, hidden under the deliberately obscuring word use or rhetoric surface. Nevertheless, the commonness of misinformation should not overshadow the fact that many of the debates in society are truly knowledge-seeking and are seriously probing into the conditions and problems of various policy fields and political decisions for the future. In those cases, a rationalising and clarifying analysis of the ideological thought-content may still be valuable to the public debate.

The secondary task in the study of ideas is to expand upon the descriptive analysis. Once a message is descriptively clarified into its skeleton of single ideas and VDP-triads, it may be exposed to systematic, rational criticism – *critical ideational analysis* (cf. the descriptions of critical analyses of discourse in Chapters 6 and 7). Descriptions may be criticised on empirical grounds (are they true and balanced?). Values and goals can be criticised on moral grounds (are they really fruitful or wanted?), but also on instrumental grounds (are the chosen means or methods effective?). Finally, the whole argumentative sequence can be criticised on logical grounds. Are there logical flaws or missing links in the argumentative sequence? In addition, prescriptions may be criticised on moral grounds; some methods are immoral, although they may seem 'effective' or 'desirable' from the actor's point of view.

In these two basic ways – the descriptive and the critical – the 'Analysis of ideas and ideological thought' approach is valuable in the study of society. If applied successfully and convincingly, the approach may contribute to a more honest and rational social and political discourse among democratic citizens.

Summary

On the usefulness of analysis of ideas and ideological content

- *Descriptive ideational analysis.* The primary aim of the approach is to single out the component ideas and the ideological thought-content of (a) an established mode of thought, (b) a message from an actor or (c) an ongoing debate or ideational strife.
- *Critical ideational analysis.* The secondary aim is to make possible a systematic, rational criticism of the ideas. Descriptive statements (D) may be criticised on empirical grounds and the values (V) on moral grounds. The prescriptions (P), or the whole sequence of reasoning (the VDP-triad), may be criticised on logical grounds.
- Both descriptive and critical analyses are enlightening and relevant for both the academic and the general public. The ultimate aim of the approach is to contribute to the rational and enlightened discussion among the citizens in society about the existing ideological alternatives and the normative tendencies for the future.

How to do it

- State your research problem and your research questions clearly. Specify the social field, the actor/agent or the discursive debate to be investigated. Be open about the limitations and the possible biases of your perspective.
- Pay attention to the representativeness and validity of your source material. Make sure your material is rich enough to support your conclusions, but do not overburden yourself with too much material.
- Do not forget other texts by the same author/agent or the surrounding discursive situation. These might be needed in the interpretation and the analysis.
- Substantial background knowledge of the field, the agent or the debate (both historical and ideational) is necessary. This may deliver essential clues in the process of interpretation.
- Read the text(s) carefully, multiple times. Take notes on key formulations and the interpretative hints you get. Start the search for V, D and P statements on the fundamental and the operative level, using the fishing net of the six-field analytical scheme (Table 3.1).
- Good advice is to start by searching for prescriptions (P) to determine what the argument is all about. Prescriptions often allow for retroductive derivation of their descriptive and evaluative premises. This may deliver clues for the further search for them.
- You must move from the sentence level to the statement level. The three basic kinds of ideas (V, D and P) normally reside below the rhetoric surface. Sometimes the language is clear and there is a

short distance between the formal sentences and their inner meaning. Sometimes the language is vague or ambiguous. When found, stylise and shorten the ideational statements and try to arrange them in accordance with the VDP-model and the six-field table.
- Search for a fundamental and an operative level of thought (see Table 3.1). Note that all six fields need not be filled out to produce a result. If the scheme turns out only half-filled or less, this is also an interesting result. Do you find any full VDP-triads? Are there any gaps or flaws in the argumentative sequences? Are there any latent assumptions, implicit factors or implicit logical steps?

Suggested reading

The VDP-model is a general theory of the inner skeleton of ideological thought-content. With its dozen or so basic analytical concepts, it presents a comprehensive analytical frame for textual analysis. In extant studies of ideas or ideologies, you usually find at least some of these analytical concepts – similar ones – at work, even though they do not employ the exact terminology of the VDP-model.

Basic textbooks on ideas and ideologies are indispensable as background knowledge (e.g., van Dyke, 1995; Heywood, 2021; Ball et al., 2021). For an in-depth background to the approach presented here, see Lindberg (2018a: 318-30; 2018b: 515-29) together with the extremely valuable Vedung (1982) or Bowell and Kemp (2015).

For further discussions about values, descriptions and prescriptions in democratic political theory, see Dahl and Shapiro (2021); in real political life, see, for example, Müller (2011). For values, descriptions and prescriptions in public policy analysis, see Majone (1989), Vedung (2000), Bacchi (2009a), Ignell et al. (2019), Syssner (2020: 11-22) or Johansson and Gabrielsson (2021). For the same in the analysis of citizens' ideological thought, see Inglehart and Norris (2003) and Norris and Inglehart (2011), and of political institutions, see March and Olsen (1989).

Studies of contemporary political ideologies are overwhelming. Here is a picky selection. For the ideas of contemporary conservatism, see Letwin (1992), Durham (2000), Skocpol and Williamson (2012). For radical parties on the right, see Widfeldt (2014), and on the left, see March (2013). For Fascism, see Gregor (2002). For Islamism, see Esposito (2016). For feminist theory (not feminist parties, though), see McLaughlin (2003) or Tong and Botts (2018). For social democracy, see Tilton (1990) or Berman (2006). For Mahatma Gandhi's influential thinking on non-violent civil resistance, see Naess (1966). For contemporary Christian political thought, see Mott (1992) or Hornsby-Smith (2006). An exemplary idea-critical study is Manea (2017) on the *Sharia* courts in Britain, delivering both an empirical and a moral criticism. For the general phenomenon of fundamentalism of today (in various ideological contexts), see Strozier et al. (2010) and the general, maybe confusing, ideological displacements in contemporary political life, see Goodwin (2023).

Exercises

Exercise 1: The operative level of the Women's Equality Party ideology

The analysis of the Women's Equality Party in this chapter found an overarching pattern of practical reasoning at the programme level, with seven core political goals G1-G7 related to seven descriptive complexes D1-D7 (see Table 3.3). But how are each of these seven chapters built up internally from the point of view of the VDP-model? In this exercise you will reconstruct the ideological thought-content at the chapter level in the party's Policy Document.

The task

Let us pick the Policy Document's chapter on *sexual violence* with its goal 'End violence against women and girls' (G6). We can see that this chapter is divided into five sections based on five aspects of the policy area 'sexual violence'. In each section we find specific descriptive accounts (D6: 1-5), making up the descriptive premises for the policy prescriptions (P6: 1-5). For example, the description in the first section of the chapter on sexual violence seems to be 'There is insufficient support and sanctuaries for women fleeing abuse' (D6: 1).

- What are the five *descriptions* of sexual violence (D6: 1-5) in the sections of the chapter? What are the accompanying five *prescriptions* for policy and legislation (P6: 1-5)? Write them down in shortened and stylised form.
- Reconstruct the sequence of practical reasoning in the chapter on sexual violence. Establish the inner GDP-triads of Chapter G6 (the D6: 1-5 and the P6: 1-5) in a table. Continue with the other chapters (G1-7), as many as you can. Use the short, stylised form of Table 3.3.

Note: Such tables are only used in the process of *investigation* to support clear thinking. If you aim to make a full presentation of the WE Party ideology, you need to narrate the whole story. However, it could be supported by the tables, in the text or in an appendix.

The texts

The Women's Equality Party Policy Document (available via the party's website: www.womensequality.org.uk).

Exercise 2: The fundamental level of the WE Party ideology

Earlier in this chapter, it was argued that one of the fundamental values in the preamble to the WE Policy Document is 'Every woman's achievement of her full potential' (see Table 3.3). It can be argued, however, that the preamble contains another set of

(Continued)

(Continued)

fundamental values. In my interpretation, there are, in fact, *three more fundamental values* in the preamble.

The task

Scrutinise the preamble to the Policy Document to see if you can find any additional values at the fundamental level.

- What are these other values? Hint: they are all tied to the idea of *'Britain as a nation'*. Try to find them.
- Interestingly, all three nationalist values lead up to almost the same prescription: 'Bring about equality for women (in Britain)!' - that is, almost the same P as emerged from the value of 'every woman's achievement of her full potential' (see Table 3.3). How can a nationalist value produce the same prescription? And what is the difference between them, considering the inner logic of the arguments?
- Reconstruct the other VDP-triads on the fundamental level, starting from the three other values (if you have found them). Insert the values you have found in a table, as in Table 3.3. Then add their respective general descriptive accounts (both D*sit* and D*me*) and check if they lead up to the general prescription to 'Bring about equality for all women (in Britain)' (P*fund*).
- Discuss the possible information strategic reasons for WE to include these three nationalist values alongside the more feminist one regarding 'every woman's achievement of her full potential'. The analysis and the arguments for it are up to you.

The texts

The Women's Equality Party Policy Document (available at the party's website: www.womensequality.org.uk).

Exercise 3: Two famous speeches on the environment and world poverty at the UN

Global warming and world poverty are two topics of great political concern. In this exercise, you will map out and compare the ideological thought-content in two famous speeches on these issues, one by the head of the Catholic Church, Pope Francis, and one by the Swedish climate activist, Greta Thunberg.

The task

In 2015, Pope Francis gave a much discussed speech before the General Assembly of the United Nations. Concentrate on the main themes of the environment and world poverty. Unpack the ideas following the VDP-model and insert them in a table in short and stylised form.

- How does the Pope describe world poverty, environmental degradation and their causes (D*sit*)? Does the Pope say something about the road to change (D*me*)?

(Continued)

(Continued)

- What are the fundamental values that inform the Pope's speech and imbues it with its remarkable action-guiding force? Is there more than one basic value? Or is it the same value seen from different perspectives? (The analysis and the arguments for it are up to you.)
- What are the Pope's prescriptions for dealing with the problems? If there is more than one fundamental value, there ought to be more than one prescription. Is this so?
- That there are values (V) on the fundamental level is self-evident. But how about the descriptions (D) and the prescriptions (P) of the speech? Do they also reside only on the fundamental level? Besides, are there not any concrete goals? The analysis is up to you.

In 2019, Greta Thunberg addressed the United Nations Climate Action Summit with a speech full of subtextual meanings and value-laden words. There is a lot of reconstructive interpretation and analysis to be done here. Unpack the ideas, following the VDP-model, and insert them in a table, in short and stylised form.

- What are the main descriptions (D*cog* and D*eval*)?
- What values and prescriptions are manifestly expressed or latently hinted at? Note: there may be more than one VDP- or GDP-triad present. If so, how do they support each other?
- Search for an over-arching, argumentative-logical VDP sequence in the speech. Is there one?
- Considering the VDP-triads or GDP-triads you have reconstructed in your tables, what similarities and differences do you find between the young, modern Greta Thunberg and the old, traditional Pope Francis?

The texts

- Pope Francis's speech address to the General Assembly of the United Nations, 25 September 2015 (available via www.vatican.va).
- Greta Thunberg's speech at the United Nations Climate Action Summit, 23 November 2019 (available via https://en.wikipedia.org/wiki/Speeches_of_Greta_Thunberg).

4

Conceptual History

Jussi Kurunmäki and Jani Marjanen

Background

The politics of language use

All political action contains partisan uses of words. We use terms like 'democracy', 'society' and 'nation' as if we all knew what they refer to, yet we often mean slightly different things when we use them. In conceptual history, such ambiguous words are referred to as 'concepts'. The disagreement about the content of these words is not just about the fact that we have not defined them carefully enough, but that we actually mean different things by these words and that their use is a way of trying to shape the world we live in. For a researcher, it is important to master this ambiguity in language. Consider, for example, a political speech that celebrates patriotism. Would our view of the speech be more nuanced if we knew that the term 'patriot' has historically referred to a republican revolutionary, a royalist, a freeholding peasant, a far-right supporter or an anarchist, among others? What about 'multiculturalism'? Does the term mean the same thing if it refers to a particular policy, describes the state of a liberal society or is used in a populist political speech? And what does 'populism' really mean: the opposite of democracy, a degenerated form of democracy or a more developed form of democracy? But despite these examples of disagreement, we talk to each other, write texts that people read, make political speeches, and so on. It seems that at least most of the time, we still understand each other enough to communicate. Conceptual history or the history of concepts focuses on this tension between shared and different meanings that concepts carry with them when they are used.

A central starting point for conceptual history is the idea of *language as a historical phenomenon*. Concepts are not timeless entities that can be defined as stable, unchanging, or common to all. As Nietzsche has said, 'definable is only that which has no history' (Nietzsche, 1892: 71; see also Koselleck, 1972: XXIII). However, despite the fact that scholars conducting conceptual history often focus on the contestation of the meaning of concepts and conceptual changes, it is important to keep in mind that the concepts we study are also carriers of continuity. As the German historian Reinhart Koselleck has noted, the historical nature of concepts and the interplay between continuity and change in their content should be understood as the coexistence of different temporal levels (*Zeitschichten, layers of time*) in concepts. Koselleck argues that past meanings of a concept persist to some extent, while new meanings are added when they are used (Koselleck, 2004: 81–2; see also Jordheim, 2017: 50–3).

A central feature of conceptual history is the questioning of linear and progressive histories of development, as these do not take into account the fact that in all times and in all contexts, people could have chosen to act in a different way. In other words, there are no automatic histories of progress when one tries to see things from the historical actors' perspective, nor are there any historical traditions that are commonly understood by all. To avoid falling into anachronistic explanatory models in our studies, we need to be aware of the different meanings of the words used in a specific historical situation. Thus, a researcher must try to analyse the use of concepts – i.e., their specific historical and rhetorical contexts (Ball, 1988: x; Skinner, 2002: 47; Koselleck, 2004: 80). Research in the history of concepts concerns the different *perspectives* that people put forward in their statements. Thus, according to a conceptual history approach, it is important to study how people viewed the democracy of their time when one tries to understand what the state of democracy was at a particular time.

It is the historicity of concepts that makes conceptual history a highly relevant method, and also for social science research on contemporary phenomena. The language we study in our own time is always also historical. For instance, it may be important for a researcher to know what the term 'citizen' has meant at different historical stages to understand the contemporary debate on immigration. A conceptual-historical sense of language can also be a central aspect of many comparative studies. Such studies may address the translations and interpretations of, for instance, different international treaties, debates on constitutional reforms, or policy programmes in different countries. That is to say, a conceptual-history approach can be rewarding for studies that examine a phenomenon in different contemporary contexts, such as different geographical settings, different cultural or intellectual traditions, and so on.

Although the starting point of conceptual history was originally in historicising central political and social concepts, the tradition has since opened up new paths for research. For example, there is a growing interest in applying conceptual history to concepts relating to ideology (Freeden, 1996; Kurunmäki and Marjanen, 2018a; 2018b; 2020), emotions (Pernau et al., 2015) and science (Goudarouli and Petakos, 2017; Kaldewey and Schauz, 2018). In principle, any building blocks of human activity can be studied through a conceptual-history perspective. Thus, issues relating to anthropology (Shoham, 2018), sexual identity (Tremblay, 2021), cultural practices or the environment and climate (Boyden et al., 2022) can serve as topics for conceptual history. Also, the scope of conceptual history has changed over the past twenty years as it has taken up new global and transnational perspectives (Pernau, 2012; Schulz-Forberg, 2014; Spira, 2015) as well as methodological know-how from corpus linguistics (cf. Chapter 7) and the digital humanities (Marjanen, 2023).

In the present, with the increased use of digitised sources, many students of text and discourse face the possibilities and challenges that are familiar to conceptual historians. As researchers often start their process by mapping a material using certain keywords, they are in fact adopting a word-centric perspective. We argue that such searches are a good start for a conceptual history analysis.

A note on concepts and words

There is a long tradition of theorising about what makes a concept a concept – for instance, within the fields of philosophy, linguistics, the history of ideas, and the study of concept formation in pedagogy and the social sciences. Although opinions differ when it comes to the difference between concepts and words, the most common starting point in the field of conceptual history is a practical one: if a concept is understood as some kind of abstract idea and a word is a single meaningful element of speech or writing, then concepts cannot be studied without making a clear connection between a concept and the word that denotes it. Hence, in practice, conceptual history studies the use of words from a historical and political point of view. We follow that practical guideline in this chapter. As Koselleck has put it, concepts are words that are always potentially ambiguous (Koselleck, 1972: xxii; 2004: 84–5). They are words that have multiple layers of meaning. Further, concepts can be understood as 'navigational instruments' that not only reflect reality but also reshape it (Koselleck, 2002: 129). (On the definition of 'concept', see 'Critical reflections' below.)

According to the conceptual-history approach, even the non-linguistic world is to a large extent mediated through language (Koselleck, 2002: 27; see also Chapter 6). The British historian of political thought, Iain Hampsher-Monk, has expressed the relationship between the linguistic and the non-linguistic in an illustrative way:

> We can indeed kill Kings with swords or axes, but it is only with words that we can abolish monarchies. In this sense, the pen is truly mightier than the sword, and to this extent too, linguistic reality and action cannot be seen as conceptually distinct from an independently existing political or social reality. (Hampsher-Monk, 1998: 48)

Reinhart Koselleck and German conceptual history

The given starting point for presenting conceptual history is the German tradition of *Begriffsgeschichte*, which was developed in the 1960s by Reinhart Koselleck (1923–2006). Koselleck's aim was to historicise both social history and the history of ideas using linguistically oriented methods (e.g., Koselleck, 2004: 81; see also Bödeker, 1998: 52; Hampsher-Monk, 1998: 47). Koselleck wanted to develop social history methods to include the historicity of language and the link between language and socioeconomic institutions. According to him, there is a reciprocal relationship between human actors and socioeconomic structures, and between actors and discourses. While structural factors constrain human actions, these actions may change the structures at the same time (e.g., Koselleck, 2002: 37). To Koselleck, then, concepts are entities in which human actions, ideas and socioeconomic structures meet each other (Koselleck, 1998: 29; 2002: 24).

Temporal layers of concepts
The idea that concepts contain multiple *temporal layers* is an important aspect of Koselleck's theory. According to him, there are always different degrees of the past, present and future in a concept (Koselleck, 1994: 11–12). This means that the central political and social concepts can be interpreted as nodes in history as well as in the present. This nodal role makes the analysis of central concepts a useful way to examine different struggles and debates. It also provides opportunities for the analysis of more general political and social changes.

Koselleck's notion of multiple temporal layers of concepts can be linked with his attempt to create a general theory of the emergence of modern political culture. Koselleck argues that the period between about 1750 and 1850 was a period of change in German political culture. Central political and social words took on so many new meanings that it has become difficult to translate the concepts used before this period (Koselleck, 1972: xv). Many scholars have identified similar threshold periods in other political cultures and languages (see, for example, Steinmetz, 2017: 63–95). Our point is not to emphasise this particular period in this chapter, but rather to highlight the possibilities that conceptual history research can offer when trying to create a larger picture of different periods of social change.

From a methodological point of view, Koselleck's characterisation of the conceptual changes surrounding the French Revolution is useful, as it spells out the *temporalisation (Verzeitlichung)* of political and social key concepts and shows that many of them became contested and took on a forward-looking character. He calls them *concepts of movement (Bewegungsbegriffe)*. According to Koselleck, *the horizon of expectation (Erwartungshorizont)* took a more central place than *the space of experience (Erfahrungsraum)* in political action. Examples of new movement concepts include 'progress', 'development' and various 'isms' such as 'liberalism', 'republicanism', 'conservatism' and 'socialism'. According to him, these 'isms' carried within them expectations of the future. Even 'conservatism' was directed towards the future in that it was created as a competitor to the forward-looking concepts of 'liberalism', 'republicanism' and 'socialism'. The most backward-looking people were then called 'reactionaries' (Koselleck, 2004: 248–75.)

Polemical concepts

Koselleck argues that political and social concepts became more polemical during the French Revolution and the following decades. He notes that they often became more abstract than they had been prior to this period, and that they were increasingly deployed as political slogans (Koselleck, 1972: xvi–xvii; 2002: 127–30). The struggle over concepts such as 'patriotism' and 'nation' during the French Revolution are good examples of how key concepts were politicised and ideologised. The early revolutionaries embraced an interpretation of 'nation' that did not include privileges stemming from estate-based society, a view that was inconsistent with the interpretation of the previous absolutist French nation. A struggle over the ownership of the correct interpretation of 'nation' ensued. In short, the dispute was about whether the concept of nation should be understood as a historical and natural entity or as something new, created by the revolutionary process. During the revolution, 'nation' was so strongly linked to the cause of the revolutionaries that the very use of the word itself could be interpreted as taking a stand for the revolution (cf. 'Semantic struggles' in Chapter 7).

Synchronic and diachronic studies

According to Koselleck, two analytical perspectives are indispensable in a conceptual-history investigation. He applies Ferdinand de Saussure's philosophy of language and argues that concepts should be analysed both synchronically and diachronically. *Synchronic* analysis means that a concept is studied in relation to other concepts that are in use at the same time. The researcher's primary focus is the selected concept's *semantic field* – i.e., how different concepts relate to each other in a specific situation. The selected concept is analysed in its linguistic and social context. One can also say that the concept is placed in its rhetorical context (Koselleck, 2004: 80). *Diachronic* analysis, on the other hand, is a historical comparison of the meaning of a concept at different points in time (Koselleck, 1972: xxi; 2004: 82–3). The idea is that the researcher tries to find out how the concept has changed over time. We would like to emphasise that both types of comparison are important. To the conceptual historian, even a study that focuses on a single case with no obvious history is a case with diachronic dimensions because the words analysed refer not only to the present but also to past uses of the word and sometimes also carry connotations to the future (see Koselleck, 1972: xxi; 1998: 30–5).

Diachronic and synchronic analyses can be carried out from two different perspectives. In the *semasiological* analysis, the different meanings of the selected words are examined. Such an analysis would, for example, pay attention to how the word 'Western' in some cases indicates a geographical distinction and in other cases refers to a certain quality that is asymmetrically opposed to something non-Western. The meanings are related, but there are differences that stem from the rhetorical situation and the beliefs and motives of the language user. Semasiological analysis tries to get at such differences in word use over time, between different people or across the political spectrum. In the *onomasiological* analysis, the question is turned around and the relevant synonyms of the target words or expressions are examined (Koselleck, 1972: xxi–ii; 2004: 75, 86). For example, it can be assumed that expressions like 'government of the people', 'popular rule' and 'democracy' refer to broadly the same thing, but it is also likely that the choice of different expressions may have been important to particular language users. It is important to start with the semasiological analysis, or there is a risk that the researcher does not connect the investigation to the word that the historical actors used.

Another methodological strategy that characterises Koselleck's conceptual history is an analysis of the *counter-concepts* that figure as opposites to the analysed concept. Typical of counter-concepts is that one of the concepts in the pair is negatively charged (Koselleck, 2004: 158). For instance, the concept of 'egoism' was for a long time commonly understood as a counter-concept of 'patriotism'. This is no longer the case, which is a sign of conceptual change. Typically, changes in counter-concepts are helpful in identifying transformations in political and social language.

Quentin Skinner and linguistic contextualism

The importance of understanding a text in its historical context

Many conceptual historians also draw on the contextualist-linguistic approach to the history of political thought advocated most famously by Quentin Skinner (and the so-called Cambridge School). The contextualist approach has focused less on historical change (diachronic analysis) and more on rhetorical strategies in particular historical situations (synchronic analysis). Skinner has examined *speech acts* (cf. 'Textual analysis and interpretation' in Chapter 1) in their historical contexts and thus contributed to our understanding of the rhetorical aspects of conceptual change. The common denominator of Koselleck and Skinner is their focus on what the concepts meant to the historical actors themselves. In other words, they share the ambition to avoid misleading hindsight or anachronistic explanations in research. In this regard, Skinner took inspiration from R.G. Collingwood, whose philosophy of history stressed that understanding historical texts requires that we first ascertain what questions the author intended to answer (Collingwood, 1939: 39).

In his polemical methodological articles since the late 1960s, Skinner has strongly questioned such anachronistic studies of the history of ideas that present political–philosophical theories as different answers to the same perennial questions, as if all historical authors had dealt with the same problems. On this point, Skinner is close to Koselleck and the German tradition of conceptual history.

Skinner stresses that the texts that for us constitute canonised classics in their own time could have been discussion pieces, usually controversial reinterpretations that had practical daily political purposes. In order to understand an author's intentions and how the text was understood in its own time, one must find out what issues were being discussed in the period in question. One should know what arguments other participants in the debate were presenting and what the author's point was in comparison to contemporary debaters. In other words, one must try to form an idea of what was possible to say, what was customary to say and what broke the unwritten rules of the period in question. Therefore, one also needs knowledge of the prevailing social and political conditions (Skinner, 2002: 47). If we approach key thinkers in political philosophy as if they were participating in a debate on perennial questions like the 'nature of the just state', we lose sight of what the actors' intentions were in their own time, but we also assume too much coherence in how the concepts of nature, justice and the state were understood in different times (Skinner, 2002: 86). Skinner thus argues that the political problems of their day set the backdrop also for political philosophers, and that we cannot understand their statements without taking their context into account.

According to Skinner, the first step in an analysis is to create an understanding of the historical context. History does not provide us with ready-made contexts, but the researcher must create the contexts in their study. Hence, contextualisation is part of the analysis (Skinner, 1978: xiii–iv). In his own studies, Skinner has placed the analysed texts in their contemporary context by examining a large number of other texts, including even anonymous contributions (Skinner, 1978, 1996a). The intention has been to understand what was being discussed and debated when the studied texts were produced, for it is clear that authors have wanted to be understood by their contemporaries (Skinner, 1978: x–xi; 1996b: 148). Skinner's approach to contextualisation is fairly text-based, but according to him social and institutional factors come into play through linguistic expression and can therefore also be studied through language (Skinner, 2002: 87).

Speech acts and rhetorical moves
Skinner's main influence on the history of concepts lies in his insistence that we should understand texts and the arguments therein as *speech acts*. He draws on Wittgenstein's later philosophy of language and especially on J.L. Austin's speech act theory. The idea is that we should not understand arguments in texts as fundamentally different from other forms of actions. Here, he follows Austin's distinction between three aspects of a speech act. First, there is the meaning of the utterance itself (the *locutionary* aspect). What do the words mean? Second, there is the performative aspect of the expression (the *illocutionary* aspect). What was the nature of the action (e.g., a statement, a question, a command)? Why did the authors write what they wrote? Third, there is the effect of the statement on those who received it (the *perlocutionary* aspect). How was the argument understood? (Skinner, 1996a: 7–8; 2002: 103–27).

We will discuss Skinner's emphasis on the synchronic aspect in the section 'Critical reflections', but it is worthwhile to point out already here that it has been quite common to criticise him for not showing much interest in the perlocutionary aspect of his studies. This also means that he has not developed a theoretical-cum-methodological approach to how one should examine the reception of language acts over time – i.e., how texts have been interpreted and reinterpreted afterwards.

Focusing on the role of the author in the historical context, Skinner has paid particular attention to the author's *intentions, rhetorical manoeuvres (moves)* or *points*. The idea is that we should understand what authors were doing when they wrote (or said) what they wrote. What questions did they want to answer? Was the text a provocation? Was it irony? (Skinner, 1996a: 7–8; 2002: 96–7, 115, 137). Skinner writes:

> To understand any serious utterance, we need to grasp not merely the meaning of what is said, but at the same time the intended force with which the utterance is issued. We need, that is, to grasp not merely what people are saying but also what they are doing in saying it. To study what past thinkers have said about the canonical topics in the history of ideas is, in short, to perform only the first of two hermeneutic tasks, each of which is indispensable if our goal is that of attaining an historical understanding of what they wrote. As well as grasping the meaning of what they said, we need at the same time to understand what they meant by saying it. (Skinner, 2002: 82)

The idea is not to identify the authors' true intentions, but to try to create a reasonable hypothesis about them to rule out historically impossible interpretations (Skinner, 1996b: 151–2).

Conceptual change

According to Skinner, concepts change because there are disputes about their meaning. He points to at least three possible ways in which disagreements about a concept can be visible: (1) how the concept (word) is usually used – i.e., what is the scope or context of the concept (*the nature and range of criteria*); (2) when it is appropriate to use the concept – i.e., when the prevailing circumstances are such that the concept fits in (*the range of reference*); (3) what can be done with the concept (*the range of attitudes*). In other words, the researcher should focus on (1) the usual criteria for use of the term; (2) when these criteria apply; and (3) the attitudes or purposes expressed by this use. As a rule of thumb, concepts can be said to have changed when an action is described and legitimised using terms that would not normally have been considered (Skinner, 1999: 66–7; 2002: 161–2).

Skinner is interested in how actors legitimise actions, decisions and opinions, not whether what is said is true or not. He talks about certain historical actors who manage to linguistically legitimate controversial actions. He calls them '*innovative ideologists*'. According to Skinner, the rhetorical task of innovative ideologists is

> to legitimise questionable forms of social behaviour. Their aim must therefore be to show that a number of favourable terms can somehow be applied to their seemingly questionable actions. If they can bring off this rhetorical trick, they can hope to argue that the condemnatory descriptions otherwise liable to be applied to their behaviour can be overridden or set aside. (Skinner, 2002: 149)

A variant of an innovative ideologist is an *apologist* whose task is to defend and preserve the existing by describing conditions in positively charged terms (Skinner, 1973: 302–3). These rhetorical strategies highlight a central theme in conceptual history research: struggles over conceptual meanings and changes in those meanings. On this point, there is no essential difference between Koselleck and Skinner, although the latter spells out the rhetorical aspect of conceptual contestation in a more detailed manner than the former (Palonen, 2003a: 47–60).

Finally, we would like to point to Skinner's notion of *rhetorical redescription*. It is a rhetorical strategy that can be interpreted as being a part of the task of the innovative ideologists and apologists, and brings Skinner's discussion thematically close to Koselleck and German conceptual history, as there is clearly a diachronic aspect in it. Rhetorical redescription is based on the idea that actors in different debates often reinterpret existing concepts by describing their histories in new ways that suit their purposes (Skinner, 2002: 178–9, 182–5; Palonen, 2003a: 8–9, 161–9). It means that positively laden terms can be used to refer to negatively valued phenomena and that negatively loaded terms can be used to refer to positively understood values. When examining rhetorical redescriptions, one can notice both the changing content of the terms and the changing contexts of their application.

Transnational conceptual history

Transnational phenomena have gained more attention among scholars in recent decades. We argue that transnational processes in the present and a higher awareness of transnationality in the past have increased the relevance of conceptual history studies, but also posed some methodological challenges (see Marjanen, 2009, 2017; Pernau, 2012). Since political key terms derive their meaning from their context of use, and since this context of use is often thought to include only one language area and one political system, the main contextual unit usually becomes one country – the nation-state. The risk is that such projects naturalise a political culture that coincides with a particular nation-state and its majority culture. Scholars critical of assuming the nation state as a natural research unit and using analytical concepts and datasets highlighting the nation, often speak of *methodological nationalism* (Beck and Sznaider, 2006: 1–6; Marjanen, 2009: 239–47). In order to avoid methodological nationalism, we must try to relate to the society or political culture under study with fresh eyes, as if it were 'a foreign country, but a country familiar to us' (Palonen, 2003b: 569). Similarly, we must pay attention to how concepts cross national boundaries and how these boundaries have been understood in different ways in the past. We can speak of the transnational dimensions of concepts.

Conceptual history is a very well-suited approach to transnational issues. Although the national perspective has dominated the social sciences and humanities, few nation-states are monolingual. More importantly, there are no languages that have not been influenced by other languages, which means that any research in the history of concepts must, in one way or another, address transnational processes of translation or etymology.

Three research perspectives on transnationality
We want to highlight three overlapping perspectives on how the transnational aspect of social and political language can be understood from a conceptual history point of view. The first is to examine the concepts that have been used to *name and describe transnationality*. We are thinking here of such terms as 'national', 'international', 'transnational' and 'global'. Studying their conceptual history would be a good way to examine how people's perceptions of the transnational, or, more broadly the border crossing, have changed. Furthermore, one could examine concepts that describe *transnational processes* themselves. This could involve examining how concepts like 'globalisation', 'regionalisation', 'integration', 'immigration', 'foreigner' and 'immigrant' have been used.

The second perspective focuses on how historical and political actors themselves have acted in ways that transcend national, cultural and linguistic contexts. Here we refer to *practices* that are present in most political and social actions, such as references to the conditions of other countries as part of the argumentation at home. One would then examine how historical actors themselves refer to other countries, political systems and cultures, and employ them as examples when they use the concepts we are interested in. This *rhetoric of comparison* should be understood as a way for these historical actors to create and reformulate the relevant context for their own purposes – i.e., a way of defining the current political agenda and reinterpreting its key concepts (Steinmetz, 2020; Kurunmäki and Marjanen, 2021). This approach also involves the study of translations and *innovative receptions* of concepts from other contexts (Leonhard, 2004). This means examining, for example, travel letters, newspaper reports from abroad or translations of official documents and international agreements. A practical way to conduct this type of research is to examine how parliamentary debates in different countries refer to examples from other countries (e.g., Ihalainen, 2017).

The third perspective is probably the most concrete way to take the transnational into account in conceptual history research. It involves examining how a concept has been used in multiple political contexts. The German historian Jörn Leonhard's study on the conceptual history of 'liberalism' in Britain, France, Germany and Italy serves as a good example. He shows that the early history of 'liberalism' in the early nineteenth century did not take place in nationally enclosed spaces, but in a constant exchange between different languages and cultures. At the same time, historical perceptions of the origins of the concept of liberalism influenced how the term could be used in certain contexts. Leonhard shows, for example, that liberalism as a concept did not take hold in British political discourse before the 1830s because the concept had previously been so strongly linked to French revolutionary and Napoleonic language (Leonhard, 2001, 2004).

These transnational perspectives show how different temporal levels of concepts and the geographical contexts of concept use intertwine. Koselleck also talks about how some historical processes seem untimely, as when a word is used in another language or country in a way that makes it feel like it belongs to a past time. We may also have the feeling that people in our current surroundings are speaking in a way that seems outdated to us or, alternatively, serves as models for the future (Koselleck, 2004: 75–92; Jordheim, 2017: 47–62; Kurunmäki and Marjanen, 2021). These examples are illustrative of Koselleck's idea of different temporal layers in a concept. The words may carry connotations to the past or the future or they may refer to past meanings a word may have held. It is always possible to reactivate old meanings that were attached to a word and such meanings often resurface when language crosses borders.

Quantitative analysis of digitised sources

Conceptual history has traditionally revolved around qualitative analysis of texts. Since more and more material is available in digital form, it has become easier to carry out quantitative analyses as well. A simple way to use digital sources is to do free-text searches that give us access to sources where the words we are interested in appear, but it is also possible to use the digital material for more advanced quantitative analyses. Even when we are not interested in an in-depth statistical analysis, the digitised material may be too extensive for one person to read in a reasonable amount of time, in which case it may help to have a statistical overview of the language used in the material (see also 'Corpus analysis' in Chapter 7.)

Word frequencies

Traditionally, conceptual history studies have paid close attention to when a concept was introduced into the language, but often it can be more informative to know when this concept became established and common. Digital text collections allow us to calculate both the absolute and relative frequency of word usage. Absolute frequency measures the occurrence of words, while relative frequency measures the occurrence of a word in relation to something else in the data – for instance, the occurrences of a word in relation to all the words in a given year in the dataset. For example, for a newspaper corpus, the number of words tends to vary annually, and a relative frequency per year offers a possibility to compare word usage historically over different time periods. Frequency analysis gives us a better picture of the impact of a word. For example, the word 'globalisation' was coined in English as early as the 1930s (James and Steger, 2014), but an analysis of relative frequency shows that the word only had a breakthrough in the 1990s. Only then did 'globalisation' appear as a word with a clear horizon of expectation and rhetorical power. Examining relative frequency thus offers an opportunity to see whether a word has made a breakthrough or become less popular in a specific time period. Still, interpreting frequencies always also requires knowledge of the historical context.

Distributional semantics

More detailed analyses are also possible. For example, we can quantitatively measure which words are more likely to co-occur together with a particular target word. In Natural Language Processing, the computer-assisted analysis and manipulation of language data, researchers often talk about *distributional semantics* or *word embeddings*, but these are actually collective names for many different methods. In general, these methods assume that words occurring in similar linguistic contexts are close in meaning, or as John Rupert Firth (1957: 179) once wrote: 'You shall know a word by the company it keeps.' Thus, by examining how the linguistic context of a word has changed over time, changes in its meaning can be accessed. We can also examine which words occur in similar linguistic contexts to find words that are likely to be close in meaning. However, newer research has shown that the sense of a word is not the only thing affecting word distributions (Kanner, 2022). In these analyses, we come close to what Koselleck meant when he spoke of *semantic fields* – that is, words that are closely related and thus create a natural context for the use of a concept (Ifversen, 2011: 71). But when working quantitatively, there is less room for interpretation of the text. Instead, we have to define a word from which we start, calculate which words occur in a defined field before and after it, and then statistically calculate which words are frequent in the semantic field around the word. The changes in the nearby words are slow and we generally do not find rapid changes in language use, but we can map out the longer trends in how language changes.

We can also study how word usage in different texts differs statistically – i.e., whether a word occurs more often in a particular text than is likely based on the whole corpus. In corpus linguistics, this is known as the *keyness method* (Scott and Tribble, 2006: 55–67). We often assume, for example, that different political parties like to use different words to convey their policies, but this is an issue that can be tested empirically and, at best, proven statistically.

A critical perspective on digitised corpora

For any quantitative analysis of word usage, it is important to know the nature of the text collection on which the analyses are based. We usually speak of a *corpus* – i.e., a defined collection of texts. The data providers who have compiled the corpus have decided what to include and what to leave out, and it is always important to check whether the corpus is suitable for your particular study. It is also worth checking whether parts of the material are restricted due to copyright.

The most advanced methods for this type of analysis have been developed in corpus linguistics and data science, but they can also be used to analyse the historical and political aspects of language. More advanced analyses often require basic programming skills. There is plenty of ready-made code online that can be adapted to new textual contexts. The principles of open science include sharing one's code so that others can use it, either in their own studies or to reproduce the studies conducted by others.

Those who do not have the opportunity to use corpus linguistic methods can make use of ready-made software for computer-driven text analysis. These are often available as online resources or as separate apps. An increasing number of digital editions also include tools for quantitative analysis of word usage. At the moment, the most extensive collection is Google Books, which includes an Ngram reader for studying relative frequencies of words and expressions in Google's text collections (cf. the section on sources in Chapter 2). However, Google Books is problematic because Google does not account comprehensively for the content and because much of the material is not fully available due to copyright (Pechenick et al., 2015). It is therefore not possible to verify the results in a completely transparent way. Still, because of its size, Google Books is very useful for grasping the main trends in language use in some of the most dominant languages in the world.

A researcher interested in the use of concepts can start from the first uses of a word, but should also form an idea of when the word became common through searches in text databases. This indicates whether historical actors were early adopters, followed a trend or used old-fashioned language. At the same time, it is important to bear in mind that individual actors did not necessarily write in a context that can be reduced to the particular corpus we are using. As Skinner constantly points out, historical actors participated in debates and often wrote against others. A macro analysis of large text datasets does not capture this dynamic, but it is often possible to examine the material in the corpus by splitting it into smaller parts.

Digitised text datasets are rarely free of errors. Large historical datasets are scanned and the text has been interpreted by a computer program. Because of the volume, the text processing cannot be checked against the original, which means that the material can contain misspellings or omissions. When reading the texts, it is usually possible to compare the text translation with images of the original, but a quantitative analysis is always based on the optically recognised version. It is therefore important to examine its quality and consider whether it is suitable for reliable quantification. As a rule, more material is better because minor errors become less significant, but one should always be aware of potential bias in text recognition.

Many conceptual history studies use a combination of quantitative and qualitative perspectives. Whether to use quantitative evidence depends on the research question and argument. If a study wants to show that a particular word became broadly used by all political parties, evidence with numbers is required.

However, qualitative rhetorical analysis may be more appropriate if one is more interested in how the different parties used the word in question. Often these perspectives are possible to combine.

Analysis

In this section, we will discuss conceptual history methods with the help of two empirical studies. The intention is to give concrete examples of the research procedure itself. We start with Koselleck's study of the concept of progress to illustrate how the semasiological and onomasiological analyses complement each other. We then present our own study of the political rhetoric of 'isms', which is an attempt to combine traditional conceptual history methods with its synchronic and diachronic analyses of the sources with a quantitative analysis of digitised material. This way, we have aimed to have a broad transnational perspective on our topic.

Koselleck's semasiological and onomasiological analysis of the concept of progress

The example of the interaction between the semasiological and onomasiological analysis comes from Koselleck's article '"Progress" and "Decline": An Appendix to the History of Two Concepts' in the collection *The Practice of Conceptual History* (2002). At the beginning of the article, Koselleck states that the analysis deals with a long historical process and that he is interested in the ways in which the word *Fortschritt* (progress) has been used over time. His starting point is the modern use of the term from the 1880s onwards, which helps him to identify the object of the analysis. He then sets out the investigation of the different meanings that have been given to the word *Fortschritt*. In other words, he makes a semasiological analysis by mapping the different meanings that the word has acquired. Furthermore, he analyses the relationship of the word to its counter-concepts such as '*Niedergang*' (decline), 'regression', 'corruption' and 'decay'. In this way, he can pinpoint changes in the meaning of 'progress'.

It is important that Koselleck combines the semasiological analysis with an onomasiological analysis. This means that he examines other words that have been used alongside 'progress' or in a similar way before 'progress' came to be commonly used. He thus makes an analysis of how other terms have been used to discuss similar things. Covering different languages and cultures from antiquity to the modern use of 'progress', his onomasiological analysis includes, for instance, the terms '*profectus*', 'perfectibility' (*Perfektibilität*) and 'advancement' (*Fortgang*) (Koselleck, 2002: 223, 227, 232).

In this way, Koselleck identifies the birth of the modern concept of '*Fortschritt*' during the late eighteenth century and the early nineteenth century, the period of political, social and cultural transformation that he calls the birth of the *Neuzeit* (modernity) (Koselleck, 2002: 218–35). According to him, 'progress' had become a concept that no longer referred to a religious process, to something perfect or to periodic fluctuations between states of progress and decay. For example, ancient teachings on different forms of government included the notion of such fluctuations. Instead, the concept was directed towards the future and began to mark a clear boundary with the past: 'The experience of the past and the expectation of the future moved apart: they were progressively dismantled, and this difference was finally conceptualised by a common word, progress' (Koselleck, 2002: 228–9).

As a result of the analysis, Koselleck points out three phases of change in the modern concept of progress. He shows how *'Fortschritt'* first became a concept with a universal character (progress in different fields), then synonymous with 'historical progress' and finally a concept that functioned as an independent subject – i.e., 'progress' as something that does things and acts by itself. *'Fortschritt'* had at this point become a catchword that could be used as a mobilising slogan (Koselleck, 2002: 218–35).

A combination of macro and micro perspectives on 'isms'

In our own studies of 'isms' and 'ideology', we have combined a diachronic conceptual analysis with a synchronic analysis (Kurunmäki and Marjanen, 2018a, b, 2021). We were interested in how concepts such as 'patriotism', 'liberalism', 'individualism' and 'feminism' belong together rhetorically because of their common suffix, even though the words belong to different spheres of life. Moreover, we have aimed to capture how the isms were identified as ideologies (Kurunmäki and Marjanen, 2021). The articles are based on both a quantitative macro analysis of digitised sources (e.g., Google Books, Hansard Corpus, the collection of digitised newspapers at the National Libraries of Sweden, Finland and Austria) and analyses of individual key texts in different languages. Both the quantitative and qualitative analyses draw attention to the transnational dimensions of conceptual use. We have examined the spread of isms in several linguistic and political contexts quantitatively, thus laying the groundwork for a closer analysis of the transnational history of isms. The most important part has been an analysis of a number of texts in which ism concepts have been in use, including academic accounts. Our aim with the articles was to develop a more rhetorical view of political ideologies and ideological traditions.

In many ways, we build on Michael Freeden's research on the conceptual history of ideology, where he analyses ideologies as more or less changing and overlapping clusters of concepts (e.g., Freeden, 1996, 2003, 2013, 2017). We also draw on Koselleck, according to whom isms are examples of modern forward-looking 'movement concepts' (Koselleck, 2004: 80). However, we argue that isms have also been important instruments for describing past traditions. There is a rhetorical power in the isms that stems from their use to categorise the world in simple words and because they share the same suffix. Like all other concepts, isms are subject to political contention, but there is an additional level to this in that the suffix itself is also contested. For example, many have argued that all isms are problematic. Such claims are usually about an author presenting themselves as being unaffected by ideological positions (e.g., Wootton, 2009 [1942]).

Our rhetorical perspective shows that the use of an ism is a way of defining a phenomenon, an ideology or a way of thinking. Isms have been used to reduce diverse and complex phenomena under one heading, often serving the purpose of setting the agenda for a debate. Ism concepts have therefore been particularly useful in political battles, which is also why they are so contested (Kurunmäki and Marjanen, 2018a).

The spread of the isms

Our quantitative analysis, based on digitised material, shows that isms have become more and more numerous after the introduction of the suffix in antiquity. They have also been adopted in a variety of areas of life from religion to politics, science, culture and popular culture. By studying previous conceptual history research, historical dictionaries and text databases, we propose five different stages of expansion in the use of isms: (1) the emergence of religious isms in the sixteenth and seventeenth centuries; (2) forward-looking isms towards the end of the eighteenth century and the beginning of the nineteenth century, a period when many ideological isms were introduced; (3) an increased number of scientific isms towards the end of the nineteenth century; (4) an association of isms with the concept of 'ideology' from the interwar years on and the emergence of 'totalitarianism' in the 1930s as an umbrella ism to cover several ideological isms under one heading; (5) a broadening of the scope in how isms were understood after the 1990s as isms such as racism, sexism, populism, neoliberalism have become more prominent in political discourse (Kurunmäki and Marjanen, 2018b).

With this rough characterisation, we also note that the ism suffix has been used in many different countries and languages. In some languages, such as Chinese, the ending is translated (Spira, 2015, 2018), but in many languages it is used as such (for example, -ism, -isme, -ismo, -ismus, -ismi). With regard to the transnational dissemination of ism concepts, we have applied Jörn Leonhard's analytical categorisation of how a conceptual transfer from one linguistic and/or political and cultural context to another can be marked. According to Leonhard, one can distinguish between an imitative, an adaptive and an integrative reception of a concept. The imitative reception means that an unfamiliar (e.g., foreign) way of using a concept is transported into a new environment without any instructions on how this concept should be understood in the new local and cultural situation. The adaptive reception involves adapting the use of concepts to the new concerns and cultural or political motives at home. The integrating reception means that a concept has become so well integrated into the new context that it is widely used without any reference to its 'original' or 'foreign' meanings (Leonhard, 2011: 252–7).

Counter-concepts in the rhetoric of ism

Paying attention to these types of conceptual transfer requires an analysis of the rhetorical use of concepts. We note in our study that the rhetoric of isms often contains counter-concepts in ism form. 'Conservatism', for example, was coined in opposition to 'liberalism' soon after the latter gained ground around 1820 (Kurunmäki and Marjanen, 2018b). Our study also shows that the ism terms often bring together several other isms, either as counter-terms or as other closely related concepts. It is common for isms to be discussed in relation to other isms, and this has also been a way of introducing new isms into the language. Many isms have initially been negatively charged labels to designate religious or ideological groupings. Indeed, the main ideological isms – 'liberalism', 'socialism' and 'communism' – were initially just such negative labels. This starting point offers the possibility of analysing interesting 'rhetorical maneuvers' (Skinner), by which the negative valuation of a term has been changed into something positive and, possibly, into a term used for a collective self-identification. In this process, too, it is common for the ism in question to be accompanied by other terms. Therefore, we have examined how different ism concepts have been linked with each other as counter-concepts or seemingly similar concepts (Kurunmäki and Marjanen, 2018b).

Isms as analytical and historical concepts

For a conceptual historian, it is important to examine in what kind of political and intellectual contexts and for what purposes analytical concepts (for example, traditions of ideas such as 'liberalism' or scientific orientations such as 'positivism') have been created. Often, traditions of an ism are considered to have a much longer history than the actual use of the ism concept.

One example that we discuss in more detail is liberalism. An established philosophical way of discussing liberalism is to start with a definition of the tradition and then examine which thinkers can be considered to belong to the tradition. Today, it is common to point to John Locke as the founder of liberalism as a tradition. A conceptual-historical way of approaching the same question is to start from all cases in which someone has tried to write the history of liberalism as a tradition and analyse on what grounds individual thinkers were included in the tradition. From such a perspective, the history of liberalism does not begin with John Locke in the late seventeenth century, but was shaped in political debates from the 1810s onwards (e.g., Rosenblatt, 2018; Freeden et al., 2019). According to Duncan Bell, Locke was only established as the 'founder' of liberalism in the 1930s in the context of the defence of liberal democracy against totalitarian doctrines. In the nineteenth century, it was rather the French Revolution that was perceived as the origin of liberalism (Bell, 2014). The rewriting of the history of liberalism is related to the way different actors wanted to redefine liberalism as something relevant for their own time.

The isms of the twentieth century

Finally, we turn our attention to how isms have been linked to ideologies in the twentieth century. Here we have drawn both on a reading of the 'end of ideology' debate (Bell, 1988) that brought ideological isms to the fore after the Second World War and on a quantitative analysis of how new ism words, like 'racism', 'feminism' and 'terrorism', became increasingly popular in the late twentieth and early twenty-first centuries. Through a reading of what selected actors did when they talked about the end of ideology, we note, for instance, that the 'end of ideology' was a rhetorical attempt to tame communism in the West rather than to promote ideological rapprochement between the Western powers and the Soviet bloc, as has often been argued (Kurunmäki and Marjanen, 2018b).

After the Second World War, ideological isms permeated the political debate. In this discussion, isms came to be equated with ideologies. This can be shown by a very concrete analysis of whether or not different isms were called ideologies. From the period after the Second World War, we see an uptick in books and other texts that discuss ideology explicitly by giving examples of individual isms. Ideology had, in effect, become a hypernym of different isms. In the present, this is no longer self-evidently true. Our analysis of how the landscape of isms has changed since the end of the Cold War shows that the relationship between ism words and what is commonly thought of as ideologies has loosened as isms such as 'feminism', 'populism', 'terrorism' and 'extremism' have become more common.

However, we are not claiming that the time of isms or ideologies is over. The political debates on Brexit in the UK ('Brexitism') and Donald Trump ('Trumpism') in recent years have reignited the discussion on ideological isms and at the same time given rise to new ones. Once again, we see that isms are concepts coined and used to try to grasp the world in a time of change.

Critical reflections

As with all methodological approaches, conceptual history faces a number of practical challenges. In this section, we discuss three interrelated difficulties: the unclear distinction between concepts and words, between concepts and contexts (or discourses), and the problem of subjectivism. We also consider how these issues emerge especially in comparative studies dealing with multiple languages or countries.

Concepts and words

The difficulty of the unclear distinction between concepts and words is about how to define the term 'concept'. In a conceptual history study, we need to be able to identify the concept under analysis, possibly over several hundred years. If we consider concepts as historical and changing objects of research, how do we know that we are investigating the same concept in different historical periods? How do we know that a transformed concept is not a completely different concept? The simplest solution would be to claim that a concept is the same as a word. However, in the conceptual history literature, a distinction is made between the two (e.g., Ball, 1988: 15–16; Farr, 1989: 27). According to Skinner, it is possible to master a concept without knowing the correct word (Skinner, 2002: 159). Koselleck has argued that a word can be unambiguous, while a concept is always ambiguous (Koselleck, 1972: xxii). How are we to understand this? If words and concepts are not linked, how can we know that a change in vocabulary means that a concept has changed and that we do not have another concept at hand? Can we examine a concept in its rhetorical context if it is not a word?

This ambiguity of the concept of 'concept' has rightly caused scholarly criticism of conceptual history (e.g., Gunnell, 1998: 645–7). Yet we need not stop here. Both Skinner and Koselleck, for instance, point out that there is a link between concepts and words. According to Skinner, the surest evidence that a new concept has emerged is the emergence of a vocabulary that makes it possible to discuss the concept (Skinner, 2002: 160). Koselleck is more definitive and argues that every concept is linked to a word, although every word is not necessarily a concept (Koselleck, 2004: 84). Our practical proposal for a solution to this unclear situation is simply to start from the word and a vocabulary around it. If we do not insist on the concepts being articulated in words, we might end up in a situation where ideas surf through history, but we do not know how they change. After all, language users associate new ideas with particular words, so it is reasonable to assume that ideational change is expressed in changes in vocabulary and that word use is where we can empirically analyse how the world has been conceptualised. A focus on words does not mean that conceptual history has to study individual words only. It can be interested in clusters of related terms, phrases or whole texts. Central to conceptual history is an interest in how ideas are articulated in language.

A related question concerns the possibility of reaching the historically relevant debates if we start only from words. We cannot just jump into history without also having an idea of what we want to find there, but when we do so, we also bring our own concepts with us. Koselleck and Skinner answer the question in accordance with an established hermeneutic tradition. They both argue that we need a prior understanding to guide us in identifying the right vocabulary. We thus have to move backwards from our own understanding of the research problem. Skinner takes the researcher's own problem formulation as the starting point, which leads the way in the search of empirical terminology (Skinner, 1989: 95–6), while Koselleck (1983: 13–14) starts from a present-day definition and links the concept we are interested in to certain words already from the beginning of the enquiry. The point is that without a prior understanding, we will not know what we are looking for. A critic might argue that a conceptual historian first chooses the contemporary definition of a concept and then searches out its history, thus creating a teleological narrative in which the goal is determined from the beginning. Therefore, it is important to ensure that the starting presuppositions do not restrict the analysis, even if we start with our own questions. A careful conceptual history analysis makes it possible to find paths *not* taken in the past, something that Koselleck called 'past futures' (Koselleck, 1979, 2004).

Concepts and contexts

The next difficulty concerns the difference between concepts and contexts (or discourses). Many find it difficult to reconcile Skinner's requirement to analyse single speech acts in a given context with Koselleck's diachronic studies. There is a risk that Skinner's focus on the contexts of speech acts results in a string of cases in which single speech acts examined in detail run one after the other. Indeed, Skinner himself notes that 'there can be no histories of concepts as such; there can only be histories of their uses in argument' (Skinner, 2002: 85).

Skinner's statement sounds as though he would categorically deny any possibility of the kind of diachronic analysis that Koselleck writes about. Nonetheless, he has written conceptual history covering several hundred years on the concepts of the 'state' (Skinner, 1989) and 'liberty' (1998). In his reply to a question about the possible similarities between German conceptual history and his own project, Skinner (2002: 187) has stated that 'Koselleck is interested in nothing less than the entire process of conceptual change; I am chiefly interested in one of the techniques by which it takes place. But the two programmes do not strike me as incompatible.' Skinner is thus not categorically opposed to writing diachronic conceptual history, but his approach to conceptual transformations is rhetorical rather than diachronic-historical (Skinner, 2002: 180). We would like to argue that although Skinner sees individual speech acts as unique, there is a diachronic aspect in his methodological approach because he has examined speech acts in relation not only to existing, but also to older linguistic conventions. His notion of 'rhetorical redescription' is a good example of a way of relating the analysis of particular texts to prior speech acts (see also Hampsher-Monk, 1998: 46).

Koselleck explains the same thing by referring to the different temporal layers of concepts (Koselleck, 1989: 649–50). He argues that historical events and language have different rhythms:

> Conceptual change is generally slower and more gradual than the pace of political events. That is to say that changes in the language of politics do not necessarily correspond to what occurs in politics. The history of language, the history of society, and the history of politics do not change at the same rate of speed. [...] Because they can be applied again and again, basic concepts accumulate long-term meanings that are not lost with every change in regime or social situation. (Koselleck, 1996: 66-7)

Cross-contextual conceptual history is thus possible because language has a different rhythm from historical events. Each event or act of language is unique, but concepts have temporal properties that make them reusable, and because of these repeated uses, they are both long-lasting and changeable at the same time (Koselleck, 1996: 62–3). However, according to Koselleck, there are political and social changes as well as intellectual innovations that cannot be captured by existing concepts, and this is where new words – *neologisms* – emerge, which in turn can open up entirely new possibilities for political action (Koselleck, 1989: 660; 1998: 31).

Comparisons between languages

The problematic nature of the relationship between concepts, words and contexts is present in studies that aim at comparing concepts in different languages or countries. For example, how do we know if we are comparing the same concepts when we compare 'education' in English, '*(ut)bildning*' in Swedish, and '*Bildung*' in German? If these words are used in a certain context and take their meaning from the contextual usage, can we still say that there is a link between them that makes the comparison relevant? Where does the connection lie, then? Is it in the shared etymology (of *bildning* and *Bildung*), or is it in the fact that the meanings of the three words can be more or less the same? Koselleck has written that, in principle, one would need a meta-language that is independent of all the languages being compared in order to make a fair comparison between languages (Koselleck et al., 1991). A meta-language is not available, but as more and more scholars have done comparative and transnational conceptual history studies, some practical solutions seem to be available. One way, for instance, is to focus on how historical actors themselves have translated words from one language to another and perhaps even commented on the differences in their use. This is one example of the transnational practices we discussed earlier in this chapter.

Conceptual history and the study of society

Since concepts are always potentially contested, it is possible to identify significant political struggles using conceptual history. In this chapter, we have argued that a conceptual-history perspective reveals that social and political phenomena that seem natural or self-evident have often been contested and politically charged. By highlighting human agency in various social and political processes – language use, rhetoric, speech acts – conceptual history differs from some branches of discourse analysis. Conceptual history methods also help us to critically examine the ways in which analytical concepts themselves have contested and changeable meanings. Our own research into isms and ideology is but one example of such ambition. Instead of serving as explanatory models, our working concepts often constitute important research objects. What is first considered a tool of analysis thus becomes an object of analysis.

Democracy studies is a field where a conceptual-history perspective helps us examine how people have understood a concept that is usually seen as a general set of values or a collection of certain political and social institutions (see, for example, Innes and Philp, 2013; Ihalainen, 2017; Kurunmäki et al., 2018). What these studies have in common is that democracy is examined as a contested concept, whose various definitions and practical applications are the result of a never-ending struggle for positions of power.

We argue that the conceptual-history approach lends itself to studying any subject involving a conceptual struggle or the use of power. Anything that can be understood as 'political' (from sexual identity to constitutional change to conceptions of useful science) has been contested throughout history and involves changing vocabularies. The conceptual-history perspective involves questioning the seemingly natural or obvious in a research object, while highlighting the political dimension of its history. It is also possible to analyse power positions in individual political debates. Often, individual political battles are about who will succeed in setting the agenda for a debate – i.e., whose concepts will control the discussion and who speaks the language that is oriented towards the future.

A concrete way for an actor to use power in debate is to describe history as a logical narrative that leads to the actor's political arguments. This is evident in the examples in the analysis section of this chapter. It is commonplace to say that each generation rewrites its history, but in a sense this possibility is present in every political struggle as well. Conceptual history makes these positions of power more visible and thus easier to understand. Such analyses help us to understand why one but not the other managed to gain the upper hand in a power struggle.

Summary

On the usefulness of conceptual history

- Conceptual history is a method suitable for studying language. Analysis of images or other semiotic expressions can be combined with conceptual history, but usually requires drawing methods also from other approaches.
- Conceptual analyses usually require large amounts of empirical sources, but it is possible to limit the scope of the source material by a well-formulated research question.
- Digitised text collections (corpora) nowadays offer good possibilities for the analysis of large amounts of source material. A macro perspective can be combined with a reading of selected texts.
- A conceptual-history perspective can be used as a complementary element in other forms of analysis. Conceptual history methods can be combined with, for example, social-historical or discourse-analytical studies.
- Conceptual history is a useful method in the analysis of long-term developmental histories such as democratisation and social change, as these processes are the result of political struggles.
- Conceptual history is a useful method in nationalism research and in various studies of collective identities, minorities, citizenship, patriotism, etc.
- Conceptual history can also be used to study changes in the way people have described emotions, scientific thinking or cultural phenomena.
- Conceptual history can be applied in comparative studies of different political entities or languages.
- Conceptual history is a way of historicising political and social science theories, political ideas and ideologies.

How to do it

- You need a research problem that leads to the identification of the vocabulary that denotes the concept. To identify a problem, you need to turn to existing research. Very often, a conceptual history study starts from identifying a discrepancy in how a particular term is used in research literature compared to historical texts. In such cases, a conceptual history study can contribute with something new about how we conceptualise the world.
- Dictionaries and encyclopaedias are usually appropriate starting points for a conceptual history study and can help in identifying discrepancies in historical semantics compared to the present.
- Digitised text databases are a good starting point to get an idea of when certain words became widely used or disappeared from use. They can also be useful in identifying debates where a term has been the focus of attention.
- The concept can be explored both diachronically between certain points in time and synchronically in a rhetorical context. This depends on your research problem.
- The concept can be examined both semasiologically (the different meanings of the word) and onomasiologically (the synonyms of the word).
- You need to create the relevant contexts for the analysis by yourself. To do so, you also need to know the relevant research literature.
- You can analyse the rhetoric of inclusion and exclusion by identifying counter-concepts to the concept explored.
- You can examine legitimation strategies by analysing descriptions of the contemporary political situation or problem, as well as the stories that are presented as descriptions of how the current situation has come to be.
- You can turn to some of the analytical concepts presented in this chapter to assist you in analysing texts. You may, for instance, ask if words seem to carry a future orientation when used in particular contexts or if some actors perform rhetorical redescriptions by using new terms to make something appear better or worse than what was commonly held at that time.
- If your study is diachronic, you may want to ask if there are different layers of meaning present in the language you are studying, or if there is a rise or drop in word frequency over time and what those changes in frequency are about.
- You may also ask if the words under analysis carry transnational connotations or if they are regarded as fully domesticated.
- When you identify changes or tensions in the words present in your research case, you can try to describe those analytically. Koselleck used concepts like temporalisation, space of experience and horizon of expectation to understand how the past and the future is present in language. You may use those concepts yourself, but can also invent your own analytical concepts if they serve you better.

Suggested reading

The best way to acquaint yourself with conceptual history is to read some of the classic texts in the field, as well as to look at some newer applications.

Reinhart Koselleck's extensive output is now partly available in English. A good overview of his methodological and historical views can be found in *Futures Past: On the Semantics of Historical Time* (2004), *The Practice of Conceptual History: Timing History, Spacing Concepts* (2002) and *Sediments of Time: On Possible Histories* (2018). A good

(Continued)

(Continued)

introduction to Koselleck's theory and intellectual development can be found in Niklas Olsen's *History in the Plural: An Introduction to the Work of Reinhart Koselleck* (2012). You may also want to consult the *Geschichtliche Grundbegriffe: Historisches Lexikon zur politisch-sozialen Sprache in Deutschland* (1972–1997) which is an almost inexhaustible source of the history of German political and social language. The methodological guidelines are found in English translation in *Contributions to the History of Concepts*, Vol. 6 (2006: 1).

The easiest way to become acquainted with Quentin Skinner's writings is to read his reworking of his old articles in *Visions of Politics I–III* (2002). The first volume deals with methodological and theoretical issues, while the two later volumes present Skinner's historical studies. An analysis of Skinner's work can be found in Kari Palonen's book *Quentin Skinner: History, Politics, Rhetoric* (2003).

An introduction to the current theoretical orientations and methodological developments of conceptual history is Willibald Steinmetz et al. (eds) *Conceptual History in the European Space* (2017), which is also an introduction to a series of books on European conceptual history. The series is published by Berghahn Books and is a growing resource for empirical studies in conceptual history. One of the best global histories of concepts is to be found in Margrit Pernau et al.'s *Civilizing Emotions: Concepts in Nineteenth Century Asia and Europe* (2015).

The main international journal in the history of concepts is *Contributions to the History of Concepts*. Other journals include *Redescriptions*, *Forum Interdisziplinäre Begriffsgeschichte* and *Ariadna histórica: lenguajes, conceptos, metáforas*.

Exercises

Exercise 1: Political words

Typically, a conceptual historian is interested in people's attitudes concerning particular words. A central part of this is to identify which words are politically charged and why people feel strongly about them. In short, the question is not only what the words mean to language users, but also what it means to them to use those words.

The task

Analyse instances of someone writing about their attitudes towards a certain word. They might be writing that they do not like a word, that they prefer another word, or that everyone is using this word right now. Note all statements revolving around that particular word that you can find. After that, discuss whether the word is politically charged in a wider discourse. Are there particular groups who use that word, whereas others prefer not to do that? This would indicate that the word is politically polarising. Or is it the case that the word feels very outdated or perhaps too modern to some users? This would indicate that the word either carries or does not carry a future orientation to certain people. The word might come across as a vehicle for a desirable or undesirable future for the language user. Is the word hard to define? Read a few examples by different

(Continued)

(Continued)

users and try to get a sense of whether they use the word in the same way. Differences in the use of the word is an indication of ambiguity. Ambiguity is in general a feature that makes words very useful for political rhetoric as it allows people to say a lot without being very precise. Finally, try to decide how long the word has been in use and for how long it has been politically charged. Here historical dictionaries and historical text datasets are useful.

The texts

Use any set of texts that are likely to contain political words, such as parliamentary records, newspapers or particular online fora, and search the particular word you want to analyse.

Exercise 2: Speech acts

Rhetorical analysis is at the heart of studying how people act politically through individual speech acts. Keeping in mind the political ladenness of words, a conceptual historian wants to understand how historical actors have redefined words or replaced them with other words in order to make their case. The important question is not only what language users meant by writing or saying something, but also what they intended while doing that.

The task

Think of the word 'Finlandisation' '(*Finnlandisierung*)', which was coined in Austria during the Cold War. In the German-speaking context, it was used as a criticism of Willy Brandt's (West Germany's influential Social Democratic chancellor, 1969-1974) new *Ostpolitik* that some saw as too lenient towards East Germany and the Soviet Union. The term invoked Finland's close relationship to the Soviet bloc as a negatively laden horizon of expectation in the West German context, but it was not designed as a diagnosis of Finnish politics. Nonetheless, the international use of the term was clearly received as irritating in Finland. Some leading Finnish politicians picked up the term and engaged in a discussion about what Finlandisation was and if the critique indeed was accurate, while others picked it up as a way of criticising those in power. In Quentin Skinner's terms, the Finnish actors were interested in the locutionary aspect of using the term, but from the perspective of rhetorical analysis the illocutionary aspect is perhaps more interesting. From the illocutionary perspective the term was used as a warning for Germans, not a criticism of Finns. After the Russian annexation of Crimea, the discussion of Finlandisation resurfaced again in Finland. In this new context, it was used as a term for discussing Finnish reactions to the annexation, but also as a term of diagnosis for other countries in Europe and their relationship to Russia.

The example highlights how any statement is bound to a certain context and that the illocutionary aspect can be understood only in that context. When a term travels to new

(Continued)

(Continued)

contexts, its illocutionary force changes. To analyse this, study whether the term is used in a pejorative way, whether it refers to Finland or whether it is rather about another political context, and if the author uses it for a specific political purpose. After that, try to situate the speech act in its specific historical context.

The texts

Use newspaper texts or parliamentary texts (e.g., minutes of chamber meetings) from a country where European politics is likely to be a common topic of discussion and search the word 'Finlandisation' or its equivalent in other languages.

Exercise 3: Understanding frequency

Arguments about changes in political language are often made by stating that certain words have become popular or have lost their position in political discourse. In the past, such arguments were often made based on reading source texts and simply presenting the impression that a word has become more common. However, to make those types of arguments, it is better to actually measure (relative) word frequency and to interpret what changed in language use.

The task

Go to the Google Ngram Viewer at https://books.google.com/ngrams/ and set the time period of interest to 1800-2000 and choose the English dataset. Although the Ngram Viewer has some significant problems for scholarly analysis, it serves as a very simple tool to assess the frequency of words and phrases. Search for the words 'ideology' and 'ideologies'. After that, search for 'ideologies/(ideology + ideologies)', which gives you the ratio of the plural form of ideology. Try to figure out why the share of ideology in the plural increases and why ideology as a term became popular in this dataset only in the twentieth century, although the word was coined already in the late eighteenth century. You can make another search with a wildcard '*_ADJ ideologies' which gives you the top word pairs, of which the first one is an adjective and the second one is 'ideologies' in the plural. Consider whether the change in the interwar period can be related to a semantic shift in how ideology was understood. If so, what kind of change?

After that, search for the word 'racism'. It is immediately clear that the frequency of the word 'racism' does not correspond to how people in the past have experienced racist practices. Try to figure out what drives the change in frequency. Why did people start to write more about racism in the 1960s and the 1980s? What were they doing linguistically when conceptualising the world through the term 'racism'?

5

Narrative Analysis

Alexa Robertson

From the moment we wake in the morning, we are immersed in a flow of narratives. The news we listen to before getting out of bed or read or watch while eating breakfast contain public accounts of what is happening in the world. Our social media feeds are replete with the stories of the private sphere that our friends tell us, and of the public sphere that we share and comment on. On our way to class or work, and on our way home, we package our experiences and reactions to what we have been told into stories of our own, without even being aware of it. Stories entertain, but they also teach lessons, socialise and create community. According to a perspective that has grown exponentially since the mid-1980s, we are better understood as narrative creatures than as the rational actors with whom social scientists were long preoccupied. It is through the stories we tell and are told that we make sense of society; it is through narratives that our situation in the political and cultural landscape, and that of everyone else, is reinforced. Making sense of our place in the scheme of things is not something that happens in a political vacuum, however. Meaning is made in context, not least in the context of certain constellations of power. The study of narratives thus provides insights into societal power dynamics. There are consequently good reasons for arguing that 'a student of social life, no matter of which domain, needs to become interested in narrative as a form of knowledge, a form of social life and a form of communication' (Czarniawska, 2004: 2). This chapter provides an introduction to the terminology, assumptions and analytical approaches of scholars who study narrative. It is organised around answers to four sets of questions:

- Why study narratives? What theoretical understandings and assumptions are entailed in this sort of research?
- What are narratives, in scholarly terms as opposed to popular parlance?

- How are narratives analysed by scholars in different fields?
- What are the implications of using a narrative approach to textual analysis?

An answer to the first question will be offered by giving an overview of the development of the field, highlighting its transdisciplinary nature and the remarkable variation in narrativist research agendas. The ingredients of a *narrative* are listed, to answer the second question, in a section that also distinguishes between the structure or the 'what' of a story and its discourse, or 'how' it is told. The section devoted to the third question, under the heading Analysis, surveys how researchers collect data, identify the object of narrative analysis, and organise their material. Two examples of narrative approaches are given, to the study of focus groups and to the analysis of television news stories. Answers to the fourth question will be offered in a section devoted to critical reflections on the narrative approach. As with the other contributions to this volume, the chapter ends with suggestions for further reading and exercises.

Background

Why study narratives?

For a long time, it was mainly historians who used a narrative approach. They sorted out the chaos of past events, and were wont to fill in any blanks left by missing evidence, by organising their primary source material into stories. This sort of work is sometimes referred to as the narrative mode of representing knowledge. Then came what has been referred to as the narrative turn. Scholars began to argue instead that social life itself, and not just accounts of it, is a matter of narrative, and that our identities and actions come into being through stories. This change in the way that scholars understood their task and their relationship to the material they analysed – sometimes referred to as a shift in focus from representational to ontological narrativity – left its mark on research conducted across the spectrum of academia, in fields as diverse as sociology, political science, public administration, organisation studies, anthropology, linguistics, gender studies, media studies, psychology, education, law, and science (Gjedde, 2000; Shuman, 2012; Raven and Elahi, 2015; Brusselaers et al., 2022; Davidjants and Tiidenberg, 2022).

Narrative analysis can be quantitative (Franzosi, 1998, 2010, 2012) but is more often associated with qualitative research, given widespread agreement across disciplines that narrative functions as a fundamental interpretive frame, helping us to organise our experiences and make the world comprehensible. Somers has stated this in no uncertain terms:

> People are guided to act in certain ways and not others on the basis of the projections, expectations and memories derived from a repertoire of available social, public and cultural narratives. (Somers, 1994: 614)

Studying narratives thus provides insights into the formation and maintenance of identity (Lieblich et al., 1998; Robertson, 2010, 2015). Stories not only provide scholars with information about something that has happened – one sort of primary source material in many case studies – but also provide insights into how individuals imbue those events and actions with meaning (Riessman, 1993: 19; Frank, 2012). Collectivities tell and share stories too. Cultures 'work "mentally" in common', through a process of 'joint narrative accrual', and continuity is provided by a 'constructed and shared social history in which we locate our Selves and our individual continuities' (Bruner, 1991: 20). This means that the study of narrative is a way of gaining analytical purchase on the power dynamics that regulate understandings in society.

There are other reasons for studying narratives. For some, it is a matter of good scholarship. Rather than producing sketchy accounts, often at high levels of abstraction, narrative attunes the analyst to nuance, helping us see things that would be overlooked in more technical readings, and making us aware of absences as well as presences (Feldman and Almquist, 2012). The approach is valuable because it 'deals with the particular and the specific, rather than the collective and statistical' (Kiser, 1996: 250) and privileges human agency. It enables scholars to be more aware of and responsive to the voices of the marginalised in society, which otherwise tend to be drowned out by the powerful and the mainstream (Carlisle, 1994). Adoption of a narrative approach has also been considered to be a way of rebelling against the straitjacket of academic praxis (Clayton, 1994; Somers, 1994).

Narratives and their ingredients

The term 'narrative' can be so vague and encompassing that Carlisle (1994) laments that it is sometimes no use at all. Roland Barthes, for example, wrote unhelpfully that narrative is any form of communication.

> The narratives of the world are numberless. Narrative is first and foremost a prodigious variety of genres [...] narrative is international, transhistorical, transcultural: it is simply there, like life itself. (Barthes, 1977: 79)

Others have made more useful contributions. A familiar definition conceives of narrative as the organisation of events into a plot (Bremond, 1980: 390; Kozloff, 1992: 69–70). Todorov (1969) described it as the passage from one equilibrium to another – from a stable situation to a disturbance to a re-established stability. This concern with plot and organisation translates into a focus on structure. It reflects the heritage of narrative analysis, which has its roots in literary analysis, coloured by Russian formalism, American new criticism, French structuralism and German hermeneutics.

It is rare to encounter a work on narrative that does not invoke the *Morphology of the Folktale*, written by the Russian formalist Vladimir Propp in 1928. A classic example of structural analysis, *Morphology* classified Slavic fairytales 'according to their component parts and their relationship to each other and to the whole'

(Propp, 1968 [1928]: 19). After analysing 100 tales, Propp was able to document a recurrence in storylines, characters (such as hero, villain, donor, helper), and what he referred to as *functions* (cf. Chapter 1, in which function is presented in more general terms), by which he meant both the actions of the characters and the consequences of these actions for the story. Propp claimed that despite the vast number of folktales in circulation, there were not more than 31 functions (which ranged from *initial situation, violation* and *hero's reaction* to *pursuit, rescue, recognition* and *punishment*).[1]

Building on Propp, early structuralist approaches were based on two assumptions. The first is that while the structures of texts might seem different on the surface, similarities can be found on abstract levels. The second is that it is important to distinguish between two stories: the series of events and the story as told by the author (De Fina and Johnstone, 2015: 153).

Improving on and streamlining Propp's formalist model, Labov and Waletsky (1967) analysed narratives in terms of their formal properties and functions. They identified six common elements. Taken together, they provide a common definition of narrative.

The *abstract* is the summary of the narrative. As De Fina and Johnstone (2015: 154) explained: it 'announces that the narrator has a story to tell and makes a claim to the right to tell it'. The setting, comprising the time, place, situation and participants or characters, is set out in the *orientation* or the referential clause of the narrative. The *complicating action* (Todorov's disequilibrium) constitutes an additional element. The *resolution* tells what finally happens and the *coda* reconnects the story with the present. The meaning of the action or series of events is commented on in the *evaluation*, or the 'story as told by the author' referred to above. Evaluative clauses are editorial and contain judgements. They 'have to do with why the narrator is telling the story and why the audience should listen to it' (De Fina and Johnstone, 2015: 153). Laying bare the power of a narrative often involves discerning and documenting the techniques used by the teller of a story to show how their words should be understood.

Evaluation can be overt or covert. In its overt form, the narrator comments on the story from the outside ('a roar of outrage erupted from the crowd at the injustice of the ruling'). In its covert form, the evaluation can be embedded in the story – for example, in information given about the characters in the orientation ('he was known to be a fair man'; 'she had a vindictive streak'). It could also be located in a comparison with alternative outcomes ('her dream of becoming a doctor and saving lives was thwarted by the senseless war').

A large body of narrative research builds on Labov and Waletsky's (1967) distinction between elements, and their insight that a story can have a referential or an evaluative function. They argued that the sequence of clauses is matched to a sequence of events, and that to move a narrative clause entails changing the order

---

[1] See Propp, 1968 [1928] or Herman and Vervaeck (2005) for a complete list.

in which the events are understood to have occurred. It is thus known as a *formal* approach to the study of narrative, and has had a strong influence on scholars working within the tradition of discourse analysis who have an interest in the linguistic, syntactic and semantic structures of narrative. But the ideas of Labov and Waletsky have also proved useful to researchers who enter the study of narrative from other disciplines, and who approach discourse in a different way. This approach looks for meaning in the way stories are told, and not just the way the component parts are assembled, and pays attention to the contexts of storytelling.

Chatman (1978) defines narrative as composed of a story *and* a discourse. The *story* (*histoire*) is familiar from the structuralist take on narrative, comprising the content of the tale or chain of events and the *existents*, or the characters and other components of the setting. Put differently, *histoire* is the 'what' of the narrative. The *discourse* (*discours*) in Chatman's operationalisation of narrative is the 'how' – the means by which the content is communicated. (Note that the term is used with a slightly different meaning from 'discourse' in the discourse analysis presented in Chapters 6 and 7.) The distinction between story and discourse is a helpful one when it comes to conducting narrative analysis in practice. The component parts of story and discourse described above are given in schematic form in Table 5.1.

The operationalisation of narrative advocated in this chapter combines several of the ideas presented above, arranged in a way that makes them amenable to empirical application. In keeping with Chatman (1978), a narrative is defined here

Table 5.1 The ingredients of a narrative

story (*histoire*) referential clause the 'what'		
	Abstract	summary of events announces that the narrator has a story to tell makes a claim that the narrator has a right to tell the story
	Orientation	sets out the time, situation, setting, participants
	Complicating action	moves the story from equilibrium to disequilibrium
	Resolution	tells what finally happened
	Coda	returns to the present
discourse (*discours*) evaluative clause the 'how'		
	Evaluation	the way in which the content is communicated the meaning of the action is commented on sense is made of the story

as an account comprising a story or a 'what' (the events and orientation referred to by Labov and Waletsky) and a discourse or a 'how' (with a focus on the way a story is communicated and not just its structure). It is thus a form of discourse in the sense that the way the story is communicated is influenced by social practices and generic conventions. Operationalised in this way, a narrative and its parsing contain at least some, but need not contain all the elements and functions stipulated by structuralist theorists.

Analysis

Narratives can give different sorts of insights, depending on where they are found. For some scholars, such as those studying personal narratives, it is the unique experience (of gender or ethnic discrimination, for example) that affords insights. For others, such as those who study organisational narratives, it is their general currency, familiarity or repetitiveness that provide insights into a given culture (Czarniawska, 1999: 8). Some stories can have a single narrator; others can be multivoiced. The approaches to analysing them must be numerous, as are the narratives themselves. There is no, and must not be, 'one best method' of narrative analysis: what works best depends on the individual researcher and the research questions guiding a given study.

Collecting data for narrative analysis

Researchers find and analyse narratives in a wide variety of contexts, from policy texts and news reports to Instagram and TikTok, to study topics as varied as protest, migration, Covid and innovation. They circulate in digital settings, often in multimodal forms. Van Dijk once wrote that they are to be found in the everyday – for example, in conversations with ordinary people, but *not* to be found in a police report, a sociological analysis, a parliamentary debate or an image (van Dijk, 1993: 123). Barthes, of course, would disagree with him, given that he viewed narrative as capable of being

> carried by articulated language, spoken or written, fixed or moving images, gestures, and the ordered mixture of all these substances; narrative is present in myth, legend, fable, tale, novella, epic, history, tragedy, drama, comedy, mime, painting (...) stained glass windows, cinema, comics, news items, conversation. (Barthes, 1977: 79)

This Barthean take on narrative has gained wider currency in a communicative landscape marked by Instagram and other platforms that privilege the visual (e.g., Davidjants and Tiidenberg, 2022). In between these two extremes, students of narratives would be well advised to look for texts that contain features outlined in Table 5.1. These can be readily found in interview transcripts and media reports, for example, and for that reason examples of such primary source material will serve as illustrations later on in this section.

Before getting around to the actual analysis of narratives, many researchers face the task of generating them. This is particularly true when working with interview material. Lieblich et al. (1998: 9) advocate the use of narrative as a way of gathering valuable data – for example, about experiences of discrimination – that would be impossible to get at otherwise. Certain kinds of open-ended questions are more likely than others to encourage narrativisation, according to Riessman (1993). It is preferable to ask questions that open up topics and allow respondents to construct answers, in collaboration with listeners, in the ways they find meaningful. In her experience, narratives often emerge when they are least expected (Riessman, 1993: 54–6). Mueller (2019) maintains that a good starting point for researchers new to the field is the episodic narrative interview, which encourages respondents to share their experiences in 'bounded' stories that are short and connected to a specific experience, in contrast to the 'big' and often sprawling stories that more often form the empirical focus.

Identifying the objects of analysis

Mueller's approach addresses the perennial problem of being able to identify a narrative in a given material. In some cases, this can be relatively straightforward: a newsreader's lead-in, for example, usually signals the start of a news story. When narratives occur in interview situations, the researcher should be attuned to 'entrance and exit talk' that indicates the beginning and end of a story. *Entrance talk* typically comprises lexical signals to the audience that a story is about to be related ('well, I'll have to back up a bit to answer the question. You see, when I was on my way to … ' or 'It happened like this … '). *Exit talk*, like the coda in the structuralist schema, returns the listener or audience member to where they were before the story began and signals that the sequence of events has closed ('and that about sums it up' or 'and the rest is history'). Consider the following excerpt from an interview with a journalist working for a global news channel. When asked to explain how she decides which images to use in conflict coverage, the journalist begins by setting out the principles of the news outlet she works for, but then resorts to telling a story.

––––––––––––––––––––– **Narrative structure** –––––––––––––––––––––

Interlocutor: When reporting a conflict, how do you decide what images to use?

Respondent: It's a question of taste. It's a question of what's right for the channel. Al Jazeera has historically had a higher threshold for gore than the BBC has – the BBC worries about offending its viewers, and in my view it often sanitises all the impact out of its package, because they don't want to upset people too much. You know, there are horrible things happening out there, I want people to understand that, I want them to see it.

(Continued)

(Continued)

Interlocutor: So those pictures out there – how gory are they?

Respondent: When I first filed from Syria back in March, we showed the body and face on an old man, lying on his kitchen floor dead. He had been shot by the Syrian army with a sniper, at random. The Syrian army has a sniper policy; it just puts guys up on the roofs, and all day they fire on to the civilian population. Not endless burst of the fire machine, otherwise people wouldn't go out; it's random, and they do it because it's a terribly easy and cheap way of keeping an entire population completely terrorised, and it costs nothing. And no one knows when they leave their door in the morning if they'll come back in the evening, because a sniper could have just decided in the moment's impulse, I'll shoot that old man, or that small boy, or that woman going out shopping. So he was 70 something, lying in the family kitchen, and the whole neighbourhood had piled in. Family members were, it was heartbreaking, cradling his old face in their hands, and I wanted the tender cradling of the old man's face, and I had no problem with us running that. His face was not disfigured, it was peaceful in death, and they blanked the face out! So I ring the newsroom, and they argue back and I go 'this is a respectful shot, it's in a context, I'm sure you understand why we show this old guy's face, he's dead but he's not disfigured. Surely our viewers can handle a dead old man?' and in the end they took the filter off.

Source: Excerpt of interview conducted for the Swedish Research Council funded project 'Europe as Other', reported in Robertson, 2015.

We enter into the story from the end (what the journalist and her team ended up showing in their report), but also the beginning (when she first started reporting on the conflict in Syria). The entrance talk ('when I first filed from Syria back in March') orients the listener by providing information about the time, the setting and the situation. The exit talk ('in the end they took the filter off') is connected with the evaluation (the assessment that Al Jazeera viewers can handle distressing images). The orientation is rich and multilayered, despite the brevity of the narrative: the time is the beginning of the respondent's assignment in Syria, but also an intimate moment in the life of a grieving family, overlaid with an irate newsroom exchange.

It could be said that how a narrative is defined and recognised in the empirical material being analysed, depends on the nature of that material. Different sorts of material contain different sorts of narratives. The narratives that interest scholars are not always as concrete as an interview transcript or other particular text. They can also be *meta-narratives*, existing at a more cumulative or 'holistic' level (Greenhalgh et al., 2005; Gelter et al., 2021), or in the taken-for-granted assumptions upon which people operate. These are often elusive in empirical terms, but make such research worthwhile. It is thus important that each person undertaking narrative analysis is clear about what they mean by narrative and how their usage relates to concepts such as discourse, story, frame, theme, and so on. Are they synonymous? Are they subordinate – i.e., components of which a narrative is made? Or are they something larger, to which several components or layered narratives contribute? How does a particular scholar recognise a narrative when encountered in the particular primary source material being analysed? Answers to such questions cannot be found in a handbook or methods textbook. Each researcher must make their own operationalisations and define their focus of analysis in a way that fits with their research question.

Organising the material

Some researchers consider it important to take a narrative on its own terms. They warn against tendencies to read simply for content, or to read a narrative as evidence for a prior theory. One way of avoiding such pitfalls is to begin with asking how the text is organised, and reflecting on why the narrator developed the tale in the way they did. Working with interview material, some start from 'the inside' (the meanings encoded in the form of talk), then explain outward, identifying the underlying propositions that make the talk sensible, including what is taken for granted (Riessman, 1993; Feldman and Almquist, 2012).

Recording and transcribing can be more than preparation of the primary source material. Going through rough drafts of interview transcripts, for example, can involve analytic induction and result in a focus for the next stage of analysis emerging from the words of the respondents. When it comes to the analysis of images and multimodal narratives (cf. Chapter 8), screenshots can be usefully incorporated into a codesheet or coding notes, while noting how image and text reinforce the message, or noting when they do not.

Lieblich et al. (1998) read, interpret and analyse narrative materials using the framework of two intersecting dimensions: *holistic* versus *categorical* and *content* versus *form*. The result of the meeting of the two dimensions is four modes of reading a narrative:

- The *holistic-content mode* of reading uses a complete story, like *The Lord of the Rings* trilogy, or a *Black Mirror* episode, or the autobiography of an ex-president, and focuses on the content presented by it. If the researcher analyses separate sections - e.g., opening or closing sequences - they analyse the meaning of the part in the light of content that emerges from the rest of the narrative.
- The *holistic-form-based mode* of analysis usually involves looking at the plots or structure of complete stories. It asks whether the story ascends towards the present moment or descends towards it from more positive periods, and whether, for example, there is a turning point or climax which sheds light on the whole development.
- The *categorical-content approach* bears a striking affinity to content analysis (see Chapter 2). Categories of the studied topic are defined, and separate utterances of the text are extracted, classified and gathered into these categories. This mode of reading focuses on the content of narratives as manifested in separate parts of the story, whatever the context of the complete story (Lieblich et al., 1998: 16). Some authors use categories made up of single words; others use a broader category of *event-explanation unit* in which narrators provide attributions to various

events in their lives (Lieblich et al., 1998: 17). Researchers engaged in media analysis break down news narratives into themes or frames, for example, or into actors and actants. In this mode, quantitative treatment of the narrative is fairly common. It is possible to ask, for example, how many times some aspect of the country's relationship to the European Union is framed as a problem, or how many times a news report of migration or asylum seekers uses the imagery of a natural catastrophe.
- The *categorical-form mode* of analysis focuses on discrete stylistic or linguistic characteristics of defined units of the narrative. It can ask what kind of metaphors the narrator uses. Are elections depicted as horse races or football matches with winners and losers in public narratives, for example? Defined instances of this nature are collected from a text or from several texts and counted.

The student who remains daunted at the prospect of an analytical framework with several intersecting dimensions should bear in mind that simplicity can be a virtue when doing research. Choose one mode of reading a narrative or, as outlined above, separate the 'what' from the 'how' and let the nature of the material and the needs of the research question guide the selection of focus.

Analysing talk: narrative analysis and focus group material

Work that builds on Labov and Waletsky's model tends to analyse narratives as texts without contexts. The model has been criticised for failing to consider the contributions the audience may make to the telling of a story. In another strain of narrative research, scholars interested in 'everyday stories' have developed what are sometimes referred to as *interactional approaches to the study of narrative*. Their focus is on the work that stories do in social action, and on the involvement of audiences in the narrative act and the construction of stories (Ochs and Taylor, 1992; Schiffrin, 1996; Ochs and Capps, 2001). This approach involves being aware of the way stories are adapted to the context in which they are told, are embedded in the conversations that surround them and unfold in one way rather than another depending on the role of the participants. One variation on the interactional approach is what has been referred to as the *small stories* paradigm (Bamberg and Georgakopoulou, 2008). Its object of analysis is underrepresented narrative activities such as the relating of ongoing events or talk about things that have yet to come and, not least, shared events. Given the emphasis on co-telling, focus group settings, which are usually designed to be informal and relaxed, are a useful site for data collection.

The following excerpt provides an illustration. It was collected for research on *cosmopolitanism*, operationalised in this case as the 'sense of being at home in the world'. While cosmopolitanism at the elite level has long been the object of theorising, less is known about 'everyday cosmopolitanism' and whether and how it can be observed in the discourse of non-elites. To find out more about this, and in particular about the intersection between their lived experience of the world beyond their national borders and their mediated experience of it as obtained through news reports, focus group interviews were undertaken with groups of people in the capital and in a small town in a rural district of Sweden.

The interview excerpted below was with a group of librarians who talked about their reactions to the news that the Swedish foreign minister, Anna Lindh, had been murdered.

Reactions to news

Librarian 1: I was in England, you see, and it was *awful*. We were a group of librarians in England who suddenly got the news. And we stood there and felt completely *outside*. We wanted to be *home* when it happened. And we *cried* together and it was ... it was *awfully* strange. And then you saw all those pictures on TV, crying people, and you felt that *that's* where we should be. It was ... strange.

Librarian 2: It's so strange when you see lots of people, because obviously, all that about 9/11, it's stuff you just stand and think about for a long, long, long time, about individual cases and so on. But otherwise it's war and so on, when you see that there are lots of people dying, and you aren't moved as much as when you see *one* single story, *one* person who tells it. You have to distance yourself.

Librarian 1: It feels so hopeless. I think you have to ... I think you have to try to distance yourself and come back to your own little reality and try, well, do the best you can with your own little life. That's where we usually end up when we discuss things. Sometimes we discuss all the misery, but we try to do what we can in our own little library.

Librarian 2: The awful thing about television news is that you stop thinking. I mean, I've almost *stopped* looking at the news because of that. I think there is *report* after *report* after *report*, and I don't have a chance to react. That it's like that. So I much prefer to watch, you know, *slower* programmes and documentaries, that allow you to, like, keep up. Because it's ... it's pure violence. I mean, it's *terror, terror, terror*. And maimed people.

Interlocutor: And you mean that it's not enough just to know what's going on, it's important to react somehow?

Librarian 1: Yes, for *me* it's important to react. Because I think sitting and being spoon-fed and not reacting, it's somehow ... well, you feel numbed. And anything at all can happen without you reacting in the end.

Source: Robertson, 2010: 70-2

This conversation can be broken down into the narrative elements set out by Labov and Waletsky, as set out in Table 5.2 below. But it also highlights the reason the model has been critiqued by narrativists interested in small stories, as there is not a single narrator. Two women participate in the telling, and use several stories to respond to a question about how the news helps them relate to world events.

Analysing small stories and focus group conversations by attending to their component features, and both the 'what' and the 'how' of the narrative, makes it possible to discern patterns across a larger corpus of primary source material and compare texts such as transcripts of live interactions.

Table 5.2 Small stories in focus group settings, parsed into their narrative elements

Story		
Orientation		
time		the moment one speaker got the news that the minister had been killed (We…suddenly got the news.)
place		far away from home, cut off from events (I was in England…completely outside. We wanted to be home.)
participants		colleagues following the news (We were a group of librarians who suddenly got the news.)
situation		trying to make sense of deaths the librarians learn about from the news (you saw all those pictures on TV, crying people… you see there are lots of people dying … there is report after report after report)
Complicating action		
		The news does not engage the speakers in the plight of distant others as they think it should. (you see that there are lots of people dying, and you aren't moved as much…You have to distance yourself…you stop thinking)
Resolution		
		The speakers decide not to deal with the misery of the world, or the news about it they get on television, but to do what they can in their own workplace. (We try to do what we can in our own little library.)
		One speaker decides to stop watching the news. (I've almost stopped looking at the news…I much prefer to watch…slower programmes and documentaries.)
Coda		
		From England and the death of the foreign minister, and from 9/11 and the deaths of many, the speakers return to their own small world. (you…come back to your own little reality and try, well, to do the best you can with your own little life. That's where we usually end up.)
Discourse		
evaluation		The speakers feel the situation is hopeless, and unsatisfactory. They think it is a problem that they are not behaving like compassionate citizens, and television news is part of the problem.

Analysing media narratives: an example of television news analysis

Discourse analysts who study news stories have sought to show that the ways journalists structure or 'emplot' reports, and the way they characterise protagonists, contribute to the dissemination of stereotypes and reproduction of power relations that disadvantage minority groups. Given that this research perspective privileges the written word, many of its analyses have been based on press coverage. While newspaper texts are relatively straightforward and easy to work with, the ubiquity of digital technologies prompts consideration of other media when looking for narratives. Scholars pursuing multimodal narrative analysis have been doing precisely this, studying narratives in television, social media (Page, 2011) and what De Fina and Johnstone (2015: 161) refer to as 'the interaction of different semiotic resources' (or multimodal texts; see Chapter 8) – i.e., sound, print, image and animation.

This section highlights television texts because they have long been where different semiotic resources have interacted and are well suited to studying the phenomena that narrative analysis seeks to explicate – power, identity and the circulation of meaning in social contexts. Television is both a 'new' and an 'old' medium. It is new in that television news content is now broadcast on website and YouTube. News stories are increasingly fashioned in packages and on platforms with the intention of making them easy to share. But television news is also 'old' in that it continues to purvey 'common, cultural references and thematic codes, incarnated in master or model narratives' that are often experienced as innocent, not because their intentions are hidden, but because they are naturalised (Barthes, 1993: 131; Birkvad, 2000: 295; Weber, 2014). What narrative analysis can get at, and what tends to elude many other forms of media analysis, is the generation of these sorts of understandings — what we take for granted or that which goes without saying.

The task facing the researcher here is to try to understand how these sorts of understandings appear natural while being so insidious and powerful. By paying attention to 'the what', it is possible to study how certain themes and values can gain prominence through the repeated, conventional dramaturgy of the news report, and to compare hundreds of news texts. By paying attention to 'the how', it is possible to study the techniques involved in telling those stories in one way rather than another, and thus giving the same events a different meaning.

Analysing the 'story' is something that different researchers do in different ways, and with different degrees of formality. One way of going about the task is simply to leverage the elements outlined in Table 5.1 by turning them into code questions to be posed to the text (be it a newspaper or website article or television news report). Examples are given in Table 5.3.

Analysing the 'how' of the narrative is less formulaic and requires drilling down from the surface information or *denotative content* of the text to examine its *connotative content*. The information that a participant in a narrative is the prime minister is denotative content, and requires no particular competence to decode. The same cannot be said of *connotation* which, in a nutshell, has to do with the associations that a word, image or phrase may evoke, when encountered by someone who is familiar with the cultural references. As developed by Barthes (1977), the term is richer and more abstract, having to do with the meeting of signs and cultural values, and the creation of meaning through complex interactions on a variety of levels. For the purposes of this practical introduction, however, connotation is perhaps easiest to grasp by way of an example. As the UK government struggled to deal with both the Covid-19 pandemic and a string of scandals in 2022, a tabloid published a critical article under the headline

Table 5.3 Coding scheme for analysing the 'story' or 'what' of television news reports

Story	
Abstract	How does the newsreader introduce the report? What do they say it will be about? What does the text at the bottom of the screen or behind the newsreader say the topic is?

Orientation	
time	Is it breaking news, or a report of something that happened earlier that day or the day before? Or is it actually about something that took place in the past (an assassination or clampdown or scandal, for example) that today's event (a funeral or the commemoration of the clampdown or a book published about the scandal) only serves as the 'news hook' for?
place	Where do the unfolding events take place? Typical answers to this question are 'at a press conference', 'outside the parliament' or 'at the scene of the earthquake'. Depending on the research question guiding the analysis, it can be worth noting whether the news story is set in a public or private space.
participants	Who speaks or acts in this story? In answering this question, distinctions can be made between: • 'real' people (Vladimir Putin; George Floyd; Prince Harry) • abstractions like states or collective actors ('Turkey shelled Kurdish forces in Syria'; 'Washington recalled its ambassador'; 'the party is divided') • characters (ruler, dissident, victim)
situation	What is the starting point or equilibrium? Here it can be useful to code for the institutional or political context of the story. Does it have to do with the local community, the nation, or with the European or world community? Is it a conflict or is the report about people's efforts to get along together? Is it about politics or the economy or society?

Complicating action	
	What happens to destabilise the equilibrium? For example, in a study of news coverage of migration, the starting point or equilibrium might be a national refugee policy that is in accordance with EU agreements and the country's humanitarian stance. A complicating action would then be: 'the government announced today it would impose border controls to stem the flow of asylum-seekers'.

Resolution	
	What finally happened? News reports are often about processes or ongoing events, so the question of what constitutes 'finally' must be connected to the 'time' coded above. But news reports tend to be formulaic, and the reporter's sign-off is a good place to look for the resolution. Examples: 'Following unprecedented protests, major Chinese cities eased covid lockdowns, whether this satisfies demonstrators remains to be seen'.

Coda	
	How does the reporter return us to the studio and the rest of the broadcast, and how does the newsreader return viewers to the present? 'We'll be hearing more from our correspondent in the days to come as we follow these ongoing developments in the field. Meanwhile...'.

'From Operation Save Big Dog to Operation Red Meat, Boris Johnson has what Baldrick might have called a cunning plan to recover from Partygate'.[2] In this context, 'cunning' connotes not only scheming – someone who tries to manipulate a situation to their own advantage – but also the unpleasant and usually foolish strategies of the characters in the popular British satirical comedy *Black Adder*. As the reference was picked up and circulated on social media, it was accompanied by an image of Johnson twinned with the unsavoury Baldrick, who was famous for perpetually hatching a 'cunning plan' (which was almost always the opposite). Connotative content is often subtler than this example, and examining it involves making visible behaviour that is otherwise invisible – i.e., the work of the audience. Chatman (1978: 41, 42) calls this work the 'reading out process', referring to our routinely employed abilities to decode from surface to narrative structures. But while it may be routine, it is also skilled work. Illusions of verisimilitude, explains Brinker (1983: 254), are based on the viewer's 'thoroughgoing familiarity with the conventions of representation' at work. Audiences recognise and interpret these conventions without being aware of them. People rarely give a thought to camera angles, but routinely and subconsciously decode the physical distance established by the filming and editing of a news story as associated with social distance. Politicians tend to appear at a respectable distance, while ordinary people tend to be shown at closer quarters, particularly if they are in distress. This convention has the effect of putting the average viewer in a more intimate relation to the sort of figures with which they are presumed to be on an equal social footing (see also Chapter 8). Table 5.4 contains an example of a code sheet designed to parse the discourse dimension of a narrative – i.e., to capture and document the 'reading out process' in an analytical rather than unconscious way.

Decades ago, Graddol (1994) made an important distinction between conventions used in storytelling with visuals that remains relevant and useful to this day. The most familiar one is *realism*, a term originally used to refer to a literary convention. The narrator in this tradition tends to be omniscient – 'one who can see things which individual characters cannot see and who is in all places at once' (Graddol, 1994: 140). Other characters can also contribute to the narrative, of course, but they are encompassed by the omniscient narrator's voice. The other tradition is that of *naturalism*. It provides 'a representation of the world as it might be directly experienced by the viewer [...]. From the naturalist perspective, a news report provides vicarious experience, an image of the world as we might expect to experience it if we were to stand where the reporter stands' (Graddol, 1994: 145). The objective, omniscient narrator's voice is absent from reports in which such narrative techniques are used and the primary definers are the people whose story is being told. An example of such a report is given in Table 5.5, which also shows how a text with video can be transcribed and organised in the first step of the analysis.

---

[2] www.mirror.co.uk/news/politics/5-cunning-plans-boris-johnsons-25961747

Table 5.4 Coding scheme for analysing the 'discourse' or 'how' of television news reports

how the story is told	What is the role of the reporter-narrator? Is he or she 'omniscient', in possession of all the facts and perhaps commenting on what is going through a participant's head? Or is the reporter a bystander, listening in on someone else's story before passing it on to us?	Is the reporter pictured in the centre of the field of vision, between the viewer and the participants? Or does the report use naturalist techniques that allow us 'direct' contact with the participants, i.e. by letting them tell the story in their own words?
	Is one side of the conflict silent or under-represented?	Are the participants on one side of the conflict only referred to, or are they pictured, and if so, how? Are they in focus or behind a fence or at sea?
	Where is the viewer situated?	Do we see events from behind the lines of the riot police, from the middle of a protest march, or from a rooftop?
	How is the audience addressed?	Are we invited, through the use of reporting conventions, to enter the room occupied by a participant? Does the journalist and camera operator place us in a position in which we can imagine conversing with the participant? Are we invited to react to what the participant or reporter tells us?
	Does the language used by the reporter-narrator suggest that participants should be understood in one way rather than another? Does he or she refer to someone as being hostile, obstinate, or aggressive – or as conciliatory, heroic or victimised?	Is there metaphorical or symbolic content in view? Look for walls and fences, and sunrises and sunsets.
evaluation	How is the story to be understood? What sense is to be made of these events, given the way they have been reported?	

Table 5.5 Transcription of 'Former Uganda child soldiers return home', broadcast on Al Jazeera English, 3 May 2014

Story	Visuals
Newsreader: In Uganda, thousands of children were kidnapped and forced to fight for the Lord's Resistance Army led by Joseph Kony. Our correspondent reports from Kitgum on one former child soldier, who is finally heading home after 13 years in captivity.	

(Continued)

Table 5.5 Continued

Story	Visuals
Reporter: When he was 10 years old, Dennis Ocan was abducted from his village in northern Uganda by rebels from the Lord's Resistance Army. That was in 2001. He was forced to become a child soldier, and to commit atrocities. It was 13 years before he could escape.	The report begins with a shot of an empty barracks, in which a young man, formally dressed, is packing his suitcase. The reporter is not in view.
Dennis Ocan (the young man): Many children were beaten to death. You have to follow the orders, or else they kill you. Children who tried to escape were killed. You have to follow orders until a chance to escape comes.	The young man is pictured sitting on the bed in the barracks. He is very still and speaks in a low voice.
Reporter: In recent weeks, this rehabilitation centre, run by the charity World Vision, has been his home. At the peak of the war, hundreds of child soldiers came through here every month. The murals they painted are still here. An estimated 10 thousand are still missing, most of them will never come home. But a trickle of former child soldiers do still escape, now grown adults. It's Christine Oroma's job to counsel them.	The reporter is not in view. Pan of walls with childlike, mural-size paintings of young people playing. Shot of piles of binders and papers, with more wall paintings in the background, of automatic rifles. Cut to a group of young men sitting on benches, in a ring, under a tree.
Christine Oroma, Counsellor, World Vision: Such kind of killing is really a problem. Psychologically they keep on recalling.	Christine Oroma is alone on screen.

The job of the narrative analyst is to make science out of the mundane, and make visible the conventions that make some narrative clauses evaluative. Asking questions about the role of the narrator, on the look-out for realist or naturalist techniques, is one way of accessing, analysing and documenting the 'how'. The study that drew on the story of Dennis, the Ugandan boy soldier, compared reporting in different global news outlets to see whether the world was – as is often claimed – narrated as a conflictual place, or whether reports contained evidence of a cosmopolitan outlook. The idea is that, if we are to feel 'at home in the world', we should be able to imagine walking beside those who are different from us, rather than be placed in (discursive) confrontation with them. The study explored how newswork could build imaginative bridges and invite connections between viewers and distant others, rather than always reinforcing conflictual frames. In the study, it was argued that the story of Dennis resonates with an outlook that understands the world in terms of cosmopolitanism rather than conflict, because the report positions the viewer in the car beside the rehabilitated soldier, and beside him as he treads on an egg and shakes the hands of other young men from the village. In so doing, the discourse of this particular narrative could be said to position the viewer – with the narrator witness – on the side of peace, freedom and reconciliation.

Critical reflections

A good place to begin reflecting on the strengths and weaknesses of a narrative approach is with this evaluation of the story of the Ugandan boy soldier. Is it reasonable to interpret the discourse of this particular narrative as resonant with a cosmopolitan outlook? When considering an answer, it should be kept in mind that there are a number of narratives at work here – or rather, narrative work taking place on different levels.

Questions of interpretation

On one level, is the narrative of the original storyteller. Has the narrative of the journalist been 'read' the way he intended it to be read? Has it been 'read' the way the intended audience is likely to make sense of it – be it the *model reader* introduced in Chapter 1 or her empirical sister in rural India, or perhaps a harassed parent, spooning meatballs into the mouth of his small offspring while the television news is on in the background? Anderton and James (2022: 11) raise important questions about what they call the 'narrow interests' of texts analysed in academic research. 'To what extent do we as cultural analysts question our own bias in the process of gate-keeping interests', they ask, 'and in the construction of analytical narratives?'

Credibility

There is another narrative at work here: the narrative of the researcher. Doing research is a matter of dialogue – with the material being analysed and with other scholars, be they world-renowned professors encountered at a conference, students in a classroom setting, or some other reader whom the student/researcher may never meet. For the dialogue to work, the analysis of the primary source material – i.e., the texts, must be transparent: the researcher should take the reader by the hand, as it were, and lead them through the material that has been analysed the way a local expert might introduce a visitor to a city or cathedral that they have never been in before. The local expert/author of the study might have the advantage of knowing the place better than the visitor/reader, but the visitor/reader may be an expert on cathedrals in another country, and is thus in a position to disagree with the local expert, or to bring a new perspective to what the latter thought they knew. The point of the story (yes, *another* narrative!) is that the discussion could never have taken place had the local expert/author of the study not taken the visitor/reader to the supposedly well-known cathedral. The dialogue on which research is based cannot take place unless the researcher shares their 'cathedral', or object of analysis, with the reader.

When the primary source material comprises hundreds of texts, comprising words and pictures, and perhaps other modalities, or transcriptions of dozens of hours of interviews, or texts in a language not likely to be accessible to the reader, the business of sharing, and maintaining transparency in the reporting of results, can be challenging. Most researchers, lacking a better solution, resort to summarising their material. Such summaries often take the form of a narrative. This approach to textual analysis can thus result in a narrative of a narrative.

Scholars approach their primary source material with their theoretical assumptions and research questions at the forefront of their minds. Those assumptions and questions may encourage them to see certain things in their material and to be blind to others. A BBC camerawoman once expressed this rather more succinctly than Gadamer (see Chapter 1) when describing how she went about filming an event: 'We see what we want to see. We film what we know' (quoted in Robertson, 2010: 145). The narrative of the researcher is thus not something to be taken at face value. As explained in Chapter 1, texts can be analysed with either the understandings of the sender (Chapter 1's *text producer*) or receiver (the *empirical reader*) in mind. What does that entail when a given text is interpreted in the context of the larger societal discourse?

Reflections on narrative analysis in general

Given these questions, it is hardly surprising that a recurrent criticism levelled at researchers using the narrative approach is that their analyses cannot be reproduced by other researchers, despite some (like Labov) taking pains to do precisely this. Not all agree that this is a problem. Bruner, for example, notes the eventuality of there being a difference between what is *expressed* in the text and what the text might *mean*, to return to issues raised at the beginning of the book. There is no ultimate solution to determining *the* meaning of a given text, he says: our best hope 'is to provide an intuitively convincing account of the meaning of the text as a whole in the light of the constituent parts that make it up' (Bruner, 1991: 8). That in itself is a goal worth trying to achieve. There is every reason to strive for good reliability in narrative analyses and, where possible, for results that can be generalised.

Lieblich et al. (1998) agree that no reading is free of interpretation. Even at the stage of procuring the text (especially in the dialogical act of conducting an interview), explicit and implicit processes of communicating, understanding and explaining constantly take place. There is a dilemma that has to do with the role of theory in listening to and explaining an account. Is the researcher a naive listener attuned only to the phenomenological world of the narrator? Or does the researcher constantly question, doubt, look for gaps, contradictions, silences, the unsaid? They offer four criteria for assessing the quality of narrative research:

- comprehensiveness of evidence. Like Riessman, they maintain that reports should be supported by numerous quotations, and alternative explanations discussed;
- coherence. This has an internal and external dimension. Internal coherence can be evaluated in terms of how the parts of the analysis fit together; external coherence in terms of how they fit with existing theories and previous research;

- insightfulness. A good study should be innovative or original in some way, in the presentation of the story and in the analysis of it;
- parsimony. As with other research, a good narrative study should be able to fulfil the preceding three criteria with recourse to a small number of concepts. It should have elegance or aesthetic appeal. (Lieblich et al., 1998: 173)

Essential to the work of evaluating narrative research is the point mentioned above: the sharing of results and interpretations with the relevant research community (be it fellow students or a tutor). Do they see the same patterns? Do they make sense of narratives differently? Do they follow the researcher's argument and find it compelling? Can they distinguish the researcher's voice from that of the narrators in the primary source material? This is known as *consensual validation* and is considered particularly significant in narrative inquiry (cf. Chapter 2 on coder intersubjectivity).

Czarniawska (1999) points out that the surge in interest in narratives has occasioned two kinds of warnings. First, some have questioned the legitimacy of work conducted by social scientists engaging in what is derogatorily referred to as 'literary work'. In this view, scholarship becomes literary criticism, and indeed a form of literary criticism that is inferior to that of literary theorists. Second, social scientists have to show that they are not only good at reading Barthes, but also at telling us something about organisations (in the case of Czarniawska's field of expertise) – or politics or culture or society or identity or power. Social scientists engaging in narrative work 'have to move across lands belonging to someone else', and this is not without its hazards (Czarniawska, 1999: 37).

Narrative analysis and the study of society

It was suggested earlier that people 'work "mentally" in common' (Bruner, 1991: 20) through the narratives circulating in society, and that the construction of such narratives thus places people in a shared social context. Because such construction work involves struggles over meaning, the study of narrative sheds light on power, and how we, as members of particular social formations, are more readily able to accept some '"realities" than others' and 'sometimes become imprisoned by these realities' (Mumby, 1993: 7). This means that, when undertaking the work of interpretation, the social scientist needs to consider how narratives are imbricated with the social realities of people experiencing inequality, violation of rights, curtailment of freedom and any number of power struggles.

Narratives exist on different levels, or in different dimensions, and can be more or less abstract. The analytical instruments presented in this chapter have been used to explicate concrete narratives – the stories a librarian or a journalist actually told and the words they used to tell them. But such analyses can only be interesting if they can give us insights into something larger or more general, and such generalisation can only take place if specific micro-level narratives are related to accumulated or macro-level and recurrent narrative themes. These often take the form of the taken-for-granted assumptions about how the world works referred to at the beginning of the chapter. These accumulated narratives go by different names. One is *public narratives*, which feature actors larger than the individual, like the 'people', the 'terrorists' or the 'market'. Another is *master narratives* (about Progress, Enlightenment, the triumph of Democracy and, increasingly, their demise) in which some scholars claim we are embedded.

Narrativity is about making sense of our place in the scheme of things, and this takes place within certain political constellations. The study of narrative thus gives us a point of entry into the distribution of power in society, particularly in affording insights into phenomena that are constructed as 'natural'; it helps us to see what is not always visible and to hear 'that which goes without saying'.

Summary

The usefulness of a narrative approach

- The starting point for this chapter has been that narrative analysis provides useful insights into society and politics, and that social actors are better understood as 'narrative creatures' than as 'rational actors'.
- The approach is characterised by considerable diversity, both conceptual and methodological. This can be a source of inspiration, but also of confusion and frustration.
- Practitioners of the approach differ when it comes to their starting points and assumptions; how they define narrative; and the uses to which narrative is put.
- Narrative is defined in this chapter as an account of something that has happened which comprises two parts: a 'story' and a 'discourse', or the 'what' and the 'how'.
- Contemporary narrative analysis has built on the work of the Russian formalists, French structuralists and literary theorists.
- Narrative analysis is now used by scholars in fields as varied as political science, law, anthropology, gender studies, psychology and science.
- By analysing concrete narratives, such as those found in interview transcripts or media texts, it is possible to get an analytical purchase on the more abstract narratives and taken-for-granted assumptions that have become so naturalised as to be almost invisible and which yet govern the way we make sense of the world.

How to do it

- In collecting material, it is important to be clear about what you mean by narrative and how you will recognise one in your primary sources. When it comes to interviews, being attuned to entrance and exit talk is a useful method. Transcription is essential. Decisions about the amount of material to be analysed should be governed partly by the nature of the research question and the material itself, partly by the researcher's ambition to focus on 'story' (in which more material can be accommodated) or discourse (which is more time-consuming).
- When analysing the narratives, it is useful to operationalise the features of the story (be they abstract, orientation, complicating actions, resolution, or whatever) as questions to be posed to the text. When analysing the discourse of the narrative, it is useful to keep the question 'how' at the fore: how is this story being told so that its content leads to a given evaluation?

- When presenting results, bear in mind the importance of being able to have a dialogue with other (student) researchers about the findings of the study. This means sharing the material in some form or other – either by making original transcripts, texts or recordings available, or by summarising the narratives and providing numerous quotes and examples – which in turn means obtaining copyright permission and written consent at the data-collection stage. When personal experiences are involved, respondents should be invited to approve the written results as well.

Suggested reading

Several textbooks on narrative can be recommended to the student who wishes to pursue the approach in more depth. They distil the often complex ideas and obscure writing style of leading narrativists in an accessible, reader-friendly fashion. One of these is Mertova and Webster's 2019 introduction to critical event narrative analysis; another is Holstein and Gubrium's 2012 anthology *Varieties of Narrative Analysis*. The *Handbook of Narrative Analysis*, edited by De Fina and Georgakopoulou, and published in 2019, contains a wide variety of applications that connect narratives in texts to the analysis of social practices, in bite-sized chapters.

The *Routledge Encyclopedia of Narrative Theory* compiled by David Herman, Manfred Jahn and Marie-Laure Ryan in 2005 (paperback version, 2008) is a valuable reference book should your library happen to have a volume.

A good source of inspiration is the *Narrative Inquiry* journal. Visiting the www.clarku.edu/~narrinq/ website and reading the abstracts published there (even if the full articles may not be available to readers) is a good way to keep abreast of developments in the field. Number 91 (2023) of *The Velvet Light Trap* is devoted to digital storytelling, and provides a good cross-section of current research into how the practice of narrative is shaped by digital platforms (and the interests of the tech giants that own and develop them). Topics include algorithm-based storytelling, virtual reality and computer graphics. Mark Davis's and Davina Long's *Pandemics, Publics and Narrative* (2020) offers a timely and prescient study of everyday, policy and media narratives of pandemics.

Exercises

Exercise 1: Big things in small stories

Historical and political events are often told in the words of the powerful, but important insights can be gained into larger societal processes by listening to the stories told by the people who experience them. The objects of analysis in this exercise are such 'small stories'.

The task

The first step in the exercise is to generate data for your analysis. Ask a grandparent if you can talk to them about living through a war or hard times, or a neighbour about migrating to a new country, or a classmate about their experience of a political protest.

(Continued)

(Continued)

The second step is to analyse one or several of the stories that emerge from your interview. Define your object of analysis by looking for entrance and exit talk, then parse it by posing questions to the transcribed text. How does the narrator signal that they have a story to tell? Do they use phrases like 'to put it in a nutshell', or 'to make a long story short', or 'in essence, what happened was … '?. What is the starting point; is there a turning point? And, most importantly, how does the narrator make sense of these events – what is the moral of the story, as they tell it?

The third step is for *you* to make sense of your respondent's story – to provide your own evaluation in the light of your research question. What can you learn about everyday experiences of war, migration or protest from the story that has been shared with you?

The texts

In many countries, there are ethnographic collections in the public domain that can be a rich source of narratives. If you decide to conduct an interview yourself, ask your respondent if they mind you recording it. Bear in mind that written consent and ethics approval is obligatory in some countries and institutional contexts. The transcription of the recording is the text to be analysed in this exercise.

Exercise 2: Analysing how a news story is told

Crime takes considerable space in public discourse, often with calls for harsher punishment, and not unusually with a racial dimension. Less attention is typically paid to acts of reconciliation and rehabilitation. Viewing the question of what should be done with the perpetrators of violent crime from different perspectives can give insights into values prevailing in a given society and how they contrast with others. Not long after the story about the Ugandan boy soldier (Table 5.5) was broadcast, another report appeared on the same channel that provides such a contrast (see URL below). Narrative analysis can be used to unpack how the texts work.

The task

The first part of the task is to analyse the news report with attention to how it is told. What is the role of the reporter-narrator? Is he 'omniscient' and at the centre of the story, as in the realist tradition? Or is he a bystander, letting participants tell the story, as in the naturalist tradition – and, if so, to what effect? Is one side silent or underrepresented? Where are you as viewer situated, and how does that make you feel?

After you have coded the text, compare it to the report about the Ugandan boy-soldier. In what way do the narratives differ? What can be said about those differences when it comes to larger issues of societal norms and social justice?

(Continued)

(Continued)

The texts

The news report can be found on YouTube, under the heading 'Rodeo show inside US prison draws flak' (www.youtube.com/watch?v=Znv2Oh7Uxeg). The story of the Ugandan boy soldier referred to in the chapter is also available on YouTube (listed as www.youtube.com/watch?v=oMFk-jNXZEQ).

Exercise 3: Stories of the nation and its place, time and space

Museums are replete with stories, ostensibly about the past, but also about the present, about how a country is to be understood in the light of its history, and how that past is told in new ways in the light of the present. These stories are often political. They can be a response to right-wing populist references to ethnically pure imagined histories, by emphasising how migrations and global connections have existed from ancient times to the present. One example – with a striking emphasis on storytelling – is how the Swedish Museum of History presents 'The Viking World' (https://historiska.se/home/). In many countries, museums are now exhibiting their artefacts in ways that acknowledge histories of racism and how the slave trade contributed to the prosperity of the nation.

The task

Choose a museum or exhibition as your object of analysis. How many stories can you find there? Whose stories are they? How is the nation's past narrated? Is it possible to discern an overarching narrative or narrative theme? If so, what would you call that theme and how does it come to expression in the way the stories are told?

The texts

Museum websites are one form of text that can be analysed. Catalogues of exhibitions are another. Museums themselves can be considered as texts and the person interested in multimodality (Chapter 8) may find them a particularly rewarding avenue of research.

6

Three Poststructural Approaches to Discourse Analysis

Linda Ekström, Göran Bergström and Hugo Faber

Background

Discourse analysis comes in many forms and shapes in the social sciences. This chapter presents three different takes on discourse analysis that are rooted in poststructuralism: *political discourse theory*, *discursive psychology* and the '*What's the problem represented to be?*' *approach* to discourse analysis. As these approaches can appear quite abstract, we will pay special attention to how they can be used in empirical research.

What is discourse?

The term 'discourse' is used in multiple research contexts and it is defined in many different ways. This can be confusing, but a first step towards greater precision is to divide discourse analysis into three different traditions (Torfing, 2005). The first tradition is linked to linguistic modes of analysis where the term 'discourse' is used in a narrow sense to denote a particular unit of spoken or written text (Fairclough, 1992: 3).

The second tradition of discourse analysis is linked to critical discourse studies, with representatives like Ruth Wodak, Norman Fairclough and Teun van Dijk. This tradition considers more dimensions than the textual one, and involves a greater focus on the context of the particular text (see Chapter 7).

The present chapter on poststructural approaches to discourse analysis belongs to a third tradition. According to this tradition, all social phenomena gain their meaning from discourses, and the term 'discourse' also includes non-semiotic aspects of social practices (Howarth, 2000: 7). The approaches can all be said to share Michel Foucault's definition of discourses as 'practices that systematically form the objects of which they speak' (Foucault, 1972: 49). Thus, discourses are inseparable from knowledge production, and they have the power to produce rather than merely describe reality as it appears to us. In line with such an understanding, Carol Bacchi and Susan Goodwin describe discourses as '*socially produced forms of knowledge* that set limits upon what it is possible to think, write or say about' a given topic (Bacchi and Goodwin, 2016: 35, emphasis in original).

Thus, in this chapter, to focus on discourse is to focus on meaning and meaning-making processes *in general*. However, in the examples used in the chapter, these meaning-making processes are mainly identified through the study of texts, as is often the case in discourse analysis. Analysing these discourses is important since they shape how we perceive situations, events, identities and practices, and determine what actions are perceived as logical and legitimate. For example, different discourses represent the COVID-19 pandemic in different ways. While the virus clearly exists independently of how we talk about it, the meaning of the pandemic – and how we are to engage with it – depends on discursive articulations. Whether a total lockdown or a more 'business-as-usual' approach is considered appropriate is ultimately a question of meaning-making and discourse.

Discourse analysis as philosophy and social theory

This section outlines a number of theoretical assumptions that the three poststructural approaches have in common.

The constitutive role of discourse

First, poststructural approaches start from the post-foundationalist assumption that, as human beings, we do not have immediate access to an objective reality. This should not be confused with idealism. The claim is not that material reality does not exist, or that its existence depends on human perception, but rather that all objects appear to us as meaningful and that their meaning is socially produced through discourse rather than given by an inherent essence (Laclau and Mouffe, 1985: 108; Bacchi and Goodwin, 2016: 33). Laclau and Mouffe (1990: 100–3) exemplify this with a stone lying in a field. They point out that the stone does not have any meaning in itself, but takes on different meanings depending on the social context. For a Stone Age warrior, the stone may be a projectile; for settlers, it may be part of a future settlement; and for some students, it may be an archaeological find. Nothing is permanent about a specific understanding of reality because it depends on discourses, which are contingent social constructions. These constructions are not fixed but involved in a process of constant construction and contestation, 'always formed in the confluence of encounters and chances, during the course of a precarious and fragile history' (Foucault, 1990: 37).

Discourse analysis and the issue of power

Second, poststructural discourse analysis stresses that language and meaning-making are saturated with power, and that instituting a particular discursive order is an inherently political practice. When a specific way of making sense of the world gains precedence, certain forms of thinking and acting are enabled, while alternatives are marginalised (Laclau, 1990: 34; Bacchi, 2009a: 35). In other words, the power of discourse lies in establishing what lies 'within the true' – i.e., what can be intelligibly said and done, even considered to be true, in a given social context (Bacchi and Goodwin, 2016: 35). Thus, the distinction between power and knowledge collapses and is replaced by the discursive practices through which we make reality meaningful. Inseparable from knowledge and discourse, power too becomes fundamentally productive: 'In fact power produces; it produces reality; it produces domains of objects and rituals of truth' (Foucault, 2020: 194). Consequently, discourse analysts pay attention to the effects that discourses may have, and the ways in which certain groups may benefit or be disadvantaged by these effects. Discourse-oriented policy theory has highlighted that discourses have concrete implications through the policies that they legitimise (Bacchi, 1999, 2009a). For example, if obesity is represented as a 'lifestyle problem', this implies that some people have made the wrong lifestyle choices and that they are individually responsible for reforming their situation (cf. Bacchi, 2016). This, in turn, is likely to affect the policies that address the issue.

Discourse analysis and social identities

Third, poststructural discourse analysis is often interested in the emergence and transformation of social identities within specific discourses. Identities such as 'woman', 'man', 'student' or 'professor' are not given, do not exist 'out there'. Nor are identity constructions exclusively internal processes that take place 'in there', in our individual psyches (Schotter, 1993; Billig, 1999; Potter and Edwards, 2001). Instead, identity constructions are seen as processes in which self-images fuse with the images of others. A specific identity, in other words, only comes about in opposition to something else – i.e., 'the other' or what the identity in question is *not* (cf. Hall, 1997). This perspective on meaning-making as *relational* is why discourse analysts often focus on distinctions such as 'us' and 'them' and are interested in how an 'us-creation' always implies a 'them-creation'.

Practices and discourses rather than actors in focus

Fourth, poststructural discourse analysis does not highlight actors and their intentions in the same way as, for example, analysis of ideas and ideological thought (Chapter 3) or conceptual history (Chapter 4) sometimes do (cf. Bacchi, 2005, 2009a, b). However, there are differences between the three different approaches in this respect. While discourse psychologists emphasise the role of actors as active mediators and negotiators of discourses, the other approaches are more interested in broader social practices and the discourses that they produce.

Discourse analytical research problems

In line with its perspective on knowledge and power, poststructural discourse analysis is not about finding objective 'truths'. Rather, it is concerned with how certain interpretations of reality become accepted as 'true' and what consequences this may have. One may be interested in how, for example, something is singled out as problematic, how certain social practices may be institutionalised to deal with the imagined problem, and how such beliefs and institutions shape and govern people. This is linked to a critical ambition. Showing how the discourse surrounding an issue is produced and maintained can show its contingency and open up different ways of making sense of the issue. This makes it possible to question the power relations that a particular discourse draws upon and reproduces, allowing us to think and act differently.

Analysis

In this section, we introduce three poststructural discourse analytical approaches. We start by describing the theoretical background to each approach, after which we offer examples to show how each approach may be used in empirical research.

Discourse analysis needs to be rigorous and thorough, but it does not follow any specific methodological procedure, and there are rarely any ready-made templates to use. Nevertheless, there are certain steps in the concrete process of analysis to which all discourse analyses must relate. We therefore conclude this section with a more concrete discussion of the steps that every discourse analytical study needs to address.

Political discourse theory (PDT)

In *Hegemony and Socialist Strategy*, the seminal work of political discourse theory (PDT),[1] Ernesto Laclau and Chantal Mouffe (1985) articulated an alternative to what they saw as essentialism and class-reductionism in Marxist social theory. They were inspired by multiple schools of thought, including Marxism, structuralism, psychoanalysis, phenomenology and pragmatism. Since then, PDT has inspired a growing literature that focuses on power, radical democracy, political mobilisation, identity and populism (e.g., Howarth et al., 2000; Mouffe, 2000; Laclau, 2005; Griggs and Howarth, 2016; De Cleen and Stavrakakis, 2017; Devenney, 2020; Persson, 2020).

Drawing on Ferdinand de Saussure's (2013 [1916]) structural linguistics and semiology, political discourse theorists think of meaning-making as a 'play of differences' (Laclau, 2005: 69). Saussure saw linguistic signs as consisting of two

---

[1]Political discourse theory is also referred to as the Essex School of discourse analysis, post-Marxist discourse theory, poststructural discourse theory, or simply discourse theory.

parts: *signifier* and *signified* (see also 'Multimodal texts, genres and discourses in Chapter 1). A signifier is a linguistic term or utterance – for example, 'cat' – and the corresponding signified is the concept that the signifier 'cat' refers to. Saussure emphasised that the relation between signifier and signified is arbitrary – there is no connection between them other than social convention. That is to say, the meaning of any signifier depends on its (socially determined) difference from other signifiers. A signifier like 'man' gains its meaning by virtue of its difference from other signifiers such as 'child' and 'woman'. In other words, languages are systems of differences, and the meaning of any signifier is contingent and relational.

Political discourse theory goes beyond Saussure by treating all social phenomena as part of similar systems of differences or *discourses*. It is not only the linguistic signifier that is at stake, but how we understand the very identity of the signified object or subject in question. Moreover, discourses are not limited to linguistic practices, but include all kinds of social practices that make up society, such as the planning and construction of infrastructure, the organisation of industry and commerce, and the laws and regulations that govern us all.

Additionally, PDT stresses that meaning-making is inherently political and always a question of power – perhaps unsurprising considering that the interpretation of reality, the organisation of society and the definition of human and non-human identities are at stake (Svärd, 2015: 25). PDT sees the world as populated by opposing political projects engaged in a constant struggle over meaning, competing to impose their own demands and to assert their own way of making sense of the world as dominant or hegemonic. It is important to note that PDT defines the political in a broad sense, including every struggle over meaning-making in society, and not only the work of parliaments, parties and governments.

Antagonism and the constitutive outside

PDT emphasises the contested and precarious nature of meaning to an even higher degree than the other approaches in this chapter. There are always alternative ways of making sense of the world, whose existence shows the contingency of our own, and it is only through their exclusion that meaning is (temporarily) fixed (Laclau and Mouffe, 1985: 113).

Just as individual signifiers attain their meaning in relation to what they are not, discourses constitute themselves as meaningful wholes by excluding other ways of making meaning. Thus, every discourse relies on an exclusion that is more radical than its internal differences (Laclau, 1996: Chapter 3). Any 'us' requires a 'them'. But this exclusion also implies the ultimate failure of establishing any particular discourse as objective. The excluded 'Other' of the discourse, its constitutive outside, is always there in the background to remind us of other ways of making sense of the world, and of the ultimate contingency of our own. The constitutive outside is a necessary part of our identities that gives them meaning, but it also reveals their arbitrary nature. Objectivity is impossible and meaning is ultimately contingent, but this contingency cannot be symbolised directly within any discourse. Instead, it manifests itself as *antagonism* towards an external threat or blockage – an 'Other' (Laclau and Mouffe, 1985: 122–5).

To illustrate, an identity as a 'socialist' is rendered meaningful by its opposition to 'capitalism', 'the right' and 'fascism'. Without the antagonism towards these 'Others', socialism would not make much sense as a concept. But they are also what blocks socialism from being fully realised, both as concrete political adversaries and in a more abstract sense as instances of other ways of making sense of the world.

Hegemony and dislocation

Despite the ultimate contingency of all meaning, partial and temporary stability can be achieved. If a political force can manage to reduce the range of possible meanings, stabilise identities and cover over antagonism, its discourse becomes *hegemonic*. It becomes taken for granted and accepted as common sense (Laclau and Mouffe, 1985: 142). Borrowing Edmund Husserl's terminology, PDT captures the institutionalisation of discursive practices with the concept of *sedimentation* (Laclau and Mouffe, 2001: viii). Sedimentation can take different forms, such as inscription into laws, routines, norms and organisations, and every social context is layered with the sediments of its own particular history. Accordingly, the concept of sedimentation indicates the contextuality and historicity of every social order.

But every order is eventually uprooted. This is captured by the concept of *dislocation*, the situation in which an event or a phenomenon breaks with our understanding of society as we know it and challenges the existing order (Laclau, 1990). Dislocations can take the form of a sudden crisis or of slow undermining, but they always lead to demands for some kind of change. Hegemonic orders can either adapt to dislocations by meeting social demands, resolving conflicts, reconfiguring meanings and practices, or undergoing more radical change or upheaval. When sedimented practices are contested and their ultimate contingency is revealed, the latent antagonism is *reactivated* (Laclau and Mouffe, 2001, viii). Concepts such as antagonism, dislocation and reactivation highlight that PDT is not only interested in hegemony, but also in resistance, counter-hegemonic struggle and change.

The struggle over meaning

So far, we have explored the Sisyphean struggle for hegemony in spite of antagonism and dislocation, a struggle that PDT envisions in terms of contingent meaning-making. But how is meaning created and how can it be studied? There are a number of concepts to describe how discourses are (re)produced and contested, and they can also be used as analytical tools.

In the vocabulary of PDT, *articulation* is the practice of instituting a relation between different signifiers, thus altering and temporarily fixing their meaning. The term *moment* refers to any signifier rendered meaningful by articulation

(Laclau and Mouffe, 2001: 105). To illustrate, it was not until the alt-right movement in the United States articulated the term 'snowflake' together with other moments that they associated with their political opponents, such as 'woke ideology', 'easily offended', 'liberal' and 'entitled', that it became a clearly defined moment with a pejorative meaning. Before that, 'snowflake' was undefined in the political sense (even if it had a definite meaning as a natural phenomenon). The fixation of moments depends on *nodal points*, privileged signifiers that act like hubs that stabilise the meaning of related identities (Laclau and Mouffe, 2001: xi, 112). For instance, in a secular discourse structured around the nodal point of 'democracy', concepts such as 'justice' or 'freedom' take on a particular meaning (including, for example, equality before the law and freedom of expression) that is different from their meaning in a religious discourse structured around, say, 'the will of God'.

The play of differences entails two opposed political logics. The *logic of equivalence* is typically associated with the creation of a collective identity in opposition to a common enemy. It refers to the process of creating *chains of equivalence* – the highlighting of similarities between a group of moments in relation to an excluded outside (Laclau and Mouffe, 2001: 127–34). This intensifies the differences instituted by the exclusion, but it also blurs the distinction between the moments within the chain as they all come to signify opposition to a constitutive outside (Laclau, 1996, 38–42). In other words, there is an element of simplification to logics of equivalence. The German Nazi discourse of the 1920s, for example, contained two chains of equivalence. National Socialism was associated with moments such as 'fatherland', 'people', 'Aryan', etc. Some moments were set against Nazism as well, such as 'Americanism', 'Bolshevism', 'foreigners', 'Jews' etc. The differences between the individual moments within each of these chains of equivalence were less important than the 'us' and 'them' that they represented. The blurring of identities within a chain of equivalence is particularly apparent in the construction of *empty signifiers*, which are nodal points that have a polarising function as they represent a whole chain of equivalence and its antagonistic relation to its outside. In the example above, 'Jews' came to represent the whole range of threats to Nazism, with links to all the other moments in the chain. 'Jew' was closely associated with 'Bolshevism' but also with 'Americanism'.

The *logic of difference* represents the countermove of breaking up a chain of equivalence and disarming an opposing discourse by emphasising the differences of its internal moments – for example, by catering to some of its demands, appeasing parts of the opposition, and assimilating parts of the opposing discourse. Employing the logic of difference against the Nazis, for example, would involve attempts to divide them by emphasising the differences and conflicts between all the identities that were articulated as the 'German people' (e.g., workers, farmers, bourgeoisie).

Two opposing political projects might both try to internalise the same moments in their own chain of equivalence. For example, they might both claim to represent 'ordinary people' or 'justice'. These signifiers will assume different meanings depending on the other moments that they are related to (e.g., 'justice' or 'ordinary people' means different things for Conservatives and Socialists). These moments are called 'floating signifiers', to capture their contested and ambiguous character (Laclau, 2005: 131; see also the description of semantic struggles over keywords in Chapter 7). Some floating signifiers, like 'progress' or 'democracy' are so ubiquitous that it is hard to think of any contemporary political project that does not try to claim them (Laclau, 1990: 28).

Human subjects are also defined through discourse. Discourses provide *subject positions* that shape our understanding of who we are (Laclau and Mouffe, 1985: 115).

Table 6.1 Key analytical concepts in PDT

Analytical concept	Definition
Articulation	Social practice through which a relation is instituted between moments, thus modifying and fixing their meaning.
Moment	Any category or identity that has been temporarily fixed through articulation.
Logic of equivalence	The practice of highlighting similarities between a group of moments to form 'chains of equivalence'. This intensifies their difference from other identities, creating an 'us' and a 'them'.
Logic of difference	The practice of breaking up a chain of equivalence by emphasising the differences between its constituent moments.
Nodal point/node	Privileged signifier that structures a discourse by acting as stabilising hub.
Empty signifier	Nodal point that comes to represent a whole chain of equivalence and serve to polarise the social space.
Floating signifier	An ambiguous signifier that different political forces struggle to capture and impart a fixed meaning to in their own discourses.
Hegemony	Situation in which a discourse is taken for granted, hard to question and accepted as common sense.
Sedimentation	The process in which established discursive practices becomes inscribed into for example laws, norms, routines, organisational patterns, etc.
Constitutive outside	The radically excluded outside or 'Other' that provides meaning to the inside. The 'them' that defines 'us'.
Antagonism	The experience of ultimate contingency/the inevitable failure of discursive closure. Often expressed as animosity towards the 'Other'.
Dislocation	Event or phenomenon that cannot be represented within a hegemonic discourse, thus challenging the existing order by revealing its contingency and foundational antagonism.
Reactivation	The process in which a sedimented practice becomes a point of contestation.
Subject positions	Discursively determined identities for people.

We live our lives through these subject positions. They enable and constrain our actions and provide a filter through which we see the world (Smith, 2003: Chapter 3). However, there is a degree of mobility in discourse, as a consequence of the ultimate instability of the social structure (Howarth, 2010: 314). Moreover, there are always multiple subject positions available to the same person – e.g., 'Christian', 'woman', 'environmentalist' or 'parent'.

How to use PDT concepts in empirical analysis

To use the concepts outlined above as tools for empirical analysis, they need to be operationalised. Often, this involves formulating analytical questions that can be posed to the empirical material. Ultimately, these questions depend on the aims and purpose of the study, but for some inspiration, consider the following questions:

- What categories and identities ('moments') are produced in your empirical material and how are they delimited from each other?
- Which moments are articulated together in 'chains of equivalence'? How does this affect the meaning of the affected moments?
- What 'outside' are they contrasted against? How is the meaning of both the outside and the inside affected by this 'antagonistic' relationship?
- Is any particular category used as an 'empty signifier' to represent a larger group of identities (e.g., used as a synonym or a symbol for a movement or cause)?
- Are any signifiers 'floating' - i.e., contested and imbued with different meanings? If so, what do they mean in each discourse? What other moments are they related to in each discourse and how does this change their meaning?
- How do different discourses respond to and affect each other? Are any attempts made to break up opposing chains of equivalence - e.g., by claiming to represent the same identities or demands? This would be an instance of the 'logic of difference'.
- What is taken for granted, considered common sense or even institutionalised ('sedimented') into formal rules?
- What human identities are produced in your material? How do these 'subject positions' affect how subjects understand themselves? How does this positioning enable and constrain their actions (e.g., what is expected, rewarded, considered typical or forbidden for a particular group of subjects, such as 'men' or 'civil servants')?

'The Gezi Park protests': hegemony, resistance and chains of equivalence

A good example of PDT in action can be found in political scientist Ayşem Mert's (2019) analysis of the protests that began in Istanbul's Gezi Park at the end of May 2013 and spread across Turkey during the summer.

The protests started as a reaction against the plan to uproot the trees of the symbolic Gezi Park and replace it with a shopping mall. But they soon turned into a mass movement of popular resistance against the government of Recep Tayyip Erdoğan and his Justice and Development Party (JDP), with its hyper-developmentalist policies, ill-planned mega-projects, authoritarian tendencies and police repression (Mert, 2019: 593).

Mert analyses interviews with protesters to explore how a discourse of popular resistance against the JDP government emerged, symbolised by the park and its trees. The study maps out the JDP discourse as well, using statements and articles in the media, in order to show how the discourse of the protesters and the JDP discourse interacted and shaped each other. In the following discussion, we highlight how Mert uses concepts from PDT to explore these struggles over meaning.

The logic of equivalence and the formation of popular resistance

The Gezi Park protests soon came to incorporate other movements of resistance against the JDP and its authoritarianism. By analysing how interviewees described the protest movement, the different identities and demands that it came to encompass, and how they related to each other and to the JDP, Mert shows how the scope of the protests expanded. A chain of equivalence was formed that included different identities, demands and groups that had not collaborated before but became unified in their opposition to JDP: the Republican elite, progressive liberals, anti-capitalist Muslims, LGBTQ activists, movements for Kurdish emancipation, feminists, environmental NGOs and many more. As one of the interviewees expressed it:

> I saw an older Republican woman and radical Kurdish leftists dancing together and thought 'only Erdoğan could bring together these people who wouldn't in a million years meet each other, let alone share a political platform'. Everyone was acting in their own way, but together. People saw these differences but kept talking to each other. I wondered whether this unity could only be organised thanks to an enemy figure such as Erdoğan, or could the Gezi spirit be maintained without him? Gezi brought together all those people 'othered' by the administration. (Mert, 2019: 602)

As the quote illustrates, this unity depended on the constitutive outside of Erdoğan and the JDP government. The differences between different groups of protesters became less important than their shared antagonism towards their common enemy, who prevented them 'from being totally themselves' (Mert, 2019: 603). Due to the socioecologically harmful hyper-developmentalism of this 'Other', the chain of equivalence came to include both nature and people. Erdoğan was charged with draining the life out of 'Istanbul', 'nature' and 'the people', thus tying these moments to the discourse of the protest movement (Mert, 2019: 601).

All the moments in the protesters' chain of equivalence came to be represented by the empty signifier of Gezi Park and its trees. As a symbol for the resistance against JDP, the trees of the park did not primarily represent the demand to protect them from destruction, but came to stand in for the whole protest movement and its antagonistic relation to the government (Mert, 2019: 601). A crucial event was the decision to stop using banners from political parties, in order to increase the appeal of the protests. As Mert argues, this was an instance of 'emptying out the signifier "Gezi Park"' (2019: 600). This highlights the blurring of identities that is inherent in the logic of equivalence and empty signifiers – Gezi Park could not have represented the whole movement if it was too closely associated with a specific moment, such as a political party.

The JDP's response

Mert also covers JDP's response to the protests by analysing how Erdoğan addressed the protests in public and how the interviewees reacted to his statements and the repression that followed. Typically, hegemonic powers respond to challenges by relying on the logic of difference. In this case, the ruling party could have undermined the emergent protest coalition by leaving the park untouched or by incorporating the demands of some groups in the hegemonic discourse. Divide and conquer, in short. However, for various reasons harking back to the JDP's populist roots, it chose to employ a logic of equivalence of its own, describing protesters as 'looters', 'leftists' and 'terrorists', and resorting to violence. This only served to solidify the opposition. The protesters could even appropriate a signifier such as 'looter' and use it ironically (Mert, 2019: 603). Calling oneself a 'looter' became just another way to represent the antagonistic polarisation between the protesters and the government.

Dislocation and the sedimentation of resistance

The protests created a dislocation that the government failed to adapt to. The antagonism that it made visible could not be covered over and several important groups that had supported JDP turned against it. The equivalential chain of the protests weakened the equivalential chain of the hegemonic discourse (Mert, 2019: 604).

JDP's hegemony was also undermined by an increased political consciousness and numerous post-Gezi protests. The protests became sedimented, institutionalised in the organisation of neighbourhood councils and continuous resistance to hyper-developmentalist projects. In this particular case, it was not the practices of the establishment that became sedimented, as is often assumed in PDT, but those of the protestors (Mert, 2019: 604).

Lessons from the study of protest

Mert's study illustrates that PDT is not only about hegemony and oppression, but also about popular resistance, collective identity formation, counter-hegemonic struggle and change. One thing that makes the study particularly valuable is that it pays attention to the discourses both of the protesters and of the hegemonic JDP, which allows us to understand how they interacted and shaped each other.

Another lesson to be learned from Mert's study is that PDT does not necessarily have to engage in detailed linguistic analysis of particular texts or the exact wording and grammar of discourse (even if such an approach could be relevant, depending on the research question). It often takes a broader view, looking at how different identities are formed, the links between them and the struggles over them. This sets PDT apart from approaches with a more distinct linguistic orientation, such as critical discourse studies (see Chapter 7).

Discursive psychology

The second poststructural discourse analytic approach, discursive psychology, emerged as a reaction to more conventional psychological approaches during the 1990s. This school of thought put into question the existence of purely 'inner' psychological processes (Potter and Wetherell, 1987; Wetherell and Potter, 1992; Harré, 1995; Billig, 1997). Instead, phenomena such as beliefs, memories or attitudes were seen as constituted through discursive practices, implying that psychological entities were socially constructed. Billig exemplifies this with the act of rudeness, and states that:

> [t]he temptations of impoliteness do not stand outside the dialogic process, but are constituted within it. The desires to be rude, to contradict, 'to speak one's mind', to have done with the constraints of politeness are formed within dialogue. Such desires cannot antedate, nor stand outside, the constrictions of politeness. In this respect, it makes sense to talk of the unconscious being dialogically constituted. (Billig, 1997: 151)

Today, discursive psychology is used in a wide range of social science settings and takes a broad interest in understanding how social actions are accomplished in interaction. Issues that have been analysed with this approach range from how identities and group identities are negotiated and established, to how 'facts' are used rhetorically by politicians. In this chapter, we mainly base our presentation in the work of Margaret Wetherell and Jonathan Potter (1992). Their analysis of racist discourse in New Zealand has received considerable attention and offers a range of analytical concepts to be used in the empirical mapping of existing discourses.

The interpretive repertoire – a small-scale discourse

In discursive psychology, analysts often focus on the micro-details of text and interaction. This small-scale focus is also evident in the way discursive psychologists conceptualise discourse. In contrast to Laclau and Mouffe's focus on broad and overarching social discourses, discursive psychologists emphasise variation and point out that human interaction is often characterised by competing views and conflicting meaning-making practices (Wetherell, 1998).

This way of looking at meaning as something fragmented is captured by the core concept of *interpretative repertoires*. These repertoires can be seen as relatively small-scale and bounded discourses that represent different ways of making sense of a practice or a phenomenon in a certain sphere of society. An interpretative repertoire consists of 'a recognizable routine of arguments, descriptions and evaluations distinguished by familiar clichés, common places, tropes and characterisations of actors and situations. Such repertoires become evident through repetition across a corpus' (Edley and Wetherell, 2001: 443). The researcher's task, therefore, is to identify the recurring descriptions, metaphors and arguments that make up the repertoires that people employ to make sense of the world. If, for example, members of a particular ethnic group are represented in four different distinguishable ways – with their associated descriptions, evaluations and familiar clichés – four different interpretative repertoires are understood to be present in the material (see, for example, Wetherell and Potter, 1992). When an interpretive repertoire has been identified in the material, it is important to clarify the specific building blocks of the repertoire. The reader wants to see, for example, the recurring definitions, metaphors or descriptions that together constitute the repertoire.

Actors matter
The concept of interpretive repertoire also implies a different view of the subject's agency compared to what we encountered in PDT. As people often have access to multiple interpretive repertoires, they typically face a choice between, and start from, different representations and understandings. This discourse analytic approach thus sees individuals as both producers of, and produced by, discourses, whereas Laclau and Mouffe see subjects primarily as products of discourses (Jørgensen and Phillips, 2002: 7). In this way, Wetherell and Potter emphasise that discourses should not be seen as independent causal agents (Wetherell and Potter, 1992: 90; Wetherell, 1998: 395). Instead, they argue that individuals use existing perceptions creatively and flexibly to create, modify or reproduce their interpretive repertoires.

This focus on people's strategic use of interpretive repertoires and the ongoing struggles to legitimate or challenge existing perspectives is inspired by rhetoric and conversation analysis (see, for example, Duranti and Goodwin, 1992; Sacks, 1992). Language use is seen as action-oriented and driven by a will to achieve specific ends. This means that the interpretive repertoires themselves cannot fully determine how they are used. Rather, they are 'available as resources to be used in a range of contrasting and sometimes surprising ways' (Wetherell and Potter, 1992: 93).

These starting points can be exemplified by Nigel Edley and Margaret Wetherell's (2001) study of how men construct feminism and feminists. By analysing men's discourses on feminism and feminists, Edley and Wetherell uncovered two competing interpretive repertoires. The first was a liberal-feminist repertoire, built around recurring descriptions of feminists as women who strive for equality. The second repertoire, feminism as extremism, was more complex and built around a larger number of recurring descriptions. In addition to 'extremism', arguments and value judgements about irrationality, anger and exaggerated feelings figured prominently in this repertoire. Together, these descriptions construed feminism as something unreasonable or excessive, antithetical to a balanced, reasonable and healthy equality (Edley and Wetherell, 2001: 446). What the existence of these two interpretative repertoires implies is that there is no ready-made understanding of what 'feminism' and 'feminists' are. Instead, there are a number of existing meaning-clusters available, and men may use these clusters/repertoires in different and unpredictable ways.

Subject positions in discursive psychology

As noted, discursive psychologists emphasise the flexible use of interpretative repertoires. In a similar vein, it is an open question whether subjects will identify themselves with the subject positions a particular repertoire provides. According to this school of thought, a subject position is a particular identity that an interpretative repertoire invites individuals to accept as their own. Subject positions represent '"locations" within a conversation … the identities made relevant by specific ways of talking' (Edley, 2001: 210). However, this does not mean that people's identities are simply determined by the way others talk about them. A repertoire may define a specific subject position, but there is always room for negotiation about the meaning of the position, and the position can be denied or resisted. This can be described as the constant existence of subject positions 'in play' (Edley, 2001: 222). Thus, even if the interpretive repertoire 'feminism as extremism' constructs feminists as 'ugly women', 'lesbians' or 'man-haters', it is unlikely that many women would adopt this subject position as their own.

This view of agency and negotiation is also relevant to how people position themselves. Our identities can be seen as created in internalised dialogues consisting both of discourses that position us based on specific categorisations (Gergen, 1994) and of our own active use of available discourses. Therefore, when analysing self-representations, we need to focus on the rhetorical organisation of text and talk to pinpoint how subjects employ existing discursive resources to constitute themselves as particular kinds of subjects. In the study of men's construction of feminism, for instance, one of the interviewees tries to distance himself from the interpretive repertoire of feminism as extremism while reproducing it at the same time. When asked about his understanding of feminism, he starts off a detailed discussion about how other men see feminism as extreme, while he sees feminism as equality. This allows him to position himself as a modern 'reconstructed' man rather than as a troublesome sexist (Edley and Wetherell, 2001: 445).

Thus, discursive psychology underlines interaction, rhetoric and competing versions of reality. But at the same time, discursive psychologists also stress how these processes always take place within broader spheres of meaning. For example, the interpretive repertoires that the interviewees put forward about feminism and feminists only become meaningful in relation to an overarching rationality in which women are seen as subordinate. In this way, discursive psychology is clearly influenced by Foucault's general understanding of the role of discourse in the creation of objects and subjects (Wetherell and Potter, 1992: 89).

In summary, discursive psychologists have tried to reach a middle position between emphasising the patterns of shared perceptions of reality on one hand, and pointing out that actors have the possibility to use these creatively in specific contexts on the other hand. This may be understood as an ambition to combine a more detailed conversational analysis with a broader Foucauldian poststructuralist approach (Wetherell and Edley, 1999: 338).

Power and ideology as objects of study in discursive psychology

Discursive psychologists have also taken an interest in power relations – for example, by focusing on the so-called ideological effects that the use of specific interpretive repertoires can have. Here, discursive psychologists draw on Foucault's view of power as something that operates through knowledge – i.e., through the creation of new categorisations of people (Wetherell and Potter, 1992: 83). Based on such an understanding, discourses can establish, maintain and reinforce oppressive power relations over those who are defined or categorised by the discourse (Wetherell and Potter, 1992: 70).

From this perspective, ideologies can be studied as situated practices. Analysing ideological effects means analysing how exploitation, power inequalities and oppressive identities are legitimised and reproduced through the use of specific interpretive repertoires (Wetherell and Potter, 1992: 103). Returning to the example of men's constructions of feminists and feminism, we can conclude that these constructions were related to ideological effects through the power relations they tend to reproduce. By legitimising and reproducing a disqualification of feminism and feminists, the prevailing power inequality between the sexes was reproduced.

How to use concepts from discursive psychology in empirical analysis

One way of making the analytical concepts from discursive psychology easy to apply in empirical research is to reformulate them as analytical questions that can be posed directly to the empirical material. Consider the following questions as a few guidelines:

- What ways of making sense of a particular group, event, or phenomenon (interpretative repertoires) can be found in the material? What recurring descriptions, arguments, tropes, clichés or metaphors define these patterns of sense-making?
- What kind of individuals or subjects are people represented to be in these discussions (subject positions)?
- How do people represent themselves in the discussions? And/or how do people actively dismiss proposed representations or subject positions (self positions)?
- To what extent do these repertoires and representations overlap, contradict, reinforce or undermine each other, and how do participants make use of these discursive resources to achieve particular results (action orientation)?
- How are specific representations constructed in relation to broader spheres of meaning? How are broader discourses evident in the small-scale repertoires (the middle position between patterns of shared perceptions of reality, and the creative language-use)?
- Do these representations and positions challenge or reinforce current patterns of power and domination (ideological effects)?

'Authentic engineers': an analysis of interpretative repertoires and positioning of selves

Silfver et al. (2021) have used discursive psychology to analyse how female engineering students present themselves as 'authentic' engineers in Swedish higher education. The authors explore how female university students' ability to present themselves as 'authentic' engineers is affected by discursive constructions of gender equality, gender and other social categories. More specifically, they take an interest in how female students position themselves within a (masculine) engineering context and how the overarching Swedish gender equality discourse influences their chances to position themselves (Silfver et al., 2021: 924). The material of the study consists of in-depth interviews and video diaries.

Three interpretative repertoires and the subject positions they create
In line with the focus of discursive psychology on small-scale discourses and variation, the authors are interested in analysing how the students draw upon different, sometimes conflicting, repertoires. The researchers identify three such repertoires in the students' talk about their situation as women in a male-dominated environment. Even though not explicitly stated in the article, this kind of work typically requires deep familiarity with the data garnered through a series of readings and rereadings of the material. Edley (2001: 199) describes this probing as a way of gradually recognising patterns across talk or texts. When the same kinds of arguments, images, metaphors and figures of speech are repeated in the material, we have identified an interpretative repertoire.

The first identified repertoire is called 'Women and men have the same value' and highlights the common assumption that women and men today are equally valued in workplaces as well as in higher education (Silfver et al., 2021: 929). This repertoire is held together by a general focus on things being 'fine' and that there are 'no problems' relating to gender in engineering class. According to the logic of this repertoire, gender does not matter; schools and workplaces are about individuals rather than gendered structures, and it is considered non-problematic for women to enter the male-dominated arena of engineering.

The next repertoire is called 'Gender equal representation', and focuses on the benefits of getting more women into the field of engineering. An increased proportion of women is described as something desired by the field and engineering education is described as advantageous for women (Silfver et al., 2021: 932). Women are described as 'needed' for the particular skills and experiences they can bring to the field.

The last interpretative repertoire is called 'A new generation'. Here, the hesitation and the potential sliding of meaning implicit in the other repertoires become more evident. In line with the discourse's psychological focus on instability, variation and contradictions, the authors focus on the respondents' tendency to hesitate and oscillate between different descriptions of their situation. This reveals that underneath the general representation of the field as gender equal, the students expressed some uncertainty about their prospects as women in engineering. For example, the students acknowledge that they have met sexist jokes about women being weaker than men, but in order to uphold the idea that gender is a non-problem, they may at the same time claim that the jokes were accurate rather than belittling or discriminatory.

It is significant for this repertoire that the awareness of sexist behaviour does not lead women to abandon the idea of an existing gender equal society. Instead, the cause of the unfulfilled ambition of gender equality is attributed to an older generation of men. To the extent that gender hierarchies remain in Sweden, their cause is located in old-fashioned ideas held by some men who are out of sync with the modern world. When these men finally retire, then we will have full gender equality (Silfver et al., 2021: 933–4). There is a parallel to be drawn here to PDT – gender equality is portrayed as blocked by a constitutive outside, an 'Other' in the form of an older generation of men.

The ambivalence about women's presence in the engineering culture is also evident in the subject positions made visible within these repertoires. For example, the authors note a 'mum' position and a 'boy' position that illustrate how women are restricted to limited roles. When discussing how the female students may approach the male students, the women concede that they need to adjust their behaviour in order to fit in. To fit in the 'boy' position, for instance, a female student has to act like 'one of the guys' to become a legitimate member of the student group. Therefore, when a female student counter-identifies with traditional femininity, it becomes less problematic to be one of the few women in the male-dominated environment of engineering (Silfver et al., 2021: 931–2).

The dual influence of the Swedish gender equality discourse

In their results, the authors show how the overarching Swedish gender equality discourse tends to influence the talk of the female students. On one hand, this discourse encourages the students to position themselves as just as good engineers as their male counterparts. On the other hand, the same discourse bars them from acknowledging their subjection to discrimination and sexism. Since there is a general understanding of Sweden as a gender equal country, contradicting experiences have to be explained as remnants from the past. In this way, power issues might be hidden or downplayed. The assumed gender equality makes us unable to see or problematise instances where gender and power still operate, since the overarching discourse stipulates that women and men today are treated as individuals of equal worth:

> [There is a] dilemma in how a perceived gender neutrality implied by the gender equality discourse can obscure remaining obstacles for women in engineering. Here, a 'no problem' position that participants take across the three repertoires signals a desire to uphold the vision of gender equality that Sweden constructs, but obscures gender troubled positions in engineering, as it so strongly assumes that Swedish women's position in engineering ought to be untroubled. (Silfver et al., 2021: 935-7)

The 'What's the problem represented to be?' approach (WPR)

The third form of poststructural discourse analysis we want to introduce is Carol Bacchi's 'What's the problem represented to be?' approach (hereafter, the WPR approach). This approach is heavily influenced by Michel Foucault's view of discourses as *'socially produced forms of knowledge* that set limits upon what is possible to think, write or speak' (Bacchi and Goodwin, 2016: 35, emphasis in original). Thus, the approach seeks to analyse how certain ways of making sense of an issue are created and legitimised as the correct or reasonable understanding, and the effects of this in terms of policy.

The WPR approach is originally a method for poststructuralist policy analysis (Bacchi and Goodwin, 2016). It was conceived as a way to deconstruct the inherent logic of policy texts such as legislative proposals, government enquiries or policy initiatives (Bacchi, 1999, 2012, 2009a). Over time, however, the WPR approach has come to be used in other fields and on other materials. Today, material such as media extracts, interview transcripts and legislative debates are frequently analysed using the WPR framework.[2]

Problem representations and their effects

In line with the theory of the construction of social problems (e.g., Spector and Kitsuse, 1977; Best, 1995), the starting point of this approach is that there is never an obvious or fixed way of looking at 'social problems' or their solutions. Rather, competing understandings of these issues arise from different discourses and, most importantly, from different *problem representations* (Bacchi, 2009a: 7, 35). For something to appear as a social or political 'problem', it must first be framed *as* a problem (and as a *particular kind* of problem at that). Take, for example, the issue of women's underrepresentation on company boards. The mere observation that there are fewer women than men in the boardrooms is not enough to render the situation problematic. It is only within a particular discourse that the situation will take on the character of a 'problem'. Moreover, different discourses will produce different problematisations. For example, one discourse may frame women's underrepresentation as a skills problem that can be ameliorated by, for example, mentor or leadership programmes, while another discourse presents the issue as an act of discrimination, which implies entirely different solutions (e.g., quotas). Some may even emphatically deny that there is a problem at all (cf. Bacchi, 2016: 1). The way an issue is problematised also has further consequences. For example, competing ways of understanding women's underrepresentation creates different subject positions for women. While the first problem representation frames women as 'insufficiently educated or competent', the second constructs them as 'competent but discriminated against'.

---

[2] In three entries on her website (https://carolbacchi.com), Bacchi herself considers how to apply WPR to these alternative sources (30 April 2021; 31 May 2021; 30 June 2021).

Because of the important effects the competing perspectives might have, the WPR approach emphasises the need to critically examine and analyse these 'problematisations' or 'problem representations' rather than taking problems for granted (Bacchi, 1999: 9–10; Bacchi, 2009a: xi–xiii). Of course, arguing that 'problems' have no objective basis does not mean denying the possible negative effects of the issue in question (see, e.g., Bacchi, 2009a: 17–18). The point is rather to make visible that these phenomena can be perceived and interpreted in different ways and that the effects brought about could have been different; other problem representation could have resulted in other 'winners' and 'losers'. Analysing problem representations can therefore access the link between discourses and the concrete effects that discourses are likely to have. As Bacchi (2009a: 35) puts it: '[d]iscourses accomplish things. They make things happen, most often through their truth status'.

Analytical questions

Unlike many other discourse theoretical approaches, the WPR approach offers very concrete guidelines for practical research. In order to analytically 'unearth' and make visible the problem representations Bacchi proposes that researchers ask the following analytical questions when working through their material (the list is modified after Bacchi 2009a: 48; Bacchi and Goodwin, 2016: 20):

- What's the 'problem' - for example, of 'problem gamblers', 'drug use/abuse', 'gender inequality', 'domestic violence', 'global warming', 'sexual harassment', etc. - represented to be in a specific policy or policy proposal?
- What presuppositions or assumptions underpin this representation of the 'problem'?
- How has this representation of the 'problem' come about?
- What is left unproblematic in this problem representation? Where are the silences? Can the 'problem' be thought about differently?
- What effects (discursive, subjectifying/objectifying, lived) are produced by this representation of the 'problem'?
- How/where has this representation of the 'problem' been produced, disseminated and defended? How has it been (or could it be) questioned, disrupted and replaced?

It is important to note that this analytical strategy requires multiple applications of the analytical questions and repeated readings of the material (Bacchi, 2015: 133). It should also be stressed that familiarity with the empirical material is not enough. The researcher also needs an insight into relevant previous research to fully answer the analytical questions and to place the results in a meaningful context.

In relation to how to structure the analysis, one can choose whether to conduct the analysis in a holistic way and answer the analytical questions continuously and integrated, or to structure the analysis according to the questions and answer them in a separate order (Bacchi, 2015: 133). On one hand, a holistic form may offer the analyst a larger room for manoeuvre, but on the other hand it risks leaving the reader without full insight into all steps of the analysis and without seeing how the analytical tool is applied in concrete terms.

The first analytical question (*What's the problem represented to be?*) is about making visible how the 'problem' is understood or classified in the material. Here, the analysis often proceeds 'backwards' (Bacchi, 2009a: 3). By examining how someone wishes to reform a particular condition, we can identify how this condition is fundamentally understood. In relation to the example on women's underrepresentation, this question aims to make visible whether women's underrepresentation is understood, for example, as a skills problem or a discrimination problem.

The second question is about examining the underlying logic of the problem representation by looking at what is taken for granted. The focus is on what makes a specific reform possible and intelligible, and the question involves a critical examination of what is understood as so obvious that it does not even prompt reflection. In relation to women's underrepresentation, this might be notions like fair competition or functioning meritocracy: we imagine from these presuppositions that whoever is best suited for a job will get it, ignoring the possibility of discrimination.

The third question focuses on the historical context and the way in which past events have contributed to the current problematisation. What has happened in the past that makes this representation appear as the only reasonable one today? The aim of the question is 'to highlight the conditions that allow a particular problem representation to take shape and to assume dominance' (Bacchi, 2009a: 11), meaning that the researcher may incorporate broader material and structural factors into the analysis. With regard to the underrepresentation of women on company boards, one could examine, among other things, the discourses that have traditionally surrounded the business world and the way in which issues of gender representation in the private sector have been regulated historically.

The fourth question focuses on what falls outside the boundaries of the problem representation. The aim of this question will thus be to highlight perspectives that do not emerge in the current problem representation. For example, in relation to our case, one could examine whether the overrepresentation of men is problematised, or whether it is simply seen as the 'natural order' of things.

The fifth question focuses on the effects that the problem representation in question is likely to produce. Bacchi calls these different types of effects *discursive, subjectifying* and *lived* effects (Bacchi, 2009a: 40). On the basis that problem representations establish a certain understanding of what is problematic, certain reforms or courses of action will appear as more or less reasonable and desirable. These are 'discursive effects'. For example, if we imagine a problem representation that assumes that women have the wrong skills to serve on corporate boards, does it make sense to propose reforms that focus on getting men to question gender-coded notions of competence?

Problem representations also create specific subject positions, which have concrete implications for those who inhabit them. These are 'subjectifying effects'. The specific way in which a particular discourse represents or shapes a problem also implies a set of specific social relations. Problem representations invite or trick us to identify with these social ontologies, a process that invariably turns us into 'subjects *of a particular kind*' (Bacchi, 2009a: 16, italics in original). Using the example of women's underrepresentation on corporate boards, we note that for a woman in business, whether she is understood (and understands herself) as discriminated against or as in need of training has significant consequences.

A recent development in the approach is Bacchi's inclusion of *objectification* effects in the analysis. The point is to highlight how not only human identities, but also the identities of objects that we typically take for granted, including places, are constituted through problem representations. This allows for an analysis of the emergence and effects of objects and places such as 'democracy', 'traffic' and 'the Western world' (Bacchi, 2022).

The last part of the fifth analysis question is about 'lived effects' – i.e., the material effects that problem representations generate. Discourses are not just 'words and talk' – they affect people's lives in highly concrete ways (Bacchi, 2009a: 17). An important aspect of this last question is to 'confront head-on the suggestion that poststructural forms of analysis are nihilistic and/or relativistic – that they do not permit assessment of governmental interventions' (Bacchi, 2021: 10). Among other things, the categorisations that a particular problem representation generates may impact people's access to different types of welfare services. Whether women in business are understood as discriminated against or inadequately educated, for example, may determine if they are able to obtain redress or other compensation.

The sixth analytical question focuses on how and where the particular representations of the 'problem' have been produced and defended, but also on how they have been (or could be) questioned, disrupted and replaced. The goal is 'to develop a sharpened awareness of the forms of power involved in the shaping of problem representations' (Bacchi, 2021: 23) – i.e., to identify the contestation surrounding various problem representations. It can also draw attention to the contradictions and ambiguities within a dominant problem representation and how they can be used to challenge it. As a last note on our example of underrepresentation of women in business, this question may illustrate how and where different understandings of the problem have clashed.

WPR scholars stress that a final and important step in the analysis is to apply these six questions to one's own problem representations. As we are all located within the limits of culturally and historically specific discourses, we need to adopt a critical stance towards our own reasoning, including our own problematisations (Bacchi and Goodwin, 2016: 24). The need for reflexivity is often repeated within qualitative social science, but WPR intends to do more than pay lip service to it: 'the WPR approach moves beyond easy-to-make declarations of the need to become "reflexive" to endorse a precise and demanding activity – subjecting one's own recommendations and proposals to a WPR analysis' (Bacchi and Goodwin, 2016: 24).

'Alcohol problems': a study of problematisations and how they affect us

Here, the WPR approach is illustrated by Carol Bacchi's own analysis of how 'alcohol problems' are problematised by the World Health Organization (WHO). In line with her assumption that 'problems' are never simply neutral descriptions, Bacchi strives to open up the taken-for-granted category of 'alcohol problem' and map what it means in the WHO discourse (Bacchi, 2015: 130–1). Bacchi is thus interested in how the term 'alcohol problem' is conceptualised by the WHO, how this underlying problematisation has come about and what effects it might have in terms of governing individuals.

The materials used in the article are formal WHO policy documents that are repeatedly read to tease out the problem representations that are embedded or nested within them. Consistent with the analytical strategy of the WPR approach, Bacchi uses the previously described analytical questions to address how the problem representations are embedded in each other (Bacchi, 2015: 138). For the sake of clarity, however, we will discuss only one of the existing problem representations in the following.

Applying the analytical questions in order to identify and analyse problem representations

In line with the first analytical question – what the 'problem' of alcohol is represented to be – Bacchi initially recognises that it is framed as a 'problem of availability'; it is too easy for people to find and consume alcohol. Bacchi reaches this conclusion by 'working backwards'. Starting from the proposed solutions, she identifies the underlying problem that the solutions are intended to fix. Again, what we decide to do about something indicates what we think needs to change. In this case, the preferred policy solutions are to impose limitations of outlets, limitations of opening hours and ensuring higher prices for alcoholic beverages (Bacchi, 2015: 135).

Turning to the second analytical question, Bacchi attends to the underlying assumptions of this problematisation. These assumptions are not explicitly stated, meaning that it is an analytical task to tease out the logic behind the recommended interventions. In this case, the policy rests on the assumption that individuals need to be steered away from consuming alcohol (via higher prices) and influenced to make better choices (Bacchi, 2015: 137). The 'problem', in other words, is primarily conceived as a matter of individual weakness, and it is individuals rather than societies that need to be reformed.

The article also addresses the third question about how the particular problem representation has evolved. Here, Bacchi prioritises the particular practices that were involved in the production of the problem as a matter of availability. This ambition lies close to Michel Foucault's (1977) genealogical approach, where the aim is to trace 'the multitude of heterogeneous factors leading to a specific development'

(Bacchi, 2015: 139). We cannot describe the historical roots that Bacchi uncovers in detail here, but the article identifies several influences such as medical frameworks and sociological frameworks that have played important roles in establishing contemporary problem representations. In the process, Bacchi highlights how research also is a political practice involved in governing processes (Bacchi, 2015: 141).

Bacchi is also interested in the silences – the discussions and arguments that are absent and the topics that remain unproblematised – within the WHO's discourse on alcohol. Since the dominant problem representation privileges certain assumptions over others, an important part of this work is to shed light on the logics and arguments that *could have* been present. By asking what is left out of the problem representation, we can visualise how certain larger social, economic and political issues are neglected. A problematisation that underlines the need to control the availability of alcohol, for example, tends to see alcohol consumption as an individual issue rather than a collective issue. Such a policy would target individual choices rather than the contextual factors surrounding, influencing or even producing the choices. Moreover, in a problem representation centring on individual choice, alcohol use is easily seen as a cause of individual problems such as poverty and unemployment. However, in a problem representation that puts focus on structural factors, it would rather be the other way around: problems such as poverty and unemployment would be seen as the cause of the alcohol problem, and consequently those situations would be the ones targeted by the policy makers (Bacchi, 2015: 137).

More than just words
These findings connect to the next analytical question about the effects of the problem representations. As previously described, these effects can be divided into discursive, subjectifying and lived effects. Starting with the discursive effects, we have already implied that the understanding of alcohol use as an individual choice tends to sideline questions about broader social change and reduce the space of reform to issues like opening hours and influencing individual customer choices.

Turning to the subject positions that are established through the problem representation, Bacchi states that the focus on availability produces subjects that 'lack either the willpower to resist the alcohol on offer or the strength of character to ignore peer pressure' (Bacchi, 2015: 136). Individuals are held responsible for determining the risks of their drinking habits (Bacchi, 2015: 140) and if they do not make sound choices they only have themselves to blame.

Steps in a discourse analysis

Regardless of which approach one choses, there are a number of steps that have to be considered when conducting a poststructural discourse analysis. After formulating a research question that is in line with this discourse analytic tradition – e.g., a question about how meaning-making is linked to power – one has to consider what material is needed to answer the question. Unfortunately, discourses are not available for researchers to observe directly. If one has decided to study, for example, the discourse of EU migration policy, one cannot simply go out and 'get' it. Discourses are primarily analytical delimitations, and one must consider and argue for the way in which one intends to delimit and collect manifestations of one's chosen discourse.

What concept of discourse to use and what texts to analyse?
In line with the broad poststructural concept of discourse, a first question to consider is whether to also include non-linguistic practices in the empirical analysis. If so, what would these be and how can they be studied? In the example of the potential study of the discourse of EU migration policy, should non-linguistic practices such as EU's external border control also be included in the analysis?

Second, even if one limits oneself to focusing on semiotic practices such as speech, pictures and written text, it is necessary to further delimit the study. Continuing with the example of EU migration policy discourse, one would need to consider which EU institutions might produce material relating to these issues, whether one should also study the various national arenas and, if so, which national authorities and institutions? Another question is where to draw the line between different issues. A study of the EU migration policy discourse could find important links to discourses around European and national identities, welfare, gender, etc. But it might not be feasible to do a full discourse analysis of all of these issue areas. It is important to clearly state the reasons for a particular selection and to make a plausible argument that the selection can tell us something about the discourse of interest.

Third, it will be important to determine the temporal boundary. What time span must be covered in a study of discursive change? How long a time span can be said to reflect the 'present'? Have there been any major turning points, and should we ensure that we include these in our sample?

Fourth, it is necessary to select the concrete texts that can be assumed to reflect the chosen discourse. Analysing the policy programmes produced by various EU institutions is of course reasonable, but without additional material it may nevertheless give a narrow view of the discourse in question. The selection of texts is also related to the type of discourse in focus – is it, for example, the public discourse in the media that is of interest, or the discourse of policy makers and experts that might be expressed in formal documents? These different choices are crucial, since failure to include a key piece of material raises the question of validity. Are we really capturing the discourse we want to analyse if the material cannot reasonably be said to reflect it? Researchers need to make clear what choices they have made and the selection principles that have prevailed.

How to organise the material overall?

To avoid being overwhelmed by your material, you will probably need a way to create themes or some overall structure in your material. To gain an overview of the material, one could, for example, use a computerised corpus analysis (see Chapter 7) to find out whether the use of certain terms says something about the content of the texts – e.g., whether texts from different actors use different language or whether language use changes over time. You can also do a broad coding of the material to bring out the themes you are particularly interested in, using QDA software for coding (see Chapter 2).

In relation to the Bacchian analysis discussed above, a first thematising step could involve identifying the extent to which the different EU reform proposals address the same migration policy problems, or whether they address different, perhaps partly overlapping, problems. In terms of PDT and discursive psychology, one could similarly start by trying to identify the broader themes in the migration discourse. For example, are the key migration policy discussions about accessing the right skills for the labour market, shutting out criminal networks or securing civil rights? And in what ways might these different ways of discussing the issues be linked?

How to select and use your analytical tools

The most important thing in choosing concrete analytical tools is that they should fit both the research question and the material. If one is interested in studying broader social discourses, PDT is a reasonable choice, while discursive psychology is well suited for analysing micro-discourses and the use of interpretative repertoires in interaction. The WPR approach, finally, is useful for studying policy and expert discourse. It can also be beneficial to combine analytical tools from different approaches.

Before getting into the empirical analysis, one's theories and concepts have to be operationalised – i.e., turned into coding categories or concrete analytical questions that can be posed to the empirical material. Consideration should be given to specifying one's analytical tools and describing how one plans to apply them. From the standpoints of PDT and discursive psychology, for example, one could ask whether there are signs or descriptions that reoccur, and how these signs relate to each other. One could also imagine examining, from all three approaches, the subject positions that emerge within the different themes. For example, are migrants portrayed as 'potential terrorists', 'fleeing asylum seekers' or as 'workers with unique skills'?

Finally, it is important to create transparency. Working with quotations to exemplify the prominent patterns that you have found is a way to both argue for your conclusions and to increase the transparency of the study. Consideration should also be given to the extent to which selected quotations are representative of the material as a whole. Do you select quotes on the basis that they most clearly illustrate your conclusions or because they are the most representative? Moreover, you can increase transparency by making the material as available as possible – for example, by providing information or links that help readers access publicly available material.

Critical reflections

In this section, we revisit the theoretical starting points discussed at the beginning of the chapter and discuss some of their implications. In so doing, we highlight several advantages and challenges of discourse analysis. We also comment on some developments in the discourse analytical approaches that we have described.

Advantages and challenges

As previously discussed, poststructural discourse analysis heavily emphasises the power-laden nature of meaning-making. Discourses define the world and the subjects in it, and affect what people do. But this is not to say that its treatment of power is without problems. A very broad definition of power can become less useful as an analytical tool. Saying that power is everywhere does not help us understand how it operates. However, the approaches covered in the chapter do offer more detailed accounts on how power operates and how to analyse it.

The emphasis on language within discourse analysis can also be seen as a potential problem. If everything is seen as shaped by language, there is no objective reality and no absolute moral principles to hold on to. This has prompted some critics to accuse discourse analysis of ontological and moral relativism. In the wake of the debate about 'alternative facts', for example, critics have charged poststructuralist epistemology with opening up a societal debate in which we no longer can distinguish between facts and lies. Discourse analysts have countered these objections by pointing out that poststructuralism may in fact be our best tool for understanding and interpreting these struggles over social reality. Poststructuralism, after all, is not about imposing a particular set of alternative facts but a way of analysing how 'facts' are constructed to begin with. Moreover, judging from humanity's track record in establishing absolute truths, a perspective that acknowledges the contingent character of knowledge is arguably more useful than a positivism that denies it. In this context, it bears emphasising that the burden of proving the existence of transhistorical, extra-discursive truths falls on the essentialists who imply that they can bypass representation and access the world 'as it is'. Discourse analysts do not (and cannot) dismiss the theoretical possibility of such an operation. They do insist, however, that it is up to the essentialists to present positive evidence for their claims – i.e., evidence that is not susceptible to discursive deconstruction.

The accusation of moral relativism can be related to Bacchi's idea that there are only competing representations of problems and no objective problems. According to the critics, such an understanding fails to consider the suffering these phenomena may cause. Take the example of alcohol consumption again: while addiction to alcohol can certainly be problematised in competing ways, the effects on people's health are real regardless of their discursive framing. Bacchi's reply is that the WPR approach in no way denies the existence of causal relationships in the social world, but stresses that we cannot understand, evaluate or address them outside of the representations through which we make sense of them. And considering that these representations determine how we respond to a particular problematic situation it is imperative that they are studied (Bacchi, 1999: 9).

Another criticism, also related to the strong emphasis on the constitutive power of language, is that problems stemming from a material sphere, such as material inequalities in terms of income, risk being deprioritised. To the extent that this is a concern, however, it does not seem to be a concern for discourse analysis alone. There is plenty of research in the humanities and the social sciences, employing a plethora of methods, that is not immediately concerned with material inequalities. Most importantly, however, there is nothing in the poststructuralist outlook that precludes an interest in economic issues. As we have stressed throughout, the three approaches presented here all insist that discourses/interpretative repertoires/problem representations are always intimately bound up with material issues. This means that discourse analytical studies are fully capable of incorporating material aspects in their analysis, even though this possibility is not always used.

The third starting point for discourse analysis was that it focuses on structures over actors. Whether this is a problem or not can be debated, but it has been argued that PDT in particular, but also the WPR approach, reduce the actors to mere products of discourse. Instead of people of flesh and blood acting intentionally, we get subject positions locked in place by structural determinism. Naturally, one answer would be to affirm this objection and say 'Yes – what else would determine subjectivity other than the discursive structure from which the subjects emerge to begin with?' Another answer, however, is that we need to rethink the category of the 'subject' altogether. Rather than assuming that the subject is a fixed, self-contained entity, poststructuralists tend to emphasise that the subject is an open place, permanently lacking in fixity. And it is precisely this lack of closure that allows for the rearticulation and change of structurally 'given' identities, as shown in Mert's (2019) study of the Gezi Park protests in Turkey and the government's response to them.

Where is discourse analysis going?

An attempt to strengthen the scientific status of PDT by adding explanatory claims is referred to as the 'logics approach'. The approach is heavily influenced by psychoanalytical theory. The logics approach does not deal with causal explanations, however. Instead it aims for *retroductive explanations*, meaning that the goal of social science should be to furnish social phenomena with plausible hypotheses for the mechanisms behind their emergence (Glynos and Howarth, 2007: 87). The goal is to provide understanding, not by using pre-existing templates, but by capturing 'the point, rules and ontological preconditions of a practice or regime of practices' through identifying the social, political and fantasmatic logics behind them (Glynos and Howarth, 2008: 32).

In relation to discursive psychology, one can point to the interest in the link between psyche and discourse developed by Wetherell (2012) in her work on emotions and affects. Drawing on the emerging 'affective turn' in social sciences and on theorists like Gilles Deleuze and Baruch Spinoza, Wetherell has pointed out that discourse 'very frequently makes affect powerful, makes it radical and provides the means for affect to travel' (Wetherell, 2012: 19). One can also point to the transition to a stronger focus on naturalistic materials, such as transcripts of courtroom interaction, telephone calls or parliamentary debates. Jonathan Potter (2012) has underlined the powerful role of the interviewer in interview studies, and has therefore proposed a shift to alternative materials.

Since Bacchi's early work (1999), the approach has turned from a constructionist approach focused on how problems are conceived, to centring on practices and performativity – i.e., how policies and other practices produce particular representations of problems (Bacchi, 2021: 7). This turn to practice has been accompanied by an increased attention to the Foucauldian concept of governmentality and the specific technologies of government that are used to categorise subjects and objects, such as 'unemployment forms, birth registers, COVID modelling, etc.' (Bacchi, 2021: 7).

Poststructural discourse analysis and the study of society

Like most textual analysts, poststructural discourse theorists assume that texts are important keys to understanding society. Texts – in a broad sense – are products of human meaning-making, and as such they say something about the societies in which they are produced. The task of discourse analysis is to reconstruct, on the basis of concrete texts, the social structures and practices from which the texts emerged. Depending on the specific research question, the focus lies on different aspects of these structures and practices. For example, this may involve examining worldviews, power relations, identity creation, conflicts, communication, patterns of interpretation or ideological systems.

Poststructuralist perspectives differ from some other text analytical approaches by extending the concept of discourse far beyond 'language' in the everyday sense. The linguistic and the material are thought to merge into structured totalities – discourses – from which specific objects and subjects emerge with a distinct meaning.

This anti-essentialist stance makes poststructuralism sceptical of generalisations and positive truth claims. Poststructuralist discourse analysis is more concerned with examining how texts build on and produce historically specific objectivities and truth effects. In essence, there is a critical ambition to show that the discourses that bind us are contingent constructions produced through political struggles.

As we have seen in this chapter, the study of discourses can be approached in different ways. PDT focuses on how objects and subjects gain meaning by being fixed in hegemonic discursive structures. With its focus on equivalences, differences and boundaries, the approach lends itself well to the study of political struggles and collective identity formation – as in the case of the Gezi Park conflict in Turkey. Discursive psychology approaches the practical communication between people and focuses on how they negotiate and try to achieve specific goals by mobilising appropriate interpretative repertoires. As the example of the female engineering students shows, the focus is often on people's attempts to navigate and make sense of meaningfully contingent situations in everyday life. The WPR approach instead emphasises the discursive construction of social and political 'problems'. The focus is often on the policy level and how people are governed by the problematisations produced there.

As we have seen, the three approaches presented here pose different concrete questions to the material to be analysed. But regardless of whether the analysis begins with an examination of chains of equivalence, interpretive repertoires or problem representations, poststructuralist analyses are based on the same core insight into the nature of social studies. People are interpretive, communicative and meaning-making beings who try to make sense of their existence in a world that is inherently lacking in meaning. To understand people and their societies, we need to pay attention to the conditions and consequences of this meaning-making.

Summary

On the usefulness of poststructural discourse analysis

- Poststructural discourse analysis is useful for studying research questions about meaning-making and how struggles over meaning affect, for example, politics, social relations, economy and culture.
- This kind of discourse analysis can be used to study, for example, debates, changes in views over time and their discursive conditions. The focus can be either on the common ground or on tensions and contradictions.
- Poststructural discourse analysis can be used to map identity constructions by, for example, analysing subject positions ('the people', 'Europeans', 'communists').
- Studies of subject positions can integrate issues of power. What scope for action does a particular subject position imply? Who benefits from a particular identity construction and who is disadvantaged?
- Poststructural discourse analysis can also address power issues by studying different types of power orders, such as cultural hegemony or gendered power structures.

How to do it

- The discourse or discourses to be examined must be delimited – for example, in terms of issue area, time period and geographical scope. These delimitations must be in line with the research question.
- The research question also determines the method. As we have seen, an investigation of discourses can be done in different ways using different discourse analytical approaches. As usual, it is important to justify the choice of approach.
- The choice of material is of central importance in defining the discourses and needs to be justified.
- Discourse analytical theories and concepts need to be operationalised into useful analytical tools – e.g., concrete analytical questions that can be posed to the empirical material.
- Since discourse analysis emphasises the importance of language, in which social relations are revealed, the material must be read very carefully. Close reading is often required, as is knowledge of the context (historical, social, political, etc.). Once an overview has been established, the material must be worked through a number of times.
- In discourse analysis, there are different ways of sorting the material. For example, textual content can be structured using overall themes or with the help of more quantitative techniques. Using Qualitative Data Analysis (QDA) software can aid in the process of categorising and coding the material, and keep your analysis grounded in the data. Whichever method is chosen, some initial themes need to be created, which can then be analysed in more detail in the next step.
- In order to gain a deeper understanding of the initial themes identified, the concrete analytical tools are brought in. In a first step, a certain overarching theme may be uncovered and in the next step one can show how this theme is given meaning by, for example, constituting a particular chain of equivalence or problem representation. In this way, the greater depths of the theme can be explored.

Suggested reading

Winther Jørgensen and Phillips (2002) provide a rich and useful account for PDT and discursive psychology. Another illustrative introduction to the general field of discourse analysis can be found in Keller (2013). The book presents a number of discourse analytic approaches in a particularly 'hands-on' way.

For those who wish to read more about PDT, see Smith (2003). The logics approach is covered in Glynos and Howarth (2007, 2008). For empirical applications, see, for example, Persson (2020), and for the relation between PDT and materiality, see Carpentier (2017) and Devenney (2020). Hansen (2014) and Marchart (2018) engage with questions of dislocation and antagonism. For more on how to use PDT for empirical research, see Marttila (2016).

If you want to read texts by Laclau and Mouffe themselves, *Hegemony and Socialist Strategy*, especially Chapter 3, is still a good starting point (Laclau and Mouffe, 1985). Laclau has continued to explore theoretical issues aspects of PDT; see, for example, Laclau (1990, 1996, 2005, 2014). See also Critchley and Marchart (2004). Mouffe has developed the themes of radical democracy and democratic pluralism in several subsequent books (Mouffe, 2000, 2005, 2013, 2018, 2022).

Regarding discursive psychology, books by Potter and Wetherell (1987) and Wetherell and Potter (1992) have played a crucial role in the emergence of the field. For more

(Continued)

(Continued)

'hands-on' guidance, we recommend a chapter by Nigel Edley in Wetherell et al. (2001), containing a pedagogical step-by-step description of how to conduct an empirical analysis. In the same anthology, Mary Horton-Salway presents an alternative approach to discursive psychology. In relation to the authors presented here, Horton-Salway emphasises even more clearly the rhetorical dimension of text and speech.

For detailed descriptions of the WPR approach, see Bacchi (1999, 2009a). These books cover both the theoretical background and the analytical questions that underpin the method. For an even more detailed description of the theoretical background of poststructural policy analysis, see Bacchi and Goodwin (2016). Bletsas and Beasley (2012) offer theoretical and methodological discussions along with empirical applications of the approach. For more applications of the approach, see for example, Bacchi (2016). Carol Bacchi also has a highly informative web page (https://carolbacchi.com) where she has gathered resources such as videos, open access articles and FAQs about the WPR approach.

Exercises

Exercise 1: Chains of equivalence and the representation of 'the Other'

This exercise is about racist and xenophobic discourse. Because of the focus on overarching discourses that define identities and establish power relations, PDT is a suitable approach.

The task

Choose a sign that represents a minority group in your country that is exposed to racism or xenophobic discrimination. Examine how the sign is filled with meaning through its connection with other recurrent moments. Find out whether there are particularly prominent moments in the discourse that might constitute nodal points. It is likely that nodal points do not only anchor the meaning of the minority, but of other moments as well. If the minority is associated with 'unemployment', it is probably tied to a discourse on unemployment that defines other moments as well – for example, related to class and education.

Search for chains of equivalence. An example could be a chain in which the minority is linked with moments such as 'crime', 'terrorism' and 'social upheaval', creating an image of the minority as a threatening 'Other' to society. It could also make sense to analyse how the exclusion of this group acts as a constitutive outside that defines the identity of the whole society. What characteristics are ascribed to 'us' when contrasted to 'them'?

You may also analyse whether this discourse around the minority is hegemonic or if there seems to be a struggle between different discourses. If you find evidence of the existence of a counter-hegemonic discourse, you could analyse the differences in how meaning is created in the two discourses and their relative weight. Are any of the discourses more prominent in certain types of material and how can you back up such a claim empirically?

(Continued)

(Continued)

The texts

First you need to consider what kind of discourse you want to analyse. For analysing public discourse, you could look at articles and statements in the traditional media. It might also make sense to look into the online discourse on internet forums, YouTube channels, etc. You may have to consider if you want to delimit your analysis to written texts, or whether you want to include, for example, images.

Exercise 2: The failure of multiculturalism and the categorisation of peoples

Despite being a societal ideal in several European and other countries for many decades, multiculturalism is today under attack and is claimed to 'have failed' (Nortio et al., 2016). In the light of such an attack, it is relevant to study how immigrants today discuss and negotiate their own group identity. Who are legitimate members of the nation state? What does one need to do in order to belong, and why are some considered insiders while others are considered outsiders?

The task

Examine how newly arrived migrants are categorised by themselves and by the majority population. In line with the theoretical points of departure of discursive psychology, the focus is not only on how people are categorised by existing discourses, but also on how people actively use language to position themselves in relation to existing cultural understandings. In relation to the different subject positions in play, it is therefore interesting to analyse how individuals may try to reject problematic subject positions that are pasted on them.

The texts

Even though it is possible to use written material such as media material or policy documents, the conversation analytical heritage of discursive psychology favours group or individual interviews. In this exercise, it is therefore possible to use open-ended interviews. You may, for example, use focus groups with newly arrived migrants and members of the majority population where you use a couple of prompts such as 'When in Rome, do as the Romans do' to start off the conversation (see, for example, Nortio et al., 2016).

Exercise 3: The problematisation of the 'PISA-crisis'

This exercise is about the search for underlying problem representations in the field of education. Due to an increased accountability culture within the educational field (Teltemann and Jude, 2019), we have witnessed a rise in the number of international testing projects in education (Heyneman and Lee, 2014). Currently, the most prominent example is the Programme for International Student Assessment (PISA), which has become a symbol for the emergence of a new testing and ranking culture. However, the increased focus on PISA scores has also led to intense debates about 'PISA crises' in countries that have witnessed a decrease in their PISA scores. Within these debates, different discourses on education are present. At stake are different perspectives on the purpose of education and different perspectives on the kind of skills and knowledges needed in today's society.

The task

Examine the problem representations that emerge in relation to a country's PISA results. Start by identifying educational policies implemented in order to 'solve' the problem of decreased PISA scores. Then apply some or all of the analytical questions of the WPR approach. For example (question 1), what kind of 'problem' is the PISA drop conceived or understood as? What 'problem' is the reform intended to 'solve'? Is it a 'problem' of individuals lacking sufficient skills in order to live a full and rich life, or is it a 'problem' of countries falling behind in the knowledge-based global economy? In relation to the particular problem representations found, you also might want to know what assumptions underpin such understandings (question 2) and what subject positions are established for students who contribute to the decreased test scores (question 5).

Finally, you may want to compare the problem representations across time or between countries. Are the problematisations – and therefore the discourses – similar or different between different countries? Has there been change over time?

The texts

The texts to be analysed can be formal policy documents from the educational sector, such as law proposals or public guidelines. When selecting policy texts, try to find texts that can be seen as key texts, rather than peripheral documents. Such texts tell us more about the most important problem representations than texts that come from very specific parts of the educational sector. However, the formal policy texts may very well be complemented by media texts where the proposed policies have been discussed and debated.

7

Critical Discourse Studies

Kristina Boréus and Charlotta Seiler Brylla

Background

The following expressions appeared in different contexts on the Internet in 2022:

'So, as a trader, how do you navigate these [...] choppy markets?'[1]
'(...) investors should consider this port in a market storm right now.'[2]
'Prepared to weather this market storm?'[3]

What views of business and markets do these sentences, with their metaphorical content, express and what does a reader learn about how markets function? According to the approach to metaphor analysis presented in this chapter, what metaphors are chosen might tell us important things about implicit ideas in discourses. The same goes for analyses of what words are chosen – the lexical aspect of texts – and how sentences are grammatically constructed. All these and other aspects of texts are studied in critical discourse studies (CDS), the framework to be introduced in this chapter.

---

[1] Daytradetheworld, downloaded 16 December 2022: www.daytradetheworld.com/trading-blog/five-simple-ways-to-navigate-the-current-choppy-markets/
[2] Neeley, Brian, *Market*, 26 September 2022: 'Morgan Stanley says investors should consider this port in a market storm right now', downloaded 16 December 2022: https://biz.crast.net/morgan-stanley-says-investors-should-consider-this-port-in-a-market-storm-right-now/
[3] Woods, Nancy, *The Globe and Mail*, 30 September 2022, 'Prepared to weather this market storm? Ask yourself these six questions', downloaded 6 December 2022: www.theglobeandmail.com/investing/education/article-prepared-to-weather-this-market-storm-ask-yourself-these-six-questions/

CDS offers a broad approach to textual analysis that is based on a number of theoretical points of departure, which we present below. Critical discourse studies – or critical discourse analysis, a previously more commonly used term[4] – has its roots in linguistics and is consequently a language-based approach focusing on how discourse is semiotically realised. Furthermore, CDS draws on the tradition of critical social research and seeks to analyse how power, difference and resistance are expressed in texts and discourses (Angermuller et al., 2014) in combination with a critical stance: 'CDA combines critique of discourse and explanation of how it figures within and contributes to the existing social reality, as a basis for action to change that existing reality in particular aspects' (Fairclough, 2015: 6). This has motivated, among other things, a particular interest in the analysis of racism, anti-Semitism and nationalism (e.g., Reisigl and Wodak, 2000; Wodak et al., 2009; Wodak and Rheindorf, 2022), sexism (e.g., Mills, 2008), populism (e.g., Wodak et al., 2013; Stavrakakis, 2017; Macaulay, 2019), neoliberalism and capitalism (e.g., Fairclough, 1993; Machin and Mayr, 2012), migration and discrimination (e.g., Krzyżanowski and Wodak, 2008; Boréus, 2020), as well as climate and environment (e.g., Krzyżanowski, 2015). The spotlight has been on how such ideas are reproduced, particularly in mass media texts, but also in political texts, policy documents (e.g., for universities, see Ledin and Machin, 2016) and in advertising.

Using tools from linguistics to analyse texts and discourses brings numerous possibilities when it comes to levels and categories to be studied. There are various comprehensive models to consider in a linguistic discourse analysis, some of which we mention below. There are also methods for analysing particular aspects of texts and discourses that have their own approaches under the umbrella of CDS, such as political discourse analysis, which is an approach to analysing argumentation (see Fairclough and Fairclough, 2012; the method is also explicated in Chapter 3 of the first edition of this book (Boréus, 2017)). In this chapter, we focus on three aspects that we consider to be potentially fruitful in social scientific studies: the analysis of metaphorical language, lexical choices and grammatical structures in texts.

CDS: inspiration and approaches

Linguists Norman Fairclough and Ruth Wodak are well-known representatives of CDS, which was developed from the 1980s onwards (Fairclough and Wodak, 1997: 261). Fairclough has described his own version of CDS as being based on Roy Bhaskar's critical realism (see Chapter 1), which makes a distinction between a

---

[4]We therefore use CDS as an umbrella term in this text, also for the approaches or studies that label(led) themselves CDA. Van Dijk (2013) recommends using the term CDS since CDA might suggest that there is *one* method (analysis) of CDA, which is simply not the case. The label critical discourse *studies* is better suited to cover the variety of theories, methods, analyses, applications and other practices of critical discourse analysts.

domain of the real, independent of our senses, and an *empirical domain* that corresponds to what our senses can comprehend (Fairclough, 2010: 355). An interpretation of Fairclough on this point is that the *true* societal power relations exist in the domain of the real, regardless of how we understand them, while the content of the texts we analyse exist in the empirical domain. It is the task of the critical discourse analyst to interpret the power relations through textual analysis. This way of looking at reality makes CDS less radically constructivist than, for example, political discourse theory (described in Chapter 6). Fairclough stresses that discourses are formed by a social structure that is characterised by 'both a discursive and non-discursive nature' (Fairclough, 1992: 64).

A linguistic approach that has influenced CDS is *speech act theory*. According to philosopher of language J.L. Austin's influential *How to Do Things with Words* (1975), speaking and writing is acting and writing, or saying something coherently is performing a *speech act*. Speaking and writing, as well as communicating with other semiotic means, are social practices embedded in other social practices. This is the basis for how several authors writing in CDS define discourse and texts (see, for example, Fairclough, 2015 [1989]: 166–8; cf. 'What is discourse?' in Chapter 6).

Critical discourse analysts distinguish between different approaches, such as the *discourse historical approach*, associated with Wodak, and Fairclough's *dialectical-relational approach*. A *sociocognitive approach*, associated with linguist Teun van Dijk, is also prominent (Fairclough, 2010; Wodak and Meyer, 2016). *Social semiotics*, and in particular *multimodal discourse analysis* (see Chapter 8), are sometimes regarded as approaches within the field of CDS (Angermuller et al., 2014).

The 'critical' in critical discourse studies

A common denominator for all CDS is the *critique*. CDS was introduced in the 1980s 'to mark a difference from an allegedly descriptive discourse analysis' (Reisigl, 2017: 50). Like other kinds of DA, CDS embraces the view that language is not a neutral instrument for communication. The idea that language represents a given reality is rejected. Instead, the formative and constitutive side of language is emphasised: language always involves a perspective on the world. In addition, language is a constitutive part of social practices, which have implications for social power relations: 'Critical discourse analysis is an instrument whose purpose is to expose veiled power structures' (Wodak, 1996: 16; cf. see also Gee, 2005: 33). The ambition of the critical social research tradition to work for social and political change can therefore also be found in CDS (van Dijk, 1997: 23).

But what does it mean to be *critical*? When CDA was introduced by Fairclough, van Dijk, Wodak and others, they had particularly the political meaning of social critique in mind:

Political critique means to judge the status quo, e.g., a specific discourse or (dis)order of discourse, against the background of an alternative (ideal) state and preferred values, norms, standards or criteria with respect to shortcomings or contradictions. (Reisigl, 2017: 50)

Reisigl and Wodak (2016) assign three tasks to their discourse-historical approach: first, a *text- and discourse-immanent critique* that is concerned with uncovering contradictions or tensions within texts. Second, a *sociodiagnostic critique* whose aim is to 'demystify' discursive practices by placing texts in their context of social and political relations and circumstances. Finally, *prognostic critique* aims to contribute to improved communication – e.g., by developing guidelines for the avoidance of sexist language (Reisigl and Wodak, 2016: 25).

Not all studies within the CDS framework engage in all three types of critique. There are also other discourse-analytical approaches rooted in linguistics that work with analytical tools similar to those used by CDA, among them *discourse linguistics* (*Diskurslinguistik* in German), which was developed mainly by German linguists (Spitzmüller and Warnke, 2011a) and the sociolinguistic approach to discourse informed by, for example, Blommaert (2007). Discourse linguistics originally stems from a framework for a historical-linguistic epistemology, drawing on Michel Foucault's earlier work. Here, the critical perspective focuses on describing and questioning how historically and culturally rooted knowledge is manifested linguistically (Spitzmüller and Warnke, 2011a: 76). Blommaert (2007) emphasises the self-reflexive stance of the researchers as an important component of the critique. This applies, for example, to treating different sets of data, combining interdisciplinary insights and opening up for other sociocultural contexts.

'Discourse' in critical discourse studies

Different CDS scholars define the term 'discourse' differently, but the definitions usually have a core of describing discourse in terms of *semiotic practices* – i.e., how people tend to express themselves semiotically through speech, writing, image or gestures. A particular discourse can then be understood as a *semiotic practice concerning some particular topic in a defined social context*. A discourse could be, for example, how the role of universities in the attempts to mitigate global warming is discussed in the universities of a particular region or country during a given period of time. This discourse definition refers to how a certain topic is discussed and negotiated in a context, but does not necessarily point to particular ideas about or perspectives on the topic in question.[5] Thus, the same discourse can contain contradictions and different perspectives. It is, for example, possible that different actors express contradictory ideas about the role of universities in the mitigation

---

[5] However, some CDS scholars use the term 'discourse', to refer to particular ideological perspectives on the topics.

of global warming, in which case the discourse is characterised by tensions or different perspectives.

The semiotic practices that a discourse analysis seeks to capture are expressed in texts produced in particular contexts. Texts relevant to a discourse on the role of universities with regard to the mitigation of climate change could be what a climate-engaged student has said at the student union meeting about the necessity of students and faculty taking action, what the university vice chancellor has written about the topic in their blog and a mural depicting climate disaster at the wall of a university building.

Why discourse analysis?

Why are discourses important to analyse? Fairclough argues that discourses do three things. First, they have an *ideational function* while 'discourse contributes to the construction of systems of knowledge and belief' (Fairclough, 1992: 64). Second, discourses have a *relational function* – i.e., they are linked to the interpersonal function of texts, cf. Chapter 1 – since they contribute to the establishment of particular relations between groups, such as between teachers and students. Third, discourses construe different *identities*, which can be seen as also linking CDA to a constructivist approach rather than to a materially based perspective.

Discourses, other social practices and social structures

In this section, we present what we believe to be a fruitful understanding of how discourses relate to other social practices and structures.[6]

Semiotic acts and discourse orders

Social practices, how people do things out of habit, as well as when they consciously follow rules, often contain semiotic elements. Fairclough takes an interest in the social order – the way that social practices are networked – for example, the neo-capitalist order or the order of education in a particular society – and refers to the semiotic aspect of the social order as an *order of discourse* (Fairclough, 2010: 265). Orders of discourse comprise three elements: genres (see Chapter 1), discourses and styles (Fairclough, 2014). While *discourses* are the practices that influence the content of texts the most – how something is talked or written about or depicted in a particular context – *genres*, i.e., the conventions for composition and design, which texts that are part of similar social actions tend to follow – have more influence on text structure. *Style* is linked to the interpersonal aspect of texts – e.g., are they informal or formal, or are they more or less polite in their address? Thus, orders of discourse are social practices of text production that influence the content, structure and mediation of the resulting texts.

---

[6]This presentation rests above all on our interpretation of various texts by Norman Fairclough.

Social practices often have other elements apart from the semiotic ones. Which recipes are found in cookbooks is influenced by a certain order of discourse, but also by economic practices – e.g., what kind of recipes in cookbooks, designed in what way, that sell the best. And by the food habits of a particular region – for example, if insects are not consumed there, there will be a scarcity of cookbooks on how to prepare them.

Social practices and structures

Social practices, with their semiotic and other elements, link actions to *structures*. What constitutes a social structure, or which structures are most important, is not agreed upon in the social sciences, but structures tend to be seen as enduring and governing social relations linked to power. In Marxism, for example, the ownership of the means of production – i.e., factories, machines, raw materials – is thought to be a structure that strongly influences the distribution of power in any society. The division of labour between women and men can also be seen as a structure that influences the distribution of societal power.

Social practices can be seen as ways of exploiting certain opportunities offered by structures at the expense of other opportunities. Language itself is a social structure (Fairclough, 2014) which offers certain possibilities – for example, how words can be combined, but closes others: we can say 'I have a book' and be understood, while 'have a I book' is not an intelligible English sentence.

Figure 7.1 shows texts as the result of semiotic acts, which are performed in relation to social practices with semiotic elements, which are constituted by certain discourse orders. Structures, which also interact with all kinds of social practices, are omitted here.[7]

The elements in Figure 7.1 can be illustrated with the social practice of guided city tours. A guide acts by showing and talking about buildings and interacts with those taking part in the tour. The guide performs a series of semiotic acts such as pointing at buildings or bridges, talking about their history and making little jokes. The guide has a certain discourse order to relate to. The genre enables certain ways of communicating and excludes others: if the guide spends the time reciting nature lyrics instead of telling about bridges and houses, it is not a guided tour. The guide also relates to certain discourses and will not randomly tell about events in the city. Perhaps the narrative will focus on the powerful people who initiated, financed and designed houses, castles or bridges. Alternatively, the narrative could concentrate on the people who physically built the city: carried the stone, laid the bricks, mixed the cement or operated the excavators. (This critical approach is expressed in the novel *The Aesthetics of Resistance* in which the famous Pergamon frieze is described from this perspective (Weiss, 2005 [1975])). Styles, finally, also set limits for what

---

[7]Figure 7.1 is inspired by, but does not follow, Figure 3.1 in Fairclough, 1992: 73.

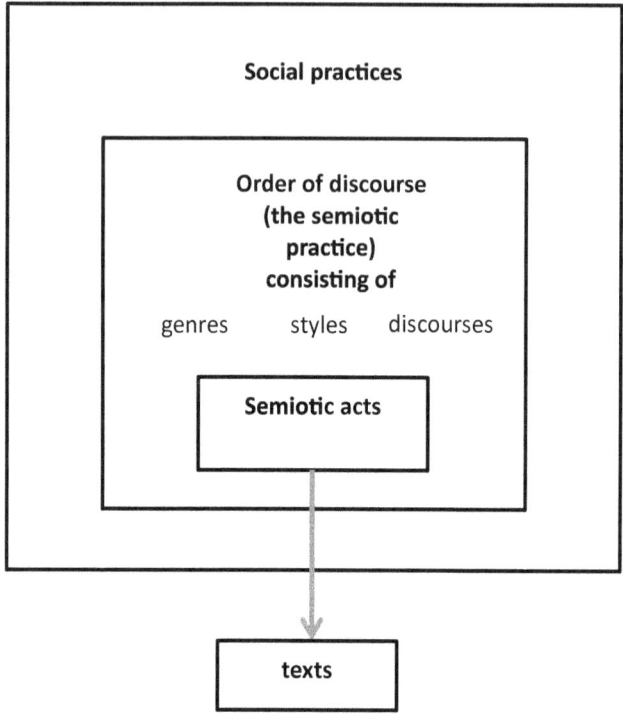

Figure 7.1 Text production in the context of semiotic and other social practices

will be said. We can, for example, distinguish between guiding where the guide is more or less inclusive in relation to those who are guided. In addition to the semiotic elements, social practice can also include other elements, such as the movement of people in urban space and the fact that the guided tour is (often) a service for which those who take the tour need to pay. This also influences the semiotic acts.

Against this theoretical background on critical discourse studies, we now move on to the analysis itself.

Analysis

We start by presenting a general approach to critical discourse studies, after which we turn to various tools for textual analysis.

Conducting critical discourse studies

Critical discourse studies often take a departure in some question of power, although the analytical tools presented in this chapter can be used for other purposes.[8] A fully developed critical discourse analysis takes all elements of Figure 7.1 into account, as well as social structures, but such studies are not common.

Let's say we want to conduct a study of which power relations guided city tours might support, if any. A source of inspiration could be the analysis of the Pergamon frieze in *The Aesthetics of Resistance*, and the research questions formulated could include which social groups' experiences of urban construction are mediated. At an early stage, research on guided tours and on other phenomena that play a role in the social practices relevant to the study should be reviewed.

Next, the discourse that should be analysed needs to be delimited. Taking departure from the discourse definition above, we might decide to do a critical discourse study of the way the building of cities is presented during guided tours in a particular city during a certain time period. The collection of texts may present a challenge. Should we join a number of guided tours and do we get permission from the guides and the people being guided to record what is said? Are there shortcuts, such as manuscripts or guidebooks from which the guides draw, that could be analysed?

We focus here on the discourse and consider knowledge of genre and style (the other elements of the discourse order) as an aid to this. A goal of the analysis will be to find patterns in the texts that reflect relevant traits of the discourse. As in other types of discourse analysis (see 'Steps in a discourse analysis' in Chapter 6), some overarching sorting tool is probably needed to address the texts, such as a simple coding of the texts that divides their content into different themes. Perhaps we are not interested in the discourse on the earliest origins of the city, but only in how the construction of houses and bridges is narrated. Once these passages have been sorted out, we can choose between different methods of analysis. Fairclough (1992 and other works) presents a comprehensive set of analytical concepts for the study of different elements in texts and discourses. Out of these, a few could be selected, such as some of those presented in this chapter. Once we find recurring patterns in different texts we can begin to describe the semiotic practices that constitute the discourses and that have influenced the texts. A final step is to relate the analysis to our overarching research question about power.

In the rest of the chapter, we present various tools for text analysis used in CDS, but which can also be used for studies not inspired by the power-critical stance of CDS. We analyse metaphors, lexical choice and grammar. We also explain how to work with large amounts of text using corpus linguistic methods.

---

[8]Fairclough (2010), Chapter 9, proposes four steps in a critical discourse analysis, the first of which is to identify a social wrong in its semiotic aspects and the second is to identify obstacles to rectifying this wrong. The third step is to analyse the wrong in relation to the overall social order and the fourth is to look for possibilities to overcome the obstacles. In this section, we take a more open approach to the task of analysis.

Metaphors we live by

To 'see the light at the end of the tunnel' and to have 'a long road ahead' might be (and usually are) metaphors. A metaphor describes something as something else that it is not, transferring meaning from one domain to another. The transfer is usually made from an area that is well known and tangible to what is more abstract. If to 'see the light at the end of the tunnel' is metaphorically meant, it refers to having found the solution to a difficult task or problem, or to a difficult situation coming to an end. The transfer is probably from more than one aspect of the experience of moving in a tunnel: the darkness of the tunnel is the difficult or disturbing situation, the light at the end is the experience of knowing that things will be right again, while the idea of the tunnel itself might transfer the experience of confinement onto the experience of not getting away from struggling with a problem.

Metaphors are one kind of figurative expressions. *Similes* – for example, 'families are like fudge' – are close to metaphors, but differ in that they state explicitly that there is a transfer of ideas. A *metonym* is an expression used for something that it is a part of or in other ways closely associated with. 'The Pink House claims' (*dice la Casa Rosada*) is seldom a literal statement – it does not mean that a building has started to talk.[9] When this phrase expresses that the president, or their spokesperson, has uttered something, the function of the expression is not to claim that the president is like a pink building; the expression is not metaphorical either. A metaphor makes a transfer between areas that are not closely associated. It is sometimes difficult to tell a metonym apart from a metaphor, and an expression can be both metaphorical and metonymic at the same time.

A guiding idea for how to tell figurative expressions apart from literal ones is to consider whether the expression at hand may be used in totally different contexts and whether a literal interpretation of that expression would appear bizarre or false in the context; if that is the case, the expression is likely to be figurative. Obviously, the expression to 'see the light at the end of the tunnel' could be used literally – e.g., by a person travelling by train. But if there is no real tunnel, it is a metaphor. Furthermore, one can consider the implications of the literal expression. If the expression were literal, it would imply that one could in principle touch the walls of the tunnel with one's hand, that the light would be dimmed if one put sunglasses on, and so on. (On how to recognise metaphors, see Rosenblatt, 1994: 25–7 and Koller, 2020a: 89.)

Metaphors are extensively studied in language studies and rhetoric. An influential line of research was introduced by the linguist George Lakoff and the philosopher Mark Johnson in their *Metaphors We Live By* (1980).

---

[9] La Casa Rosada, Argentina's government building.

The theory of conceptual metaphors: CMT

According to Lakoff and Johnson and followers, metaphors are not just embellishments in language but tools we use, consciously and unconsciously, to understand the world around us. Our conceptual system, which influences how we think and act, is metaphorical in nature. The metaphors used in a given linguistic community say something about how the world is interpreted there. Furthermore, metaphors can influence how we perceive social phenomena. This way of understanding the role of metaphors is called *CMT, conceptual metaphor theory*, after the central concept of conceptual metaphor, explained below. Analysis influenced by CMT has been adopted under the umbrella of CDS, in that context referred to as *CMA, critical metaphor analysis* (Koller, 2020a).

CMT, which challenges a view of metaphors as primarily rhetorical devices, is arguably now the dominant way to comprehend metaphor use (Gibbs, 2014; Koller, 2020a). Since the breakthrough of Lakoff and Johnson's book, hundreds of studies have shown how systematic patterns of linguistic expression reveal underlying conceptual metaphors in a large number of languages. Many studies have, for instance, demonstrated the role of conceptual metaphors in thinking across academic disciplines (philosophy, mathematics, physics, chemistry, architecture, political science, geography, law, economics and others) (Gibbs, 2014).

Metaphorical expressions and conceptual metaphors

We distinguish between *metaphorical expressions* ('metaphors'), such as the phrase 'to see the light at the end of the tunnel' when used metaphorically, and *conceptual metaphors*.[10] Conceptual metaphors are collective ideas in a linguistic community according to which a phenomenon is conceptualised in terms of something it is not. Conceptual metaphors are expressed by metaphorical expressions in a language, both by set expressions like the tunnel metaphor in English and by freshly made up metaphors that are understandable exactly because they express shared ideas. Conceptual metaphors might also be expressed by non-figurative language.

Lakoff and Johnson (1980: 7–9) use metaphors in the English language to lay bare the conceptual metaphors that structure mundane activities in the English-speaking world. The conceptual metaphor TIME IS MONEY[11] is expressed in many different ways in English – e.g., 'You're *wasting* my time', 'How do you *spend* your time these days?', 'That flat tyre *cost* me an hour', 'He's living on *borrowed* time'. All these expressions refer to time as if it were money, an entity that we can save, spend etc. Several other languages use corresponding expressions, which indicate

---

[10] What we refer to as 'conceptual metaphor' can also be referred to as 'metaphor' (Lakoff, 1993: 209).

[11] Following the conventions of some linguistic literature, all conceptual metaphors in this chapter are typed in SMALL CAPS. The metaphors that express them are marked with *italics*.

that they too use the conceptual metaphor TIME IS MONEY. The expressions reveal a particular way of conceiving time that is related to how the concept of work has developed in modern industrialised societies, in which work is often associated with the time it takes to carry it out and one gets paid for work according to time units. They strongly structure our everyday activities. We act as if time were a precious good, a scarce resource, and we understand it in that fashion.

Conceptual metaphors like TIME IS MONEY and the metaphors that express them highlight certain aspects of phenomena but hide others and they may steer our thoughts in certain directions. According to the metaphors with regard to markets at the beginning of this chapter, markets can get *choppy* when you *navigate* them, *market storms* might blow up and the markets need to be *weathered*; even seeking a *port* should be considered. The conceptual metaphor MARKETS ARE OCEANS/LARGE WATERS seems to be at work. Highlighted by that conceptual metaphor are qualities of markets such that when people invest in them, they take risks because the markets are uncontrollable, like the stormy sea. Markets are like natural forces in relation to which humans can take precautions (navigate to a port), but which they cannot control. What this particular conceptual metaphor conceals is that, unlike a stormy ocean, what happens in the markets is the result of human actions. It also steers thought away from the fact that political decisions can regulate markets in a way that they cannot regulate oceans.

Metaphors and cancer

You cannot only live, but also die by metaphors. Semino et al. (2017) examined metaphor use in the blogs of cancer patients in the UK, the background being that UK policy documents[12] deliberately avoided the use of metaphors that relate to violence and struggle (HAVING CANCER IS A BATTLE), favouring those based on the idea of a journey (HAVING CANCER IS A JOURNEY).[13] Expressions such as dying after 'a long fight against cancer' had become controversial for their associations with violence and since not getting well is presented as a defeat. In line with the travel metaphors (patients make a 'cancer journey' and different treatments are different 'paths' that the journey can take), cancer presumably becomes a fellow traveller rather than an enemy. Despite this policy choice in UK healthcare there were no studies on how patients spontaneously use metaphors, the authors claim.

The aim of the study was to compare the frequency of expressions of the two conceptual metaphors in online texts by cancer patients and healthcare professionals, and to investigate how patients with cancer use these metaphors. For the

---

[12] Such as the 2007 NHS Cancer Reform Strategy.

[13] The authors do not use the term 'conceptual metaphor' in the article, but we use it here since the researchers refer to CMT theory and since overarching beliefs expressed through metaphors in texts were studied.

study, two corpora were compiled: one from a British online forum for cancer patients and another one from a forum for healthcare professionals.

The analysis was carried out in several manual and computerised steps and broadly followed the procedure proposed by Charteris-Black (2004), described in the section on corpus linguistics below. In the initial manual analysis, the coders placed the metaphors they found into semantic fields, which can also be described as classifying them as expressions of certain conceptual metaphors. The researchers searched for metaphors that were motivated by the conceptual metaphors that understand cancer either as a battle or as a journey. For example, when one patient described how she was 'fast becoming a chemo veteran' (Semino et al., 2017: 60), 'veteran' was coded as belonging to the semantic field of war. In order to ensure good reliability (cf. Chapter 2), the expressions were analysed first by a main coder and then by two other coders independently of each other. A qualitative analysis then explored how patients used the metaphors to express their experiences, particularly in relation to feelings of power and powerlessness in the context of illness.

The result showed that patients used metaphors related to both the conceptual metaphor of cancer as a battle and that of cancer as a journey more frequently than did healthcare professionals. The researchers interpreted this to mean that the metaphors did indeed help patients express different aspects of their experiences. Furthermore, the results showed that patients used both types of conceptual metaphors to express both empowerment and disempowerment. As for the battle metaphors, there were examples of how the disease was thought to fight the patient: it was said to 'attack from within' and 'invade the body'. Patients who did not get better felt like losers: 'I feel such a failure that I am not winning this battle' (Semino et al., 2017: 63). But patients also used this kind of metaphor to express agency and pride: 'my consultants recognised that I was a born fighter' (Semino et al., 2017: 63). The journey metaphors were sometimes used to express a sense of control, but they could also be used to express powerlessness – e.g., when patients described themselves as travellers forced out on trips they did not want to take. Thus, despite the problems attributed by the profession to the use of combat metaphors their use proved complex. The researchers used the results to give advice to the medical profession on how they should express themselves in conversations with cancer patients.

Other studies have found that battle metaphors are also common in Swedish texts about cancer, often including expressions such as 'invasive cancer', 'aggressive treatment' and 'weapons in the fight against cancer' and that different conceptual metaphors are used in many complex ways by people living with cancer (Gustafsson and Hommerberg, 2018; Gustafsson et al., 2020).

All three cancer metaphor studies referred to take a critical approach in line with CDS. Semino et al. (2017) critically examine a particular discourse – the way the medical profession talks about patients with cancer – and attempts to interpret how the discourse affects the social reality of the patients affected and make an active attempt to influence the language used by health professionals – what Reisigl and Wodak (2016) call 'prognostic criticism'. Neither of the studies relate as clearly to what lies outside the discourse as would be possible from Figure 7.1. From metaphor analysis we now move to the study of word choice.

Analysing lexicon

The analysis of words and other lexical items such as names is one way to study implicit meaning (Machin and Mayr, 2012: 30). As language users, we often make all kinds of lexical choices to represent the world, and negotiate social identities and relations. The words we choose to describe the world and the phenomena around us greatly influence our and others' perception of them. How we name an act can also have both political and legal consequences, as in the case of 11 September 2001, when George W. Bush declared a 'war on terrorism'. Words also help us to categorise the world around us, thereby laying the foundations for a particular way of looking at things. If a regular and binary use of the categorisations 'natives' and 'migrants' can be observed in many texts on migration, this distinction will have an impact on the discourse, and hence the way we look at migration and integration (cf. Boréus, 2020). Certain keywords may shape discourses significantly by evoking frames and intertextual relations. Some words appear particularly frequently in certain discourses, others become disputed and thus prominent. In both cases, the words shape the discourse and we will therefore look closer at what characterises such lexical units that may serve as representatives and signals for central concepts in the discourse.[14]

Word categories

Three types of lexical units are of particular interest as objects of discourse analysis: *proper nouns* (for example, names), *species* and *collective nouns*, and *keywords*. Analysing the use of names in different contexts can be a fruitful entry point into discourse. Both *personal names* (anthroponyms) and *place names* (toponyms) carry meaning and fulfil an important function in the discourse. The names of the two German states during the Cold War may serve as an historical example: in the German–German competition to represent the 'rightful' Germany, it was important for both countries that their official names – German Democratic Republic or Federal Republic of Germany, respectively – were used, whereas the names East or West Germany were rejected, as well as strategically deployed by both states about the other. By using

---

[14]Moreover, words are not only relevant to discourse as singular units, but also word groups such as collocations or recurring word combinations are worth analysing. Word groups have a lot in common with metaphors, as one has to understand their transferred meaning (Spitzmüller and Warnke, 2011b: 140). Formally speaking, metaphors are to be considered as lexical units, but they also have specific features that justify treating them as a category of analysis in their own right (Böke et al., 2005: 260).

different names, the states were able to position themselves and simultaneously call into question the legitimacy of the 'other' Germany (Seiler Brylla, 2019).

The so-called species and collective nouns are also interesting from a discourse analytic perspective (Spitzmüller and Warnke, 2011b: 141). The grouping of phenomena into categories and species (e.g., humans and animals) or into collective groups (e.g., population, police) is a cognitive procedure, but it also contributes to the evaluation and the perspectivation of these phenomena. Categorisation is not inherently given, but something we language-users do. How we order and categorise people into 'women', 'men', 'Swedes', 'foreigners', 'students', 'workers' also influences how we look at the world.

However, it is the third type of lexical units, the so-called keywords, that we would like to highlight as particularly applicable for discourse analysis and to which we now turn.[15]

Keywords

Keywords are words with complex semantics that are capable of expressing the ideals and beliefs of an entire group, a party or even a time period or epoch. These words can, under certain circumstances, form the core of communication because they are perceived as particularly significant and their meaning is negotiated by the participating language-users (cf. discussions on feminism, security or sustainability). By using certain keywords, language users can posit themselves socially and politically.

In view of such significance for capturing discourses, Schroeter et al. (2019) introduces the concept of *discourse keywords*. Here, they draw on two different research fields: on one hand the Anglophone tradition of cultural keywords (Williams, 1985; Wierzbicka, 1997) and on the other hand, the Germanophone conceptual history as established by Reinhart Koselleck (Brunner et al., 1972ff.; see further Chapter 4). Common for both traditions is that they consider keywords (or basic concepts – *Grundbegriffe*, as Koselleck calls them) as simultaneously shaping and reflecting reality. Koselleck (1972: XXIIIf.) argued that central concepts are not only indicators of social and historical processes, but also factors with the potential to influence the development of society. This keyword concept has been further developed within a discipline called *'discourse semantics'*, which is a linguistic elaboration of Koselleck's conceptual history. An analysis at the word level in discourse analytic studies can largely be based on conceptual-historical methods, but a crucial difference is that a discourse-semantic approach means that the word is considered as embedded in a discourse and focus is on the *function* of the word in the discourse. In other words, the reason why lexical units lend themselves as a category of analysis is their relevance to the discourse

---

[15] In German linguistics, there are a number of competing terms or subconcepts to keywords such as catch words, signal words, slogans, stigmatised words, etc. For an overview, see Hermanns (1994).

and here keywords are particularly intriguing because of their ability to represent the thinking, attitudes, programmes and goals of different groups or eras while tending to have a semantic flexibility (Böke et al., 2005: 258–9). Keywords are significant in the public debate and as such they often are sites of struggle for meaning (Schroeter et al., 2019: 14).

Keywords can strike us as significant by being frequently used in a particular discourse, but it is a relative frequency: keywords are not frequent in comparison with, for example, auxiliary verbs (become, must) and function words (and, but). In addition, keywords seem to be semantically (re)productive and to a greater extent than other words give rise to new word formations, which is an indication of their central function and contested meanings. Words for disputed phenomena such as immigration or climate generate new compounds as a consequence of their central status. Keywords thus act as a kind of signal in communication and can structure the message and highlight particularly important aspects. Their capacity as 'container terms' also makes them particularly dynamic in relation to context and language users. The meaning of a word is always dependent on its context, but this is even more true for keywords.

Semantic struggles

There is a constant negotiation about the meaning of keywords, which is evident not least in their varying connotations – i.e., the added meanings, emotions and associations we connect with the words. Evidently, it depends on the speaker whether 'feminism' is used with positive or negative connotations. But also labelling practices are the subject of negotiations. We can think of the reluctance of many speakers to call 'climate change' a 'climate crisis'. This constant (re)negotiation makes keyword theory speak of a 'semantic struggle' (Böke, 1996: 42). Actors try to seize the prestige words (positive signal words) and to fill them with semantic content that corresponds to the actor's own ideological message. In German linguistics, even the war metaphor of 'occupy concepts' (Klein, 1991) is used. Similarly, it is a matter of defining the opponents' keywords in negative terms or providing their ideas with stigmatising designations (negative signal words) and thus taking a stand against the object of reference. An example from the post-war period is the Berlin Wall, which was given the ideological label 'the anti-fascist protective wall' by the GDR regime, while the Federal Republic called the border between West and East Berlin a 'wall of shame'. The semantic struggle can also be about claiming a word by defining and filling it with a particular ideological content. This is the case, for example, with keywords such as 'peace', 'freedom' and 'democracy', with which most parties or groups want to be associated.

The competition for meaning and designation is particularly visible when expressions such as 'x means y' are used in texts and debates. Other ways of highlighting central or contested concepts or launching new meanings are metalinguistic markers such as quotation marks, the addition of 'so called' or by means of layout such as boldface, italics, framing, larger type, etc. (Brylla, 2003: 38f.). This is usually how we can find the keywords in the texts we examine. Thus, we should look for words that somehow attract attention, that are the focus of the communication and thus shape the discourse.

Keywords

Overall, it is typical for keywords that:

- they have a relatively high frequency of use;
- they can act as carriers of ideas;
- they are significant in the public debate;
- they are semantically (re)productive;
- they introduce new meanings or connotations;
- they are thematised (or emphasised) in the discourse, i.e., they have a metalinguistic character;
- they are part of a 'semantic struggle'.

Analysing keywords in discourse

In the following, we will illustrate how to analyse and interpret keywords in discourse by briefly presenting a comparative study of the keywords 'multicultural' and 'multiculturalism'. The study of Schroeter et al. (2019) uses a comparative approach in analysing what the authors call discourse keywords. They look into discourses about migration in four countries through the lens of keywords in combination with corpus assisted discourse analysis. The study examines the use of the keywords 'multicultural' and 'multiculturalism' and is based on corpora from British, French, German and Italian newspaper articles covering the time span 1998–2012, collated from one conservative and one left-liberal national newspaper in each language.

Despite some methodological issues related to comparing keywords from different language communities, Schroeter et al. (2019: 17) argue for the advantage of using discourse keywords for comparative research:

> [it] lies in their salience, their frequency of occurrence across a range of texts in public discourse, their phenomenologically distinct form – as opposed to the analytical level of 'strategy' or 'argumentation'.

The research group collected a thematic migration discourse corpus consisting of the four newspaper corpora mentioned above. The four corpora were then uploaded to a database where they were linguistically annotated.[16] In order to analyse the data in terms of frequency of occurrence, collocations etc., the database

---

[16] To annotate a corpus means to add notes to, for example, words or phrases, giving explanations or comments.

was linked to a corpus analysis tool (see Schroeter et al., 2019: 21ff. for the specific steps of the process).

This comparative analysis of migration discourses in four European countries shows commonalities as well as differences in the use and salience of the keywords 'multicultural' and 'multiculturalism' (see Schroeter et al., 2019: 37–8 for a discussion of the results). However, across the languages, the results show that 'multicultural' is used mostly as descriptive, typically without negative evaluation, whereas 'multiculturalism' is associated with more negative discourse connotations, which emerge through collocates (words that particularly frequently appear nearby, see below) such as 'failure'. Above all, the authors demonstrate that 'multicultural(ism)' is a node of debates in public discourses about migration across different European countries and languages. The study takes a critical stance by anchoring the corpus linguistic methodology in CDS. Its comparative research interest in how multicultural(ism) is used in each country's discourse has social relevance and attempts to respond to the ambitions of CDS in terms of sociodiagnostic critique. How we talk about a phenomenon can have consequences for policies in the relevant field, and vice versa. The differences in the respective discourse on multicultural(ism) can be explained with reference to the migration histories and political responses to immigration in the respective countries.

Instead of investigating a keyword selected in advance in a particular corpus/context – contrastive or not – a study of keywords can also be done by departing from a corpus or a database where keywords are identified on the basis of the criteria we indicate above (see also the section on corpus analysis below and Exercise 2 at the end of the chapter). Having examined the important role of lexicon in discourse analysis we will now turn to the function of grammar in discourse.

Analysing grammar

The analysis of grammar in CDS can be seen as a methodological legacy from *critical linguistics*. *Language and Ideology* by Gunther Kress and Robert Hodge (1979) is an early and seminal book in this area. According to the authors, language is a social construction of fundamental importance for how we understand reality; the grammar of a language can be considered as a theory of reality. In the critical linguistics approach to the analysis of grammar – which takes its starting point in M.A.K. Halliday's systemic functional grammar (SFG) – the basic idea is that each language contains a number of different models of thought for describing what happens and how things are (Halliday and Matthiessen, 2014).[17] By describing something that took place (or is taking or will take place), one chooses between existing models, and, by that, one also chooses a perspective on what happened.

---

[17] Halliday's framework is known by both the abbreviations SFL (systemic functional linguistics) and SFG (systemic functional grammar). We use SFG here when referring to grammatical analysis according to Halliday.

Which model is used is signalled by sentence structure and word choice which are interdependent categories and therefore conceptualised as lexicogrammar in the SFG framework. Discourse analysts are interested in what functions language has in particular contexts and how its use helps to create particular meanings; the SFG provides concrete methods for analysing exactly that.

In this chapter, we focus on what is called the 'analysis of *transitivity*', an important lexicogrammatical tool in the analysis of representation.[18] Transitivity relates to the *ideational metafunction* (see Chapter 1) and is a way of exploring what choices speakers and writers make to represent the world. The conceptual apparatus distinguishes between *processes* (descriptions of actions, of things that happen and of different kinds of states), *participants* (those who are grammatically involved in these events or states) and *circumstances* (which tell us more about the how, when, where and why of the actions, events and states). In other words, transitivity is about what is going on and who is involved as represented in a clause.

We explain the different elements with the help of the newspaper article below (*The Local*, 17 November 2022).

Train collision in northern Germany causes nationwide travel delays

A collision between two freight trains in Lower Saxony is causing widespread disruptions along one of the busiest stretches of Germany's rail network.

The accident occurred on Thursday morning on a stretch of track near Gifhorn in Lower Saxony, around 20 km from Wolfsburg and 60 km from Hanover.

According to the local fire service, a cargo train had stopped at a railway signal when a second cargo train ploughed into it from the back.

The driver of the second train was badly injured and has been taken to hospital, while the driver of the first train sustained light injuries, a spokesperson said.

As a result of the impact, two carriages holding propane gas were overturned while a further two were derailed, causing a major gas leak in the area.

However, authorities say local residents should not be affected as the accident occurred in a stretch of forest outside the town.

The second cargo train had been transporting propane gas tanks in 25 carriages in total, the fire service explained.

The reasons for the collision are so far unclear but the incident has caused largescale disruption on one of the most widely used sections of Germany's railway track.

Emergency services have said it will take at least a day to start clearing the area following the collision. Authorities now have to wait for the gas canisters to empty before they can start the clean-up operation.

Source: *The Local* (German): www.thelocal.de/20221117/train-collision-in-northern-germany-causes-nationwide-travel-delays/

---

[18] In traditional grammar, the term 'transitivity' means something different – namely, if the verb takes no, one or two objects (cf. Koller, 2020b: 58).

Processes

By analysing transitivity, the focus lies on the process, which in turn determines what roles participants have. Circumstances can be important as well in order to represent the world, but they are not in the same ways as participants dependent on the processes. Processes can be of different kinds: *actions*, *events* and *states*.[19]

An *action* is something that is done more or less intentionally by someone, usually a human being, and is under their control (but not always, as we can see in the examples below). We say that the clause has an *actor*. In the news text above, we see instances of action right from the beginning: 'a cargo train *had stopped* at a railway signal when a second cargo train *ploughed into* it from the back.' We can distinguish between actions that affect other participants and those that do not. The first clause above is an example of the latter type of action, as the first train only stops at the railway signal, while the second clause is an example of how one actor affects a second one by ploughing into it. Here one could object that a train is no real actor, that there must be a driver, but *grammatically speaking*, the train has agency, which is decisive here. An *event* is a change in the world that occurs without anyone's conscious action (or that has no agent) and is not under anyone's control. Described as an event is the clause 'The accident occurred on Thursday morning on a stretch of track near Gifhorn in Lower Saxony'. Whereas both actions and events relate to changes in the world, there are also *states*, processes that imply no change: 'The reasons for the collision are so far unclear'. States are often described with the verbs 'be' or 'have'. Clearly, the grammatical choice of describing a process as an action, event or a state can provide different versions of what is going on.

Actions and events might be of different types as well. Here, we distinguish between *material*, *verbal* and *mental* process types.[20] A material verb process is something tangible and external to a person, something that could be observed by somebody else. Material processes in the text about the train collision are, for example, *transport*, *injure*, *plough* and *take*. Verbal processes are referred to by verbs to do with speech and expressions – in the train story we have several examples of the verb '*say*', which is a verbal action. Mental processes, finally, are about somebody imagining, thinking or believing. 'I dreamed about a train last night' would be an example.

Text producers' choice of process types influences how we grasp and interpret what we hear and read. High frequency of material verb processes can, for example,

---

[19] In the following, we draw on Fowler's (2013 [1991]) terminology for analysing transitivity and transformation. In addition, we also use some concepts from Halliday and Matthiessen (2014) who have a much more elaborated model for describing processes.

[20] Again, we rely on Fowler's (2013 [1991]) terminology. Halliday and Matthiessen (2014) differentiate between six process types, where, for example, states are described as two kinds of relational processes (for a comprehensive overview, see Koller, 2020b: 61).

give the impression of an active setting, but to explain this more in detail we have to introduce the participants connected to the different processes.

Participants
Different process types determine different *participant roles* and a relevant distinction is between participants who carry out the processes and those who are affected by them. In a material process, the participants are divided into *actors* and *goals*. The process starts from the actor and the goal is the object of the action or event. Actors as well as goals can be human or non-human. In the clause 'the incident has caused largescale disruption', 'incident' is the actor and 'disruption' is the goal of the action. There may also be other participants in material processes who are somehow affected by the process and whom we call the *recipient*. The clause 'She gave him his glasses' needs another participant besides the goal (his glasses) – namely, the recipient (him). In the text we can imagine different recipients (who are not mentioned though) such as the train company, passengers etc.

In verbal processes, we have a *sayer* as the first participant, while the second participant can be a *receiver* or a *verbiage*. In the example 'authorities say local residents should not be affected', authorities is the sayer in the verbal process 'say' and what they say (= local residents should not be affected) is the verbiage. However, we can also imagine a receiver of the statement, who is not included in the text.

Mental processes have *sensers* as first participants and *phenomena* as second participants as in the example: 'I (senser) dreamed about a train (phenomenon) last night'. This terminology may seem complex and academic, but can be helpful in interpreting the processes. Let's say we have a text with several material process types, then we will also see a number of *actors*. By contrast, texts dominated by mental and verbal process types or by states will instead show us *sensers* and *sayers*, which in turn may influence how we perceive the text.

Also, in the process type state there are different participants bound together by the verbs 'have' or 'be'. Here, the first participant is usually called *carrier* or *identified* depending on the type of state described and the second participant *attribute* or *identifier* (Björkvall, 2003: 62; Halliday and Matthiessen, 2014: 259ff.). In 'The reasons for the collision are so far unclear', 'reasons' is *carrier* and 'unclear' is *attribute*, since it is about categorising and describing the reasons. We also have identifying states such as 'Anna is the leader of the group', where Anna is the identified and leader of the group the identifying. In some states (existential) there is only one participant as 'it' in 'it exists in the whole country'. They are often combined with different kinds of circumstances ('in the whole country'), to which we finally turn.

Circumstances
The third element distinguished by Fowler is *circumstance*, referring to *when*, *where*, *how* and *why* something happened. In the text above, we learn that the accident

occurred on Thursday morning (when) on a stretch of track near Gifhorn in Lower Saxony (where). There is also information on the consequences – for instance, that the driver of the second train was 'badly injured' (how). However, the article cannot tell us anything about the reasons for the accident (why). The circumstances are not as linked to the processes as the participants and can thus be combined with different process types. The analysis of the circumstances can show us what the text producers wanted to make explicit and what they did not.

Tables 7.1 and 7.2 summarise the conceptual framework we have presented here.

Transformations

The lexicogrammar model described above makes clear that the text producer's choice of process types, participants and circumstances will have an impact on the representation – just like the choice of words, as shown above. Moreover, it can tell us a lot about the speaker's or writer's epistemological and/or ideological viewpoint. The basic idea of critical linguistic analysis is then to contrast the expressions of the existing text with other possible ways of describing the same sequence of events. Here, critical linguistics uses the concept of *transformation* (Fowler, 2013 [1991]: 76). It is based on the idea that there are descriptions of what is going on in the world that have a more basic or complete form than others. For example,

Table 7.1 Process types and participant roles

Process types	Participant roles	Examples	Action/event/state
Material	**Actor**	**She** gave <u>him</u> *his glasses*.	Action
	Goal	**The incident** has caused *largescale disruption*.	Action
	<u>Recipient</u>		
		The accident occurred.	Event
Mental	**Senser**	**I** dreamed about *a train*.	Event
	Phenomenon		
Verbal	**Sayer**	**Authorities** say <u>to the local press</u> *residents should not be affected*.	Action
	Verbiage		
	<u>Receiver</u>		
States	**Carrier/identified**	**The reasons** are *unclear*.	State
	Attribute/identifier	**We** have *a new car*.	
		Anna is *the leader of the group*.	

Table 7.2 Circumstances

Circumstances	Question	Example
Time	When?	The accident occurred on *Thursday morning*.
Place	Where?	The accident occurred *in a stretch of forest*.
Manner	How?	The driver of the second train was *badly* injured.
Cause	Why?	The school remained closed *due to Covid-19*.

some descriptions do not include participants, even though it is clear that there were participants involved in the process. We will give some examples of how transformation could be explored using the categories above.

As mentioned above, it may be interesting to examine whether a process is described as an action or as an event. Describing something as an action implies that certain participants in the processes are given responsibility for something occurring, which is not the case if the process is described as an event. In the news article we can read that '[t]he accident occurred on Thursday morning', which does not reveal if somebody was responsible. A little further on in the article, we learn that one cargo train has hit another, but 'the reasons for the collision are so far unclear'. Throughout the article, the train remains the only actor and we are told nothing about any possible human actors. Backgrounding and exclusion of actors can be conducted in different ways (Koller, 2020b: 62) and grammatically, *nominalisation* and *passivisation* are two significant ways of making participants invisible.

Nominalisation means that verbs that can be used to describe processes are replaced by nouns. The article talks about 'train collision', 'train delays' and 'disruptions' instead of using the verbs 'collide', 'delay' and 'disrupt' which would have needed some kind of participants. Nominalisations allow participants to be removed from the processes and thus transform what is said. As for the train accident, it might still be unknown whether the accident was caused by a technical error or a human mistake. However, there can be other, more ideological reasons for excluding the actors: The 'closure' of a company may look like an event caused by natural forces rather than the presence of a CEO, a board of directors or shareholders behind the decision 'to close' the company (cf. the discussion on market metaphors above). Furthermore, processes may be perceived as more materialised if they are referred to by nouns. A 'closure' thus becomes something that seems to have a life of its own rather than a process that has participants who both influence and are influenced.

The distinction between events and actions also creates an interest in who does what in the verb processes. As for the human participants, we saw above that they can have different roles whether they are responsible or the object in the process. A transformation of interest in this context is called *passivisation* – that is, agentless passives, as in the clause 'The driver of the second train was badly injured and has been taken to hospital'. Passive statements allow hiding the agent, leaving responsibility unspecified and foregrounding the process and the goal of the action (what happened to the driver?).

Analysing transitivity in discourse

How could a transitivity analysis be put into practice? As can be seen from the complex framework above, this method is quite time-consuming. Data and research questions should therefore be carefully matched. Sari Pietikäinen (2003) applies this method in a study of how the indigenous Sami people are represented in the

Finnish news discourse. Inspired by Fairclough's (1992) box model of discourse as a three-dimensional phenomenon, the study examines how the journalists utilised textual and linguistic resources available to them, how journalistic practices limited and enabled choices made and, finally – and at this point at the core of our interest – how the textual choices in the news texts contributed to the representations. For the analysis of Sami representations in the news texts, transitivity was used in order to disclose the attribution of agency and process to the various participants in the news texts analysed (Pietikäinen, 2003: 581–603). The study shows how the distribution of grammatical roles evoke an opposition between the Sami and the Finns in the news discourse. Whereas the Finnish majority was depicted as active and capable of action, the Sami were represented as affected by these actions. Pietikäinen's study is a significant example of how a political issue such as minority status can be explored through the analysis of verb processes and participants. All the types of analysis presented in this chapter could be conducted on single texts, as well as on large corpora with the help of suitable software, which is the topic of the next section.

Corpus analysis

Like other fields, CDS can benefit from databases and software to analyse data. Charteris-Black (2004) demonstrates how metaphor analysis can be carried out using corpus analysis, although parts of the analysis have to be performed manually. In a first step, the analyst reads a number of texts drawn from the context of interest in order to identify possible metaphors. Words used to express these metaphors are then searched for in the corpus. After that, it is necessary to read the expressions found in context to judge whether they are, in fact, metaphors (2004: 35–7). A similar method is to predefine words related to the target domain, search for them and then go through them in context. (For the last step, see below on concordances.) There is also particular software that can be used to combine word searches with annotation of meaning, creating semi-automated methods to find the metaphors (Koller, 2020a). Corpus analysis is also very useful for studying lexical aspects of discourse.

A first step in corpus analysis is to find or construct a corpus that can be used to answer certain research questions. Sometimes existing archives or full-text databases – for example, for daily press or parliamentary documents (see the section on sources in Chapter 2) can be used – while sometimes the best solution is for the researcher to collect texts for a special corpus. In the latter case, already digitised texts may be used or texts may be scanned.

Qualitative text analysis software (*Qualitative Data Analysis* programs, QDA, also known as *Computer Assisted Qualitative Data Analysis Software*, CAQDAS) can then be used to examine various lexical patterns in the texts. One technique is *frequency analysis*. The program counts the frequency of all words in the corpus. Frequency analysis can be used, for example, to identify the topics covered in similar ways as in a content analysis. Frequency analysis is suited for a first comparison of different corpora.

However, as discussed in Chapter 2, the programs are insensitive to the meaning of words, as long as they are used on corpora where the words are not tagged or annotated according to their meaning. A *concordance list* is a list of the occurrences of the word of interest with a chosen number of words before and after it, thus offering an easy way to interpret the word in its local context. Concordance lists could, for example, be created with the freeware program AntConc.

Another function of these applications is called *collocation*, which lists with which other words a particular word tends to occur in the corpus – i.e., next to or with only a few words in between. AntConc can be used for this purpose as well. Baker (2006: Chapter 5) used this technique to study which words tended to occur in the vicinity of 'spinster' and 'bachelor', respectively. After disregarding a number of words of no interest and grouping the remaining words, he concluded that 'bachelor' collocated more frequently with words with a positive value, or words that themselves tended to collocate with words with a positive value, than did 'spinster'. The interpretation might be that the life of an unmarried man tends to be constructed in a more positive way than the life of an unmarried woman.

There are additional useful techniques to exploit in corpus linguistics, including *keyness*, which is a way of comparing when a word occurs statistically more often in one set of texts than in another.

For social scientific discourse analysis techniques of this kind are very useful, not least since social scientists often work with large numbers of texts. The techniques facilitate finding patterns that point to characteristics of the discourse of which the texts are manifestations. They can be of great help in getting an overview of the texts. The computerised techniques are also good for avoiding drawing too strong conclusions on the basis of a few texts.

There are also limitations to these techniques that discourage their use as the sole basis for a discourse analysis. Among these limitations are issues discussed in 'Critical reflections' in Chapter 2. Besides, working with corpora consisting of digitised texts means limitations from the outset (Baker, 2006): existing databases tend to have newer rather than older material, written texts rather than spoken, and texts from rich rather than poor parts of the world.

Critical reflections

Criticism of CDS

Even though CDS has proved fruitful in many contexts and is widely used, it is still partly controversial in linguistics. The normative positioning that characterises many CDS studies has been criticised as being ideologically biased, tendentious and unscientific from the standpoint that science should be objective and descriptive. Such a critique clashes with a critical research tradition, according to which objectivity is hardly possible and researchers *should* use their knowledge and privileged positions to critically examine societal power relations.

A further point of criticism concerns the homogeneous choice of themes and research material by CDS researchers: with few exceptions, they analyse contemporary political and social problems of post-industrial First World societies. For a long time, CDS showed little interest in resistance and counter-discourse, focusing instead on oppressive discourses. By presenting and thereby repeating expressions of oppressive discourse, the research risks reproducing it.

CDS has also been criticised for not paying due attention to the actors who produce the discourse the way ethnographically inspired discourse analysis (Blommaert, 2007) and discourse linguistics (Spitzmüller and Warnke, 2011a, b) do. These approaches focus more strongly on discourse regulating actors (*ideology brokers*) and to which actors have a *voice* in the discourse. Such a perspective opens up for an analysis beyond the identification of discrimination and asymmetrical power relations by ensuring the potential to also consider these discursive representations as resources for resistance and change.

One of Blommaert's (2007) key criticisms of CDA is its linguistic bias – i.e., the focus on linguistic-textual analysis, more specifically on systemic-functional linguistics, that may overlook the ways in which language is embedded in broader social structures and practices. Also, the emphasis on linguistic analysis presupposes a fixation with available discourses. This, in turn, is the basis for the homogeneous choice of topics and data mentioned above, and there is a risk of missing much of the discourse, which is not linguistically encoded.

Criticism of CMT

The notion that metaphors in language really express an underlying pattern of thought has been questioned and it has been asked how this could be investigated (see Gibbs, 2014 for details of this critique).

Furthermore, it has been argued that many expressions analysed as metaphorical in the CMT tradition may be perceived by language users as literal. This applies to *dead* or *inactive metaphors* – i.e., expressions that used to be metaphors but are no longer perceived as such by most language users – e.g., 'to stand behind a proposal', or many expressions that make transfers from the human body to dead objects: 'table leg', 'needle eye' and 'foot of a mountain'. As for the examples in this chapter, the metaphor 'choppy market' is in specific enough use to have a proper definition: 'A choppy market refers to a market condition where prices swing up and down considerably', which indicates that the metaphor is on its way towards inactivity or death.[21]

Another kind of critique is that CMT underestimates the role that metaphorical language plays in rhetorical interactions between people: although there are

---

[21] www.investopedia.com/terms/c/choppymarket.asp, downloaded 20 December 2022.

conceptual metaphors that operate subconsciously, metaphorical language is also important in conscious and planned attempts to persuade others. While this criticism exists, recent research based on psychological experiments has reinforced the idea that conceptual metaphors, as underlying beliefs, are indeed linked to the use of linguistic metaphors in people's imaginations (Gibbs, 2014).

A different and broader view of the role of metaphors in thinking is represented by the theory of *blending* developed by Gilles Fauconnier and Mark Turner (2003) who argue that our way of thinking is far richer and more flexible than the languages we use. The human brain creates new meaning from language in a variety of ways that allow us, often quickly and unconsciously in a specific situation, to expand and multiply the meaning of words. In such processes, there may be more than one source domain.

Critical discourse studies and the study of society

Critical discourse studies in which discourses are seen as semiotic practices anchored in other social practices are by definition interested in social phenomena outside the texts. Yet, to maintain the link between texts and society outside the texts might be challenging, perhaps particularly so when conducting the kind of critical grammatical analysis described above. A 'common pitfall' when working with this method is, according to Koller (2020b: 25), to 'fail to advance beyond description' of text content. When departing from texts in studies of social phenomena, this pitfall needs indeed to be watched out for.

An example of a descriptive grammatical analysis that could well be used in a more comprehensive study of societal phenomena is the analysis of participants, nominalisations and agency in an Indian president's address, held on International Women's Day. The analysis revealed certain patterns in the text.[22] While the speech problematised violence against women and emphasised solutions that included various actors' cooperation for the empowerment of women, the grammatical analysis showed that men were completely deleted as actors of violence against Indian women, while women, despite being mentioned frequently in the texts and urged to demand their rights, were in the majority of cases not referred to as actors but as receivers/recipients. This kind of analysis points to interesting societal issues but is not yet a social scientific study. It would become one, however, if it were included in a larger study motivated by research questions about elite discourse at a national level and how it relates to societal issues such as Indian women's rights. To qualify as a study in the social-scientific field, the linguistic analysis should normally be related to theories about society and its structures, agents or relations between agents.

---

[22] The analysis is demonstrated in Chapter 9 of the first edition of this book, Boréus and Bergström (2017).

Summary

The usefulness of critical discourse studies

- CDS is a broad umbrella that spans several linguistics-inspired methods for analysing different aspects of texts in different genres from a critical perspective.
- The methods of analysis presented in this chapter can be used to disclose perspectives and ideological messages that are not explicitly expressed.
- Conceptual metaphors highlight some aspects of a phenomenon but hide others, which can lead thoughts in certain directions. Therefore, a CMT-inspired analysis can be used to critically examine prevailing beliefs about and perspectives on social phenomena.
- Systematic studies of keywords or other lexical units in texts can be used to critically study how a phenomenon is illuminated from a particular viewpoint.
- Grammatical analysis in the form of a transitivity analysis is useful for uncovering the different perspectives adopted when describing events, actors, relationships and circumstances. Whether something that has occurred is described as an action or an event has implications for whether different participants can be given responsibility for what has occurred.
- Transformations such as nominalisation and passivisation can be examined to show whether actors are present and/or involved in the represented actions and events. Some participants may be more active, whereas others are completely excluded. The analysis can be used to examine what is emphasised or left implicit in discourses.
- Grammatical analyses are time-consuming and do not allow the processing of large amounts of text. They require a basic knowledge of grammar, which can be an obstacle for non-linguists.
- Corpus linguistics can be used for both metaphor analysis and lexical analysis and can be an integrated part of critical discourse studies.

How to do it

- The research question(s) should guide what kinds of (linguistic) tools are applied in the analysis. Make sure you have a clear aim for your study before choosing the tools.
- The kind of analysis presented in the chapter should be combined with an initial, 'ordinary', kind of reading of the texts (all of them if possible, some of them in a larger corpus) to get at the meaning you pick up without particular analyses being conducted.
- In a fully developed critical discourse study, the analysis of texts and discourses is related to other social practices and to social structures. Even in more limited CDS analysis, one should relate text and discourse analysis to a social context.
- A way to recognise a metaphor is to ask whether the literal meaning of the expression would be false or bizarre in the context where it appears. If so, it is a metaphor (or some other figurative expression, such as a metonym).
- Conceptual metaphors are collective notions in a language community according to which a phenomenon is conceptualised in terms of something it is not. They are sought by studying which metaphorical expressions seem to express the same overall notion (TIME IS MONEY).
- By studying keywords in a text, we gain an insight into what the text producer considered important and from what perspective this is portrayed.
- Transitivity analysis studies how events, actors and relations are described by analysing the different elements of clauses and their relations to each other. A conceptual framework drawn from functional grammar is used for this purpose.
- The choice of perspective indicated by the transitivity analysis is contrasted with other possible perspectives on events, actors and relations in a critical analysis.

Suggested reading

A seminal work within CDS is *The Routledge Handbook of Critical Discourse Studies* (Flowerdew and Richardson (eds), 2017). It provides a state-of-the-art overview of the central theories, frameworks, concepts and applications of CDS. The applicability of CDS in various fields such as politics, education, legal and media sciences is demonstrated. In *Methods of Critical Discourse Studies* (Wodak and Meyer (eds), 2016) various strands within CDS, such as the Discourse-Historical Approach and the Dialectical Relational Approach, are presented.

For those who want to deepen their theoretical understanding of the role of metaphors presented here, Lakoff and Johnson (1980) is a good start, clear and well written. It demands some effort from its reader, but it is well worth it, one of the rewards being to have read a classic of the genre. An accessible text on how to conduct metaphor analysis inspired by CMT is Koller (2020a) in a volume edited by Christopher Hart (2020): *Researching Discourse: A Student Guide*.

Machin and Mayr (2012) provide a usable toolbox to analyse lexicon and grammar within the CDS framework. There are several studies using lexical analysis to be inspired by. In a study of the German parliamentary debates on the 1973/1974 oil crisis, historian Ann-Judith Rabenschlag (2021) examines how the keyword 'the West' is deployed as a contested concept. Daniel Wojahn (2023) studies how refugees, migrants and asylum seekers are categorised and denominated in the Swedish Press, 2015-2017, by combining methods from corpus linguistics and CDS. Fowler (2013 [1991]), referred to in the section on grammar analysis, offers a simplified model for examining grammatical relations within critical linguistics. Koller (2020b) and Thompson (2014) are very much recommended introductions for anyone new to systemic functional grammar. After a theoretical background, Koller provides step-by-step instructions on which research questions and which data are suitable for a transitivity analysis. An analysis of leaflets during the 2019 EU election in the UK is carried out to illustrate the use and significance of processes and participants. Those who want to delve deeper into systemic functional grammar can consult Halliday and Matthiessen (2014), which, however, demands advanced grammatical knowledge from its readers.

A good introduction to corpus linguistics is Baker (2020). Baker (2006) is an excellent start for anyone who wants to learn more about techniques in corpus linguistics, while Baker (2009) is a collection of different texts on how corpus linguistics can be used. Charteris-Black (2004) shows corpus linguistic metaphor analyses of religious and political texts as well as sports and financial reports. Koller (2009) shows how metaphor analysis can be carried out on a corpus using specific software in a study of religious and political metaphors in corporate discourse.

The journals *Discourse and Society, Critical Discourse Studies, Discourse & Communication, Journal of Political Communication, Multimodality & Society* and *Visual Communication* regularly publish articles on CDS-oriented discourse analysis, including studies of metaphor and grammar.

Exercises

Exercise 1: The nation, metaphorically speaking

This exercise is about expressions of nationalism, a well-researched topic (see, for example, Wodak et al., 2009). Political elites use public speeches to convince people to rally round the flag and the national leadership, and to convey the qualities of their nation to outsiders. This is done differently in different countries, due to countries' varying history and the ideas that dominate in the public spheres. The expressions of nationalism and of what the nation is and represents also vary over time and might be contentious within a country.

The task

Examine the metaphors and other figurative language used by national elite persons (prime ministers, presidents, party spokespersons, royalties, ministers or others) to refer to the nation in two different countries. Start by listing all the metaphors for the nation/country in the texts. Then analyse which conceptual metaphors for the nations that seem to be at work. An example of what you might find is the conceptual metaphor NATION X IS A PERSON, often expressed by statements about a nation *doing* or *feeling* what only persons can do or feel, such as that the nation 'is striving for' something or 'is prepared to stand up for' some value. Consider also expressions such as 'nation-building' and what conceptual metaphors for the country or nation they might express. Discuss what these conceptual metaphors highlight and what they conceal. Finally, compare your findings for the two countries and point out similarities and differences. Discuss further how similarities and differences found could be explained.

The texts

Use the Internet to find transcripts of speeches by elite persons from two countries. You can compare speeches from two different English-speaking countries, but to compare speeches in different languages might be more rewarding. Speeches are preferable since they often contain more figurative language than do documents. It might be necessary to analyse a number of speeches before interesting metaphors for the country or nation are found.

Exercise 2: Keywords of our time

The COVID pandemic, which spread across the world in spring 2020, is to be considered a historical event. How was this crisis conceptualised in public discourse? To explore this huge question, a keyword analysis that considers the features of central concepts can be used as an entry point.

(Continued)

(Continued)

The task

Our primary research interest here is to find out which keywords emerged in public discourse during the pandemic. But we also want to know how these keywords were used - i.e., with what meanings, with what values and in what context they appear in different texts. To identify the keywords in texts, use the characteristics listed in the section on keywords above. Since it will be necessary to consult several different texts for the analysis, it may be advisable to use corpus analysis software - for example, AntConc. The analysis of the keywords must be done manually, but the first step can advantageously be done automatically. AntConc can provide both word frequencies and collocations. After removing function words or similar, keywords can be identified and their use analysed in detail with the help of concordance lists. What meanings do you identify? Do they have negative or positive connotations? Are the keywords differently used and part of semantic struggles? The findings may show what ideologies, attitudes and policies the keywords indicate.

The texts

We are interested in how the pandemic was represented in public discourse through certain keywords. The aim is therefore to analyse texts that we can assume have determined the discourse to some extent and that are publicly accessible on, for example, online platforms. Conceivable examples would be speeches by members of the government, information from the public health authority or editorials in newspapers with large circulation. A contrastive perspective can be fruitful for this exercise by comparing texts from, for example, different countries.

Exercise 3: Who is visible in history?

In this exercise, we use functional grammar (especially transitivity analysis) to analyse how social actors are represented in history textbooks. Textbooks are powerful producers of knowledge as they are read by many students and thus shape their ideas about, for example, the history of a nation.

The task

Taking a critical perspective on what is taught through textbooks, we can ask the following questions: Which social actors are represented in the texts? How are they portrayed? What processes are ascribed to them? And what consequences do these (chosen) representations have for how we look at history? Use the transitivity analysis presented above to systematically list the participants and processes that appear in the texts. Who takes an active role and who is rather backgrounded or even invisible? For example, there might be differences in the participant roles that women and men or natives and migrants have in the texts. The analysis of participants and processes could

(Continued)

(Continued)
provide information about the roles attributed to different groups in the historiography of a nation that in turn influences today's discourse on, for example, gender and migration.

The texts

Textbooks in history for grammar/secondary schools are suitable for this analysis. These may be available online, but can otherwise be obtained through the library or second hand. Since grammatical analysis is time-consuming, it is advisable to focus on specific sections. A comparison between textbooks from different regions or countries can be fruitful, as well as a combination with the multimodal analysis presented in Chapter 8, as textbooks contain many visual elements.

8

Multimodal Discourse Analysis

Anders Björkvall

Background

The rationale for this book is that the analysis of texts is of key importance for our understanding of a number of issues in society at large. However, in many texts language alone does not create meaning. Instead, images, illustrations and information graphics play key roles for the production and interpretation of meaning. This is obviously the case in contemporary mass media and social media texts, on many websites and in advertisements, but also, for instance, in pamphlets and leaflets from political parties, governments and organisations as well as in textbooks and reports in various formats. Such texts are often referred to as multimodal texts. The concept of text is extended to include modes of communication other than just writing or speaking (cf. Chapter 1). Too strict a focus on the linguistic parts of these texts comes with the risk of missing out on other relevant meanings conveyed by other modes, such as images. Any student or researcher in the social sciences who is interested in conducting a more detailed analysis of texts may thus have use for analytical tools that connect to linguistic text analysis, but at the same time go beyond the written parts of the text.

Figure 8.1 shows the cover of a report (Wallace, 2010) that the public interest group GeneWatch UK has produced for Greenpeace International. Figure 8.2 presents a page from a brochure produced by the Swedish Nuclear Fuel and Waste Management Company. Both texts deal with the same topic: the handling and disposal of nuclear waste and its consequences. In addition, images are of key importance for the communicative functions of both texts, but from the perspective of this chapter, the differences between the two texts are more interesting. The texts present two totally different perspectives on the handling of nuclear waste, an increasingly present environmental, economic and societal challenge in many parts of the world. And it is through the combination of images, illustrations and language that these differences become most obvious.

The Swedish Nuclear Fuel and Waste Management Company is responsible for the 'safe' disposal of spent nuclear fuel in Sweden, a country that has had nuclear power plants since the 1960s. The text in Figure 8.2 (Swedish Nuclear Fuel and Waste Management Company) contains a schematic illustration of how different types of spent fuel are transported between power plants and their final disposal. Arrows in different colours systematically connect the different units. Such illustrations can give the impression of scientific precision and accuracy. In addition, this illustration is placed at the top of the page, thus setting a tone of 'technical reliability' for the rest of the page. Just below the illustration there is a caption which reads 'Sweden has a well-functioning system for managing and disposing of various types of radioactive waste'. The illustration of the nuclear-waste management system and the verbal confirmation that the system is 'well-functioning' complement each other: the illustration shows how the different units of the system are dynamically connected and the writing is used to evaluate the functionality of the system. This relation between the illustration and the linguistic statement is what Roland Barthes called 'relay' in one of the most

Figure 8.1 Cover of a GeneWatch UK report for Greenpeace

influential papers ever written on image–language relations: 'Rhetoric of the image' (1977: 32–51). In other words, the illustration of the nuclear-waste management system and the sentence that evaluates the system create a combined meaning at a higher level than if they were to be interpreted separately. This complementary view of image–language relations is one of the cornerstones of the model for multimodal discourse analysis presented in this chapter.

The cover of the GeneWatch UK report for Greenpeace in Figure 8.1 presents a different view of the disposal of spent fuel. Despite the fact that this is a report presenting research findings – the subtitle of the report is 'A scientific review of

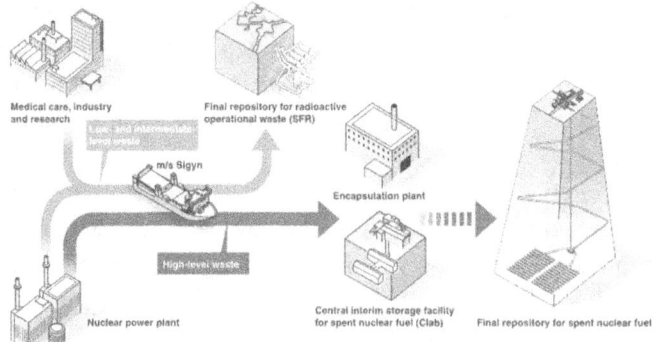

Figure 8.2 Page from a brochure by the Swedish Nuclear Fuel and Waste Management Company

geological disposal of high-level radioactive waste' – there are no information graphics in the text. Instead, there is a sepia-coloured photograph of a stone with an inscription. There is also a question at the top of the page, 'Rock Solid?', which is also the main title of the report, and the question is set in a colour that matches the sepia tone of the photograph. Colour is thus used as a means for emphasising the connection between the critical question and the stone with the inscription. This top-placed question frames the rest of the messages found in Figure 8.1: can we really trust rock as a final repository for spent nuclear fuel? The inscription on the stone has a salient warning, 'CAUTION–DO NOT DIG', followed by information saying that 'radioactive material from nuclear research' is 'buried' in the area. This danger of 'buried' nuclear waste is further emphasised by the stone's visual resemblance to a tombstone. Is the human race digging its own grave when burying nuclear waste underground? This type of *semiotic sign* (see Chapter 1), based on resemblance, is what the founding father of semiotics, Charles Sanders Peirce, called an *iconic sign*.

Even though both Peirce and Barthes, who along with Ferdinand de Saussure and Umberto Eco are two of the most influential names in general semiotics, have been mentioned in the introduction to this chapter, the aim of the chapter is not to present a classic semiotic account of the analysis of images. Instead, it introduces one version of *multimodal discourse analysis*, which offers tools for analysing texts such as the ones in Figures 8.1 and 8.2 – but also many other multimodal texts – as multimodal ensembles. The theoretical and methodological framework comes from the work by Gunther Kress and Theo van Leeuwen, mainly from their book *Reading Images: The Grammar of Visual Design* (3rd edn, 2021). The basic assumption is that *discourses*, defined as 'socially constructed knowledges of (some aspect of) reality' (Kress and van Leeuwen, 2001: 4), can be expressed in many shapes and forms – in many communicative modes – which calls for analytical frameworks that can handle multimodal texts.

However, since the groundbreaking book *Reading Images* came out in its first edition in 1996, the field of multimodal discourse analysis has expanded and developed. Two developments are worth noting here. First, there has been a movement from primarily extending linguistic models for text analysis to images and other visual representations (diagrams, tables, etc.) to the full range of multimodal meaning making through, for instance, architecture, sculptures and monuments, dance, or digitally mediated touch. This development is also reflected in how key journals for multimodal discourse analysis, such as *Visual Communication*, are now complemented with journals titled *Multimodal Communication* and *Multimodality & Society*. However, because of the scope of this book, the present chapter is mainly concerned with visual dimensions of texts, as defined above, rather than, for instance, dance.

Second, and related to the first development, there have been debates regarding the usefulness of the *metafunctions of language* (cf. Chapter 1) for the analysis of visual and other types of multimodal communication. In a rather heated debate in the journal *Critical Discourse Studies*, Ledin and Machin (2018a) argued that applying the metafunctions to other modes of communication than language comes with the risk of just 'ticking off' a number of meaning potentials in multimodal texts based on very strong theoretical assumptions, mostly valid for language. Instead, they suggest that every multimodal analysis must be based on the practices of, for instance, photography and how those practices have shaped the materialities and, thus, potentials for (and restrictions of) meaning making in that particular mode.

With reference to the overall scope of this book, the present chapter *is* structured in relation to the metafunctions (Chapter 1) and, thus, also relates closely to the chapters on discourse analysis (Chapter 6) and critical discourse studies (Chapter 7). However, the metafunctions should be understood as a means of exploring how *interactional*, *representational* and *compositional* aspects of multimodal texts can have meaning potential rather than as a model for describing how visual communication always works.

As mentioned, the major part of the concepts introduced in the chapter comes from Kress and van Leeuwen (2021). Not all of the concepts can, of course, be included in this chapter, and some analytical concepts have been merged, all in order to make the chapter accessible to readers who have little or no previous knowledge of discourse analysis and linguistics. The chapter begins with an introduction to how symbolic *interaction* can be analysed. This part focuses on the interactive potential set up between a producer of a text, or a depicted person, and the reader or viewer. The analysis relates to issues of power, as well as exclusion and inclusion from social interaction. For instance, depicted persons can be presented as if they are inferior, superior or equals to the person looking at an image. They can also be depicted in a way that symbolically includes or excludes them from the social world or social group of the viewer. The analysis of such symbolic interactions can be performed in relatively close connection to what is described as the *interpersonal* function of texts in Chapter 1 of this book.

Then follows a description of how *representations* of goings-on in the world can be analysed from a multimodal perspective. This analysis relates to what is called the *ideational* or *representational* function of texts in Chapter 1 (Halliday and Matthiessen, 2014: 30). Depicted persons, and sometimes objects, will be called *participants* in this analysis, and the participants can be represented as active or passive in texts. This dynamic, or the lack thereof, is expressed as *processes*: who does what to whom or what other type of relation is set up between participants represented in a multimodal text? The analysis of processes and participants can give insights on how different versions of goings-on can be construed in multimodal texts depending on, for example, the interests of the producers of texts and the dominating ideologies and discourses in various realms of society.

The last part of the analysis presented in the chapter deals with *composition*, related to the *textual* metafunction as described in Chapter 1. One difference between verbal language and images is that images are *spatially* organised, whereas language is primarily organised according to a *temporal* and *linear* logic. In other words, a linguistically oriented text analysis will often include answering the question of 'in what order?' since the linear order of words is highly meaningful. 'Will I see you tomorrow?' has a different meaning from 'I will see you tomorrow', just as 'the protesters were threatening the police' is fundamentally different from 'the police were threatening the protesters'. In the analysis of the composition of images, the guiding question is 'where?' – in other words, the placement of an element in an image, but also of elements on a larger page such as those in Figures 8.1 and 8.2, carries meaning. It matters whether an element in a visual composition is placed high or low, to the left, to the right, or in the centre. It also matters whether it is larger or smaller in relation to other elements in the composition.

The analysis of symbolic interaction, representations of goings-on in the world and composition all aim at identifying different types of meaning in multimodal texts. Such an analysis can form the foundation for further investigations into issues of gender, power or ethnicity: 'How are masculinities, femininities and ethnicities construed in election pamphlets in India and Canada?', 'Why are women construed as less active than men in advertising?', 'Why are citizens positioned as powerless in texts from public authorities when they are supposed to be empowered?', or 'Why does the format of Instagram always place the images above the writing, and how does that affect the social and political potential of this particular social medium?'

Even though the focus on meanings of multimodal texts can be rewarding when investigating issues in the social sciences, it requires careful epistemological and methodological considerations right from the start of the analysis. Meanings in and of texts are by no means static or given since they are intrinsically connected to the social, cultural and historical contexts of the texts, and to the interests and interpretative strategies of the producers of texts and their readers. In multimodal discourse analysis, just as in critical discourse studies, *meaning potential* (or *semiotic potential*; see van Leeuwen, 2005: 4) is the preferred term when talking about texts. The assumption is that texts contain a number of potential meanings that the reader recognises, does not recognise or, perhaps, chooses to ignore when interpreting the text. In order to know which of these meaning potentials are actualised when a reader meets a certain text, the processes of actual reading and interpretation have to be studied. That type of analysis requires different methodological tools from the text analytical tools presented in this chapter, such as interviews, questionnaires and ethnographic studies of how texts are brought into social practices. The point is that anyone who analyses multimodal texts – or any text – based on the terminology introduced in this chapter must recognise that they can only identify potential meanings, rather than fixed meanings of texts that are relevant for anyone, anywhere, at any given point in time. For the sake of simplicity, the term *meaning* will still be used in this chapter, keeping in mind that the explanatory value of the analysis cannot go beyond potential meanings. This also means the analysis presented here above all relates to the interpretation strategies of 'preferred readings' and 'constructions of text internal reader identities' presented in Table 1.2 in Chapter 1.

A short analysis of one of the features of the text from GeneWatch UK for Greenpeace in Figure 8.1 may illustrate the difference between meaning potentials and meanings that are actualised by readers of the text. The multimodal text has the headline 'Rock Solid?' and both the headline and the photo of the stone are sepia toned. The use of the same colour for many elements in a multimodal text can create *cohesion*, connecting the elements. More specifically, images and written elements that have the same colour have the meaning potential of 'we belong together' or 'we are connected' is referred to as *visual rhymes* in multimodal discourse analysis. In that way, the critical question in the headline, 'Rock Solid?', is connected to the image and its content. The critical question is explicitly supported by the image: radioactive material is detrimental to the environment and dangerous, or even lethal, to humans. At the same time, it is by no means certain that all readers will acknowledge or notice this visual, colour-based connection between the headline and the image. For instance, to some readers the difference between the mode of writing and image will overshadow the meaning potential of colour as a cohesive resource. The fact that the solidity of the rock can actually be questioned just by looking back at historical nuclear experiments – in this case, in the USA – is then a meaning potential of the multimodal text that may not be recognised or actualised by the reader.

Accordingly, the method for analysis presented in this chapter can result in reasonable interpretations of texts based on what we know from text and discourse analytical research regarding how texts are constructed, but also how they tend to be interpreted. Thus, the method can offer descriptions of preferred readings and interpretations, which do not in any way exclude other readings.

Analysis

Qualitative methods for analysis usually require a toolbox with many analytical concepts and terms, even though not all of them will become relevant for every single study. The sample analyses below contain a number of multimodal texts from different parts of the world, but only certain aspects of these will be analysed, always with the aim of showing how the basic analytical concepts can be employed in order to answer questions relevant to the social sciences.

Interaction

Many multimodal texts contain images of persons, and there is a potential for symbolic interaction between the depicted persons in an image and the person that actually looks at the image, located outside the image; this person will be referred to as the reader of a multimodal text.

The majority of relations between human beings involve power; this is also the case in the type of symbolic interaction discussed here. Power relations between depicted persons and a reader can be of three main types. First, the relation can be set up as if power is attributed to the reader. Second, power can be given to depicted persons, and, third, an equal power relation can be set up. *As if* is a key expression here, since the analytical interest is directed toward symbolic relations of power. We usually know very little about the actual power relations between the reader of a multimodal text (or of any text for that matter) and the people depicted in it.

The most important resource for expressions of *symbolic power relations* is the camera angle, what is sometimes referred to as the *perspective* of an image or another visual representation. There are three main vertical perspectives in images (Kress and van Leeuwen, 2021: 138–40):

- from above;
- from below;
- eye-to-eye.

In the *from above perspective*, the reader is symbolically placed in a position that looks down on the depicted person. This gives symbolic power to the reader. In the *from below perspective*, power is attributed to the persons in the image. Finally, the *eye-to-eye perspective* is the perspective of 'equality'.

Figure 8.3 shows a multimodal text posted on a wall in central Cape Town, South Africa. Someone has glued a paper advertisement from the City of Cape Town, featuring the (now former) mayor Patricia De Lille, to the wall. De Lille is depicted slightly from below, thus attributing power to the mayor, but not too obviously. She is a democratically elected mayor, and it would possibly be too challenging to further increase the 'from below' perspective in which the reader is positioned.

In the case of the De Lille text, the vertical camera angle is used to underline the authority of the mayor in office, but at the same time she is addressing the citizens of Cape Town as part of a social group that she herself is or wants to be part of. If for a minute we disregard the adjustments (the speech bubble and the red marker blurring) that someone has made to the text in Figure 8.3, De Lille states that 'I have a drug problem, and so do you' and that 'we may not use them, but they still affect us'. In the first statement, the personal pronoun 'I' is matched with 'you' – the reader. In the second sentence, De Lille and readers of the poster are grouped together as 'we' and 'us'.

The linguistically expressed meanings are matched with interactional meanings expressed in the image in Figure 8.3. These meanings have to do with symbolic *inclusion* and *exclusion* in a social group, and with symbolic *distance*. Whereas the vertical perspective in an image was described as the perspective of symbolic

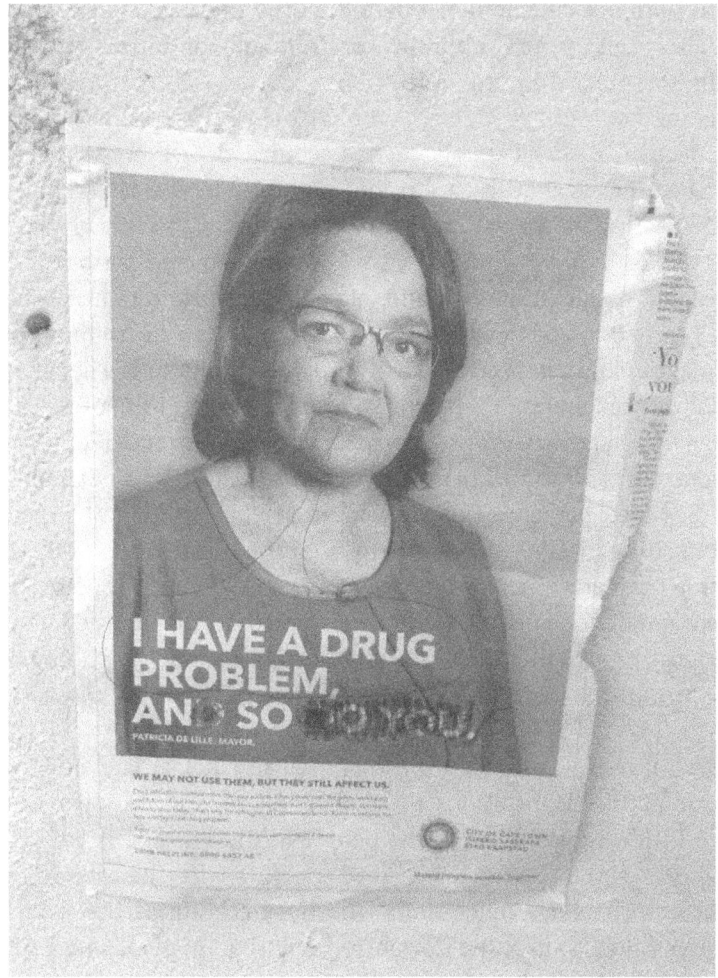

Figure 8.3 Patricia De Lille in a Cape Town street

power, the horizontal perspective is that of inclusion or exclusion. Three main options are available (see 'involvement', Kress and van Leeuwen, 2021: 133–8):

- full frontal;
- rear view;
- side view.

In the *full frontal perspective* the reader is placed in a horizontal position right in front of the depicted person. This is the perspective of 'social involvement' and it is illustrated by the full frontal image of mayor De Lille in Figure 8.3. The horizontal perspective of this image makes the reader look straight at the mayor, symbolically including her in their social group. This is in line with the visually most salient sentences in the text where the drug problem is described as something that affects all in the community, even the mayor. In this way, the interactive meanings expressed by the horizontal perspective in the image support the written statements.

The perspective of social involvement becomes clearer if compared with the two other perspectives that to various degrees exclude the depicted person from the reader's social world or group. The first example is the rear view perspective, the perspective of 'full detachment', in which the depicted persons are excluded from the reader's social group. It would, of course, be absurd to make the reader of the text in Figure 8.3 face De Lille's back, but it is not an uncommon perspective in media images. This perspective assigns full anonymity to the depicted persons, thus symbolically excluding them from the social world of the reader.

The side view perspective is also a perspective of exclusion, but of 'partial' rather than 'full' detachment. In this perspective the reader is placed in an oblique angle facing the depicted persons. This camera angle shows a certain interest in the depicted, but still partially excludes them from the social group of the reader. For instance, this perspective can be recognised from early anthropological photography where indigenous people were often depicted from the side view perspective, symbolically excluding them from the social world of the photographer and, accordingly, from that of the viewer of such images (see Kress and van Leeuwen, 2021: 133–5).

The lower image in Figure 8.2 from the Swedish Nuclear Fuel and Waste Management Company also positions the reader in the side view perspective. This may seem a little strange: why are the people in the image not fully included in the social group of the reader? When read together with the caption, the reason becomes clearer: 'It is the generations who have consumed the electricity from nuclear power who also bear the responsibility for safely managing and disposing of the spent nuclear fuel.' In other words, the persons in the image are part of the group that are responsible for the management and disposal of spent nuclear fuel. It is not assumed that the reader of the texts is or wants to be part of that social group. Another aspect of the image is that the depicted persons seem to look at something far away; perhaps they look towards the future. This, however, is a representation of the goings-on in the world that will be discussed in the next section of this chapter.

There is another noticeable difference between the image of De Lille in Figure 8.3 and the group of people in Figure 8.2. The reader encounters the depicted persons at different distances with De Lille at a personal distance and the group of people at a longer distance. The category of *symbolic distance* in images (see 'Social distance', Kress and van Leeuwen, 2021: 123–9) is inspired by the theories of the anthropologist Edward T. Hall (1966). Put briefly, Hall suggested that the physical distances that human beings keep between each other in social life are directly related to the social relation between the persons involved in interaction. For instance, one can usually keep a closer physical distance to one's father than to one's superior at work. These physical distances vary between cultures and subcultures, and so does the enactment of social roles, but the point here is that Hall's way of thinking can be helpful when analysing symbolic distances in multimodal texts.

Kress and van Leeuwen (2021: 123) suggest that *size of frame* is the main resource for expressing symbolic distance in images. Depending on how the image is cropped, the depicted persons stand out as more or less distanced from the reader. Figure 8.4 presents a number of different symbolic distances that can be expressed through size of frame. The figure is a simplification of the different distances presented by Kress and van Leeuwen (2021: 123–9).

The depicted persons are found at the centre of Figure 8.4. When a *personal distance* is expressed, the image of a person is cropped in a way that no more than the head and shoulders are visible, or sometimes even less, such as the face or parts of the face only. In relation to Hall's description of enacted social distances, this framing of an image would symbolically place the reader at a distance that we can keep only to persons that we know well, such as close friends or family.

At a *social distance* the depicted persons would be cropped at the waist or at the knees; the image can also be cropped in such a way that a person's entire body, but not much more, is shown within the frame of the image. Here, the reader is symbolically positioned as if they are at a farther distance from the persons in the image than in the case of personal distance. Social distance is the distance which in Western culture is usually upheld between, for instance, colleagues at a workplace. Finally, at an *impersonal distance*, persons can also be depicted in full figure, but they will only occupy less than half of the total image space and be presented as if they were strangers or more distant acquaintances.

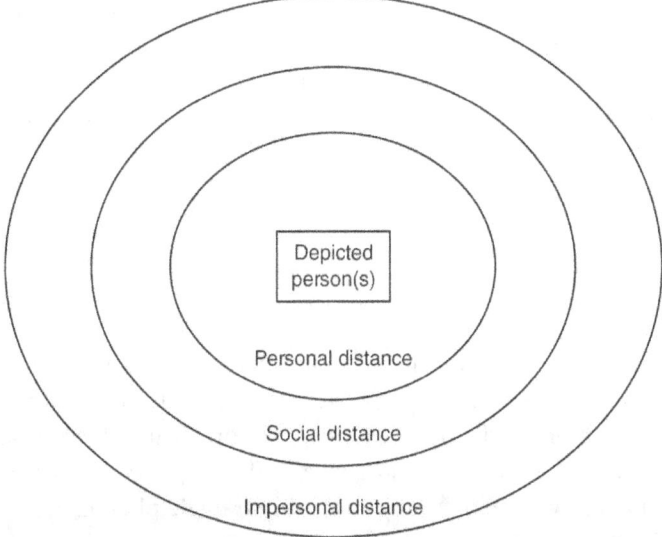

Figure 8.4 Symbolic distance in images

The use of size of frame for expressing symbolic distance is illustrated in both Figures 8.2 and 8.3. The lower image of a group of people in Figure 8.2 expresses impersonal distance between the reader and the depicted persons. They are all shown in full figure, but the persons occupy less than half of the space of the full image. This is actually in line with the interactional meanings expressed in the rest of this multimodal text. The text is dominated by rather formal statements that, for instance, lack personal pronouns that can sometimes give a text more of a dialogic, or interactive, character.

It is today's generations that have created the energy requirement and have consumed electrical energy. It is Sweden as a nation that has benefitted from energy production. The nuclear-waste issue is both a national and a local matter.

The persons in the photograph are not presented as friends of the reader or as someone who wants to be close to the reader; they are distant representatives of a generation that 'have consumed electrical energy' and of 'Sweden as a nation'. It is probably also the case that the topic of the multimodal text – 'the nuclear-waste issue' – is not a personal issue – at least, it is not presented as such in the text. Rather, it is a present, but also future, responsibility for an entire generation, of which the distant persons in the image are representatives.

In Figure 8.3, Mayor De Lille is depicted as if she were at a social, almost personal, distance in relation to the reader. As mentioned, the writing in this multimodal text directly addresses the reader through the use of personal pronouns and includes the reader in the social group of 'we' and 'us'. Thus, the less distanced interaction set up by the image is in line with the other choices made in the text, including the full frontal perspective. The topic, drug use, may also play a role here as something more personal and close, affecting members of the community in a more direct way than nuclear-waste disposal.

The text in Figure 8.3 also illustrates the last feature of the analysis of symbolic interaction: *speech* and *image acts*. In *systemic functional linguistics*, the theory of language that underpins some of the analytical tools in, for instance, critical discourse studies (see Chapter 7), a distinction between four basic speech acts is made (Halliday and Matthiessen, 2014: 135–8):

- statements;
- questions;
- offers;
- commands.

A *statement*, 'Joe Biden won the election', implies that the speaker or writer *offers information* to the listener or reader. Information can also be *demanded*, 'Did Joe Biden win the election?', which is a *question*. Not only can information be offered or demanded through the use of language, but also *goods* and *services*. To offer goods and services, 'Please, have a look at our strategic plan' is, not surprisingly, called an *offer*, whereas demanding goods and services is described as a *command*, 'Give me a copy of the constitution'.

There are a number of other, more specific, speech acts as well – for instance, *warnings* or perhaps *insinuations* – but in principle, these can all be sorted under one of the basic speech acts: the warning is a type of command – 'watch out' – and the insinuation is a type of statement – 'I saw you with your ex-husband yesterday'. However, from the perspective of the analysis of texts in the social sciences, such semantic and to some extent grammatical categorisations are usually of lesser importance. More interesting is the fact that the basic speech acts presuppose a specific *response*, which is relevant for the type of interaction that a reader of a text is invited to. Statements presuppose some kind of *consideration* as a response, or at least an *acknowledgement* on the behalf of the listener or the reader, even if such an acknowledgement can be almost unnoticeable: 'Joe Biden won the election.' – 'Oh, really?'. Questions presuppose *answers*, whereas the preferred response to an offer would be an *acceptance*: 'Please, have a look at the constitution of our party' – 'Yes, I will'. Commands require some kind of *action* that does not need to be verbally expressed, even though it can be accompanied by language or gesture: 'Give me a copy of the constitution' – 'Here you are.'

These are all examples of preferred responses to the various speech acts, but again, it is difficult to know how an actual reader will react to a text that is dominated by, for example, questions or commands. It is any reader's privilege to 'read against' a text. What an analysis of speech acts in a text can provide is a description of its preferred response structure. Such a response structure can offer an indication of whether a text tends to be open for interaction – if it invites the reader through its response structure – or if it is more closed to interaction. A text dominated by statements has the lowest interactive potential in terms of response structure; it only presupposes that the reader acknowledges its offer of information. Offers (of goods and services) are slightly more interactive; the reader has at least to accept or reject these. Commands and questions are the most interactive speech acts since they presuppose actions and answers from the listener or reader.

Kress and van Leeuwen (2021: 115–23) argue that just as there are speech acts that can be expressed in speech and writing, there are *image acts* that can be expressed in the visual mode. However, they also argue that the resources for expressing image acts are not as specified as those used for speech acts. The analysis of image acts is therefore less complex and only includes *offers* and *demands*. Offers are expressed in the visual mode when the gazes of depicted persons are not directed toward the reader, as in the lower image in Figure 8.2. In that image the reader is just offered to watch the persons; the interactive potential of the image is low.

In Figure 8.3, Patricia De Lille is looking straight at the reader and the image act of demand is expressed. Exactly what De Lille is demanding is hard to say, but perhaps she is demanding attention, or social interaction of some kind. The human gaze is a powerful interactional resource, and it would be difficult for any reader to totally avoid the demand character of this and similar images.

A brief analysis of the image act in Figure 8.3, together with the most salient speech acts in the text, can show how image acts and speech acts combine in multimodal texts, but also how changing one single speech act may completely change the interactive meanings into a humoristic critical commentary. As mentioned, the text was posted on a wall in Cape Town and it is unclear whether the person posting the text actually made the changes to it or not. It could also have been a process of different people adding elements to the text once it was posted. Originally, the larger, top positioned and framed part of the text consisted of the demand image in which De Lille demands something from the reader along with the sentence 'I have a drug problem, and so do you'. The sentence is a type of statement that could be interpreted more specifically as a *confession*. The original preferred response structure thus implies that the mayor seeks attention visually and then verbally states facts that the reader is expected to acknowledge.

Three noticeable changes have then been made to the multimodal text: the 'do you' including the full stop has been blurred by a red marker pen; the 'd' in 'end' has been blurred in the same way, and a speech bubble has been added encircling the statement 'I have a drug problem'. The speech bubble further connects the statement to the mayor – there is no doubt that she is the speaker. From the perspective of speech acts and image acts, the second part of the sentence is turned into a question: 'an so' (the reason for blurring the 'd' in 'and' is probably to turn the mayor's language into a slightly more vernacular version of English). This adjustment to the print also strikes out the 'you', the reader in this section of the text, and all the focus is directed towards the problems of the mayor. In the new multimodal ensemble of image and writing, the mayor still seeks attention through a visual demand, but then she produces the confession that she is a drug addict, which is completed with the 'an so' question, asking the reader what the problem is with that.

Thus, the text in Figure 8.3 is an example of how different visual and verbal resources can be combined in order to invite a reader to a specific kind of interaction. It also illustrates what can happen with the meanings of a text when other resources – in this case, mostly visual resources – are added: information from a public institution such as the City of Cape Town can be turned into a critical commentary regarding the mayor's drug policy or into political caricature, making fun of a politician with power.

Representations of goings-on in the world

The second, broader type of meaning making through multimodal texts has to do with representations of goings-on in the world; of the dynamic actions or non-dynamic states that participants represented in a text are engaged in. It is important to stress the term *representation*. The version of multimodal discourse analysis presented here rests on the assumption that versions of reality are created in texts, and these versions depend on, among other things, the interests of the persons behind the text or normative discourses. In other words, a going-on in the world – for example, an action by someone towards someone else – can be represented in many, sometimes contradictory, ways. The tools for analysis of representations presented below can be employed in order to say something about various representations rather than making statements about a 'reality' outside the texts.

The relation between *participants* in an image – for instance, depicting US soldiers or Taliban fighters – can be represented in relation to *processes* of different types. A participant can be represented as an *actor* in an *action process*. An actor is a participant that initiates and is active in a dynamic going-on; a soldier can 'threaten' another soldier with a gun, and the threatened soldier is represented as the *goal* in the action process. An analysis of such and related representations can point to ideological choices in a text – for example, when people of a specific ethnicity or gender are always represented as actors and people of another ethnicity or gender are always represented as goals.

Even though they are not identical, the analytical tools presented here connect to the analysis of *transitivity* presented in Chapter 7 of this book (see Tables 7.1 and 7.2). Kress and van Leeuwen (2021: 44–112) have developed a detailed account of participants and processes that can be visually represented. A selection has been made for this chapter, based on the relevance for students in the social sciences when analysing multimodal texts.

Although there can be no exact mapping between transitivity in language and in image, action processes are the visually expressed processes that are most similar to the *material actions* described in Chapter 7. These are processes that take place in the outer, material world and not, for instance, in the human mind. In language, the processes are expressed by verbs, most commonly a finite verb, in a clause: 'the soldier *shoots* at the enemy'. In that clause, 'the soldier' is the actor, 'shoots' expresses the process (a material action in the terminology of Chapter 7) and 'the enemy' is the goal. If a similar process were to be expressed in an image, this could be done as in the example in Figure 8.5, a screenshot from the popular computer game *Call of Duty*.

The function of the finite verb in language, 'shoots', is carried by the rifle in Figure 8.5. The rifle functions as a *vector* (Kress and van Leeuwen, 2021: 45) and connects the actor – the soldier who 'shoots' – with the goal, the enemy in the building. A vector is formed by an arrow or a line in an image that creates dynamic meanings revolving around 'movement' and 'action'. Usually, but not always, vectors emanate in one participant, the actor, and point to another participant, the goal. An example would be when participants in a public rally or demonstration are represented as either actors – for example, raising their arms with the function of vectors in the direction of a goal, such as the police, or when the police (actors) are represented as pointing their weapons (vectors) at a protesting crowd of people (goals). There are less dramatic examples of action processes, of course, and also those that do not explicitly involve human participants. *MS Sigyn*, the ship at the

Figure 8.5 Vectors in an action process

top of the illustration in Figure 8.2, where it is explained how radioactive waste is transported, is dynamically connected to, for example, the 'final repository for radioactive operational waste' and the 'encapsulation plant' through the use of arrows. In other words, *MS Sigyn* is represented as the actor that 'transports' the waste to the other, non-human, goals in this action process.

From the perspective of broader issues addressed in the social sciences, it is relevant that the participant roles in action processes in images are the results of choices made by someone with a specific interest at a specific point in time. A public rally for whatever purpose can be represented as including active protesters or active law-enforcement representatives. An analysis of such representations can say something interesting, not only about power relations in a society, but also about access to the public sphere for different groups of people. Further, the action process of handling nuclear waste could be visually represented as a process involving human participants in the roles of actors or goals, but in Figure 8.2 it is not. Instead, all the participants are non-human, from the actor, the ship *MS Sigyn*, to the goals: 'encapsulation plant', 'final repository for radioactive operational waste' and ultimately 'the final repository for spent nuclear fuel' (see Table 7.1). This may make the process seem safer and more controlled than what would have been the case if human actors had been explicitly represented in the illustration. Again, such an analysis can be broadened to ask questions of how 'risks' are handled and dealt with in different areas of society.

A few other types of participants in action processes need to be mentioned. If a vector does not point in a specific direction, or if it has the shape of a double-edged arrow, both emanating in and pointing to participants, it is hard to say if the participants are actors or goals. In such cases, and they are quite common, both the participants are called *interactors*. A typical example would be two heads of state photographed when shaking hands at the final press conference of a state visit. Again, from the perspective of representation of power, it matters whether a head of state is repeatedly represented as only a goal at the state visit, or as an interactor or actor.

In other cases, a vector points at a goal, but the participant in which it emanates is not in the image, or the origin of a vector in an image lies in an empty space. In other words, no actor that initiates the process. The vector still represents a dynamic process, but it represents an *event* rather than an action (see Chapter 7, 'Analysing grammar'). Objects that 'fall' may, for example, leave speed lines; 'to fall' is not an action, but rather a dynamic process without an explicitly represented initiator.

Events, just like action processes, take place in an outer reality whereas *reaction processes* and *mental processes* take place on the inside of human beings, in their minds. In reaction processes, the human gaze functions as a vector, connecting depicted persons in a multimodal text. The participant that 'looks' is analysed as a *reacter*, and the participant towards which the gaze is directed is the *phenomenon*. The participant doing the looking *reacts* to something in the world – the phenomenon; the gaze connects the outer world phenomenon with the inner reality of the reacter. In some cases, as in the lower image in Figure 8.2, the phenomenon is not in the image. The gazes of the depicted persons are directed towards an invisible phenomenon. This opens up for slightly more abstract interpretations. Are the persons in the image envisaging the future of nuclear power; are they looking at future generations, reflecting on the responsibility of their own generation?

Another example of reaction processes are the cases when two participants are looking at each other; they become *interreacters* (similar to interactors in action processes). This is illustrated in the image in Figure 8.6 that is part of a multimodal text that includes print ('Sexuality, it's not just about sex' and 'Gender') and handwriting – for instance, 'What is the difference between sex and gender?' and 'It's still love'.

The two men are represented as interreacters in a reaction process; they are reacting to each other. The multimodal text in Figure 8.6 is part of a number of texts that were exposed on the University of Cape Town campus in order to raise awareness about disability, gender and relationships. The reaction process in the image is used as a resource for normalising love and sexuality between persons of the same gender.

However, it is difficult just from looking at the image in Figure 8.6 to interpret the exact content of the reaction process; we have to go to the context of the image and its relation to the written parts of the text in order to come to the conclusion that the reaction is probably best described as 'love'. Similarly, in Figure 8.2, we had to make a well-informed and contextually motivated guess at the more exact nature of the phenomenon, as well as the reacters' reflections on it.

Figure 8.6 Gaze as vector in an interreaction process

In *mental* processes, the content of goings-on in the minds of represented participants are made explicit, just as it is possible to do in language – for example, in 'the representatives of the present generation think about the future of nuclear power'. The visual resource for expressing such mental processes is the thought bubble in which the content is placed, either as writing or as another visual representation. In mental processes, the human participant from which the vector emanates is called a *senser* and the content in the thought bubble is called the *phenomenon* (cf. participants in verbally realised mental processes in Chapter 7).

The thought bubble as a resource for expressing mental processes was developed and is most commonly used in comics, and the same is true for the last type of dynamic process to be introduced in this chapter: the *verbal* process (see Table 7.1). What can be expressed in language as 'the representatives of the present generation say that nuclear power has done its duty' could be expressed visually by, for example, adding a speech bubble with the content 'nuclear power has done its duty' next to the depicted persons at the bottom of Figure 8.2. In verbal processes there is a *sayer*, with the *utterance* represented in the speech bubble.

What all the processes presented so far have in common is that they are expressed through the use of vectors of different kinds, and that these vectors add some kind of movement and dynamics to the visual representation. Kress and van

Leeuwen (2021: 44–75) call these *narrative representations*. However, there are also other types of visual representations of goings-on in the world that present the world as less dynamic and that do not make use of vectors. These can be viewed as visual versions of verbally expressed *states* of affairs like 'she *is* the CEO of a multinational company' rather than the more active and dynamic 'she *directs* a multinational company' (see 'states' in Table 7.1). These processes represent what somebody or something *is* or *has*, and Kress and van Leeuwen (2021: 76–112) refer to them as *conceptual representations*. Such processes of 'being' and 'having' can be of two basic types that relate participants to each other in terms of, on one hand, part–whole structures, and on the other, super- and subordination. The first type is called *analytical processes* and the second *classificational processes*.

Analytical processes actualise two participants: the *carrier* and the *attributes*. Maps are examples of multimodal texts that usually express analytical processes. In a map of Europe, for instance, Europe as a continent would be the whole – the carrier – and the different national states would be the attributes – the parts that make up the whole. Of course, analytical processes of this kind are often challenged. How big is Europe and what should its attributes be? And in times of political turmoil and conflicts: what are the relations between the attributes? What counts as a country rather than a region in maps of Europe as a whole?

Representations of identities are commonly expressed in analytical processes. Such representations are often the results of ideological choices that draw on different types of normative discourses. In Figure 8.5, not only is an action process realised through the machine gun as a vector, but the uniforms, as well as the weapons, are attributes that make up the carrier of 'soldier'. Another attribute is also visible in Figure 8.5. The head of the goal in the action process can be seen if one looks carefully. A head covered in a 'keffiyeh' – an Arab headscarf – is visible as a part of the analytical process that makes up the whole of the enemy's identity as 'Arab', or at least having a Middle Eastern identity. In this case, the analytical processes are used as a means of assigning identities to participants in the multimodal texts, but probably also for promoting loyalty with one of the identities rather than another. How this is done, and above all why this is done in a particular way, could be questions for further research.

Analytical processes are sometimes connected to gendered discourses of the human body. For instance, the advertising business is often accused of representing women in analytical, static, processes as a set of bodily attributes to be evaluated by the male gaze. Men in advertising, on the other hand, tend to be represented as actors in action processes, with attributes that symbolise power (ties, suits) or activity such as sports equipment (cf. classic studies such as Goffman, 1979 and Williamson, 1978). A totally different analytical representation of men is shown in Figure 8.7.

The multimodal representation in Figure 8.7 comes from a publication on female self-defence from CREA (Creating Resources for Empowerment in Action).

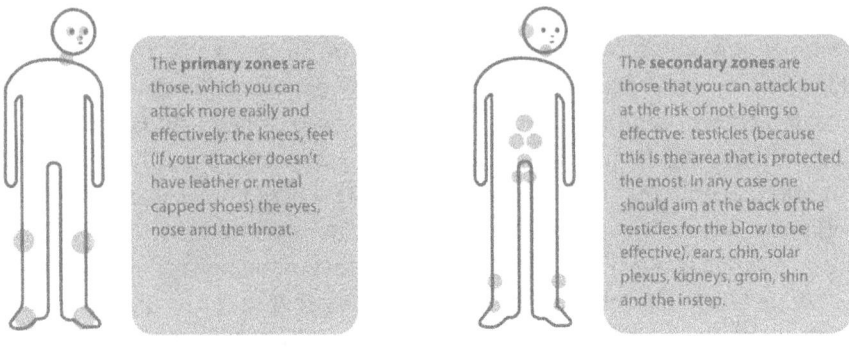

Step 8: Learn how to react to any attack.

Figure 8.7 Analytical process: *Self-Care and Self-Defence Manual for Feminist Activists*

CREA is a feminist human rights organisation that is based in India. In this illustration, the body is represented as a carrier that is not made up of power attributes such as big muscles or expensive clothing; the attributes that make up the carrier – presumably a male aggressor – are the zones of the body that are most sensitive to physical attacks by a woman. In fact, it is interesting to see how the primary zones for a successful attack are so salient in the representation that they become the main attributes of the male body. Figure 8.7 shows how analytical processes in images can be used in order to empower a very large group of people – in this case, women in the developing world and beyond – who face the risk of being attacked and sexually abused by men.

Another multimodal aspect of the representations in Figure 8.7 is that the illustrations and the written parts can complement each other because of their spatial and linear organisation. If we look at the writing to the left in Figure 8.7, the linear organisation of language allows for a definition of the body's 'primary zones' (boldface in the original), and these are the zones 'which you can attack more easily and effectively: the knees, feet (if your attacker doesn't have leather or metal capped shoes) the eyes, nose and the throat'. However, it is very difficult to use language in order to show *where* those body parts are located, so the visual representation that is spatially organised is used to do this 'showing', and it is done through an analytical process.

The final type of processes presented in this section is the classificational processes that represent super- and subordination rather than part–whole structures. Super- and subordination have to do with power and hierarchies, and these types of representations are often found when organisations, public authorities, corporations or businesses present their internal structure. The analysis of classificational processes can also be fruitful if one wants to, for example, compare how political systems are represented in different multimodal texts.

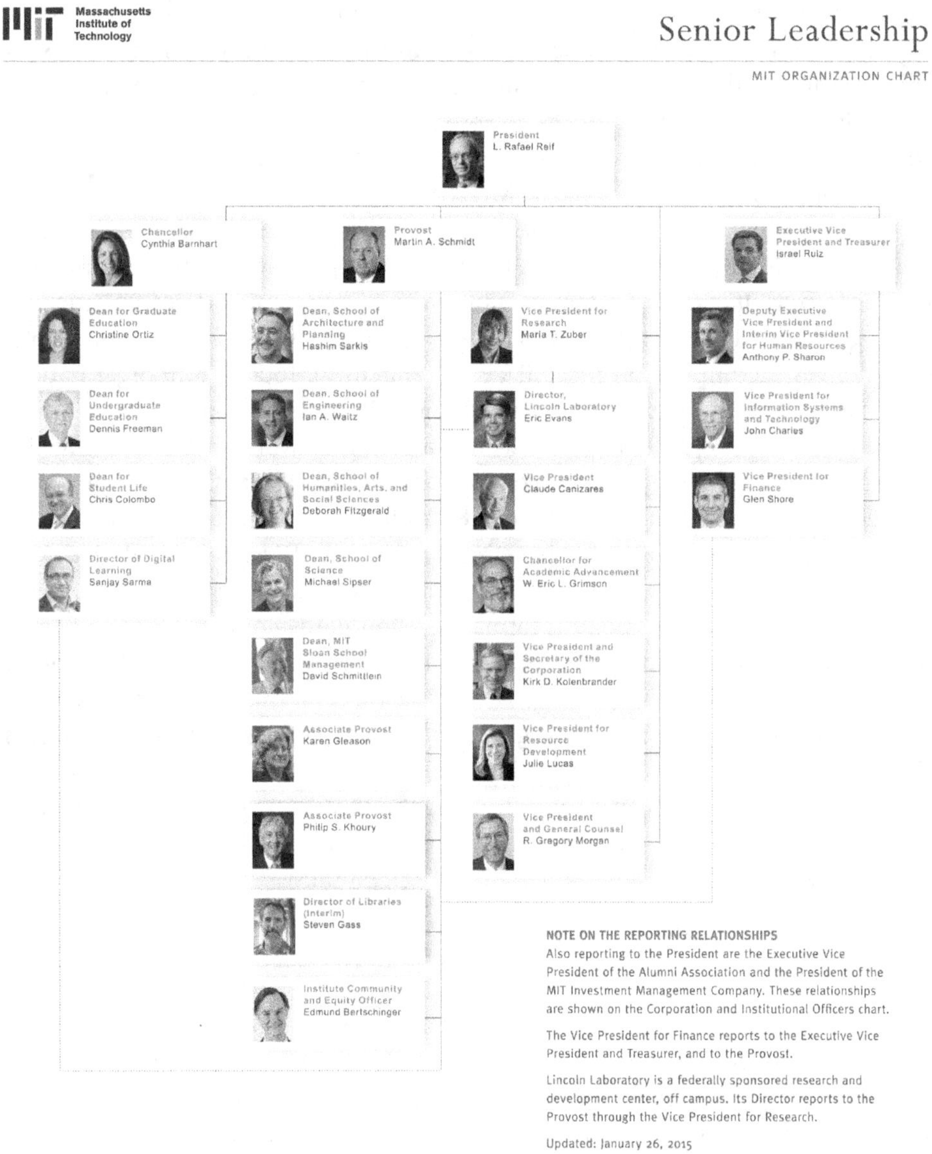

Senior Leadership

MIT ORGANIZATION CHART

Figure 8.8 Classificational process: MIT's organisational chart

The tree structure is the typical shape of classificational processes. In Figure 8.8, the leadership structure of the Massachusetts Institute of Technology (MIT) is represented as an 'organisation chart'. The participants in classificational processes are *superordinate* and *subordinate*, concepts that capture the hierarchical and power infused nature of these types of representations. At the top of the tree structure in Figure 8.8 is the President of MIT, L. Rafael Reif, represented as a superordinate participant. His subordinates are the Chancellor, the Provost and the Executive

Vice President and Treasurer. But these three are not only subordinates, they are also, in turn, represented as superordinate in relation to a number of other subordinates in the organisation. The hierarchical nature of this multimodal text is also reflected in the writing in the lower right-hand corner in Figure 8.8, where additional information is given concerning who 'reports' to whom, with reference to other organisational charts of the MIT.

From the perspective of the social sciences, it is important to remember that the classificational process in Figure 8.8 is a representation of a power structure. In other words, it is one of many possible ways to represent this power structure, but it is the one that MIT, for various reasons, wants to be the public one. However, it gives the impression that MIT is a hierarchical, top–bottom organisation. That may also be the case if one were to empirically study and analyse how power and control are employed at MIT, but such an analysis would most certainly also show that there are many hidden connections and structures that are not visible in the classificational process in Figure 8.8. For instance, some of the subordinates at the bottom of Figure 8.8 may have power over certain agendas that would, in practice, give them more power than is represented in the organisational chart. There would certainly be many informal decision paths going back and forth in ways that may be too complicated to be represented in a chart like the one in Figure 8.8. However, comparing such actual decision paths and informal connections between employees in an organisation with the classificational processes that often give only the official version of the power structures can give insights that are relevant to many different fields in the social sciences. And finally, one may ask, why does MIT – a world-leading research and educational institution – want to present itself as a highly hierarchical organisation?

Composition

Composition has to do with how parts of a multimodal text can communicate different meanings based on where they are placed for example, the cover of a magazine or a newspaper page. One implication is that when textual elements such as images, illustrations, headlines or written paragraphs are placed as part of a textual composition, they are assigned other, complementary, sometimes even contradictory meanings than the interactive and representational meanings that they communicate as separate elements. According to Kress and van Leeuwen (2021), elements placed towards the top of a page tend to be assigned meanings such as 'ideal' or 'general', whereas those placed towards the bottom can be assigned meanings like 'real' or 'specific'. There is also a left–right dimension that can be used to create meaning in multimodal texts, assigning meanings such as 'given' to elements placed to the left and 'new' to those to the right. The left–right dimension is related to the semiotic principle of reading and writing from left to right in Western cultures, and does not apply to cultures where this principle is not present. The analysis of the top–bottom and left–right dimension is called an 'analysis of *information value*' (Kress and van Leeuwen, 2021: 185–98).

However, the composition of a multimodal text can be meaningful in other ways as well. *Framing* of elements in a text can create meanings of *connection* and *disconnection*. For example, in Figure 8.1, the sepia tone was used as a device that connected the heading and the image of the 'tombstone'. They were presented as if they belong together. A contrasting colour between the elements would have had the opposite effect, disconnecting the two elements semiotically.

The final analysis to be introduced here is that of *salience*. This aspect of composition relates to the extent to which different elements in a text are foregrounded in relation to other elements. This is related to meanings of 'importance': a more salient element in a multimodal text is presented as if it were more 'important' than other elements in the same text.

Returning to the analysis of information value, an understanding of the underlying assumptions behind that analysis is needed in order to strengthen its validity. Figure 8.9 presents a model for the information values of some multimodal texts. The model has an outer frame that should be read as the boundaries of a semiotic space: a newspaper page, an advertisement, or a cover of a brochure or a pamphlet. As shown, elements placed in the top space are assigned the information value of 'ideal', with related values of 'general' and 'abstract'. Elements placed towards the bottom are presented as if they are 'real' or 'specific' and 'down to earth'. Broadly speaking, the *ideal–real dimension* of multimodal texts has an *experiential* provenance in human environments. Whereas the sky is far away and difficult to touch, the earth is highly tangible and has a direct physical presence for human beings. These experiences of high and low are also used in texts, thus making possible a distinction between the information values of textual elements such as 'ideal', 'general' and 'abstract' vs. 'real' or 'specific'.

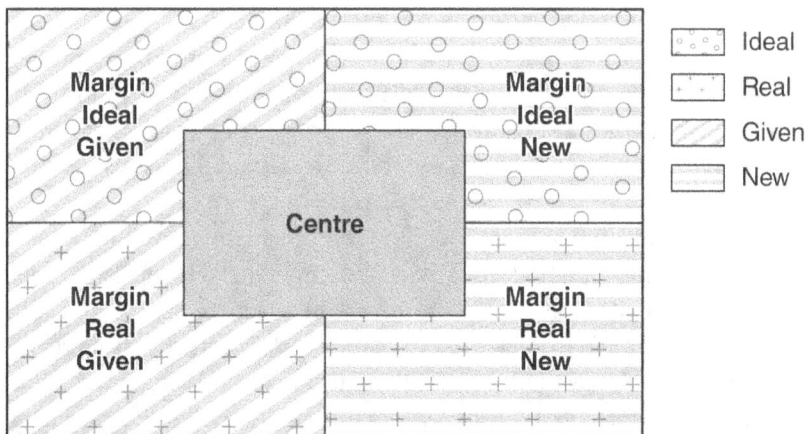

Figure 8.9 Information value (inspired by Kress and van Leeuwen, 2021: 203)

As mentioned, elements placed to the left in the semiotic space are assigned the information value of 'given' and those to the right 'new', following a linear principle of semiotic organisation in language. Finally, there are the information values of 'centre' and 'margin'; elements that surround a centred element tend to represent aspects of the centred element – not necessarily subordinate in relation to the centred element – as when in an ice-cream advertisement the centred image of the ice cream is surrounded by key words describing it as 'delicious', 'refreshing', 'produced locally in Vermont' or perhaps 'organically produced'.

In relation to the model in Figure 8.9, it should be pointed out that this is neither an absolute model of compositional meaning making in multimodal texts, nor a 'how to' guide to assigning specific meaning potentials to elements in a text. The model is an attempt to illustrate how elements are likely to be presented and interpreted in multimodal texts. There will be exceptions, and there are a number of text types for which the model is less relevant, such as, for instance, strictly linear texts and websites that show a different layout depending on how the reader scrolls them or the size of the device they are viewed on. In addition, it is important to remember that the dimensions of information value may or may not be realised through the composition of any given multimodal text. For the distinction between 'ideal' and 'real' and 'given' and 'new' to be relevant, there needs to be some kind of framing device, like a line or space, separating different elements in the semiotic composition. If there are no devices that distinguish, for example, left from right in a text, we would have to say that this potential of meaning making was just not actualised.

In the text from the Swedish Nuclear Fuel and Waste Management Company in Figure 8.2, there are framing devices that separate top from bottom. It shows a text box with a darker background that emphasises this distinction, and the white background of the illustration separates it from the photo at the bottom. In other words, there are framing devices that are put to use in order to realise the ideal–real dimension in this text. Thus, the top-placed elements – those that make up the illustration – and those placed at the bottom in the photo of persons from different generations are attributed with additional meanings other than their interactive and representational meanings. The technical process of handling spent nuclear fuel is presented as an 'ideal', whereas the depicted persons are presented as more 'real'.

Even if the text in Figure 8.2 may have the rhetorical aim of 'selling' the Nuclear Fuel and Waste Management Company as a competent actor to the public, it is above all an information brochure. In advertising, where selling products and services is always the final goal, persons and products in social environments of different types are usually idealised in the top position. Figure 8.10 shows an advertisement published in *Woman*, one of Britain's best-selling magazines targeted at middle-aged women.

Just as in Figure 8.2, there is a framing device in Figure 8.10 that separates top from bottom, 'ideal' from 'real': the pink background at the top half of the advert multimodal discourse analysis | 223

(which unfortunately is not possible to see in the black-and-white reproduction) creates a symbolic distinction in relation to the white background at the bottom. In other words, the personal medical problem, 'I felt my stomach was going to explode!' and the photo of a smiling woman at a symbolic distance between 'social' and 'personal' (see the section on interaction above) are presented as if

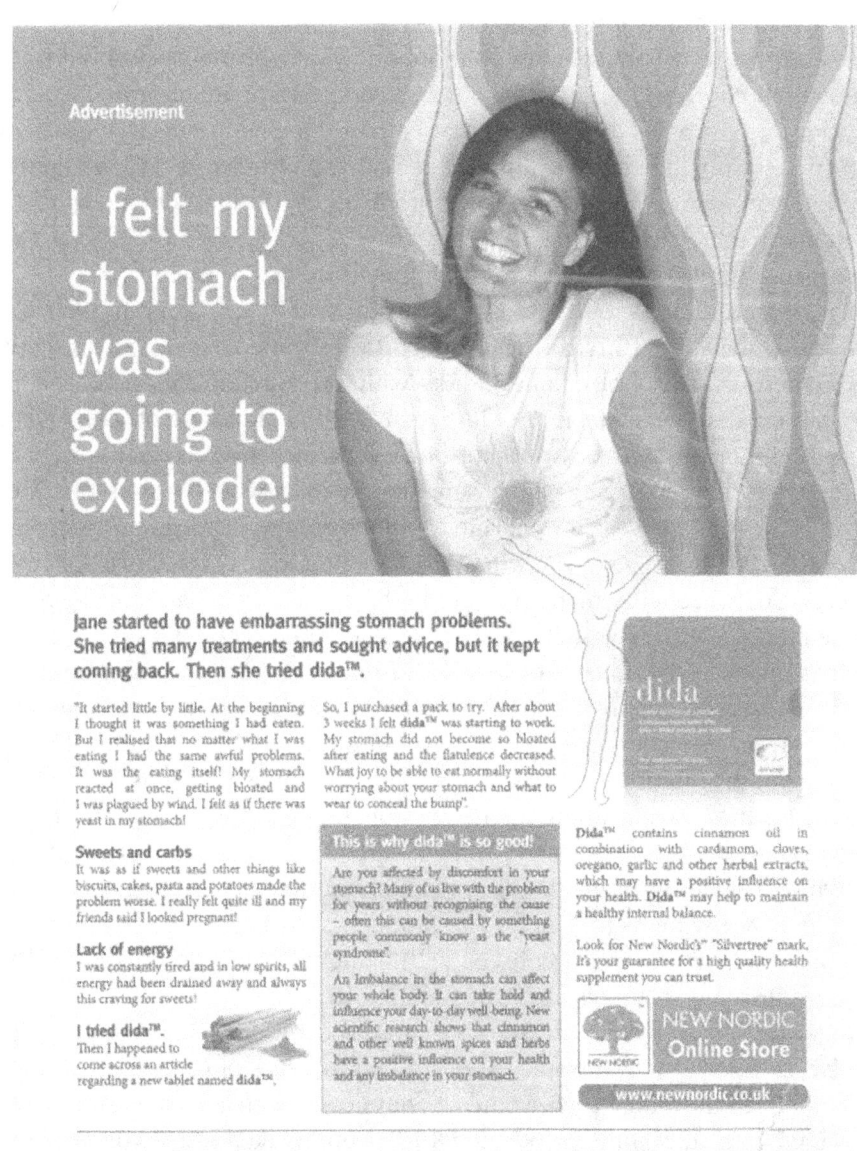

Figure 8.10 New Nordic advertisement, *Woman* magazine

they have the information value of 'ideal'. At the bottom of the page, the 'real' information is presented: a written narrative about how 'Jane' developed stomach problems, the solution, a product called 'dida™' (a food supplement), and a more technical description of the content and functions of 'dida™'. There is specific information on where the 'dida™ tablets' can be purchased as well as telephone numbers and a website address. On the lower, 'real', space of the page there is also a photo of the package of the product.

The point with the two analyses of information value in Figures 8.2 and 8.10 is to show that choices in terms of layout and composition are meaningful, sometimes ideological or at least argumentative or rhetorical. There is a difference between presenting technical solutions as an 'ideal', as in Figure 8.2, and presenting photos of persons and their personal problems as the 'ideal', as in Figure 8.10 and in many other advertisements.

Another example of how the ideal–real dimension can be used is found in Figure 8.6 where the two interreacters – the two men that look at each other – are presented as the 'ideal' through the layout of the multimodal text. The distinction is set up between the photo frame and the white background formed by the bed. The written parts, 'Sexuality, it's not just about sex', 'Gender' and other handwriting are presented as 'real', as a specification of the meanings in the photo of the two men. In addition, it may be relevant that the idealised relation in this South African text is that between a black and a white man.

To some extent, the given–new (left–right) dimension is also actualised in the top section of the advertisement in Figure 8.10. There is no obvious framing device, but the mode of writing vs. the visual mode (the photo), creates a sort of distinction that is recognised from many other advertisements, not least from those that specifically target women. To the left, a severe stomach problem is presented as a 'given' that many readers can identify with. In other words, it is assumed that at least some of the readers of *Woman* have experienced these problems. The 'new' in the advert is the image of a smiling, happy woman, presented as 'Jane' in the bottom part of the text. This is a 'new' woman who no longer has stomach problems. This type of use of the given–new dimension in multimodal texts is prototypically found in advertisements for weight-loss products showing an overweight person to the left and a slimmer version to the right (which would be reversed in cultures where reading and writing is not done from left to right).

The pattern in Figure 8.10 relates to a more general compositional pattern of problem–solution that is to some extent related to issues of gender. In advertisements targeted at middle-aged women, a physical 'problem' (often an aesthetic 'problem' or a medical one, as in Figure 8.10) is often taken as a starting point, as a given for the entire advert that has to be worked on by women and solved with the help of the product advertised.

More generally, the given–new dimension relates to change, not only from 'medical problem' to 'solved problem' but, for example, from 'poor' to 'rich', from 'immigrant' to 'citizen', or from 'child' to 'adult'. This raises the critical question of what is presented as a desirable change in a text and what is not. Or, for example, whether the change is concerned with all members of a society, or only a selected few?

Returning to Figure 8.10, the 'given' stomach problem and the 'new' Jane are connected through an illustration of a female body that overlaps both the image of Jane and that of the 'dida™' package. This is related to another aspect of composition that Kress and van Leeuwen (2021: 204–5) call *'framing'*. As mentioned, the top and bottom part of the advert in Figure 8.10 are disconnected through the use of *contrasting* backgrounds. Semiotically, they are presented as if they do not belong together – they have different information values. However, through the use of *overlapping*, this distinction is partially downplayed as the illustration of the female body connects the advertised product to the happy woman depicted in the top section. Through the layout of the advertisement, the product is explicitly connected to the given–new dimension: the product is what made the transformation from problem to solution possible.

There are a number of devices that can be used to connect or disconnect elements in multimodal texts:

- overlapping;
- framing;
- distance;
- visual rhyme;
- contrast.

All these devices can be used in order to present elements in a text as if they belong together or as if they do not. As mentioned, overlapping between elements was used to connect the photo of the smiling Jane to the product in Figure 8.10. In the same text, there are also examples of framing devices used for disconnecting elements. For example, there is a framed rectangle with a pink background that separates the information under the headline, 'This is why dida™ is so good!' from the rest of the written elements at the bottom of the advert. This separation is probably motivated by the fact that the information in the rectangle is quite normative and gives a short version of the advantages explained more extensively elsewhere in the 'real' section of the advert. Another device for symbolically connecting or disconnecting elements in a text is placing them on shorter or longer *distances* from each other.

Returning to the use of colour in Figure 8.10, the background is pink (again, unfortunately it is not possible to see the colour in the black-and-white reproduction). This sets up a visual rhyme with other pink elements in the advertisement. Visual rhymes are often used to symbolically connect elements in a multimodal text that are placed at some distance from each other. The use of the same typeface – boldface, italics or other types of shapes – also creates such cohesion between elements. In Figure 8.10, a pink colour is used to connect the lower rectangle with the short description of why 'dida™' is so good, to the 'idealised' elements (the statement about the stomach problem and the happy Jane), and to the packaging of the product. Actually, it is possible to grasp the key points of the advertisement just by reading these rhyming elements.

An example of how visual rhyme and *contrast* tend to interact is found in Figure 8.11. Contrast has quite the opposite semiotic function as visual rhymes: elements in contrasting colours, typefaces or shapes are symbolically disconnected. Figure 8.11 contains multimodal texts that are found on three consecutive pages in an online pamphlet called *COVID-19 Toolkit: Information on how to stay safe and healthy from COVID-19*, published by the New Mexico Department of Health in the USA (2022). Each of the texts revolve around the same theme: 'How to get COVID-19 testing, vaccine, and treatment in New Mexico (...)'. However, they present different scenarios depending on the medical insurance level of 'private insurance', 'Medicaid' or 'no insurance'. Medicaid is a type of financial support for medical care in the state of New Mexico (also referred to as 'Centennial Care') for persons meeting certain eligibility criteria – for instance, income below a certain amount (www.hsd.state.n m.us/LookingForAssistance/centennial-care-overview/).

In terms of visual design, the three texts are very similar: the headlines and the bullet point lists as well as the backgrounds of the lists are coloured in either orange, teal green, violet or blue. All the orange parts in the three texts also contain an illustration of a person with a temperature, the teal green parts a COVID-19 test kit, the violet ones a vaccine container and a syringe, and the blue parts two pills: COVID-19 medicine. In addition, the final phrase of the main headings in all the three texts is highlighted in marine blue. In sum, all these designs create visual rhymes across the three texts, and a person reading the full *COVID-19 Toolkit* encounters a meaning potential of 'the themes and subthemes across these three texts are closely connected: all citizens of New Mexico have access to COVID-19 health care'.

However, these rhymes interact in visually quite intricate ways with contrasts. The bullet points in the lists under each of the headings contain symbols. These symbols are rhythmically connected through the same background colour, but the symbols contrast between the three texts. For instance, in the text targeting the uninsured, the violet and blue set of bullet points contain dollar signs, embedded in the overall colour rhythm. The dollar signs are followed by the writing 'Federally Qualified Health Centers can give you COVID-19 vaccine without insurance, but you might have to pay a fee' and 'Federally Qualified Health Centers can help you get COVID-19 treatment but you might have to pay a fee'. The dollar sign is also found in the text targeting those with private insurance, but followed by 'You might have to pay a co-pay or deductible fee [for medicine]' whereas the text targeting those with Medicaid contain no dollar signs.

More precisely, an overall visual design of connectedness through visual rhymes ('we all have access to COVID-19 health care') is presented in this pamphlet with all citizens of New Mexico as a target group, but embedded in this design are elements of contrasts related to the fundamentally different situations of the citizens. In other words, a type of medical equality is presented on the visual surfaces of these texts, but existing, quite substantial differences between the health care plans of the readers of the pamphlet are embedded in the design, producing meaning potentials of 'difference'. An analysis of devices for connecting or disconnecting elements in multimodal texts can lay bare how texts can play down and at the same time reflect economic and social status in a society.

How to get COVID-19 testing, vaccine, and treatment in New Mexico with private insurance

Testing if you feel sick or were exposed to COVID-19

Get tested at a healthcare location or pharmacy that takes your insurance. Your insurance plan will pay for this service.

Your private insurance will repay you for up to 8 COVID-19 home tests a month.

Go to findatestnm.org or call 1-855-600-3453 to find a testing location or order COVID-19 home tests.

Testing for work, travel, or other reasons

Some people may have cost sharing for COVID testing. Check with your insurer if you have health insurance.

You can order COVID-19 home tests for free from Project ACT.

Go to findatestnm.org or call 1-855-600-3453 to find a testing location or order at-home COVID-19 tests. .

Getting a COVID-19 vaccine

Get the COVID-19 vaccine from your usual medical provider or pharmacy. The cost of getting a vaccine is paid for by private insurance.

Everyone can also get COVID-19 vaccine for free at New Mexico Department of Health vaccine events.

Go to vaccinenm.org or call 1-855-600-3453 to find a vaccine near you and set up an appointment.

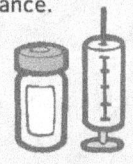

Getting COVID-19 medicine

Schedule an appointment with a doctor or medical provider that takes your insurance. Online video appointments are also available.

You might have to pay a co-pay or deductible fee.

Go to findatreatmentnm.com or call 1-855-600-3453 to find a medical provider or pharmacy near you.

Figure 8.11 *COVID-19 Toolkit*, New Mexico Department of Health

How to get COVID-19 testing, vaccine, and treatment in New Mexico with Medicaid

Testing if you feel sick or were exposed to COVID-19

 Get tested at a healthcare location or pharmacy that takes your Medicaid plan. Medicaid will pay for this service.

 You can get COVID-19 home tests at a pharmacy for free with your Medicaid insurance.

 Go to findatestnm.org or call 1-855-600-3453 to find a testing location or order COVID-19 home tests.

Testing for work, travel, or other reasons

 Medicaid will pay for your COVID-19 test.

 You can order COVID-19 home tests for free from Project ACT.

 Go to findatestnm.org or call 1-855-600-3453 to find a testing location or order COVID-19 home tests.

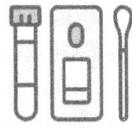

Getting a COVID-19 vaccine

 Get the COVID-19 vaccine from your usual medical provider or pharmacy. The cost of getting a vaccine is covered by Medicaid.

 Everyone can also get COVID-19 vaccine for free at New Mexico Department of Health vaccine events.

 Go to vaccinenm.org or call 1-855-600-3453 to find a vaccine event near you or set up an appointment.

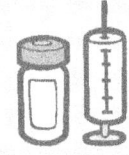

Getting COVID-19 medicine

 Schedule an appointment with a doctor or medical provider that takes Medicaid. Medicaid should pay for all medication fees.

 Go to findatreatmentnm.com or call 1-855-600-3453 to find a medical provider or pharmacy near you.

 Online video appointments are also available. Go to welcome.netmedical.com.

How to get COVID-19 testing, vaccine, and treatment in New Mexico with no insurance

Testing if you feel sick or were exposed to COVID-19

 Get tested at a Curative or NetMedical Xpress location. If you do not have insurance, funds may be available for testing.

 You can order COVID-19 home tests for free from Project ACT.

 Go to findatestnm.org or call 1-855-600-3453 to find a testing location or order COVID-19 home tests.

Testing for work, travel, or other reasons

 You can order COVID-19 home tests for free from Project ACT.

 Go to findatestnm.org or call 1-855-600-3453 to find a testing location or order COVID-19 home tests.

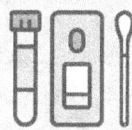

Getting a COVID-19 vaccine

 Everyone can also get COVID-19 vaccine for free at New Mexico Department of Health vaccine events or at Public Health Offices.

 Federally Qualified Health Centers can give you COVID-19 vaccine without insurance but you might have to pay a fee.

 Go to vaccinenm.org or call 1-855-600-3453 to find a vaccine event near you or set up an appointment.

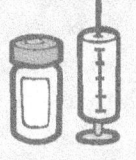

Getting COVID-19 medicine

 Federally Qualified Health Centers can help you get COVID-19 treatment but you might have to pay a fee.

 Go to findatreatmentnm.com or call 1-855-600-3453 to find a medical provider or pharmacy near you.

 Net Medical Xpress will provide free online video appointments for people who are uninsured. Go to welcome.netmedical.com.

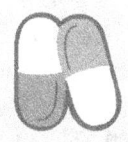

People who are uninsured can apply for Special COVID Medicaid. People who are not U.S. citizens can apply for Emergency Medical Services for Non-Citizens. Go to www.yes.state.nm.us or call 1-800-283-4465

Salience is the final aspect of the composition of multimodal texts: is an element presented as if it is more or less important in relation to other elements in the same text? The main resources for creating relative salience are presented below (see Kress and van Leeuwen, 2021: 210–16):

- size;
- colour;

- overlapping;
- contrasting typeface;
- cultural symbols.

Relative *size* is the most straightforward device for assigning salience to an element in a multimodal text: the larger the element, the more 'important' it is. In Figure 8.10, the largest elements are the top-placed statement about the stomach problem and the image of the woman along with the photo of the product packaging. These elements are presented as the most 'important' ones. Other elements in the texts are smaller, and thus presented as 'less important', even though some of them are given salience through other layout choices. As mentioned, pink is used as a type of signal *colour* in the advertisement that gives salience to the rectangle explaining why 'dida™' is so good, to other 'idealised' elements and to the package. In other words, these elements are not only framed as belonging together, they are also presented as quite 'important' in the advertisement.

Salience can also be given to an element by making it *overlap* other elements. For instance, the drawing of the female body in Figure 8.10 overlaps with both the photo of Jane and part of the packaging of the product, and it gains some salience through this. This is also the case for the golden rectangle in Figure 8.2 with the headline 'a question of responsibility'; it overlaps the photo of the depicted persons at the bottom of the page. A *contrasting typeface* can also be used as a device to give salience to an element in a text. The use of boldface in headlines is perhaps the most obvious example. Finally, well-recognised cultural symbols tend to gain attention and thus become 'important', even if they are neither large, colourful nor overlapping. It is difficult to give examples of such symbols since they vary between cultures and subcultures, but religious symbols, flags or politically loaded symbols fall into this category.

Critical reflections

When the analytical tools presented in this chapter are combined, they can be used to answer specific questions about multimodal texts – for example, how ethnicity or gender is construed in advertising or social media. Perhaps more importantly, such an analysis can open up questions relevant for our understanding of, for example, power relations and other discursive formations at higher levels of abstraction. However, there are a number of aspects of the presented method that need to be critically attended to; a few of these are discussed below.

Language and image

This chapter has introduced an extended concept of text that includes, for example, writing, image, illustrations, information graphics and colours. The discussion of the interactive as well as the representational function of images was related to how those functions can be expressed in language. This has at least one obvious methodological advantage: we can talk about meanings expressed in images in a similar way – with a similar terminology – as we can speak of meanings expressed in language. For example, we can talk about processes and participants in images as well as in linguistic clauses (see Chapter 7), and we can talk about combinations of image acts and speech acts when analysing the interactive functions of multimodal texts.

But there are significant differences between how language and image can be used for meaning making. In addition to the aforementioned critique of the use of metafunctions for analysing communicative modes beyond language (Ledin and Machin, 2018a), Machin (2014) argues that images are very different from language since they create meaning above all through their iconic resemblance to something else in the world as we know it. An image of a house means 'house' because we recognise the house from our experience of the world outside the image. Based on this assumption Machin (2014) argues that it can be problematic to deconstruct an image into components such as vectors, participants and compositional fields with various information values. When analysing language, this type of deconstruction into components is motivated because language has a grammar that relies on, among other things, linear semiotic principles where one component follows after another. But if images are above all iconic representations that create all meaning at once, so to speak, can they really have a grammar similar to that of language?

This may seem like a semiotic discussion with less relevance to text-oriented researchers and students in broader fields of the social sciences, but it is important to consider the explanatory value of any method for analysis. The linguistically inspired and well-defined analytical categories may seem to give high reliability to the analysis of any multimodal text, but questions of validity must also be kept in mind. If one thinks that images, just like language, create meaning through combinations of different elements, an analysis of action processes in, for example, a history textbook, may provide high validity when examining how a certain type of participant is acting upon other participants. Vectors must be identified, and participants are then categorised as either actors or goals, and conclusions can be drawn.

On the other hand, if one believes that images create meaning above all through their direct resemblance to something in the world and that they cannot be deconstructed into predefined, grammar-like categories, such an analysis would, of course, have a lower validity. It would then be better to base the analysis of the images on one's own experience of the world or to invite readers from a number of social groups in society into the interpretative process. For instance, based on one's knowledge of the world, an image of football hooligans could be interpreted as if they are actively 'threatening' other people, even if they do not show any raised weapons or other vector-like objects.

Different types of multimodal texts

All the texts that have been presented in this chapter have in common that their semiotic space is limited by a rather predictable and stable format – for instance, the front of the GeneWatch UK report for Greenpeace, the torn-out text from the City of Cape Town, the photo of the two men attached to a bed with writing on it or the COVID-19 pamphlet. However, many texts do not have such stable boundaries. The format of, for instance, Facebook displayed on a computer screen partially depends on the size and settings of the web browser window. In relation to the analytical concepts presented in the chapter, this mainly becomes problematic when analysing composition. Dimensions of high–low and centre–margin become relative to the size of the browser window – how it crops the displayed multimodal text or image – and how the reader scrolls it. Items placed at the bottom of the page may then not be visible at all, which invalidates the analysis of information value presented in this chapter (see Knox, 2007 for an alternative model for the analysis of web-based newspapers).

Another example would be longer, printed text such as textbooks or reports. These types of texts often make use of images, illustrations and information graphics, but the texts as a whole are dominated by the sequential and temporal principle of organisation of writing. Images and illustrations are often placed next to the written parts that they are semiotically connected to. Again, the analysis of composition – especially information value – loses some of its explanatory value. An image placed at the top of such text may not at all have the information value of 'ideal'; it is just connected to the chunk of written text that is placed there. For example, it would be misleading to say that a table showing the US annual deficits is 'idealised' just because it has been placed at a top position in one of the pages of the budget of the United States Government. Such issues require critical considerations on behalf of the researcher or student doing the analysis, all in order not to employ the presented method too mechanically and in that way reduce its explanatory capacity.

Doing multimodal discourse analysis in practice

Initially, it may be challenging for a student in the social sciences to employ concepts of multimodal discourse analysis without any previous experience of discourse analysis (Chapter 6), critical discourse studies (Chapter 7), semiotics or general linguistics. On the other hand, all of the concepts and terms presented in this chapter have been developed in order to be concrete rather than abstract concepts, allowing for a practical analysis of texts.

Further, multimodal discourse analysis is better adapted to the qualitative analysis of smaller rather than larger corpora of texts. As discussed above, a number of qualitative considerations are necessary throughout the process of analysis in order to keep the validity of the analysis at an acceptable level, and it is generally more rewarding to analyse texts from all of the perspectives presented above (interactive, representational and compositional), which is a time-consuming process. Then again, it is, of course, possible to select just one or two analytical categories and employ these in an analysis of a larger corpus of texts. An example would be to select the human gaze as a resource for expressing reaction processes in a large corpus of COVID-19 brochures from different cultures. Who is presented as the reactor and who is the phenomenon? Is the medical staff more often the reactor with the COVID-19 patient as phenomenon, and how does this differ between cultures? And why do such patterns differ between cultures? Some qualitative data analysis applications now offer the possibility to code pictures, which is helpful when analysing larger corpora.

Multimodal discourse analysis and the study of society

Even though all the text analytical examples in this chapter have dealt with texts in different contexts of society, they have done so through a quite detailed analysis, very close to the text itself. The main point of the analyses has been to offer ways to penetrate multimodal texts in a more systematic and perhaps also formal way than what is usually possible by just intuitively reading and interpreting without an arsenal of text analytical concepts at hand.

Issues of social relations and power can usually be analysed directly through multimodal analysis of interactive meanings in texts. The chapter has shown how point of view in images can be used as a maker of power. Depicted persons can be represented as if they are superior or inferior to the reader, or as if they are included or excluded from the social world of the reader. Symbolic distance is another category which can be related to power, and so can the use of speech acts and image acts: is the reader asked to do something or not? And who is the depicted person who has the power to command or demand?

The analysis of representations of goings-on in the world and that of composition can also be connected to the study of society and power. Different representations depend not only on the power of text producers in relation to the readers, but also on the power of normative discourses to regulate what it is possible to represent in a text and what it is not. In other words, who does what against whom in a multimodal text is not randomly determined. The fact that the 'goal' in the action process in Figure 8.5 is wearing a 'keffiyeh' and sits in a building with a sign in Arabic is a result of discourses that construct Arabs as enemies and Western soldiers as good actors in many conflicts. Such discourses can be more systematically identified and dissected through a thoroughgoing analysis of recurring representations in multimodal texts.

In a similar way, the analysis of composition can point not only to what is regarded as 'ideals' in texts of certain types (information value), but also to what is presented as most 'important' (salience) and 'connected' or 'disconnected' (framing). The chapter has shown how the technical side of nuclear power is 'idealised' in the text from the Swedish Nuclear Fuel and Waste Management Company (Figure 8.2); a compositional choice that can have further relevance in the analysis of discourses around nuclear power in many societies. The analysis of the given–new dimension in the advertisement in Figure 8.10 showed how it related to a gendered problem–solution pattern that is relevant in many other domains of society where female problems continuously have to be worked upon, often through the use of commercial products. Finally, the rather straightforward analysis of salience can point to patterns in what is construed as if it is important in society: is it commercial products, beauty, freedom, liberty, gender equality? Thus, the analysis of salience can be a powerful tool for an analysis of value systems in cultures and subcultures. Framing can often say something about categorisation: which social groups or categories of things or ideas are presented as belonging together and which are symbolically separated? And what does that say about a society at a specific point in history?

Summary

The usefulness of multimodal discourse analysis

- Multimodal discourse analysis can be used in order to analyse meanings in multimodal texts in a more detailed and less intuitive manner, grasping both the meanings expressed through language and those expressed through images and illustrations. It is possible to combine the method with those of critical discourse studies analysis presented in Chapter 7.
- Multimodal discourse analysis can also be combined with other approaches to the analysis of texts presented in this book – for example, discourse analysis (Chapter 6).
- By analysing interaction represented in multimodal texts, it is possible to draw conclusions about, for example, power, inclusion and exclusion.
- The analysis of visual representations of goings-on in the world can help to categorise texts as more or less dynamic and also to systematically identify who does what to whom. This analysis can be used to answer questions such as 'How are relations between persons in an organisation represented?', 'How can maps be directly related to ideological and political tensions in a given part of the world?' or 'What are the markers of identity in a given text and to whom are they attributed?'
- The analysis of the composition of multimodal texts can say something about the ideological motivations behind a certain layout. Elements placed to the left in a text are often presented as if they are 'given' in relation to elements placed to the right, but 'given' to whom and under which circumstances? Elements placed in a top position in a multimodal text are 'ideal' in relation to lower elements, but why is something idealised at the expense of something else? And why are certain elements salient, and thus presented as if they are important, while others are not? This type of analysis can give input to discussions about ideologically driven choices in multimodal texts.

How to do it

- Only a restricted number of texts can be analysed if all the three meta functions (interaction, representation and composition) are to be analysed qualitatively. If only a few analytical categories are selected, the number of texts analysed can be increased.
- Multimodal discourse analysis as a text analytical method is often successfully combined with research questions relevant to the fields of gender studies, rhetoric and discourse analysis in general.
- Precision is of key importance, and so are consistency and clear definitions of the concepts applied in the analysis. This type of text analysis has to be detailed before it can be abstracted to a level that is usually required for making it relevant in the social sciences.

- It is important to have a clear aim for the analysis and not to over-interpret the results. Multimodal discourse analysis is a method for analysing and producing reasonable and well-founded interpretations of texts; it is not a method for making statements about how producers or interpreters of texts think.

Suggested reading

The main source for this chapter is Gunther Kress's and Theo van Leeuwen's book *Reading Images: The Grammar of Visual Design* (2021). The book presents not only a detailed exploration of resources for meaning making in multimodal texts, but also critical discussions of, for example, the differences between language and image. Ledin and Machin (2020) is a comprehensive presentation of multimodal analysis of not only images, but also, for instance, typography, texture and materiality – for example, in interior design. The book is highly accessible, also to readers with no prior knowledge of linguistics or discourse analysis. As mentioned above, Ledin and Machin (2018b) is a book that argues for a multimodal analysis oriented towards the shaping of materialities in social and professional practices. In the book, *affordance* (Gibson, 1977) – the potentials and restrictions of communicative modes – is used as a key concept for analysing, for instance, photographs, films, packaging and interior design.

Halliday (1978), Hodge and Kress (1988), van Leeuwen (2005), Kress and van Leeuwen (2001) and Kress (2010) are books that discuss *social semiotics*, the overarching theoretical framework for the concepts and methods presented in this chapter. Van Leeuwen (2022) analyses identity from the perspective of multimodality, and Zhao et al. (2018) contains a number of chapters that all apply concepts and approaches inspired by the social semiotic and discourse analytical work of van Leeuwen. The linguistic application of social semiotics – *systemic functional grammar* – is introduced in Halliday and Matthiessen (2014), a book that requires some previous knowledge of linguistics from its readers.

The Routledge Handbook of Multimodal Analysis (2014, edited by C. Jewitt) contains articles on multimodality from researchers in many different disciplines, including anthropology, education, linguistics and cognitive science. The leading academic journals in the field of multimodality are *Visual Communication, Social Semiotics, Multimodality & Society* and *Multimodal Communication*.

Exercises

Exercise 1: Affect in political communication

One of the main points with doing discourse analysis in general and multimodal discourse analysis in particular is to try to reveal meaning potentials that are not obvious at first sight and to try to grasp the complexity of multimodal texts. Affective meanings in texts are sometimes treated as a type of 'add on' to the, perhaps, more rational, logical or informative meanings. However, affects often play a key role in political communication.

(Continued)

(Continued)

The task

Take a closer look at how semiotic resources are employed in order to create affective meanings such as 'happiness', 'anger' or 'engagement' in political communication. Which resources are used to represent affects multimodally – are they primarily verbal or visual? Why, do you think?

The texts

Visit the websites of two political parties and identify and analyse multimodal ensembles in which images combine with writing. There will almost certainly be some kind of affective meaning communicated in such ensembles, but they will vary in terms of affective intensity and the semiotic resources employed. Try to look at the websites of political parties with different ideological roots.

Exercise 2: Multimodal texts in the urban landscape

Multimodal texts such as political stickers never exist in geographical isolation: they are located somewhere, in a certain location in a specific environment. This is sometimes rather broadly referred to as 'context', but try here to think of it more concretely, as locations in urban environments that affect the meaning potential of texts.

The task

Visit an urban area and identify three environments that differ in terms of, for example, function (institutional building vs. commercial building vs. a parliamentary building, for instance), dominating socioeconomic groups that move around in the environment (bank district vs. university campus) and location in a city (central or on the outskirts of town). Look for multimodal texts exposed in each environment that contain political or other ideologically driven messages. To what extent would you argue that the meaning potential of these texts are affected by the environment in which they are posted?

The texts

Visit urban environments as the ones described above and document multimodal texts *in situ*. Remember that it is not only the overall environment (e.g., a commercial mall) that may affect the semiotic potential, but also the more immediate one: is the text posted in a shape of a note on a public noticeboard? Is it framed and strategically placed at an entrance, which gives it an official and authorised touch? Is the text part of an ensemble of other texts as part of an advertising campaign in a public square? Texts to look out for include political and ideologically coloured stickers, election posters (if you are lucky enough to do this exercise during an election campaign), or invitations to religious, political or other meetings on noticeboards.

Exercise 3: Negotiating monuments and other symbols of historical persons and events

In recent years there have been student protests at the University of Cape Town campus in South Africa under the slogan of 'Rhodes Must Fall'. The slogan refers to the decolonisation of higher education in general, but also to the specific statue of the British colonialist Cecil Rhodes, placed in a central position in the university campus. At many other universities and educational institutions across the world there are still many monuments representing historical persons or other symbols of historical events such as wars. Sometimes these are not so centrally placed as the Rhodes statue in Cape Town, and they remain quite unnoticed to students and staff; in other cases, they become an issue of intense media (or social media) discussions of the presence or removal of symbols of the past in contemporary educational spaces.

The task

Analyse how visual resources are employed in multimodal texts that address the presence or removal of historical monuments or symbols in educational environments (schools and campuses). In what ways are contemporary or historical photos of the monuments, statues or symbols used to support, contradict or more fully mediate the opinions put forward?

The texts

Identify a social media hashtag similar to the #rhodesmustfall of the University of Cape Town protests, such as hashtags related to the removal of a Confederate monument at University of Mississippi in the USA in 2020. Collect a number of Instagram or Twitter posts advocating the removal of the symbols from the educational spaces and a number of posts that argue for preserving them. Alternatively, or in combination with the social media texts, you can collect multimodal texts from student newspapers or the local press with the same themes.

References

Anderton, C. and James, M. (eds) (2022) *Media Narratives in Popular Music*. London: Bloomsbury.

Angermuller, J., Maingueneau, D. and Wodak, R. (2014) *Discourse Studies Reader*. Amsterdam: John Benjamin Publishing Company.

Archer, J. and Jockers, M.L. (2016) *The Bestseller Code: Anatomy of the Blockbuster Novel*. New York: St. Martin's Press.

Archer, M. (2000) *Being Human: The Problem of Agency*. Cambridge: Cambridge University Press.

Audi, R. (2001) *The Architecture of Reason: The Structure and Substance of Rationality*. New York: Oxford University Press.

Austin, J.L. (1975) *How to Do Things With Words*. J.O. Urmson and M. Spisà (eds). Oxford: Clarendon.

Avelino, F. (2021) 'Theories of power and social change: power contestations and their implications for research on social change and innovation', *Journal of Political Power*, 14 (3): 425–48.

Bacchi, C. (1999) *Women, Policy and Politics: The Construction of Policy Problems*. London: Sage.

Bacchi, C. (2005) 'Discourse, discourse everywhere. Subject "agency" in feminist discourse methodology', *NORA – Nordic Journal of Women Studies*, 13 (3): 198–209.

Bacchi, C. (2009a) *Analysing Policy: What's the Problem Represented to Be?* London: Pearson Education.

Bacchi, C. (2009b) 'The issue of intentionality in frame theory: the need for reflexive framing', in E. Lombardo, P. Meier and M. Verloo (eds), *The Discursive Politics of Gender Equality: Stretching, Bending and Policymaking*. London: Routledge, pp. 19–35.

Bacchi, C. (2012) 'Introducing the "What's the problem represented to be?" approach', in A. Bletsas and C. Beasley (eds), *Engaging with Carol Bacchi: Strategic Interventions and Exchanges*. Adelaide: University of Adelaide Press, pp. 21–24.

Bacchi, C. (2015) 'Problematizations in alcohol policy: WHO's alcohol problems', *Contemporary Drug Problems*, 42 (2): 130–47.

Bacchi, C. (2016) 'Problematization in health policy: questioning how problems are constructed in politics', *Sage Open*, 6 (2): 1–16.

Bacchi, C. (2021) 'Introducing WPR: a work in progress'. Available at: www.kau.se/files/2021-10/BACCHI%20KICKOFF%20PRESENTATION_1.pdf

Bacchi, C. (2022) *Keynote address*. Delivered at the WPR Symposium on Critical Policy Studies – Exploring the Premises and Politics of Carol Bacchi's WPR Approach, 17 August. Karlstad University, Sweden. Available at: www.kau.se/files/2022-09/BACCHI%20Symposium%20Keynote%20FINAL.docx

Bacchi, C. and Goodwin, S. (2016) *Poststructural Policy Analysis: A Guide to Practice*. London: Palgrave Macmillan.

Bail, C.A. (2014) 'The cultural environment: measuring culture with big data', *Theory and Society*, 43 (3–4): 465–82.

Baker, P. (2006) *Using Corpora in Discourse Analysis*. London: Continuum.

Baker, P. (ed.) (2009) *Contemporary Corpus Linguistics*. London: Continuum.

Baker, P. (2020) 'Corpus-assisted discourse analysis', in C. Hart (ed.), *Researching Discourse: A Student Guide*. London: Routledge.

Ball, T. (1988) 'The changing face of power', in *Transforming Political Discourse: Political Theory and Critical Conceptual History*. Oxford: Basil Blackwell, pp. 80–105.

Ball, T., Dagger, R. and O'Neill, D.I. (2021) *Political Ideologies and the Democratic Ideal* (11th edn). New York: Routledge.

Bamberg, M. and Georgakopoulou, A. (2008) 'Small stories as a new perspective in narrative and identity analysis', *Text & Talk*, 28: 377–96.

Barthes, R. (1977) *Image, Music, Text*. London: Fontana.

Barthes, R. (1993) *Mythologies*. London: Vintage.

Bateman, J.A., Wildfeuer, J. and Hiippala, T. (2017) *Multimodality: Foundations, Research and Analysis: A Problem-oriented Introduction*. Berlin: De Gruyter Mouton.

Bechdel, A. (1986) *Dykes to Watch Out For*. Ithaca, NY: Firebrand Books.

Beck, U. and Sznaider, N. (2006) 'Unpacking cosmopolitanism for the social sciences: a research agenda', *The British Journal of Sociology*, 57 (1): 1–23.

Bell, D. (1988 [1960]) *The End of Ideology: On the Exhaustion of Political Ideas in the Fifties. With a New Afterword*. Cambridge, MA: Harvard University Press.

Bell, D. (2014) 'What is Liberalism?', *Political Theory*, 42 (6): 682–715. DOI: 10.1177/0090591714535103

Benton, T. and Craib, I. (2011) *Philosophy of Social Science: The Philosophical Foundations of Social Thought* (2nd edn). Basingstoke: Palgrave Macmillan.

Berger, P.L. and Luckmann, T. (1966) *The Social Construction of Reality: A Treatise in the Sociology of Knowledge*. New York: Anchor Books.

Berman, S. (2006) *The Primacy of Politics. Social Democracy and the Making of Europe's Twentieth Century*. Cambridge: Cambridge University Press.

Best, J. (1995) *Images of Issues: Typifying Contemporary Social Problems*. New York: De Gruyter.

Bhaskar, R. (1998) *The Possibility of Naturalism*. London: Routledge.

Bhaskar, R. (2008 [1978]) *A Realist Theory of Science*. New York: Harvester Press.

Billig, M. (1995) *Banal Nationalism*. London: Sage.

Billig, M. (1997) 'The dialogic unconscious', *British Journal of Social Psychology*, 36: 139–59.

Billig, M. (1999) *Freudian Repression: Conversation Creating the Unconscious*. Cambridge: Cambridge University Press.

Birkvad, S. (2000) 'A battle for public mythology: history and genre in the portrait documentary', *Nordicom Review*, 2: 291–304.

Björklund, S. (1970) *Politisk teori [Political Theory]*. Stockholm: Aldus Bonniers.

Björkvall, A. (2003) *Svensk reklam och dess modelläsare*. Dissertation. Stockholm University, Stockholm.

Björkvall, A. (2020) 'The critical analysis of genre and social action', in A. De Fina and A. Georgakopoulou (eds), *The Cambridge Handbook of Discourse Studies*. Cambridge: Cambridge University Press, pp. 601–21.

Blaikie, N. and Priest, J. (2019) *Designing Social Research*. Cambridge: Polity Press.

Bletsas, A. and Beasley, C. (2012). *Engaging with Carol Bacchi. Strategic Interventions and Exchanges*. Adelaide: University of Adelaide Press. https://library.oapen.org/bitstream/handle/20.500.12657/33181/560097.pdf?sequence=1&isAllowed=y

Blommaert, J. (2007) *Discourse: A Critical Introduction* (4th edn). Cambridge: Cambridge University Press.

Bloor, K. (2010) *The Definitive Guide to Political Ideologies*. Milton Keynes: Author House.

Bödeker, H.E. (1998) 'Concept – meaning – discourse: Begriffsgeschichte reconsidered', in I. Hampsher-Monk, K. Tilmans and F. van Vree (eds), *History of Concepts: Comparative Perspectives*. Amsterdam: Amsterdam University Press, pp. 51–64.

Böke, K. (1996) 'Politische Leitvokabeln in der Adenauer-ära. Zu Theorie und Methodik', in K. Böke, F. Liedtke and M. Wengeler (eds), *Politische Leitvokabeln in der Adenauer-Ära*. Berlin, New York: Mouton de Gruyter, pp. 32–50.

Böke, K., Jung, M., Niehr, T. and Wengeler, M. (2005) 'Vergleichende Diskurslinguistik: Überlegungen zur Analyse national heterogener Textkorpora', in M. Wengeler (ed.), *Sprachgeschichte als Zeitgeschichte*. Hildesheim: Olms, pp. 247–83.

Boréus, K. (1997) 'The shift to the right: neo-liberalism in argumentation and language in the Swedish public debate since 1969', *European Journal of Political Research*, 31: 257–86.

Boréus, K. (2017) 'Argumentation analysis', in K. Boréus, and G. Bergström (eds), *Analyzing Text and Discourse: Eight Approaches for the Social Sciences*. Los Angeles: Sage, pp. 53–85.

Boréus, K. (2020) *Migrants and Natives – 'Them' and 'Us': Mainstream and Radical Right Political Rhetoric in Europe*. London: Sage.

Boréus, K. and Bergström, G. (2017) 'Suggested analysis', in K. Boréus and G. Bergström (eds), *Analyzing Text and Discourse: Eight Approaches for the Social Sciences*. Los Angeles, London, New Delhi, Singapore, Washington, DC, Melbourne: Sage, pp. 242–261.

Bourdieu, P. (2013 [1977]) *Outline of a Theory of Practice*. Cambridge: Cambridge University Press.

Bowell, T. and Kemp, G. (2015) *Critical Thinking: A Concise Guide*. London: Routledge.

Boyden, M., Basirat, A. and Berglund, K. (2022) 'Digital conceptual history and the emergence of a globalized climate imaginary', *Contributions to the History of Concepts*, 17 (2): 95–122. DOI: 10.3167/choc.2022.170205

Brecht, A. (1959) *Political Theory: The Foundations of Twentieth Century Political Thought*. Princeton, NJ: Princeton University Press.

Bremond, C. (1980) 'The logic of narrative possibilities', *New Literary History*, 11: 387–411.

Brinker, M. (1983) 'Verisimilitude, conventions and beliefs', *New Literary History*, 14: 253–67.

Bruner, J. (1991) 'The narrative construction of reality', *Critical Inquiry*, 18: 1–21.

Brunner, O., Conze, W. and Koselleck, R. (eds) (1972–1997) *Geschichtliche Grundbegriffe: Historisches Lexikon zur politisch-sozialen Sprache in Deutschland*. 8 vols. Stuttgart: Ernst Klett Verlag.

Brusselaers, N., Steadson, D., Björklund, K., Breland, S., Sörensen, J.S., Ewing, A., Bergmann, S. and Steineck, G. (2022) 'Evaluation of science advice during the COVID-19 pandemic in Sweden', *Humanities & Social Sciences Communications*, 9 (91). Available at: www.nature.com/articles/s41599-022-01097-5

Brylla, C. (2003) *Die schwedische Rezeption zentraler Begriffe der deutschen Frühromantik: Schlüsselwortanalysen zu den Zeitschriften Athenäum und Phosphoros*. Dissertation. Stockholm University, Stockholm.

Burr, V. (2003) *Social Constructionism* (2nd edn). London: Routledge.

Butler, J. (2006) *Gender Trouble: Feminism and the Subversion of Identity*. New York: Routledge.

Carlisle, J. (1994) 'Introduction', in J. Carlisle and D. R. Schwarz (eds), *Narrative and Culture*. London: University of Georgia Press, pp. 1–12.

Carnap, R. (2003) *The Logical Structure of the World and Pseudoproblems in Philosophy*. Chicago: Open Court.

Carpentier, N. (2017) *The Discursive-Material Knot: Cyprus in Conflict and Community Media Participation*. New York: Peter Lang Publishing.

Charteris-Black, J. (2004) *Corpus Approaches to Critical Metaphor Analysis*. Basingstoke and New York: Palgrave Macmillan.

Chatman, S. (1978) *Story and Discourse: Narrative Structure in Fiction and Film*. Ithaca and London: Cornell University Press.

Chouliaraki, L. and Fairclough, N. (1999) *Discourse in Late Modernity: Rethinking Critical Discourse Analysis*. Edinburgh: Edinburgh University Press.

Clayton, J. (1994) 'The narrative turn in minority Fiction', in J. Carlisle and D.R. Schwarz (eds), *Narrative and Culture*. London: University of Georgia Press, pp. 58–76.

Collier, A. (1994) *Critical Realism: An Introduction to Roy Bhaskar's Philosophy*. London: Verso.

Collingwood, R.G. (1939) *An Autobiography*. Oxford: Oxford University Press.

Connolly, W.E. (1983) *The Terms of Political Discourse*. Oxford: Martin Robertson.

Critchley, S. and Marchart, O. (eds) (2004) *Laclau: A Critical Reader*. New York: Routledge.

Crowley, S. and Hawhee, D. (1999) *Ancient Rhetorics for Contemporary Students*. Needham Heights, MA: Allyn & Bacon.

Czarniawska, B. (1999) *Interviews, Narratives and Organizations*. Gothenburg: GRI Raport: 8.

Czarniawska, B. (2004) *Narratives in Social Science Research*. London: Sage.

Dahl, R. and Shapiro, I. (2021) *On Democracy*. Dublin: Penguin Books.

Davidjants, J. and Tiidenberg, K. (2022) 'Activist memory narration on social media: Armenian genocide on Instagram', *New Media & Society*, 24 (10): 2191–206.

Davis, M. and Long, D. (2020) *Pandemics, Publics and Narrative*. Oxford: Oxford University Press.

De Cleen, B. and Stavrakakis, Y. (2017) 'Distinctions and articulations: a discourse theoretical framework for the study of populism and nationalism', *Javnost – The Public*, 24 (4): 301–19.

De Fina, A. and Georgakopoulou, A. (eds) (2019) *The Handbook of Narrative Analysis*. Oxford: Wiley Blackwell.

De Fina, A. and Johnstone, B. (2015) 'Discourse analysis and narrative', in D. Tannen et al., *The Handbook of Discourse Analysis* (2nd edn). New York: John Wiley & Sons, pp. 152–67.

Derrida, J. (2001) *Writing and Difference*. London: Routledge.

Devenney, M. (2020) *Towards an Improper Politics*. Edinburgh: Edinburgh University Press.

Dovring, K. (2009) 'Quantitative semantics in 18th century Sweden', in K. Krippendorff and M.A. Bock (eds), *The Content Analysis Reader*. Los Angeles, CA: SAGE Publications, pp. 4–8.

Durham, M. (2000) *The Christian Right, the Far Right and the Boundaries of American Conservatism*. Manchester: Manchester University Press.

Durranti, A. and Goodwin, C. (eds) (1992) *Rethinking Context: Language as an Interactive Phenomenon*. Cambridge: Cambridge University Press.

Eco, U. (1984) *The Role of the Reader: Explorations in the Semiotics of Texts*. Bloomington, IN: Indiana University Press.

Eco, U. (1994) *Six Walks in the Fictional Woods*. Cambridge, MA: Harvard University Press.

Edelman, M. (1977) *Political Language: Words that Succeed and Policies that Fail*. New York: Academic Press.

Edelman, M. (1988) *Constructing the Political Spectacle*. Chicago and London: Chicago University Press.

Edley, N. (2001) 'Analysing masculinity: interpretatative repertoires, subject positions and ideological dilemmas', in M. Wetherell, S. Taylor and S.J. Yates (eds), *Discourse as data: a guide to analysis*. London: Sage and the Open University, pp. 189–228.

Edley, N. and Wetherell, M. (2001) 'Jekyll and Hyde: men's constructions of feminism and feminists', *Feminism and Psychology*, 11 (4): 438–57.

Esposito, J. (2016) *Islam: The Straight Path*. New York: Oxford University Press.

Evans, V. (2009) *How Words Mean: Lexical Concepts, Cognitive Models and Meaning Construction*. Oxford: Oxford University Press.

Fagerholm, A. (2013) 'Towards a lighter shade of red? Social Democratic parties and the rise of Neo-liberalism in Western Europe, 1970–1999', *Perspectives on European Politics and Society*, 14 (4): 538–61.

Fairclough, I. and Fairclough, N. (2012) *Political Discourse Analysis: A Method for Advanced Students*. London: Routledge.

Fairclough, N. (1992) *Discourse and Social Change*. Cambridge: Polity Press.

Fairclough, N. (1993) 'Critical discourse analysis and the marketisation of public discourse: the universities', *Discourse & Society*, 4 (2): 133–68.

Fairclough, N. (1995) *Critical Discourse Analysis: A Critical Study of Language*. London: Longman.

Fairclough, N. (2003) *Analyzing Discourse: Textual Analysis for Social Research*. London: Routledge.

Fairclough, N. (2010) *Critical Discourse Analysis: The Critical Study of Language* (2nd edn). London: Longman.

Fairclough, N. (2014) 'A critical agenda for education', in J. Angermuller, D. Maingueneau and R. Wodak (eds), *Discourse Studies Reader*. Amsterdam: John Benjamins Publishing Company, pp. 378–388.

Fairclough, N. (2015 [1989]) *Language and Power* (3rd edn). London and New York: Routledge.

Fairclough, N. and Wodak, R. (1997) 'Critical discourse analysis', in T.A. van Dijk (ed.), *Discourse as Social Interaction. Discourse Studies: A Multidisciplinary Introduction*. Vol. 2. London: Sage, pp. 258–84.

Fairclough, N., Jessop, B. and Sayer, A. (2002) 'Critical realism and semiosis', *Alethia*, 5 (1): 2–10. DOI: 10.1558/aleth.v5i1.2

Farr, J. (1989) 'Understanding conceptual change politically', in T. Ball, J. Farr, R.L. Hanson (eds), *Political Innovation and Conceptual Change*. Cambridge: Cambridge University Press, pp. 24–49.

Fauconnier, G. and Turner, M. (2003) 'Polysemy and conceptual blending', in B. Nerlich, Z. Todd, V. Herman and D.D. Clarke (eds), *Polysemy*. Berlin: De Grutyer, pp. 79–94.

Feldman and Almquist (2012) 'Analyzing the Implicit in Stories', in J.A. Holstein and J.F. Gruber (eds), *Varieties of Narrative Analysis*. London: Sage, pp. 207–28.

Fernández Galeote, D., Legaki, N.Z. and Hamari, J. (2022) 'Avatar identities and climate change action in video games: analysis of mitigation and adaptation practices', CHI Conference on Human Factors in Computing Systems (CHI '22), 29 April–5 May. New Orleans, LA. DOI: https://doi.org/10.1145/3491102.3517438

Firth, J.R. (1957) 'A synopsis of linguistic theory 1930–1955', in F.R. Palmer (ed.), (1968) *Selected Papers of J.R. Firth 1952–1959*. London: Longman, pp. 180–212.

Fisher, D.R., Leifeld, P. and Iwaki, Y. (2013) 'Mapping the ideological networks of American climate politics', *Climatic Change*, 116 (3): 523–45.

Flowerdew, J. and Richardson, J.E. (eds) (2017) *The Routledge Handbook of Critical Discourse Studies*. London: Routledge.

Foucault, M. (1972) *The Archeology of Knowledge*. London: Tavistock Publications.

Foucault, M. (1977) 'Nietzsche, genealogy, history', in D.F. Bouchard (ed.), *Language, Counter-Memory, Practice: Selected Essays and Interviews*. Ithaca: Cornell University Press, pp. 139–64.

Foucault, M. (1980) *Power/Knowledge: Selected Interviews and Other Writings 1972–1977*. Brighton: The Harvester Press.

Foucault, M. (1990) *The History of Sexuality (Vol. 1): The Will to Knowledge*. Harmondsworth: Penguin.

Foucault, M. (1994) *Essential Works of Foucault 1954–1984. Vol. 3: Power*. V. Marchetti and A. Salomoni (eds). London: Verso.

Foucault, M. (1997) *The Politics of Truth*. New York: Semiotext(e).

Foucault, M. (2001 [1967]) *Madness and Civilization: A History of Insanity in the Age of Reason*. London: Routledge.

Foucault, M. (2020) *Discipline and Punish: The Birth of Prison*. London: Penguin Classics.

Fowler, R. (2013 [1991]) *Language in the News: Discourse and Ideology in the Press*. London: Taylor & Francis.

Frank, A.W. (2012) 'Practicing dialogical narrative analysis', in J.A. Holstein and J.F. Gruber (eds), *Varieties of Narrative Analysis*. London: Sage, pp. 33–52.

Franzosi, R. (1998) 'Narrative analysis – or why (and how) sociologists should be interested in narrative', *Annual Review of Sociology*, 24: 517–554.

Franzosi, R. (2010) *Quantitative Narrative Analysis*. London: Sage.

Franzosi, R. (2012) 'On Quantitative Narrative Analysis', in J.A. Holstein and J.F. Gruber (eds), *Varieties of Narrative Analysis*. London: Sage, pp. 75–96.

Freeden, M. (1996) *Ideologies and Political Theory: A Conceptual Approach*. Oxford: Clarendon Press.

Freeden, M. (2003) *Ideology – A Very Short Introduction*. Oxford: Oxford University Press.

Freeden, M. (2013) 'The morphological analysis of ideology', in M. Freeden et al. (eds), *The Oxford Handbook of Political Ideologies*. Oxford: Oxford University Press, pp. 115–37.

Freeden, M. (2017) 'Conceptual history, ideology and language', in W. Steinmetz et al. (eds), *Conceptual History in the European Space*. New York: Berghahn Books, pp. 118–38.

Freeden M., Fernández Sebastián, J. and Leonhard, J. (2019) *In Search of European Liberalisms: Concepts, Languages, Ideologies*. New York: Berghahn Books.

Friedrich, C.J. (1963) *Man and his Government: An Empirical Theory of Politics*. New York: McGraw-Hill.

Gadamer, H.-G. (1989) *Truth and Method* (2nd edn). New York: Crossroad.

Gee, J.P. (2005) *An Introduction to Discourse Analysis: Theory and Method*. London and New York: Routledge.

Gelter, J., Lexhagen, M. and Fuchs, M. (2021) 'A meta-narrative analysis of smart tourism destinations: implications for tourism destination management', *Current Issues in Tourism*, 24 (20): 2860–74.

Gemenis, K. (2013) 'What to do (and not to do) with the comparative manifestos project data', *Political Studies*, 61 (1 suppl.): 3–23.

George, A.L. (2009) 'Propaganda analysis: a case study from World War II', in K. Krippendorff and M.A. Bock (eds), *The Content Analysis Reader*. London: SAGE Publications, pp. 21–7.

Gergen, K.J. (1994) *Realities and Relationships: Sounding in Social Construction.* Cambridge, MA: Harvard University Press.

Gibbs, R.W., Jr (2014) 'Conceptual metaphor in thought and social action', in M. Landau, M.D. Robinson and B.P. Meier (eds), *The Power of Metaphor: Examining its Influence on Social Life.* Washington: American Psychological Association, pp. 17–40.

Gibson, J. (1977) 'The theory of affordances', in R. Shaw and J. Brandsford (eds), *Perceiving, Acting, and Knowing: Toward an Ecological Psychology.* Hillsdale, NJ: Erlbaum, pp. 62–82.

Giger, N. and Schumacher, G. (2015) *Integrated Party Organization Dataset (IPOD)*, Harvard Dataverse, version 1.

Gjedde, L. (2000) 'Narrative, genre and context in popular science', *Nordicom Review*, 21 (1): 51–7.

Glynos, J. and Howarth, D. (2007) *Logics of Critical Explanation in Social and Political Theory.* London: Routledge.

Glynos, J. and Howarth, D. (2008) 'Critical explanation in social science: a logics approach', *Swiss Journal of Sociology*, 34 (1): 5–35.

Goffman, E. (1979) *Gender Advertisements.* London and Basingstoke: Macmillan.

Goffman, E. (1986) *Frame Analysis. An Essay on the Organization of Experience.* Boston: Northwestern University Press.

Goodwin, M. (2023) *Values, Voice and Virtue.* Dublin: Penguin Books.

Goudarouli, E. and Petakos, D. (2017) 'Translating the concept of experiment in the late eighteenth century: from the English philosophical context to the Greek-speaking regions of the Ottoman Empire', *Contributions to the History of Concepts*, 12 (1): 76–97.

Graddol, D. (1994) 'The visual accomplishment of factuality', in D. Graddol and O. Boyd-Barrett (eds), *Media Texts: Authors and Readers.* London: Open University Press, pp. 136–57.

Greenhalgh, T. et al. (2005) 'Storylines of research in diffusion of innovation: a meta-narrative approach to systematic review', *Social Science & Medicine*, 61 (2): 417–30.

Gregor, J. (2002) *Phoenix: Fascism in our Time.* New Brunswick and London: Transaction Publishers.

Griggs, S. and Howarth, D. (2016) *The Politics of Airport Expansion in the United Kingdom: Hegemony, Policy and the Rhetoric of 'Sustainable Aviation'.* Manchester: Manchester University Press.

Gunnell, J.G. (1998) 'Time and interpretation: understanding concepts and conceptual change', *History of Political Thought*, 19: 641–58.

Gustafsson, A.W. and Hommerberg, C. (2018) '"It is completely ok to give up a little sometimes": metaphors and normality in Swedish cancer talk', *Critical Approaches to Discourse Analysis across Disciplines*, 10 (1): 1–16.

Gustafsson, A.W., Hommerberg, C. and Sandgren, A. (2020) 'Coping by metaphors: the versatile function of metaphors in blogs about living with advanced cancer', *Medical Humanities*, 46: 267–77.

Haar, M. (1971) 'Nietzsche and metaphysical language', *Man and World*, 4 (4): 359–95. DOI: 10.1007/BF01579032

Habermas, J. (1991) *The Theory of Communicative Action. Vol. I: Reason and the Rationalization of Society*. Cambridge: Polity Press.

Hall, E.T. (1966) *The Hidden Dimension*. New York: Doubleday & Company.

Hall, S. (1994) 'Encoding/Decoding', in D. Graddol and O. Boyd-Barrett (eds), *Media Texts: Authors and Readers*. London: Open University Press, pp. 200–11.

Hall, S. (1997) 'The work of representation', in S. Hall (ed.), *Representation: Cultural Representation and Signifying Practices*. London: Sage, pp. 13–74.

Halliday, M.A.K. (1978) *Language as Social Semiotic: The Social Interpretation of Language and Meaning*. London: Edward Arnold.

Halliday, M.A.K. and Hasan, R. (1976) *Cohesion in English*. London: Longman.

Halliday, M.A.K. and Matthiessen, C.M.I.M. (2014) *Halliday's Introduction to Functional Grammar* (4th edn). Abingdon and New York: Routledge.

Hampsher-Monk, I. (1998) 'Speech acts, languages or conceptual history?', in I. Hampsher-Monk, K. Tilmans and F. van Vree (eds), *History of Concepts: Comparative Perspectives*. Amsterdam: Amsterdam University Press, pp. 37–50.

Hansen, A.D. (2014) 'Laclau and Mouffe and the ontology of radical negativity', *Distinction: Scandinavian Journal of Social Theory*, 15 (3): 283–95. DOI: https://doi.org/10.1080/1600910X.2014.973895

Harré, R. (1995) 'Discursive psychology', in J.A. Smith, R. Harré and L. van Langenhove (eds), *Rethinking Psychology*. London: Sage, pp. 143–59.

Hart, C. (ed.) (2020) *Researching Discourse: A Student Guide*. London: Routledge.

Hartwig, M. (2008) 'Introduction', in R. Bhaskar, *A Realist Theory of Science*. London: Routledge, pp. ix–xxiv.

Harvey, D. (2005) *A Brief History of Neoliberalism*. Oxford: Oxford University Press.

Hatakka, N., Niemi, M.K. and Välimäki, M. (2017) 'Confrontational yet submissive: calculated ambivalence and populist parties' strategies of responding to racism accusations in the media', *Discourse & Society*, 28 (3): 262–80.

Hempel, C.G. (1970) *Aspects of Scientific Explanation: And Other Essays in the Philosophy of Science*. New York: Free Press.

Herman, D., Jahn, M. and Ryan, M.-L. (eds) (2008) *Routledge Encyclopedia of Narrative Theory*. London and New York: Routledge.

Herman, L. and Vervaeck, B. (2005) *Handbook of Narrative Analysis*. Lincoln, NE and London: University of Nebraska Press.

Hermanns, F. (1994) *Schlüssel-, Schlag- und Fahnenwörter: zu Begrifflichkeit und Theorie der lexikalischen 'politischen Semantik'*. Heidelberg/Mannheim: Institut für Deutsche Sprache.

Heyneman, S.P and Lee, B. (2014) 'The impact of international studies of academic achievement on policy and research', in L. Rutkowski, M. von Davier and D. Rutkowski (eds), *Handbook of International Large-Scale Assessment*. Boca Raton, FL: CRC Press, pp. 37–75.

Heywood, A. (2021) *Political Ideologies: An Introduction* (7th edn). London: Red Globe Press.

Hodge, R. and Kress, G. (1988) *Social Semiotics*. Cambridge: Polity Press.

Holstein, J.A. and Gubrium, J.F. (eds) (2012) *Varieties of Narrative Analysis*. London: Sage.

Horn, A. (2019) 'Can the online crowd match real expert judgments? How task complexity and coder location affect the validity of crowd-coded data', *European Journal of Political Research*, 58: 236–47.

Hornsby-Smith, M.P. (2006) *An Introduction to Catholic Social Thought*. Cambridge: Cambridge University Press.

Horton-Salway, M. (2001) 'The construction of M.E.: the discursive action model', in M. Wetherell, S. Taylor and S.J. Yates (eds), *Discourse as Data: A Guide for Analysis*. London: Sage, pp. 147–88.

Howarth, D. (2000) *Discourse*. Buckingham: Open University Press.

Howarth, D. (2010) 'Power, discourse, and policy: articulating a hegemony approach to critical policy studies', *Critical Policy Studies*, 3 (3–4): 309–35, DOI: 10.1080/19460171003619725

Howarth, D. and Stavrakakis, Y. (2000) 'Introducing discourse theory and political analysis', in D. Howarth, A.J. Norval and Y. Stavrakakis (eds), *Discourse Theory and Political Analysis: Identities, Hegemonies and Social Change*. Manchester: Manchester University Press, pp. 1–23.

Howarth, D., Norval, A.J. and Stavrakakis, Y. (eds) (2000) *Discourse Theory and Political Analysis: Identities, Hegemonies and Social Change*. Manchester: Manchester University Press.

Hsieh, H.-F. and Shannon, S.E. (2005) 'Three approaches to qualitative content analysis', *Qualitative Health Research*, 15(9): 1277–88.

Ifversen, J. (2011) 'About key concepts and how to study them', *Contributions to the History of Concepts*, 6 (1): 65–88.

Ignell, C., Davies, P. and Lundholm, C. (2019) 'A longditudinal study of upper secondary school students' values and beliefs regarding policy responses to climate change', *Environmental Education Research*, 25 (5): 615–32.

Ihalainen, P. (2017) *The Springs of Democracy: National and Transnational Debates on Constitutional Reform in the British, German, Swedish and Finnish Parliaments, 1917–1919*. Helsingfors: Finnish Literature Society.

Inglehart, R. and Norris, P. (2003) *Rising Tide: Gender Equality and Cultural Change Around the World*. Cambridge: Cambridge University Press.

Innes, J. and Philp, M. (2013) *Re-imagining Democracy in the Age of Revolutions: America, France, Britain, Ireland, 1750–1850*. Oxford: Oxford University Press.

Jacobs, A.M., Matthews, J.S. and Hicks, T. (2021) 'Whose news? Class-biased economic reporting in the United States', *American Political Science*, 115 (3): 1016–33.

Jakobson, R. (1960) 'Closing statement: linguistics and poetics', in T.A. Sebeok (ed.), *Style in Language*. Cambridge, MA: MIT Press, pp. 350–77.

James, P. and Steger, M. (2014) 'A genealogy of globalization: the career of a concept', *Globalizations*, 11: 417–34.

Jameson, F. (1989) *The Political Unconscious: Narrative as a Socially Symbolic Act*. London: Routledge.

Jewitt, C. (ed.) (2014) *The Routledge Handbook of Multimodal Analysis* (2nd edn). London and New York: Routledge.

Jockers, M. (2014) *Text Analysis with R for Students of Literature*. Berlin: Springer.

Johansson, J. and Gabrielsson, J. (2021) 'Public policy for social innovations and social enterprise – what's the problem represented to be?', *Sustainability*, 13 (14): 65–84.

Jordheim, H. (2017) 'Europe at different speeds: asynchronies and multiple times in European conceptual history', in W. Steinmetz et al. (eds), *Conceptual History in the European Space*. New York: Berghahn Books, pp. 47–62.

Jørgensen, M. and Phillips, L. (2002) *Discourse as Theory and Method*. London: Sage.

Kagan, D., Chesney, T. and Fire, M. (2020) 'Using data science to understand the film industry's gender gap', *Palgrave Communications Humanities/Social Sciences/Business*, 6: 92.

Kaldewey, D. and Schauz, D. (eds) (2018) *Basic and Applied Research: The Language of Science Policy in the Twentieth Century*. New York: Berghahn Books.

Kanner, A. (2022) *Meaning in Distributions: A Study on Computational Methods in Lexical Semantics*. Helsinki: University of Helsinki. Available at: http://urn.fi/URN:ISBN:ISBN%20978-951-51-8067-4

Keller, R. (2013) *Doing Discourse Research: An Introduction for Social Scientists*. London: Sage.

King, G., Pan, J. and Roberts, M.E. (2013) 'How censorship in China allows government criticism but silences collective expression', *American Political Science Review*, 107: 326–43.

Kiser, E. (1996) 'The revival of narrative in historical sociology: what rational choice theory can contribute', *Politics and Society*, 24 (3).

Kitcher, P. (2002) 'Scientific knowledge', in P.K. Moser (ed.), *The Oxford Handbook of Epistemology*. Oxford: Oxford University Press, pp. 385–407. DOI: 10.1093/0195130057.003.0014

Klein, J. (1991) 'Kann man "Begriffe besetzen"? Zur linguistischen Differenzierung einer plakativen politischen Metapher', in F. Liedke, M. Wengeler and K. Böke (eds), *Begriffe besetzen: Strategien des Sprachgebrauchs in der Politik*. Opladen: Westdeutscher Verlag, pp. 44–69.

Knox, J. (2007) 'Visual–verbal communication on online newspaper home pages', *Visual Communication*, 6 (1): 19–53.

Koller, V. (2009) 'Missions and empires: religious and political metaphors in corporate discourse', in A. Musolff and J. Zinken (eds), *Metaphor and Discourse*. Basingstoke: Palgrave Macmillan, pp. 116–34.

Koller, V. (2020a) 'Analysing metaphor in discourse', in C. Hart (ed.), *Researching Discourse: A Student Guide*. London: Routledge, pp. 77–96.

Koller, V. (2020b) 'Discourse analysis and systemic functional linguistics', in C. Hart (ed.), *Researching Discourse: A Student Guide*. London: Routledge, pp. 54–76.

Koselleck, R. (1972) 'Einleitung', in O. Brunner, W. Conze and R. Koselleck (eds), *Geschichtliche Grundbegriffe: Historisches Lexikon zur politisch-sozialen Sprache in Deutschland*. Band 1. Stuttgart: Ernst Klett Verlag, pp. XIII–XXVII.

Koselleck, R. (1979) *Vergangene Zukunft: Zur Semantik geschichtlicher Zeiten*. Frankfurt am Main: Suhrkamp.

Koselleck, R. (1983) 'Begriffsgeschichtliche Probleme der Verfassungsgeschichsschreibung', *Der Staat, Sonderheft 6*.

Koselleck, R. (1989) 'Linguistic change and the history of events', *Journal of Modern History*, 61: 649–66.

Koselleck, R. (1994) 'Some reflections on the temporal structure of conceptual change', in W. Melching and V. Velema (eds), *Main Trends in Cultural History: Ten Essays*. Amsterdam: Rodopi, pp. 7–16.

Koselleck, R. (1996) 'A response to comments on the geschichtliche grundbegriffe', in H. Lehmann and M. Richter (eds), *The Meaning of Historical Terms and Concepts. New Studies on Begriffsgeschichte*. Washington, DC: German Historical Institute, pp. 59–70.

Koselleck, R. (1998) 'Social history and begriffsgeschichte', in I. Hampsher-Monk and T. van Vree (eds), *History of Concepts: Comparative Perspectives*. Amsterdam: Amsterdam University Press, pp. 23–35.

Koselleck, R. (2002) *The Practice of Conceptual History: Timing History, Spacing Concepts*. Stanford, CA: Stanford University Press.

Koselleck, R. (2004) *Futures Past: On the Semantic of Historical Time*. New York: Columbia University Press.

Koselleck, R. (2018) *Sediments of Time: On Possible Histories*. Redwood City, CA: Stanford University Press.

Koselleck, R., Spree, U. and Steinmetz, W. (1991) 'Drei bürgerliche Welten? Zur vergleichenden Semantik der bürgerlichen Gesellschaft in Deutschland, England und Frankreich', in H.-J. Puhle (eds), *Bürger in der Gesellschaft der Neuzeit*. Göttingen: Vandenhoeck & Ruprecht, pp. 14–58.

Kozloff, S. (1992) 'Narrative theory and television', in R.C. Allen (ed.), *Channels of Discourse, Reassembled: Television and Contemporary Criticism*. London: Routledge, pp. 67–100.

Kress, G. (2010) *Multimodality: A Social Semiotic Approach to Contemporary Communication*. London and New York: Routledge.

Kress, G. and Hodge, R. (1979) *Language as Ideology*. London: Routledge & Kegan Paul.

Kress, G. and van Leeuwen, T. (2001) *Multimodal Discourse: The Modes and Media of Contemporary Communication*. London: Arnold.

Kress, G. and van Leeuwen, T. (2021) *Reading Images: The Grammar of Visual Design* (3rd edn). London and New York: Routledge.

Krippendorff, K. (2019) *Content Analysis: An Introduction to Its Methodology*. Thousand Oaks, CA: SAGE Publications.

Krippendorff, K. and Bock, M.A. (eds) (2009) *The Content Analysis Reader*. London: Sage.

Krzyżanowski, M. (2015) 'International leadership re-/constructed? On the ambivalence and heterogeneity of identity discourses in European Union's policy on climate change', *Journal of Language and Politics*, 14(1): 110–33.

Krzyżanowski, M. and Wodak, R. (2008) *The Politics of Exclusion: Debating Migration in Austria*. New Brunswick: Transaction Publishers.

Kuckartz, U. (2014) *Qualitative Text Analysis: A Guide to Methods, Practice and Using Software*. London: SAGE Publications.

Kunelius, R. and Roosvall, A. (2021) 'Media and the climate crisis', *Nordic Journal of Media Studies*, 3 (1): 1–19.

Kurunmäki, J. and Marjanen, J. (2018a) 'A rhetorical view of isms: an introduction', *Journal of Political Ideologies*, 23 (3): 241–55.

Kurunmäki, J. and Marjanen, J. (2018b) 'Isms, ideologies and setting the agenda for public debate', *Journal of Political Ideologies*, 23 (3): 256–82.

Kurunmäki, J. and Marjanen, J. (2020) 'How ideology became isms: a history of a conceptual coupling', in H. Haara, K. Stapelbroek and M. Immanen (eds), *Passions, Politics and the Limits of Society*. De Gruyter Oldenbourg, pp. 291–318. DOI: 10.1515/9783110679861-017

Kurunmäki, J. and Marjanen, J. (2021) 'Catching up through comparison: the making of Finland as a political unit, 1809–1863', *Time & Society*, 30 (4): 559–80. DOI: 10.1177/0961463X21990349

Kurunmäki, J., Nevers, J. and te Velde, H. (eds) (2018) *Democracy in Europe: A Conceptual History*. New York: Berghahn Books.

Labov, W. and Waletzky, J. (1967) *'Narrative Analysis: Oral Versions of Personal Experience,' Essays on Verbal and Visual Arts*. Seattle, WA: University of Washington Press, pp. 12–45.

Laclau, E. (1990) *New Reflections on the Revolution of Our Time*. London: Verso.

Laclau, E. (1996) *Emancipation(s)*. New York: Verso.

Laclau, E. (2005) *On Populist Reason*. London and New York: Verso.

Laclau, E. (2014) *The Rhetorical Foundations of Society*. London: Verso.

Laclau, E. and Mouffe, C. (1985) *Hegemony and Socialist Strategy: Towards a Radical Democratic Politics* (1st edn). London and New York: Verso.

Laclau, E. and Mouffe, C. (1990) 'Post-Marxism without apologies', in E. Laclau (ed.), *New Reflections on the Revolution of Our Time*. London and New York: Verso, pp. 97–134.

Laclau, E. and Mouffe, C. (2001) *Hegemony and Socialist Strategy: Towards a Radical Democratic Politics* (2nd edn). London: Verso Books.

Lakoff, G. (1993) 'The contemporary theory of metaphor', in A. Ortony (ed.), *Metaphor and Thought*. Cambridge: Cambridge University Press, pp. 202–51.

Lakoff, G. and Johnson, M. (1980) *Metaphors We Live By*. Chicago, London: The University of Chicago Press.

Lasswell, H. and Kaplan, A. (1950) *Power and Society: A Framework for Political Inquiry*. New Haven, NJ and London: Yale University Press.

Laver, M. and Garry, J. (2000) 'Estimating policy positions from political texts', *American Journal of Political Science*, 44 (3): 619–34.

Ledin, P. and Machin, D. (2016) 'Performance management discourse and the shift to an administrative logic of operation: A multimodal critical discourse analytical approach', *Text & Talk*, 36 (4): 445–67. DOI: 10.1515/text-2016-0020

Ledin, P. and Machin, D. (2018a) 'Doing critical discourse studies with multi-modality: from metafunctions to materiality', *Critical Discourse Studies*, 16 (5), 497–513. DOI: 10.1080/17405904.2018.1468789

Ledin, P. and Machin, D. (2018b) *Doing Visual Analysis: From Theory to Practice*. London: Sage.

Ledin, P. and Machin, D. (2020) *Introduction to Multimodal Analysis* (2nd edn). London: Bloomsbury.

Leifeld, P. (2013) 'Reconceptualizing major policy change in the advocacy coalition framework: a discourse network analysis of German pension politics', *Policy Studies Journal*, 41 (1): 169–98.

Leifeld, P. (2016) *Policy Debates as Dynamic Networks: German Pension Politics and Privatization Discourse*. Frankfurt: Campus Verlag.

Leonhard, J. (2001) *Liberalismus: zur historischen Semantik eines europäischen Deutungsmusters*. Munich: Oldenbourg.

Leonhard, J. (2004) 'From European Liberalism to the languages of Liberalisms: the semantics of Liberalism in European comparison', *Redescriptions: Yearbook of Political Thought and Conceptual History*, Vol. 8. Department of History, University of Jyväskylä, Finland.

Leonhard, J. (2011) 'Language, experience and translation: towards a comparative dimension', in J. Fernández Sebastián (eds), *Political Concepts and Time*. Santander: Cantabria University Press, pp. 245–72.

Letwin, S.R. (1992) *The Anatomy of Thatcherism*. London: Fontana.

Lieblich, A., Tuval-Mashiach, R. and Zilber, T. (1998) *Narrative Research: Reading, Analysis and Interpretation*. Applied social research methods series, vol. 47. Thousand Oaks, CA: Sage.

Lindberg, M. (2018a) 'The VDP-triad in ideational analysis: toward a general theory of ideological thought-content in social and political communication, debate, thought and language – beyond the concepts "ideology", "culture", "belief system", "discourse" and "policy" (Part I)', *Statsvetenskaplig Tidskrift*, 120 (2): 277–362.

Lindberg, M. (2018b) 'The VDP-triad in ideational analysis: toward a general theory of ideological thought-content in social and political communication, debate, thought and language – beyond the concepts "ideology", "culture", "belief system", "discourse" and "policy" (Part II)', *Statsvetenskaplig Tidskrift*, 120 (3–4): 435–556.

Lukes, S. (2005) *Power: A Radical View* (2nd edn). London: Palgrave Macmillan.

Macaulay, M. (ed.) (2019) *Populist Discourse: International Perspectives*. Cham: Springer International Publishing.

Machin, D. (2014) 'Multimodality and theories of the visual', in C. Jewitt (ed.), *The Routledge Handbook of Multimodal Analysis* (2nd edn). London and New York: Routledge, pp. 217–26.

Machin, D. and Mayr, A. (2012) *How to Do Critical Discourse Analysis: A Multimodal Introduction*. London: Sage.

Majone, G. (1989) *Evidence, Argument and Persuasion in the Policy Process*. New Haven, NJ: Yale University Press.

Manea, E. (2017) *Women and Shari'a Law: The Impact of Legal Pluralism in the UK*. London: I.B. Tauris.

March, G. and Olsen, P. (1989) *Rediscovering Institutions: The Organizational Basis of Politics*. New York: The Free Press.

March, L. (2013) *Radical Left Parties in Europe*. London: Routledge.

Marchart, O. (2018) *Thinking Antagonism: Political Ontology after Laclau*. Edinburgh: Edinburgh University Press.

Marjanen, J. (2009) 'Undermining methodological nationalism: historie croisée of concepts as transnational history', in M. Albert et al. (eds), *Transnational Political Spaces: Agents, Structures, Encounters*. Frankfurt: Campus, pp. 239–63.

Marjanen, J. (2017) 'Transnational conceptual history, methodological nationalism and Europe', in W. Steinmetz et al. (eds), *Conceptual History in the European Space*. New York: Berghahn Books, pp. 139–74.

Marjanen, J. (2023) 'Quantitative conceptual history: on agency, reception, and interpretation', *Contributions to the History of Concepts*, 18 (1): 46–67. DOI: 10.3167/choc.2023.180103

Martin, J. (2014) *Politics and Rhetoric: A Critical Introduction*. London: Routledge.

Marttila, T. (2016) *Post-foundational Discourse Analysis: From Political Difference to Empirical Research*. Basingstoke: Palgrave Macmillan.

Mayring, P. (2019) 'Qualitative compontent analysis: demarcation, varieties, developments', *Forum: Qualitative Social Research*, 20 (3): 1–26.

McGowan, K. (2006) 'Structuralism and semiotics', in S. Malpas and P. Wake (eds), *The Routledge Companion to Critical Theory*. London: Routledge, pp. 3–13.

McLaughlin, J. (2003) *Feminist Social and Political Theory*. Basingstoke: Palgrave Macmillan.

McMillan, S.J. (2009) 'The Challenge of Applying Content Analysis to the World Wide Web', in Krippendorff, K. and Bock, M.A. (eds), *The Content Analysis Reader*. London: Sage, pp. 60–7.

Mert, A. (2019) 'The trees in Gezi Park: environmental policy as the focus of democratic protests', *Journal of Environmental Policy & Planning*, 21 (5), 593–607, DOI: 10.1080/1523908X.2016.1202106

Mertova, P. and Webster, L. (2019) *Using Narrative Inquiry as a Research Method*. London: Routledge.

Miller, C.R. (1984) 'Genre as social action', *Quarterly Journal of Speech*, 70: 151–67.

Mills, S. (2008) *Language and Sexism*. Cambridge: Cambridge University Press.

Mott, S.Ch. (1992) *A Christian Perspective on Political Thought*. Oxford: Oxford University Press.

Mouffe, C. (2000) *The Democratic Paradox*. London: Verso.

Mouffe, C. (2005) *On the Political*. London: Verso.

Mouffe, C. (2013) *Agonistics: Thinking the World Politically*. London: Verso.

Mouffe, C. (2018) *For a Left Populism*. London: Verso.

Mouffe, C. (2022) *Towards a Green Democratic Revolution: Left Populism and the Power of Affects*. London: Verso.

Mueller, R.A. (2019) 'Episodic narrative interview: capturing stories of experience with a methods fusion', *International Journal of Qualitative Methods*, 18. DOI: 10.1177/1609406919866044

Müller, J.W. (2011) *Contesting Democracy: Political Ideas in Twentieth Century Europe*. New Haven, NJ: Yale University Press.

Mumby, K. (1993) *Narrative and Social Control: Critical Perspectives*. London: Sage.

Munzert, S., Rubba, C., Meißner, P. and Nyhuis, D. (2014) *Automated Data Collection with R: A Practical Guide to Web Scraping and Text Mining*. London: John Wiley & Sons.

Myrdal, G. (1996 [1944]) *An American Dilemma: The Negro Problem in the American South. Vol. I–II*. New Brunswick and London: Transaction Publishers.

Naess, A. (1965) *Gandhi and the Nuclear Age*. Totowa, NJ: The Bedminster Press.

Naess, A. (1966) *Communication and Argument*. London: Allen & Unwin.

Nietzsche, F. (1892) *Zur Genealogie der Moral*. Leipzig.

Nietzsche, F.W. (1976) 'On truth and lie in an extra-moral sense', in W. Kaufmann (ed.), *The Portable Nietzsche*. New York: Penguin Books, pp. 42–7.

Norris, P. and Inglehart, R. (2011) *Sacred and Secular: Religion and Politics Worldwide*. Cambridge: Cambridge University Press.

Nortio, E., Varjonen, S., Mähönen, T. A., and Jasinskaja-Lahti, I. (2016) 'Interpretative repertoires of multiculturalism – supporting and challenging hierarchical intergroup relations', *Journal of Social and Political Psychology*, 4 (2): 623–45. DOI: https://doi.org/10.5964/jspp.v4i2.639

Norton, A. (2004) *95 Theses on Politics, Culture, and Method*. New Haven, NJ: Yale University Press.

Nyman, J. (2016) 'Horsescapes: space, nation, and human–horse relations in Jane Smiley's horse heaven', in D. Herman (ed.), *Human–Animal Relationships in Twentieth- and Twenty-First-Century Literature*. Palgrave Macmillan, pp. 218–39.

Ochs, E. and Capps, L. (2001) *Living Narrative*. MA: Harvard University Press.

Ochs, E. and Taylor, C.E. (1992) 'Family narrative as political activity', *Discourse & Society*, 3: 301–40.

Ogden, C.K. and Richards, I.A. (2013 [1923]) *The Meaning of Meaning: A Study in the Influence of Language upon Thought and of the Science of Symbolism*. Mansfield Centre, CT: Martino Publishing.

Olsen, N. (2012) *History in the Plural: An Introduction to the Work of Reinhart Koselleck*. Oxford: Berghahn Books.

Olson, J. D, McAllister, C., Grinnell, L. D., Gehrke Walters, K., and Appunn, F. (2016) Applying constant comparative method with multiple investigators and inter-coder reliability', *The Qualitative Report*, 21 (1): 26–42. DOI: https://doi.org/10.46743/2160-3715/2016.2447

Oren, I. (2006) 'Can political science emulate the natural sciences? The problem of self-disconfirming analysis', *Polity*, 38 (1): 72–100.

Orgad, S. and De Benedictis, S. (2015) 'The "stay-at-home" mother, postfeminism and neoliberalism: content analysis of UK news coverage', *European Journal of Communication*, 30 (4): 418–36.

Page, R. (ed.) (2011) *New Perspectives on Narratives and Multimodality*. London: Routledge.

Palonen, K. (2003a) *Quentin Skinner: History, Politics, Rhetoric*. Cambridge: Polity.

Palonen, K. (2003b) 'Europoppalaiset poliittiset käsitteet suomalaisissa pelitiloissa', in M. Hyvärinen et al. (eds), *Käsitteet liikkeessä: Suomen polittisen kulttuurin käsitehistoria*. Tampere: Vastapaino, pp. 569–87.

Parsons, T. (1951) *The Social System*. London: Routledge & Kegan Paul.

Pechenick, E.A., Danforth, C.M. and Dodds, P.S. (2015) 'Characterizing the Google Books corpus: strong limits to inferences of socio-cultural and linguistic evolution', *PLoS ONE*, 10 (10): e0137041. DOI: https://doi.org/10.1371/journal.pone.0137041

Peirce, C.S. (1998) *The Essential Peirce: Selected Philosophical Writings, Vol. 2*. Bloomington: Indiana University Press.

Pernau, M. (2012) 'Whither conceptual history? From national to entangled histories', *Contributions to the History of Concepts*, 7 (1): 1–11.

Pernau M., Jordheim, H., Bashkin, O. et al. (2015) *Civilizing Emotions: Concepts in Nineteenth Century Asia and Europe*. Oxford: Oxford University Press.

Persson, S. (2020) *Corporate Hegemony through Sustainability: A Study of Sustainability Standards and CSR Practices as Tools to Demobilise Community Resistance in the Albanian Oil Industry*. Dissertation. Södertörn University, Huddinge.

Pietikäinen, S. (2003) 'Indigenous identity in print: representations of the Sami in news discourse', *Discourse & Society*, 14 (5): 581–609.

Potter, J. (2012) 'Re-reading Discourse and Social Psychology: Transforming social psychology', *British Journal of Social Psychology*, 51, 436–55.

Potter, J. and Edwards, D. (2001) 'Discursive social psychology', in P. Robinson and H. Giles (eds), *The Handbook of Language and Social Psychology*. Chichester: Wiley, pp. 103–18.

Potter, J. and Wetherell, M. (1987) *Discourse and Social Psychology: Beyond Attitudes and Behaviour*. London: Sage.

Propp, V. (1968 [1928]) *Morphology of the Folktale*. Austin, TX: University of Texas Press.

Rabenschlag, A-J. (2021) 'Semantic struggles in the face of crisis: "The West" as contested key concept in West German parliamentary debate (1973/74)', *Redescriptions: Political Thought, Conceptual History and Feminist Theory*, 24 (2): 150–65.

Ramage, D., Rosen, E., Chuang, J., Manning, C. D. and McFarland, D. A. (2009) 'Topic modeling for the social sciences', *NIPS 2009 workshop on applications for topic models: text and beyond*, 5 (27): 1–4.

Raven, P.G. and Elahi, S. (2015) 'The new narrative: applying narratology to the shaping of futures outputs', *Futures*, 74: 49–61.

Reisigl, M. (2017) 'The discourse-historical approach', in J. Flowerdew and J.E. Richardson (eds), *The Routledge Handbook of Critical Discourse Studies*. London: Routledge, pp. 44–59.

Reisigl, M. and Wodak, R. (2000) *Discourse and Discrimination: Rhetorics of Racism and Antisemitism*. London: Routledge.

Reisigl, M. and Wodak, R. (2016) 'The discourse-historical approach', in R. Wodak and M. Meyer (eds), *Methods of Critical Discourse Studies* (3rd edn). London: Thousand Oaks, CA and New Delhi: Sage, pp. 23–61.

Richardson, H.S. (2002) *Democratic Autonomy: Public Reasoning about the Ends of Politics*. Oxford and New York: Oxford University Press.

Riessman, C.K. (1993) *Narrative Analysis*. London and New Delhi: Sage.

Robertson, A. (2010) *Mediated Cosmopolitanism: The World of Television News*. Cambridge: Polity.

Robertson, A. (2015) *Global News: Reporting Conflicts and Cosmopolitanism*. New York and London: Peter Lang.

Rorty, R. (1989) *Contingency, Irony, and Solidarity*. Cambridge: Cambridge University Press.

Rose, J. and Johnson, C. (2020) 'Contextualizing reliability and validity in qualitative research: toward more rigorous and trustworthy qualitative social science in leisure research', *Journal of Leisure Research*, 51 (4): 432–51.

Rosenblatt, H. (2018) *The Lost History of Liberalism: From Ancient Rome to the Twenty-First Century*. Princeton, NJ: Princeton University Press.

Rosenblatt, P.C. (1994) *Metaphors of Family Systems Theory: Toward New Constructions*. New York and London: The Guilford Press.

Rudder, C. (2014) *Dataclysm*. New York: Crown Publishers.

Sabine, G. and Thorson, T. (1973) *A History of Political Theory*. Hinsdale, IL: Dryden Press.

Sacks, H. (1992) *Lectures on Conversation* (Vol. 1). Oxford: Blackwell.

Saussure, F. de. (2013 [1916]) *Course in General Linguistics*. London: Bloomsbury.

Sayyid, B. and Zac, L. (1998) 'Political analysis in a world without foundations', in E. Scarbrough and E. Tanenbaum (eds), *Research Strategies in the Social Sciences*. Oxford: Oxford University Press, pp. 250–68.

Schiffrin, D. (1996) 'Narrative as self-portrait: sociolinguistic constructions of identity', *Language in Society*, 25: 167–203.

Schleiermacher, F. (1998) *Hermeneutics and Criticism and Other Writings*, translated and edited by A. Bowie. Cambridge: Cambridge University Press.

Schotter, J. (1993) *Conversational Realities*. London: Sage.

Schreier, M. (2014) 'Qualitative content analysis?', in U. Flick (ed.), *The SAGE Handbook of Qualitative Data Analysis*. London: SAGE Publications, pp. 170–83.

Schreier, M., Stamann, C., Janssen, M., Dahl, T. and Whittal, A. (2019) 'Qualitative content analysis: conceptualizations and challenges in research practice – introduction to the FQS special issue "Qualitative Content Analysis 1"', *Forum: Qualitative Social Research*, 20 (3), 1–26. DOI: 10.17169/fqs-20.3.3393

Schroeter, M., Veniard, M., Taylor, C. and Blaette, A. (2019) 'A comparative analysis of the keyword multicultural(ism) in French, British, German and Italian migration discourse', in L. Viola and A. Musolff (eds), *Migration and Media Discourses About Identities in Crisis*. Amsterdam: John Benjamin Publishing Company, pp. 13–44.

Schulz-Forberg, H. (eds) (2014) *A Global Conceptual History of Asia, 1860–1940*. London: Pickering & Chatto.

Scott, M. and Tribble, C. (2006) *Textual Patterns: Key Words and Corpus Analysis in Language Education*. Philadelphia, PA: J. Benjamins.

Seiler Brylla, C. (2019) 'Strategische benennungen: zur sprachgeschichte des geteilten Deutschland in einem deutsch-schwedischen kontext', *Zeitschrift für Literaturwissenschaft und Linguistik*, 49 (2): 279–301.

Seliger, M. (1976) *Ideology and Politics*. London: George Allen & Unwin.

Semino, E., Demjén, Z., Demmen, J., Koller, V., Payne, S., Hardie, A. and Rayson, P. (2017) 'The online use of violence and journey metaphors by patients with cancer, as compared with health professionals: a mixed methods study', *BMJ Supportive & Palliative Care*, 7 (1): 60–6.

Shapiro, G. and Markoff, J. (1997) 'A matter of definition', in C.W. Roberts (ed.), *Text Analysis for the Social Sciences: Methods for Drawing Statistical Inferences from Texts and Transcripts*. Mahwah, NJ: Lawrence Erlbaum Associates, pp. 9–34.

Shoham, H. (2018) 'The conceptual and anthropological history of Bat Mitzvah', *Contributions to the History of Concepts*, 13 (2): 100–22.

Shuman, A. (2012) 'Exploring narrative interaction in multiple contexts', in J.A. Holstein and J.F. Gruber (eds), *Varieties of Narrative Analysis*. London: Sage, pp. 125–50.

Silfver, E., Gonsalves, A.J., Danielsson, A.T. and Berge, M. (2021) 'Gender equality as a resource and a dilemma: interpretative repertoires in engineering education in Sweden', *Gender and Education*, 34 (8): 923–39.

Simpson, P. (1993) *Language, Ideology and Point of View*. London and New York: Routledge.

Skinner, Q. (1973) 'The empirical theorists of democracy and their critics: a plague on both their houses', *Political Theory*, 1: 287–306.

Skinner, Q. (1978) *The Foundations of Modern Political Thought. Vol. 1: The Renaissance*. Cambridge: Cambridge University Press.

Skinner, Q. (1988a) 'Meaning and understanding in the history of ideas', in J. Tully (ed.), *Meaning and Context: Quentin Skinner and his Critics*. London: Polity Press, pp. 29–67.

Skinner, Q. (1988b) 'Language and social change', in J. Tully (ed.), *Meaning and Context: Quentin Skinner and his Critics*. London: Polity Press, pp. 119–34.

Skinner, Q. (1989) 'State', in T. Ball, J. Farr and R.L. Hanson (eds), *Political Innovation and Conceptual Change*. Cambridge: Cambridge University Press.

Skinner, Q. (1996a) *Reason and Rhetoric in the Philosophy of Hobbes*. Cambridge: Cambridge University Press.

Skinner, Q. (1996b) 'From Hume's intentions to deconstruction and back', *The Journal of Political Philosophy*, 4: 142–54.

Skinner, Q. (1998) *Liberty before Liberalism*. Cambridge: Cambridge University Press.

Skinner, Q. (1999) 'Rhetoric and conceptual change', *Finnish Yearbook of Political Thought*, 3. Jyväskylä: SoPhi, University of Jyväskylä.

Skinner, Q. (2002) *Visions of Politics. Vol. I: Regarding Method*. Cambridge: Cambridge University Press.

Skocpol, T. and Williamson, V. (2012) *The Tea Party and the Remaking of Republican Conservatism*. New York and Oxford: Oxford University Press.

Smith, A.M. (2003) *Laclau and Mouffe: The Radical Democratic Imaginary*. London: Routledge.

Somers, M.R. (1994) 'The narrative constitution of identity: a relational and network approach', *Theory and Society*, 23: 605–49.

Spector, M. and Kitsuse, J. (1977) *Constructing Social Problems*. New Brunswick: Transaction Publishers.

Spira, I. (2015) *A Conceptual History of Chinese -Isms: The Modernization of Ideological Discourse, 1895–1925*. Leiden: Brill.

Spira, I. (2018) 'Chinese isms: the modernization of ideological discourse in China', *Journal of Political Ideologies*, 23 (3): 283–98. DOI: 10.1080/13569317.2018.1502937

Spitzmüller, J. and Warnke, I.H. (2011a) 'Discourse as a "linguistic object": methodical and methodological delimitations', *Critical Discourse Studies*, 8 (2): 75–94.

Spitzmüller, J. and Warnke, I.H. (2011b) *Diskurslinguistik. Eine Einführung in Theorien und Methoden der transtextuellen Sprachanalyse*. Berlin: de Gruyter.

Stavrakakis, Y. (2017) 'Discourse theory in populism research: three challenges and a dilemma', *Journal of Language and Politics*, 16 (4): 523–34.

Steinmetz, W. (2017) 'Multiple transformations: temporal frameworks for a European conceptual history', in W. Steinmetz et al. (eds), *Conceptual History in the European Space*. New York: Berghahn Books, pp. 63–95.

Steinmetz, W. (2020) 'Introduction: concepts and practices of comparison in modern history', in W. Steinmetz (ed.), *The Force of Comparison: A New Perspective on Modern European History and the Contemporary World*. New York and Oxford: Berghahn Books, pp. 1–32.

Strozier, C.B. et al. (eds) (2010) *The Fundamentalist Mindset*. Oxford: Oxford University Press.

Svärd, P.-A. (2015) *Problem Animals: A Critical Genealogy of Animal Cruelty and Animal Welfare In Swedish Politics 1844–1944*. Dissertation. Stockholm University, Stockholm. Available at: http://urn.kb.se/resolve?urn=urn:nbn:se:su:diva-121356

Syssner, J. (2020) *Pathways to Demographic Adaptation*. Cham: Springer.

Teltemann, J. and Jude, N. (2019) 'Assessments and accountability in secondary education: international trends', *Research in Comparative and International Education*, 14 (2): 249–71. DOI: https://doi.org/10.1177/1745499919846174

Thompson, G. (2014) *Introducing Functional Grammar*. Abingdon: Routledge.

Tidwell, C. (2016) '"A little wildness": negotiating relationships between human and nonhuman in historical romance', in D. Herman (ed.), *Human–Animal Relationships in Twentieth- and Twenty-First-Century Literature*. London: Palgrave Macmillan, pp. 152–71.

Tilton, T. (1990) *The Political Theory of the Swedish Social Democracy. Through the Welfare State to Socialism*. Oxford: Clarendon Press.

Todorov, T. (1969) 'Structural analysis of narrative', *Novel*, 3: 70–6.

Tong, R. and Botts, T.F. (2018) *Feminist Thought: A More Comprehensive Introduction*. New York and London: Routledge.

Torfing, J. (2005) 'Discourse theory: achievements, arguments, and challenges', in D. Howarth and J. Torfing (eds), *Discourse Theory in European Politics*. Basingstoke: Palgrave Macmillan, pp. 1–32.

Tremblay, S. (2021) 'Rosa Winkel et Pink Triangle: comprendre la mémoire collective homosexuelle de la répre', *Revue d'Allemagne et des pays de langue allemande*, 53 (2): 379–96. DOI: 10.4000/allemagne.2840 van Dijk, T. (1993) 'Stories and racism', in D.K. Mumby (ed.), *Narrative and Social Control: Critical Perspectives*. London: Sage, pp. 121–42.

van Dijk, T. (1998) *Ideology: A Multidisciplinary Approach*. London: Sage.

van Dijk, T. (2013) 'CDA is NOT a method of critical discourse analysis.' Available at: www.edisoportal.org/debate/115-cda-not-method-criticaldiscourse-analysis

van Dijk, T.A. (1997) 'The study of discourse', in T.A. van Dijk (ed.), *Discourse as Structure and Process. Discourse Studies: A Multidisciplinary Introduction*. Vol. 1. London: Sage, pp. 1–34.

van Dyke, V. (1995) *Ideology and Political Choice: The Search for Freedom, Justice, and Virtue*. Chatham: Chatham Publishers.

van Leeuwen, T. (2005) *Introducing Social Semiotics*. London and New York: Routledge.

van Leeuwen, T. (2022) *Multimodality and Identity*. London and New York: Routledge.

Vedung, E. (1982) *Political Reasoning*. London: Sage.

Vedung, E. (2000) *Public Policy and Program Evaluation*. New Brunswick and London: Transaction Publishers.

Volkens, A., Lacewell, O., Lehmann, P., Regel, S., Schultze, H. and Werner, A. (2011) *The Manifesto Data Collection*, edited by Manifesto Project (MRG/CMP/MARPOR). Berlin: Wissenschaftszentrum Berlin für Sozialforschung (WZB).

von Beyme, K. (2013a) *Liberalismus: Theorien des Liberalismus und Radikalismus im Zeitalter der Ideologien 1789–1945*. Wiesbaden: Springer.

von Beyme, K. (2013b) *Konservatismus: Theorien des Konservatismus und Rechtsextremismus im Zeitalter der Ideologien 1789–1945*. Wiesbaden: Springer.

von Beyme, K. (2013c) *Sozialismus: Theorien des Sozialismus, Anarchismus und Kommunismus im Zeitalter der Ideologien 1789–1945*. Wiesbaden: Springer.

Wallace, H. (2010) *Rock Solid? A scientific review of geological disposal of high-level radioactive waste*. Buxton, UK: GeneWatch UK.

Walton, D. (2008) *Informal Logic: A Pragmatic Approach*. Cambridge: Cambridge University Press.

Weber, C. (2014) *International Relations Theory: A Critical Introduction*. New York and London: Routledge.

Weber, M. (2009) 'Towards a sociology of the press: an early proposal for content analysis', in K. Krippendorff and M.A. Bock (eds), *The Content Analysis Reader*. London: SAGE Publications, pp. 9–11.

Weiss, P. (2005 [1975]) *The Aesthetics of Resistance*, Volume 1. Durham, NC: Duke University Press.

Wetherell, M. (2012) *Affect and Emotion: A New Social Science Understanding*. London: Sage.

Wetherell, M. and Edley, N. (1999) 'Negotiating hegemonic masculinity: imaginary positions and psycho-discursive practices', *Feminism and Psychology*, 9 (3): 335–56.

Wetherell, M. and Potter, J. (1992) *Mapping the Language of Racism: Discourse and the Legitimation of Exploitation*. New York: Harvester Wheatsheaf.

Wetherell, M. (1998) 'Positioning and interpreting repertoires: conversation analysis and post-structuralism in dialogue', *Discourse & Society*, 9 (3): 387–412.

Wetherell, M., Taylor, S. & Yates, S.J. (eds) (2001) *Discourse as Data: a Guide for Analysis*. London: Sage, in association with the Open University.

Widfeldt, A. (2014) *Extreme Right Parties in Scandinavia*. London: Routledge.

Wierzbicka, A. (1997) *Understanding Cultures Through Their Key Words: English, Russian, Polish, German, and Japanese*. Oxford: Oxford University Press.

Williams, R. (1985) *Keywords: A Vocabulary of Culture and Society*. New York: Oxford University Press.

Williamson, J. (1978) *Decoding Advertisements: Ideology and Meaning in Advertisements*. London and New York: Marion Boyers.

Wodak, R. (1996) *Disorders of Discourse*. London: Longman.

Wodak, R. and Meyer, M. (2016) *Methods of Critical Discourse Studies* (3rd edn). London: Sage.

Wodak, R. and Rheindorf, M. (2022) *Identity Politics: Past and Present*. Exeter: University of Exeter Press.

Wodak, R., de Cilla, R., Reisigl, M. and Liebhart, K. (2009) *The Discursive Construction of National Identity*. Edinburgh: Edinburgh University Press.

Wodak, R., KhosraviNik, M. and Mral, B. (eds) (2013) *Right-wing Populism in Europe: Politics and Discourse*. London and New York: Bloomsbury.

Wojahn, D. (2023) 'Refugees, migrants and asylum seekers in the Swedish press: the discursive construction of mobile humans during the so-called European refugee crisis, 2015–2017', in Fábián, A. (ed.), *The Representation of Refugees and Migrants in European National Media Discourses from 2015 to 2017: A Contrastive Approach (Corpus Linguistics)*. Berlin and Heidelberg: J.B. Metzler/Springer, pp. 307–346.

Wootton, B. (2009 [1942]) 'A plague on all your isms', *The Political Quarterly*, 80.

Zhao, S. and Zappavigna, M. (2017) 'Beyond the self: intersubjectivity and the social semiotic interpretation of the selfie', *New Media & Society*, 20 (5): 1735–54. DOI: 10.1177/1461444817706074

Zhao, S., Djonov, E., Björkvall, A. and Boeriis, M. (2018) *Advancing Multimodal and Critical Discourse Studies: Interdisciplinary Research Inspired by Theo van Leeuwen's Social Semiotics*. London and New York: Routledge.

Journals

Ariadna Histórica. Lenguajes, conceptos, metáforas. The Basque Country: University of the Basque Country.
Contributions to the History of Concepts. New York & Oxford: Berghahn Journals.
Critical Discourse Studies. Milton Park, Abingdon-on-Thames: Taylor & Francis.
Discourse & Communication. London & New York: Sage.
Discourse & Society. London & New York: Sage.
Forum Interdisziplinäre Begriffsgeschichte. Berlin: ZfL (Leibniz Center for Literary and Cultural Research).
Multimodal Communication. Berlin: De Gruyter.
Multimodality & Society. London & New York: Sage.
Narrative Inquiry. Amsterdam: John Benjamins Publishing Company.
Political Communication. Milton Park, Abingdon-on-Thames: Taylor & Francis.
Redescriptions. Helsinki: Helsinki University Press.
Social Semiotics. Milton Park, Abingdon-on-Thames: Taylor & Francis.
The Velvet Light Trap. Austin: The University of Texas Press.
Visual Communication. London & New York: Sage.

Index

action
  defined, 186
  events and, 189
  and ideas, 55
  orienting, 52
action guiding, 52
action-guiding thought, 54
The Aesthetics of Resistance (Weiss), 173, 175
Alcohol problems
  analytical questions, 156–157
  more than just words, 157
  problem representations, 156–157
  study of problematisations, 156–157
American new criticism, 113
American Public Media Archive, 29
analysis of ideas and ideological thought, 8
analytical distinctions, 67–68
analytical instruments, 32
analytical processes, 217
  attributes, 217
  carrier, 217
analytical scheme of ideological thought, 65–66
Anderton, C., 128
antagonism, 140, 142
  and constitutive outside, 139–140
arbitrariness, 4
Archer, J., 27
articulation, 142
Austin, J.L., 170
authentic engineers
  interpretative repertoires, 150–151
  positioning of selves, 150–151

Bacchi, C., 136, 152, 153, 155, 156–157, 162
banal nationalism, 17
Barthes, R., 5, 113, 116, 123, 130, 200
Bateman, J.A., 5
Bechdel test, 26–27
Begriffsgeschichte, 88
Bell, D., 101

Bhaskar, R., 12, 169
Björklund, S., 59–60
Black Adder, 125
Blommaert, J., 171, 192
Boréus, K., 28
Brinker, M., 125
Bush, G.W., 180

cancer and metaphors, 178–180
Carlisle, J., 113
categorical-content approach, 119–120
categorical-form mode of analysis, 120
category guidelines, 31
chains of equivalence, 141–142, 143–146
Charteris-Black, J., 179, 190
Chatman, S., 115, 125
code form, 31
coding
  computerised, 30
  consistency, 33–34
  content analysis, 30, 32–34
  manual, 30
  type-building qualitative, 43–45
coding frame, 25
coding instructions, 31
coding scheme, 31
cognitive assertions (D*cog*), 61–62
cohesion, 5, 205
Collingwood, R.G., 90
collocation, 180, 183, 191
complete idea system, 66
complicating action, 114
composition
  multimodal discourse analysis, 220–230
  of multimodal text, 220–223
  semiotic, 222
  visual, 204
comprehensive ideal types, 56–57
comprehensive ideologies, 56
comprehensive political Islam (Islamism), 56
conative function, 6

concepts
  vs. context, 104–105
  defined, 85–86
  historicity of, 86
  note on, 87
  polemical, 89
  temporal layers of, 88–89
  vs. words, 102–104
conceptual change, 92–93
conceptual history, 8–9
  analysis, 98–99
  critical reflections, 102–105
  digitised sources, 95–98
  German, 88–90
  macro and micro perspectives on 'isms,' 99–102
  overview, 85–87
  and study of society, 105–106
  transnational, 93–95
conceptualization of power, 2–3
conceptual metaphors, 177–178
conceptual metaphor theory (CMT)
  criticism of, 192–193
  tradition, 177, 192
conceptual representations, 217
concordance list, 191
conflictual ideas, 53
connotative content, 123, 125
consensual validation, 130
conservatism, 101
constitutive outside, 142
constitutive role of discourse, 136
constructivists, 11–12
content analysis, 8, 24–51
  analytical instruments, 32
  analytical tools, 31
  choosing and collecting texts, 28
  coding, 30, 32–34
  defined, 25
  limitations and challenges, 45–47
  overview, 24–28
  qualitative, 25
  quantitative, 25
  recording and sampling units, 31–32
  and software, 35–36
  sources, 28–30
  steps and concepts in, 28–35
  and study of society, 47
  summarise quantitative analyses, 34–35
  uses of, 26–28
context
  vs. concepts, 104–105
  and ideas, 70–71
  unit, 31–32
Corbyn, J., 70
corpora, 27–28
  digitised, 96–98

corpus, 96
corpus analysis, 190–191
cosmopolitanism, 120
counter-concepts, 90
  in rhetoric of isms, 101
COVID-19 Toolkit, New Mexico Department of Health, 226–229
credibility, and narrative analysis, 128–129
Critical Discourse Studies (journal), 203
critical discourse studies (CDS), 3, 6, 9
  analysis, 174–191
  conducting, 174–175
  corpus analysis, 190–191
  'critical' in, 170–171
  critical reflections, 191–193
  criticism of, 191–192
  'discourse' in, 171–172
  inspiration and approaches, 169–170
  overview, 168–174
  and the study of society, 193
critical ideational analysis, 52, 79
'critical' in critical discourse studies, 170–171
critical linguistics, 184
Critical Metaphor Analysis (CMA), 177
critical realism, 3, 12
cultural keywords, 181
cultural wars, 53
Czarniawska, B., 130

datasets
  digitised text, 97
  historical, 97
dead or inactive metaphors, 192
deductive coding, 45
De Fina, A., 114, 123
Deleuze, G., 162
De Lille, P., 206–208, 210, 211–212
democratic decision-making, 68
denotative content, 123
descriptions, 52, 54
  argumentative combination of, 58–59
  double-sidedness of, 61–62
  hierarchical chains of, 64–65
  types of, 61–63
descriptive ideational analysis, 52, 79
descriptive statements, 62–63
diachronic studies, 89–90
dialectical-relational approach, 170
digitised corpora, 96–98
digitised sources
  quantitative analysis, 95–98
  word frequencies, 95–96
discourse, 7–8, 135–136
  analysing keywords in, 183–184
  analysing transitivity in, 189–190
  constitutive role of, 136
  in critical discourse studies, 171–172

discourse, *cont.*
  neoliberal, 7
  and other social practices, 173–174
  racist, 7
  and social structures, 172–174
discourse analysis (DA), 9
  analysis, 138–160
  analytical tools, 159–160
  concept of discourse to use, 158
  critical reflections, 160–162
  importance of, 172
  and the issue of power, 137
  organise the material, 159
  overview, 135–138
  as philosophy and social theory, 136–138
  poststructural approaches to, 135–163
  and social identities, 137
  steps in, 157–160
discourse analytical research problems, 138
discourse historical approach, 170
discourse keywords, 181
discourse linguistics, 171
discourse orders, 172–173
discourse-oriented policy theory, 137
discourse-oriented strategy, 17
'discourse semantics,' 181
discursive network analysis, 39–42
discursive psychology, 146–149
  actors matter, 147–148
  interpretive repertoire, 146–147
  power and ideology as objects of study in, 149
  small-scale discourse, 146–147
  subject positions in, 148–149
  using concepts in empirical analysis, 149
dislocation, 140, 142
  hegemony and, 140
  and sedimentation of resistance, 145
distributional semantics, 96
double coding, 33

Eco, U., 202
economic democracy, 57
Edley, N., 147, 150
egoism, 90
empirical analysis
  using concepts from discursive psychology in, 149
  using PDT concepts in, 143
empirical reader, 15
empirical social science, 58
empiricists, 10–11, 13
empty signifiers, 141–142
entrance talk, 117, 118
epistemology, 10
Erdoğan, R.T., 143, 145
evaluations *vs.* values, 63
evaluative judgements (*Deval*), 61–62

events, 186
  and actions, 189
'everyday cosmopolitanism,' 120
exit talk, 117

Fagerholm, A., 37
Fairclough, N., 3, 135, 169–170, 175, 190
Farage, N., 70
Fauconnier, G., 193
feminism, 147–148
Fernandez Galeote, D., 26, 43
field-specific ideologies, 57
finality, 5
floating signifier, 142
focus group material, 120–122
Fortschritt, 98–99
Foucault, M., 2–3, 136, 149, 152, 156, 171
Fowler, R., 187
Freeden, M., 99
French structuralism, 113
frequency analysis, 190–191
Friedrich, C. J., 55
functional text(s), 5–6
fundamental level, ideological thought, 63

Garry, J., 28, 46
general social theory, 58
GeneWatch UK, 199, 201
genres, 7–8, 172
German hermeneutics, 113
'The Gezi Park protests'
  dislocation and sedimentation of resistance, 145
  hegemony, 143–146
  JDP's response, 145
  lessons from study of protest, 145–146
  logic of equivalence and formation of popular resistance, 144–145
  resistance and chains of equivalence, 143–146
globalisation, 95–96
goals, 64
Goodwin, S., 136
Google Books, 97
Graddol, D., 125
grammar
  analysing, 184–188
  circumstances, 187–188
  participants, 187
  processes, 186–187
grammatical multifariousness, 71

Hall, E. T., 208–209
Hall, S., 16
Halliday, M., 6–7, 184
Hampsher-Monk, I., 87
Hatakka, N., 26

hegemony, 142, 143–146
   and dislocation, 140
Hegemony and Socialist Strategy (Laclau and Mouffe), 138
hermeneutics, 15
Hodge, R., 184
holism, 78–79
holistic-content mode of reading, 119
holistic-form-based mode of analysis, 119
How to Do Things with Words (Austin, J.L.), 170
Huckleberry Finn (Twain), 79
Husserl, E., 140

iconic sign, 202
idea-criticism, 52
idealism, error of, 77–78
ideas
   and actions, 55
   analysis of, 68, 79–80
   conflictual, 53
   grammatical multifariousness, 71
   and institutions, 55
   multilayered/ambiguous sentences, 69–70
   and politics, 52–54
   and society, 52–54
   three basic kinds of, 58–59
idea systems, 54
ideational metafunction, 6
identifying the objects of analysis, 117–119
ideological change, 28
   counting expressions of ideas as measure of, 36–39
ideological thought, 52
   analysis of, 79–80
   content, general theory of, 54–55
   dimensions, 54
   levels of, 63–67
   two-level analytical scheme of, 65–66
ideologies, 52–53
   field-specific, 57
   as objects of study in discursive psychology, 149
   organisation-specific, 57
images
   language and, 230–231
   multimodal discourse analysis, 230–231
   and power, 2
   symbolic distance in, 208–209
impersonal distance, 209
innovative ideologists, 92–93
institutions, and ideas, 55
interactors, 214–215
interdiscursively, 17
interpersonal metafunction, 6
interpretation
   discourse-oriented strategy, 17
   empirical reader, 15
   hermeneutics, 15

interpretation, *cont.*
   issues, 47
   model reader, 15
   producer-oriented strategy, 15
   reader-oriented strategy, 16–17
   and textual analysis, 13–17
interpretative repertoires, 146
   small-scale discourse, 146–147
   and subject positions they create, 150–151
intersubjectivity, 20, 34
intrasubjectivity, 20, 33
isms
   as analytical and historical concepts, 101
   counter-concepts in rhetoric of, 101
   macro and micro perspectives on, 99–102
   spread of, 100
   of the twentieth century, 102

Jacobs, A.M., 27
Jakobson, R., 6
James, M., 128
Jameson, F., 17
Jockers, M.L., 27
Johnson, B., 125
Johnson, M., 176, 177
Johnstone, B., 114, 123
Justice and Development Party (JDP), 143–145

Kagan, D., 26
keyness, 191
keyness method, 96
keywords
   analysing, in discourse, 183–184
   lexicon, 181–182
Koller, V., 193
Koselleck, R., 9, 86, 103, 181
   German conceptual history, 88–90
   onomasiological analysis of concept of progress, 98–99
   semasiological analysis of concept of progress, 98–99
Kress, G., 4, 184, 202, 203, 209, 211, 216–217, 220
Kuckartz, U., 25

Labov, W., 114–116, 120–121
Laclau, E., 136, 138, 146
Lakoff, G., 176, 177
language(s)
   comparisons between, 105
   constructivist view, 11–12
   empiricists on, 10–11
   as a historical phenomenon, 86
   and images, 230–231
   multimodal discourse analysis, 230–231
   politics of use, 85–87
   textual analysis, 10–13

Language and Ideology (Kress and Hodge), 184
Laver, M., 28, 46
Ledin, P., 203
Leifeld, P., 39
lexicon
   analysing, 180–184
   analysing keywords in discourse, 183–184
   keywords, 181–182
   semantic struggles, 182–183
   word categories, 180–181
liberalism, 101
Library of Congress, 29
Lieblich, A., 117, 119, 129
linguistic contextualism, 90–93
Linguistic Inquiry and Word Count (LIWC), 27
linguistic philosophy, 58
'lived effects,' 155
locations of power, 2
Locke, J., 101
logical positivism, 10–11
logic of difference, 141, 142
logic of equivalence, 141, 142
   and formation of popular resistance, 144–145
'logics approach,' 161–162
Lukes, S., 2
Luther, M., 77

Machin, D., 203, 231
Madness and Civilization (Foucault), 3
Man and his Government (Friedrich), 55
manifesto coding, 46
Manifesto Project Database, 36
manifest textual aspects, 25
Marxism, 138
Marxist social theory, 138
master narratives, 131
material
   artefacts, 10
   organising, 119–120
materiality, 5
Mayring, P., 25
meaning potentials, 4, 15
means–ends descriptions (Dme), 61
media narratives
   analysing, 122–127
   example of television news analysis, 122–127
memos, 32–33
Mert, A., 143, 144–145, 161
metafunctions of language, 202
meta-narratives, 118
metaphorical expressions, 177–178
metaphors, 176
   and cancer, 178–180
   conceptual, 177–178
   dead or inactive, 192

Metaphors We Live By (Lakoff and Johnson), 176
meta-theories of science, 14
methodological nationalism, 93
metonym, 176
micro-physics of power, 2
model reader, 15
moment, 140–141, 142
moral relativism, 161
Morphology of the Folktale (Propp), 113
Mouffe, C., 136, 138, 146
movement concepts, 99
Mueller, R.A., 117
multiculturalism, 85
Multimodal Communication (journal), 202
multimodal discourse analysis, 9–10
   analysis, 205–230
   composition, 220–230
   critical reflections, 230–233
   different types of multimodal texts, 231–232
   doing, in practice, 232–233
   interaction, 205–212
   language and image, 230–231
   overview, 199–205
   representations of usage in the world, 212–220
   and the study of society, 233–234
Multimodality & Society (journal), 202
multimodal texts, 4–8
   different types of, 231–232

narrative analysis, 9, 111–131
   analysis, 116–127
   collecting data for, 116–117
   credibility, 128–129
   critical reflections, 128–130
   and focus group material, 120–122
   organising the material, 119–120
   overview, 112–116
   questions of interpretation, 128
   reflections on narrative analysis in general, 129–130
   and the study of society, 130–131
narratives
   reasons for studying, 112–113
   representations, 217
   structure, 117–118
   and their ingredients, 113–116
narrativity, 131
naturalism, 125
Nazism, 141
neoliberal discourses, 7
neutral observation language, 10–11
Ngram Viewer, 29
Nietzsche, F., 86
nodal point/node, 141–142

nominalisation, 189
non-decision making, 2
nultilayered/ambiguous sentences, and ideas, 69–70

Obama, B., 70
objects of analysis, 117–119
onomasiological analysis, 90
ontological narrativity, 112
ontology, 10
operative level, ideological thought, 63
organisation-specific ideologies, 57
organising the material, 119–120
'Other,' 139–140

passivisation, 189
patriotism, 90
Peirce, C.S., 4, 202
personal distance, 209
phatic function, 6
phenomenology, 138
philosophy, discourse analysis as, 136–138
pictures, and power, 2
Pietikäinen, S., 189
pilot study, 32
poetic function, 6
polemical concepts, 89
political discourse theory (PDT), 138–143
　antagonism and constitutive outside, 139–140
　articulation, 140
　hegemony and dislocation, 140
　struggle over meaning, 140–143
　using PDT concepts in empirical analysis, 143
political ideologies, 54
political language, 57–58
　analytical distinction, 68
　interpretation of, 68–72
political philosophies, 54
political unconscious, 17
politics
　and ideas, 52–54
　of language use, 85–87
Politisk teori (Political theory, Björklund), 60
popular resistance
　formation of, 144–145
　and logic of equivalence, 144–145
poststructural discourse analysis
　advantages and challenges, 160–161
　analysis, 138–160
　critical reflections, 160–162
　overview, 135–138
poststructuralism, 12
poststructuralists, 12–13
Potter, J., 146, 147, 162

power, 2
　discourse analysis and the issue of, 137
　first dimension of, 2
　Foucault on, 2
　and images, 2
　as objects of study in discursive psychology, 149
　and pictures, 2
　second dimension of, 2
　and text, 3
　third dimension of, 2
practical reasoning, 59
　argumentative pattern of, 59
　formal VDP-model of simple, 59–60
　unorganised/fragmented, 69
The Practice of Conceptual History (Koselleck), 98
pragmatism, 138
preferred reading, 17
prescriptions, 52, 54
　argumentative combination of, 58–59
　hierarchical chains of, 64–65
producer-oriented strategy, 15
'prognostic criticism,' 180
prognostic critique, 171
progress
　onomasiological analysis of concept of, 98–99
　semasiological analysis of concept of, 98–99
Propp, V., 113–114
psychoanalysis, 138
public narratives, 131

QDA (Qualitative Data Analysis) software, 30, 33, 35, 190
qualitative content analysis, 25
quantitative content analysis, 25
　limitation of, 45
quantitative questionnaires, 58
quasi-sentences, 37

racist discourses, 7
reactivation, 142
reader-oriented strategy, 16–17
Reading Images: The Grammar of Visual Design (Kress and van Leeuwen), 202
realism, 125
reconstructive interpretation, 69
referential function, 6
Reisigl, M., 171, 180
reliability, 20
representational metafunction, 6
resistance, 143–146
　dislocation and, 145
　sedimentation of, 145
retroductive explanations, 162
rhetorical moves, 91–92

rhetorical redescription, 93
Riessman, C.K., 117
Rudder, C., 30
Russian formalism, 113

salience, 228–230
sampling unit, 31–32
Saussure, F.D., 4, 89, 138–139, 202
Schreier, M., 25
Schroeter, M., 181, 183
scientific socialism, 56
sedimentation, 140, 142
semantic fields, 89, 96
semantic struggles, 182–183
semasiological analysis, 89
Semino, E., 178, 179
semiotic acts and discourse orders, 172–173
semiotics, 4
    sign, 202
    social, 4
signified, 4, 139
signifiers, 4, 138–139
    empty, 141–142
    floating, 142
signs, 4
    iconic, 4
    indexical, 4
    symbolic, 4
Silfver, E., 150
similes, 176
simplicity, 22
situational descriptions (D*sit*), 61
Skinner, Q., 15–16, 103
    conceptual change, 92–93
    linguistic contextualism, 90–93
small-scale discourse, 146–147
small stories, 120
social distance, 209
Social doctrine of the Catholic Church, 56
social identities, 137
social science
    analysing text in, 1–22
    textual analysis in, 18–21
social semiotics, 4
social structures, 173–174
social theory, 136–138
society
    and ideas, 52–54
    study of, 79–80
sociodiagnostic critique, 171
software and content analysis, 35–36
Songs of Zion, 24
source material, 57–58
speech acts, 91–92
    commands, 210
    offers, 210
    preferred responses to, 211

speech acts, *cont.*
    questions, 210
    statements, 210
speech act theory, 170
Spinoza, B., 162
Springsteen, B., 70
structuralism, 138
subject positions, 142
    in discursive psychology, 148–149
summative content analysis, 25
Swedish gender equality discourse, 151
Swedish Media Archive, 29
Swedish Media Database, 29
Swedish Nuclear Fuel and Waste Management
    Company, 199–200, 201, 208, 222, 233
symbolic distance in images, 208–209
symbolic power relations, 206
synchronic studies, 89–90
syndicalism, 57
systemic functional linguistics, 210

talk analysis
    focus group material, 120–122
    narrative analysis, 120–122
    television news analysis, 122–127
temporal layers of concepts, 88–89
text(s)
    analysing, in social science, 1–22
    conventions, 7
    finality, 5
    functional, 5–6
    materiality, 5
    multimodal, 4–8
    myriad, 1
    and power, 3
    understanding, in historical context, 90–91
text- and discourse-immanent critique, 171
textual analysis
    approaches to, 8–10
    and interpretation, 13–17
    language, 10–13
    learning, 10–13
    in social sciences, 18–21
textual metafunction, 7
theory of conceptual metaphors, 177
Todorov, T., 113
transformations, 188–190
transitivity, 213
    analysing, in discourse, 189–190
transnational conceptual history, 93–95
transnationality, 94–95
triangulation, 19
Trump, D., 63, 70, 102
trustworthiness, 19
Turner, M., 193
Twain, M., 79
type-building qualitative coding, 43–45

validity, 19
  and content analysis, 46
  problems, 46
value dimensions, 64
values, 64
  argumentative combination of, 58–59
  vs. evaluations, 63
  hierarchical chains of, 64–65
van Dijk, T., 116, 135, 170
van Leeuwen, T., 202, 203, 209, 211, 216–217, 220
VDP-triads, 54–55
  combination of, 66–67
  incomplete, 72
verbose reasoning, 71
visual rhymes, 205

Waletzky, J., 114–116, 120–121
'war on terrorism,' 180
Weber, M., 24
Wetherell, M., 146, 147, 162

'What's the problem represented to be?' approach (WPR approach), 152–155
  analytical questions, 153–155
  problem representations and their effects, 152–153
Wodak, R., 135, 169, 170, 171, 180
Woman (magazine), 222–224
Women's Equality Party (WE)
  descriptions of social fields, 74–75
  fundamental philosophical assumptions, 75–76
  objectives of party, 73–74
  policy document, 72–77
  two-level analytical scheme, 76–77
  VDP-triad of, 75
words, 87
  categories, 180–181
  vs. concepts, 102–104
  embeddings, 96
  frequencies, 95–96
World Health Organization (WHO), 156–157

www.ingramcontent.com/pod-product-compliance
Lightning Source LLC
Chambersburg PA
CBHW051350070526
44584CB00025B/3709